The Fiction of
LeRoi Jones/
Amiri Baraka

The Fiction of
LeRoi Jones/ Amiri Baraka

FOREWORD BY GREG TATE

6 Persons edited and introduced by Henry C. Lacey

Lawrence Hill Books

Library of Congress Cataloging-in-Publication Data

Baraka, Imamu Amiri, 1934–

    [Selections. 2000]

    The fiction of Leroi Jones/Amiri Baraka / foreword by Greg Tate.

    p.   cm.

ISBN 1-55652-346-7 (cloth). — ISBN 1-55652-353-X (pbk.)

1. Afro-Americans Fiction.   I. Title.

PS3552.A583A6   2000

813'.54—dc21

                                    99-25770

                                     CIP

"Suppose Sorrow Was a Time Machine" originally appeared in *Yugen,* no. 2 (1958), pp. 9–11.

"Round Trip" originally appeared in *Mutiny* 2, no. 2 (Autumn 1959), pp. 79–81.

"The Man Who Sold Pictures of God" originally appeared in Stanley Fisher, ed. *Beat Coast East: An Anthology of Rebellion.* New York: York /Excelsior Press, 1960, pp. 91–96.

The System of Dante's Hell was originally published by Grove Press, Inc. © 1963. Portions of *The System of Dante's Hell* have appeared in the following publications: The first seven Circles in *The Trembling Lamb;* "Hypocrites" and "Thieves" in *The Moderns;* "The Eighth Ditch" in *The Floating Bear,* © 1961 by Diane Di Prima and LeRoi Jones; "The Christians" and "The Rape" in *Soon One Morning;* "The Heretics" in *New American Story.*

Tales was originally published by Grove Press, Inc. © 1967. A number of the stories in *Tales* have appeared in *Evergreen Review, Pa'lante, The Moderns, Transatlantic Review,* and *Yugen.* © 1967 LeRoi Jones

"God and Machine" originally appeared in Sonia Sanchez, ed. *We Be Word Sorcerers: 25 Stories by Black Americans.* New York: Bantam, 1973, pp. 9–12.

The first chapter of *6 Persons* ("I") originally appeared in *Selected Plays and Prose of Amiri Baraka / LeRoi Jones,* New York: Morrow, 1979, pp. 194–208.

Published by Lawrence Hill Books

An imprint of Chicago Review Press, Incorporated

814 North Franklin Street

Chicago, Illinois 60610

ISBN 1-55652-346-7 (cloth)

ISBN 1-55652-353-X (paper)

Printed in the United States of America

5 4 3 2 1

Contents

Foreword

Vicious Modernism

There are many great writers whose work, when imposed on the unsuspecting reader, will not suffer for lack of biographical details. The subject of this essay is not one of them. To read Amiri Baraka is to read someone who has written as romantically about his social passions, prejudices, and bodily functions as Joyce wrote of Bloom's. He is also a man who has led a public life full of political furor and controversy, and has never excluded those activities from the arena of his art. The juggling of avant-garde literature and grassroots rabble-rousing form the heart and marrow of his life, and might even be said to *be* his life. Though the performance has not always been graceful, the performer continues to intrigue those who've followed our good brother's progress since the sixties.

Like Bertolt Brecht, Baraka has strung the chewy "literary value" of his output around the harder nut of his theories about political art. Reading Baraka for pleasure requires that one swallow whole his hatreds, his poesy, and his sarcastic wit. One's gender category or ethnic group might turn one into the target of his ire, which has made many readers ask, Why should I bother?

But assessing Baraka's prowess as a poet, novelist, playwright, and essayist without bringing his prejudices into the matter is akin to appraising a jazz musician's sense of harmony without considering his or her sense of rhythm, taste, and history. Baraka's literary forms are so rich and provocative *because* of his personality, not in spite of it. As could also be said of hip-hop MCs, Baraka's best art puts a premium on projecting his bad attitude.

* * * * *

In the matter of LeRoi Jones/Amiri Baraka, then, the facts are roughly these: born Everett Leroy Jones to a postal supervisor father and a social worker mother on October 7, 1934, in Newark, New Jersey, the future father of the Black Arts movement grew up lower middle class in an integrated neighborhood. He attended a high school heavily populated by Italians and Jews, excelled academically, played team sports, and graduated at the tender age of sixteen. He attended Rutgers for a year before transferring to Howard University, an institution he left after two years to join the Air Force and train as a bombardier (an experience he later portrayed as an "Error Farce"). After service he moved to New York and took up residence on the Lower East Side to pursue a writing career. In a short time he became a close friend and confidant of several leading lights of the American avant-garde, including but not exclusive to the Beat and Black Mountain groups. In 1958 he married his first wife, the former Hettie Cohen, a writer/editor/educator best known as the author of *How I Became Hettie Jones*, generally regarded as one of the better memoirs of the era. This union produced two daughters: Kellie, now an internationally known fine arts curator, and Lisa, an accomplished journalist and screenwriter, known for film adaptations of work by Toni Morrison, Dorothy West, and Terry McMillan and for the black feminist essay collection *Bulletproof Diva*.

Jones's first book of poems, *Preface to a Twenty-Volume Suicide Note*, published in 1961, was rapidly followed by *The Dead Lecturer* (1964) and *Black Art* (1966). *Blues People*, published in 1963, is now generally regarded as the most trenchant book of critical theory about African American musical history. *Black Music*, published in 1967, is an equally influential compilation of essays about sixties experimental jazz. In 1964 Baraka had three major plays produced: *The Toilet, The Slave*, and, most notably, *Dutchman*, which won that year's Obie award. Also to be reckoned with in this prolific period are *Home* (1966), a sharp-tongued volume of essays, and the legendary production of his play *Slaveship* (1967) by his company Spirit House Movers.

In 1965, propelled by the assassination of Malcolm X, Jones uprooted himself from his bohemian life downtown and moved to Harlem, leaving wife and children behind, to pursue a course of activism that estranged and alienated him from many of his white friends, admirers, and fellow travelers. By 1967 he had become the era's most vociferous black cultural nationalist, had taken the name Imamu Amiri Baraka (Swahili for "spiritual leader, blessed prince"), and embarked down a concomitant political and literary path.

Later that year, during the Newark riots of 1967 he was beaten bloody by Newark police, then arrested and charged with sedition. During his trial two poems were entered as evidence of his guilt. In 1970 he was instrumental in the election of Newark's first African American mayor, Kenneth Gibson. In 1972 he became a dedicated Marxist-Leninist, a move that alienated him from many of his friends, followers, and fellow travelers in the cultural nationalist camp. A few months before the Newark rebellions, Baraka married his second wife, dancer, painter, poet, and activist Amina Baraka (the former Sylvia Robinson). They produced five children, Obalaji, Ras (already a well-known poet and political activist), Shani, Amiri Jr., and Ahi. Together with Amina's two daughters from a previous marriage, Vera and Wanda, they composed the Baraka family.

In the ensuing decades Baraka has continued writing, lecturing, teaching, and organizing—most recently in support of his son Ras's campaign for mayor of Newark.

In the estimation of literary scholar Arnold Rampersad, Baraka is one of four major figures—the others being Paul Laurence Dunbar, Langston Hughes, and Richard Wright—who have shaped the course of African American literature. Baraka has sustained his prominence outside mainstream American literary circles—a feat unto itself, since his writing and politics have at various points been unfriendly if not downright hostile toward Jews, gays, white men and women, and the black middle class. Yet his most popular works—the poems, *Blues People*, and *Dutchman*—have never long been out of print, and he continues to find receptive imprints for current work as well.

* * * * *

This collection unites the two known volumes of fiction in the Baraka canon, *The System of Dante's Hell* (1965) and *Tales* (1967), with four uncollected short stories and the never-before-published *6 Persons* (1973–74). Baraka's narrative writing tends not to be as well known or as widely discussed as his essays, plays, poetry, and mercurial politics. Partly this is because fiction is the one medium where he didn't ignite and incite the core audience as volubly as he did those for drama, poetry, and music criticism. But in fiction Baraka has been at his most inventive, vulnerable, and self-critical. To be sure, these books are anything but light reading. As polemically charged as any of Baraka's other writing, they are also more taxing of a reader's time, patience, and powers of comprehension than even the more vaunted black experimental fictions of Ishmael Reed and Clarence Major. There is the added rub that while the average reader of experimental fiction may find much formally enticing about the books, he or she may also be turned off by the antiwhite, antigay, anti-Semitic, and misogynistic sentiments that pepper them liberally. For all but the most devoted Barakaphiles, these may be the least inviting of his major works, and so have come to reside in a kind of literary limbo. Their ideal readers are folks with equal admiration for the man's fearless black socialism and his restless assaults on literary convention.

The degree to which *Dante's Hell*, *Tales*, and *6 Persons* read as a warped strain of autobiographical literature is the degree to which they yield the most pleasure. Céline, Miller, and Burroughs seem probable models here, as does the general twentieth-century trend of writing about cities as if they were protagonists, where the narrator figures both as topographer and as a character living in the head of the metropolis. This tendency, first seen in the poetry of Baudelaire, was further evolved by Joyce and Proust, adumbrated by Walter Benjamin, counter-acculturated by Samuel R. Delany in *Dhalgren*, and recently redirected at the field of urban planning by architect-theorist Rem Koolhaas.

Like those writers' texts, Baraka's fictions are unapologetically diaristic, demanding that we allow Baraka as much room for naked honesty, casual observation, offhand brilliance, and utter human failure as any fictional character we may have ever loved or loathed. With the possible exception of Delany, no African American writer has laid as much of his sexual anxiety between covers. In "The Screamers" he contradicts any notion of him as a lifetime hipster with the confession that during slow dances "amateurs like myself, after the music stopped, put our hands quickly into our pockets and retreated into the shadows. It was as meaningful as anything else we knew."

It may indeed be the self-lacerating nature of Baraka's fiction that keeps readers who are hostile to his militancy as much at bay as sympathizers. Who wants to know about the angst of a militant black monster? But Baraka's fiction vitally demands that the ferocity of black rage and the fragility of the black individual's neuroses be given equal sympathy.

> My brother stands there beat and bleary eyes. His friends with him
> shambling, a rude group, a motion, a place in the universe. "We

demand to be loved. We demand to be alive. We demand to be looked at like human beings. We demand that we are always so beautiful. And dirty. And bent. And drunk. And ignorant. . . . Our friend here is hurt. Is injured. Help him lady."

And he stands there with his opening of the sweater, and his droopy pants, and shows the stab wounds. The blood and tearing gap. His heart just beneath it, throwing the blood to the top. ("No Body   No Place," p. 210)

Baraka's life has not been so atypical of other American bad boys who rerouted the national culture (especially those who lived to a ripe old age rather than burned out before age thirty)—early recognition for youthful genius and promise, an Oedipal period of rebellion, followed by rejection for vociferous public displays of social disruption. The intertwining of the private and public selves is perhaps matched in American letters only by Allen Ginsberg and Norman Mailer, who have also become bigger names in the public imagination than have any of their books. They are all also linked to the most explosive of sixties rhetoric, and through the activism of that time have come to signify three different responses to the gauntlet the decade threw down to writers of conscience and extreme charisma.

Many of the spiritual crises lined out in *Dante's Hell* and *Tales* have to do with Baraka's turmoil over whether thinking or feeling is a more honest and radical response to American society—particularly for the black outsider, who, whether deified or demonized by whites, is perpetually the victim of misunderstanding. Baraka's fiction is, if nothing else, a rebuke to the refusal to recognize the consciousness and complexity of African American culture's human by-products.

As history has shown, what he couldn't work out on his fiction's pages he would work out on the barricades. But the interior battles described in his fictional prose are acutely resonant of the times they were written in, when every value white America held as sacrosanct was being challenged and overturned, if not pillaged and burned. Because of the social history of his evolution into a writer and activist, Baraka had a unique vantage point on that burning question of the day: the role of the artist in the revolution. The fictions document his slow docking in the bay of self-consciousness and worldliness—his initial uncertainty about where he belonged in the struggle, and just who were His People, really?

* * * * *

Though earmarked early as a bright middle-class black boy headed for
the Respectable Professional Negro track, Baraka jumped ship to seek
out an earthier reality among the lumpen proletariat of Newark's ghettoes. It is this Diogenian search for truth in experience that fuels *The
System of Dante's Hell*, a bildungsroman stylistically like no other in African
American literature, but thematically not so different from those found
in the most famous works of the Black Novel's big three—Wright, Ellison,
and Baldwin. Not least of the similarities is the way each relates the tor-
ment visited upon young black men stuck between two worlds that had
little use and few answers for their schizophrenic psyches.

In the chapter called "The Eighth Ditch (is Drama," the Jones of the
sixties bickers with his adolescent predecessor. The cadence and mode of
address is not so far removed from those found in *Dutchman*:

> 64—What do you know? You sit right now on the surface of your life. I
> have, at least, all the black arts. The smell of deepest loneliness.
> (*Moves his fingers on the other's shoulders*) I know things that will split
> your face & send you wild-eyed to your own thoughts!

> 46—Oh? I'm stronger than people think. I'm an athlete, and very
> quick-witted. Ha, I'll bet you wdn't play the dozen with me.
> (*Looking up*)

> 64—No. . . . I wdn't do that. You'd only make me mad and I'd have to
> kick your ass. I want more than yr embarassment! (p. 76)

Dante's Hell is the book whose creation Baraka credits with the cesaren
birth of his singular voice. Joyce's *Ulysses* is an obvious influence on
Baraka's experimentations, not just syntactically but in the obsession with
viewing the folkways of his birthplace through a consciously artsy lens.
The book also marks him stepping away from the influence of Charles
Olson and Robert Duncan. In interviews Baraka has said Olson's theories
of a Projective Verse encouraged his desire to write poetry that spoke
about his life and didn't obey the patented gentility of the then-domi-
nant *New Yorker* school. Duncan's early novels, as critic Robert Elliot Fox
has pointed out, contain prose constructions and syncopations that read

like textbook Baraka. The role of Dante, whose *Inferno* Baraka studied extensively at Howard, lies in providing a structural and moralistic grid Baraka purports to invert from the very outset:

> I put The Heretics in the deepest part of hell, though Dante had them spared, on higher ground.
>
> It is heresy, against one's own sources, running in terror, from one's deepest responses and insights . . . the denial of feeling . . . that I see as basest evil.
>
> We are not talking merely about *beliefs*, which are later, after the fact of feeling. A flower, turning from moisture and sun, would turn evil colors and die. (Contents, p. 17)

From there the book proceeds in ways that are maddeningly referential to the author's Newark upbringing, jumping back and forth in time between incidents, personalities, and social rituals. Some passages are little more than character sketches of folks Baraka encountered during what seemed to have been a convulsive rite of passage from childhood to adolescence.

The writing is lush in description, full of lyrical feeling in the more episodic moments, and displays a tendency typical of Baraka's work at this stage to collapse philosophical, carnal, poetic, and racial epiphanies into a litany of self-affirmation and self-loathing:

> We danced, this face and I, close so I had her sweat in my mouth, her flesh the only sound my brain could use. Stinking, and the music over us like a sky, choked any other movement off. I danced. And my history was there, had passed no further. Where it ended, here, the light white talking jig, died in the arms of some sentry of Africa. Some short-haired witch out of my mother's most hideous dreams. I was nobody, now, mama. Nobody. Another secret nigger. No one the white world wanted or would look at. (p. 108)

What the book captures in embryonic formation is Baraka's lifelong rage against bourgeois respectability. To some degree that battle is also against that most respectable of literary endeavors, the Negro Novel, which by the sixties had become a cornerstone of American race relations. Baraka's novel is, in its experimental bent and exploded views of mental minutiae, a sort of mockery of the prevalent notion that the job of the Negro novelist was to explain black men to white men. If this novel has an agenda it is to be so far up its own ass as to only be concerned with what one young black man has to say to himself. While for Ellison, the tradition of the novel wears the status of a national hero, Baraka's critical writing barely deems it worth examining at all. The exception is an essay included in *Home* in which he berates the state of so-called Negro writing. There is a degree to which Baraka is actually upholding a tradition of Oedipal infighting, initiated by Wright and brought to a boil by Baldwin and Ellison—of mainstream-approved black writers banishing their competing brethren and sistren to the land of the wannabes.

Reading that essay today reminds one that Baraka was once as much of an elitist as Ellison. The willful difficulty of *Dante's Hell* only shows just how precious he could get. Yet like Ellison, Baraka had no interest in writing that did not embrace his folkways and his bookish concerns. He seems bent on demonstrating to his white colleagues the ways in which being an African American allowed him to expand the provinces of American fiction. Baraka was not just mimicking his influences, but passionately inventing forms that addressed his readings in Western literature and philosophy as well as his abiding passion for black working-class culture. Eschewing racial polemics in favor of self-revelation, Baraka used his fiction, as he would his other mediums, to stab away at American middle-class existence as not just corny but sterile, moribund, and inhuman. Like Wright, Ellison, and Baldwin, Baraka reveals the existential dimensions of black Americanness—the mental anguish that evolved from trying to see oneself as fully human under American apartheid. The fondness and tenderness with which Baraka writes of whores, junkies, winos, and criminals is all about humanizing people whose capacity for intelligence and feeling belie the stereotypes. *Dante's Hell* magnificently illuminates the consciousness of America's ghettoes—all the deep thinking about Being and Nothingness hidden beneath the surface. The book demands to be read as a flow of verbal energy rather than as a linear narrative, though the last chapter, where his young seviceman incarnation encounters a willful and motherly prostitute named Peaches, settles so comfortably into straight narration as to seem calculated to quiet those who'd bark that he wrote experimental prose because he couldn't tell a story. Of course he could, and in his inimitable style, too.

* * * * *

If *The System of Dante's Hell* is Baraka's *Ulysses, Tales* is his *Dubliners*, a loose collection of short narrative vehicles that display Baraka's capacity for sociological introspection to great advantage. "The Alternative" details the harassment of two gay men by students in an all-male dorm in Howard University in the fifties. Like the Eighth Ditch chapter of *Dante's Hell*, it is a play thinly dressed up in fictional trappings. More conventional stories—"Salute," "Uncle Tom's Cabin: *Alternate Ending*," and "Heroes Are Gang Leaders"—work his time in the Air Force and the Village into driving, suspenseful scenarios rife with deft character descriptions and incisive dialogue. Some are little more than thumbnail sketches for Baraka to show how brilliant he can be conducting a jam session with his own pen. As in his poetry, there are lines that scream their origins from Baraka's singular sense of wit, syntax, and life-affirming sarcasm. They remind one of Thelonious Monk and Miles Davis in their commitment to an elliptical, disjunctive, darting attack, one very much at odds with the verbose rhythmic cascade generally asociated with the so-called jazzy writing of Jack Kerouac. Just as jazz musicians converted stentorian Western concert instruments into vessels of spontaneous broken rhythms and lightfooted virility, Baraka used short prose to resonantly capture his most fleeting sense-impressions.

The most outstanding piece of *Tales* is "The Screamers," a story many critics and readers consider to be Baraka's best piece of short fiction. It is certainly a masterpiece of concision; in six pages Baraka reports of a riot that jumped off during a rhythm and blues performance in fifties Newark while simultaneously providing an anthropological precis on the ritual importance of fashion, gesture, music, and manners in a roughneck urban juke joint. The prose itself is a wonder of cinematic detail, sociological revelation, music criticism, and poetic illumination. As in many a Baraka work, the language is the protagonist, though the central story in this instance would be compelling in the hands of a hack. Baraka the adult sophisticate and Baraka the virgin explorer of forbidden spaces converge to create a pungent hybrid:

> The dancers ground each other past passion or moved so fast it
> blurred intelligence. We hated the popular song, and any freedman

could tell you if you asked that white people danced jerkily, and were slower than our champions. One style, which developed as Italians showed up with pegs, and our own grace moved towards bellbottom pants to further complicate the cipher, was the honk. The repeated rhythmic figure, a screamed riff, pushed in its insistence past music. It was hatred and frustration, secrecy and despair. It spurted out of the diphthong culture, and reinforced the black cults of emotion. (p. 184)

Tales is arranged in two sections, which demarcate Baraka's life and thinking in bohemia versus what it was becoming after the move to Harlem and the adoption of cultural nationalism. Two pivotal stories from the latter portion are "Words" and "Answers in Progress." The former is most notable for the meditative instructions it concludes with—an eerie Afro-Zen contemplation of Black militancy as a form of spiritual asylum.

> We do not need to be fucked with.
> We can be quiet and love the silence.
> We need to look at trees more closely.
> We need to listen. (p. 194)

"Answers" juxtaposes alien tourists and Harlem Mau Mau in a manner that now seems typical of spaced-out sixties radicalism. The story's concluding lines carry a Baraka trademark—revolutionary prophecy lyrically combined with mundane sensuality:

> White came in with the design for a flag he'd been working on. Black heads, black hearts, and blue fiery space in the background. Love was heavy in the atmosphere. Ball wanted to know what the blue chicks looked like. But I didn't. Cause I knew after tomorrow's duty, I had a day off, and I knew somebody waitin for me at my house, and some kids, and some fried fish, and those carrots, and wow.
>   That's the way the fifth day ended. (p. 222)

* * * * *

6 Persons, written after Baraka's conversion to Marxist-Leninism, is a fascinating contribution not only to his fictive oeuvre but to his autobiographical writings as well. More frenzied and stylistically daring than *The Autobiography of LeRoi Jones*, it is a freewheeling (if not cartwheeling) examination of his evolutionary arc—from the fanciful childhood fan of comic books and radio plays to the teenage urban drifter and bebop aficionado to studious college boy to displaced Air Force pilot to aspirant New York intellectual to Black Power advocate to Black Marxist. For Baraka followers, the record of changes won't seem revelatory, but the telling is an extraordinarily artful and mercilessly sarcastic attack on his own past. Of his feeble attempts at becoming a regular college Lothario, he recalls,

> You were outside on the balcony with this Delta pledgee, an art student, with short wavy dirty blond hair, and lightskinned bumpy complexion. She was weird tho. And then, you kept drinking, LJ, and you cdn't drink then, going back into the kitchen for more. And you and this babe were mated off by the others, and you were getting dizzy, LJ, and it seemed to you you were really getting over, and you had on a brand new Brooks Brothers grey flannel vine, rich white boy style, and suddenly LJ, the pretty babe was drifting, drifting, away . . . and then, my man, hey cat, you were drunk and on the floor and vomiting all over everything. . . .
>   You remember that, LJ? (p. 262)

Of his stumble through the prevailing currents of progressive American cultural politics of the late fifties and early sixties he writes:

> Anglo-Germanic rebellion was called Blk Mountain. Also crammed in its juicier times with Monk and Sonny Rollins. Pound vs Whitman was what it came down to. The same king of jazz, this time with a beard and boy-jones. For the immigrants to rally behind. Pound right back to Germanic Anglo correct vision and version. The fact that Pound was a fascist made him the true object of niggers' worship. The fact that he sd outright he hated them made him the object of fond regard. Damn, how pure can they get?? These particular niggers here whose story this is. Anything totally esoteric they dug. And even the fact that Pound was s'posed to have thot niggers simple barbarians. There was even dudes like light-skinned Steve J in Bostown who was absolutely Poundian and wrote exactly, even letters, like him, and echoed the same exact anti-nigra tone. (p. 322)

For its complexity, invention, confessional recklessness, and abiding contribution to complicating the African presence in American letters, the fiction of Amiri Baraka deserves a closer read from contemporary audiences. Distant from the furor that surrounded the author when the stories were first published, today's readers should be able to give these major works the copious attention they have always deserved.

Greg Tate
New York, 1999

Suppose Sorrow Was a Time Machine

Here is Dothan, Alabama, U.S.A. 1898. This is of value. What is to be said about the place, Dothan, and the time, 1898. It is of value, but it doesn't matter what becomes of the telling, once it is told.

Say that you are Tom Russ. It is Dothan, Alabama, U.S.A. 1898. You are a Negro who has felt the ground vibrate, and you are trying to interpret the vibration. You are trying to interpret the vibration, and what it means in 1898 Dothan. I know you Tom. You are my grandfather. I am not born yet but I have felt the ground vibrate too. And I too would like to know exactly what it means, here in Alabama 1898, 34 years before I am born. Fifty years before I realize you knew about the vibration, 50 years before I knew that I possessed the knowledge of your knowing. But now is what we are concerned with.

The store is burning, Tom. They have burnt your store, Tom. What does it mean? Is the burning another vibration? Interpret this one, Tom. Let your unborn grandchild know what his dead, whistling grandfather thought of the burning. If I were you, Tom, I would have cried. Did you cry, Tom? No, I suppose not. Not with the vibration still moving the ground in front of you. What was crying that it could erase a knowledge of what everything meant? How obscure is enlightenment? As obscure as dust kicked up on a path nobody walks on, as obscure as birds falling off trees with no god to catch them. All this is O.K., Tom, but what about the unholy bastards who are killing you? I hear they dropped a street-light on your bald head and scattered your brains. Is that true, Tom? That's the lie your wife told me when I watched you sitting by the wood stove, unable to make your hurts vocal. Rocking back and forth like the rocking chair would carry you clear to paradise, so you could finally find out about them 50 year old vibrations.

You built that store back up. You knelt down and scraped the black parts of the wood away and stuck them poles in the ground and got the thing up so fast folks thought you had hypnotized them, and there wasn't really any store at all, only the insane intensity of your vision. So they burned this one too, and said they were going to run you out of town.

1

And just to spite them you knelt back down in those ashes and scraped the black off again, and built again. "It's the biggest funeral parlor in the county. . .got 3 horse drawn hearses. . .belongs to that nigger Tom Russ." A vibration can carry a man a long ways. Fancy Tom Russ, funeral parlor so fancy, the niggers killing each other so they can get an excuse to go to it. But the other folks got tired of all that noise, and burned it again. What can a man do? One vibration ain't the world. Your unborn grandson says leave this pisshearted town, Tom. Pack up and move on, Tom. Vibrations are like anything else—there's more wherever you go. Goodbye, crackers, Tom Russ is leaving your town. His grandson'll be back to correct your grammar and throw stones in your wells. Fifty years ain't so long.

Here is Beaver Falls, Pennsylvania, 1917. Tom and Anna Russ, son George age 20, daughter Anna Lois age 16. No vibrations here. Sell eggs, produce. Best liquor in the county. Send my grandson's mother to college. She's got to know 'bout them vibrations. Got to tell him when he gets here, write it down. We're going north, Anna. Got to hunt them vibrations down. Got to find out where the music goes when we don't hear it no more. Got to know about the silence at the top of our screams. Gonna find out what part of the world is fashioned in my image. Gonna make a myth for my unborn grandson, who'll surely like to know. The signs read "Goodbye Tom & Anna Russ." Goodbye and God bless you, sorry to see you go. Three Negroes, 2 with horns, the third with a battered drum. Tah, tah, tat, tah, yippeee, hoorah, Tom Russ, Tom Russ. Good ol' Tom Russ. Sure am sorry to see 'em go.

Here is Newark, New Jersey, 1925. Can't hardly walk for all the movement between me and the ground. This'll be good, Anna. "Russ Produce—Super General Store," "Music While You Shop," George Russ on the piano, rags and stomps, victrola requests played if possible. It's nice here, one vibration can carry a man a long way if he knows just how to handle it. Can make a man realize why there's such a thing as spring. I sit here and see Tom smiling at me, winking, knowing full well I hear everything he's saying. He stands there being sworn in to the Board of Elections, winking, grinning at me, daring me to understand what all this has got to do with the Dothan vibrations. And what it's all got to do with me. Tom Russ, standing there trying to remember some of his unborn grandson's poems. Hearing a few words and shaking his head up and down, staring me square in the eyes. He should only realize how beautiful he is. Although he probably does know that vibrations don't come to the unworthy. I hope he knew that.

1929, the streets of Newark are littered with tophats and striped pants and a few bankers with holes in their temples. Tom grins and closes the doors of "Russ Super General Store." The wind moves a few leaves down Boston Street as Tom goes to see his daughter and her husband. He is a quiet man, industrious, thin as a string and painfully shy. Tom looks him up and down and asks him is he a good man. This is my father who nods and slides his arm around Tom's daughter. Tom wonders will I look like him, and I nod yes, and he is satisfied and takes out his cigars and chats about the depression.

I hear they finally hit you in the head with a street lamp, Tom. Is that so? Gave you a cane and a wheelchair, and made you sit by the wood stove nodding and spitting, trying desperately to remember exactly when and where it was the ground vibrated. But do you realize that your unborn grandson has finally got here? Or is it that he's still unborn and only the body has managed to make it right now. Have you got time, Tom? Can you remember any of those lines, Tom? Tell the saucereyed boy at your feet. Maybe they'll do him some good.

Here is Greystone Sanatorium, 1943. Tired, eh Tom? Lying there so still and manageable. What's up there on the ceiling that you have to stare at it so hard? Is it written up there about the vibrations? Tell the 11 year old foot-sitter about them, Tom. Have you got time? Why are your hands so pale, Tom? You must be doing a lot of heavy thinking to be so quiet. Look how the boy looks at you, Tom. He looks scared. Smile at him, Tom. Just a tiny smile of recognition. Brighten this bleak rust room. Show him the suns you used to carry around in your pocket. Whisper something funny to him, Tom. Did you know he was your grandson, Tom. Did you know he fell down on the floor and screamed and kicked his feet when they said they were taking you to this loony pen. Did you know that in only a few years he'll recognize you as his "before everything conversationalist" and want to go to wherever it is you'll want to go after this short detour. Just a phrase, Tom. It'll make things better when your daughter cuts down your black overcoat so he can have something to wear at his grandfather's funeral. Tom, are you going to let him cry like that? Are you going to let the me that was, before the stoneage metamorphosis, suffer? Have you no feeling for the child? A sympathy for the post-prebirth enlightenment, the pre-promethean banality of childhood? The boy is sensitive, Tom, say something before you move on to grounds more fertile for random vibrations. Tom, are you listening? Don't stare like that. Tom. Tom. O my god.

Round Trip

He'd come out of the alley only at dusk. Then, only to overturn a few garbage cans and browse a bit for delicacies. If he found any, he would gobble them down right on the spot. He was never one for hoarding anything. Sometimes he'd find some great things in those cans, too. Once I remember, when I was over for dinner, he had a chicken, some hors d'oeuvres, and a couple of half emptied bottles of champagne. It was a real feast. But he always took pains about his stomach. A real gourmet.

Well, I heard him sing many times. Mostly late in the evening it was. He'd clear away the stuff that was left over from the evening meal, then while he was picking his teeth he'd begin to hum. Sometimes he'd leave it at that; the humming. But then sometimes he'd break into a great aria or something. I never could recognize the particular opera it came from, but, Christ it was beautiful. He'd stand up and throw out his chest, and let go with a real high, shiny kind of note. Then he'd let it roll right down till he had near hit bottom. I never heard nothing like it before or since. Sometimes he'd sing for hours, and then sometimes, if he wasn't feeling too well, he'd cut it off after one song. His voice? Well, it's hard to describe. First thing it'd sound like was some kind of trumpet or cornet playing high and steady. Then when he'd drop it down real low it was almost like the rumble of one of them big engines. Sometimes it was as if there wasn't really any sound at all. You know like when an organ goes so low you can't hear it, just feel the vibrations. When it did that, it was really scary. But great as hell. I always wondered how he picked that up.

In the winter he'd bring a lot of cardboard boxes into the alley to block some of the wind. But I never heard him complain about the cold, not once. And you know that winter we had last year. All that snow, remember? I think it began snowing the day after Christmas, and didn't let up till two or three weeks later. Well, every day I'd come by the alley, and he'd be there smoking his pipe, or ordering his papers or something. Real calm about the whole thing. He'd make me sit down and take a meal with him, and he'd talk about the usual things; music, his trip to Puerto Rico, or how beautiful the sea is off Greece. But nothing about the weather.

He never talked about his family or anything. I don't even know exactly where he came from. He looked kind of European. You know like the ambassadors in the films—thin, straight, with this heavy beard covering most of his face. I used to wonder if maybe he wasn't rich or something, or maybe a writer just living in the alley like that to get ideas for a book. I asked him a few times about himself, but all he'd ever say was that he was a young man and there was still a long time to go before what he was would be clear to him. No, that's what he said. It struck me so funny that I kinda memorized it. I never understood what he meant, but I didn't pester him about it. I guess he had a reason for it. I used to think, too, that it was a woman that had caused him whatever trouble he must have been in, to be living like that. But he certainly never mentioned anything about no female. Not at all. Whenever I saw him, he was sitting cross-legged like he always did, writing in a little notebook. I don't know how he could understand what he was writing—the pencil just barely had a point. But there he'd be writing away. Head down, very interested in what he was doing. I asked him what he was writing and he'd look at me very seriously and say, "I'm trying to understand what the error is." That's all he'd say, just that. "I'm trying to understand what the error is."

When he didn't want to be bothered with my foolishness, he'd meet me at the entrance to the alley and shake his head. I knew right away what it was, and I'd turn around and go home. It wasn't often he did that though. Most of the times we'd sit and chew the fat for hours and hours, after he'd sung. Then when it was time for me to go, he'd pat me on the shoulder and walk with me right out almost to the street. He was the kindest, quietest fellow I ever knew.

Strange, the way I met him. I was going through my rounds, pushing the broom down the curb—not making any headway at all, you know how dirty this damned city is, when I see this fellow poking around in the wire refuse cans on the corner. I went over to stop him, and when I touched him on the shoulder he turns around and says that it's all right because he's not throwing stuff on the ground, just eating it. I thought he was a bum or something, but then he invites me to dinner. I thought I'd puke, but he just laughed and asked me about dirt. I asked him what he meant; so he says, describe dirt. I try, and he laughs again and says, describe clean. I laugh, and he walks away into the alley. After that, I'd stop on my rounds each night and talk to him, or listen to him sing.

I knew him about a year before that thing happened. Yeh, just about one year exactly. What thing? You didn't read about it in the papers? Well, I guess it was easy enough to miss. It was only about eight or nine lines in the 'Mirror.' I was the one who found him, too. I remember, it was later than I usually came around. So when I first called to him, I figured he might have been asleep. Then I went up a little ways into the alley and there he was, sprawled out on the ground half-naked, blood all over. I almost died it was so gruesome. His face was caked with blood and his eyes were still open, staring straight up. Somebody had stabbed him in the side and God knows where else. I ran for the cops. They came and carried him away . . . said he was a bum and that he was probably in a brawl. Stupid bastards, what do they know? They never heard him sing.

Funny I should tell this now, seldom thing about it. But, God, sometimes I see him in my sleep, dead like that—his arms and legs spread wide apart. Whoever done it must of been crazy or something. They stabbed him all over. Even his feet and hands had stab marks in 'em. Can you imagine?

the man who sold pictures of god

He, the man, was on the side of the entrance to the park. Around him, stretching away from him on all sides, as lies from the transcendental ego, were canvases. Myriads of convases; all sizes. 9 x 12's, 18 x 24's, 36 x 48's, 72 x 96's. . . . Thousands of canvases. All the same color. All the canvases were white. (reflect on that for a second. The whiteness of the canvases was *purely* symbolic.) There was absolutely nothing on them, believe me! I, playing the fool as usual, stopped to look. I was attempting to make some sense of this. Of course, I could have passed the devil by, unmindful (or rather more mindful of the obvious consequences of any indiscretion)—or merely attributed the whole phenomenon to economics, sayin that the fellow was probably just a canvas salesman. Can you imagine that? A canvas salesman.

I was not alone when I made this discovery. I mean, there was another person with me, walking alongside me whom I knew, when I came upon the canvas salesman. (You see, I've tried to slip that idea across already.) She did not see the man.

Yes, I pointed, gesticulated, insulted her. . .was on the point of actually striking her. .but she insisted she could not see him. So I finally accepted the lie. We were not close enough to the man at the time to hear, (or take part in) the altercation that arose over her inconsistency.

A likely story, I screamed. A likely story. She only smiled attractively and remained more or less mute.

When we did reach the man, I began the argument over again at the top of my voice. A likely story, I ranted. A likely story. She smiled again, more attractively than before, but remained essentially mute.

The canvas salesman (watch me closely now) turned his head towards me, AND WITH SLOW (agonizingly slow) ALMOST FELINE

9

MOVEMENTS RAISED HIS LEFT HAND AND POINTED TOWARDS ONE OF THE CANVASES. You like the pretty canvases, he asked? I craned my head towards him as if I hadn't heard the first time. He repeated the question. You like the pretty canvases?

I howled. I fell down on the pavement clutching my sides in merriment. The man repeated the question. You like the pretty canvases? I rolled over into the gutter laughing uncontrollably. The man remained unsmiling. The woman (my companion) smiled graciously, but remained for the most part quite mute. The man repeated the question. You like the pretty canvases?

After I had composed myself, brushed off my clothes, wiped the tears from my eyes, adjusted my umbrella, took out my pipe and emptied it against my shoe, recovered my hat which had rolled off my head and into the gutter, popped two sen sen under my tongue, I turned and faced the man squarely, uttering in my most cultivated voice, I'm afraid I don't understand what you mean. The man smiled. I turned to the woman. She also smiled. This was no time to admit defeat. I could still bring a victory (albeit of a rather pyrric nature) from this chaos.

The man was dressed in what appeared to be army coveralls, but these coveralls had some kind of red and white stripes on them. I don't think they were sewn on rather they looked as if someone had taken tubes of oil paint and made lines hurriedly and quite sloppily, vertically from shoulder to ankle. He wore a very stylish tweed cap. Very 'English' looking. Very correct (the cap). Quite sporty. He also wore the most elegant shoes. Cordovans they were; very expensive looking dress shoes. He watched me look him over from head to toe. He said nothing, continued to smile. The woman also continued to smile, although she remained (I would say) quite mute.

The man and I chose to stare at each other for a few more moments. When I turned to the woman, SHE HAD STRANGELY ENOUGH, STOPPED SMILING. (When she had accomplished this, I am not quite certain). HER MOUTH WAS MOVING AS IF IN SOME SUPREME EFFORT TO SPEAK. I turned back to the man. By this time he had crawled beneath some of the canvases and was lying there under 10 or 12 pounds of canvas, unmoving. I immediately turned back to the woman. HER MOUTH HAD STOPPED, BUT SHE WAS NOT SMILING NOW. . NO, NOT AT ALL. Meanwhile, the man had started to whistle.

I shouted to him, come out from under those canvases. No answer. He continued to whistle. I decided to change my strategy. I whispered, please, sir come out from under those heavy canvases or you will surely hurt yourself. He immediately scrambled to his feet, and stood rigidly before me in what could have been taken as an attitude of sincere reverence. (I was not fooled, however).

Enough of this foolishness, I screamed. What is the meaning of these bare canvases, my friend? His tinny little eyes glittered and became animate, like the water in a commode when it is flushed. He beckoned me to come closer. I did. The woman stood motionless. It was getting to be twilight. The sheepish old sun was growing rapidly senile. I edged toward the man. A thin vein of saliva rolled down out of the side of his mouth.

My name is Maurice, he said. I stared blankly. Do you like the pretty canvases, he continued? I continued staring. Suddenly, he grabbed me by the shoulders and screamed into my face, DO YOU LIKE THE PRETTY CANVASES? I was dumbfounded; thunderstruck; virtually speechless. He screamed at me again. DO YOU LIKE THE PRETTY CANVASES? His eyes seemed to be spinning around like roulette wheels. .for one mad second I thought I could actually see numbers on his eye balls. Sweat was pouring into my mouth. My whole being was aflame with a feeling of eminent disaster, but I knew I couldn't turn back now. I couldn't renege. I had to go through with the whole farce. Even if it meant execution. I shuddered at that prospect. EXECUTION. The man shouted again. And again. His words were Egyptian dancers in the bright sun pirouetteing beneath the godly sphinx. Now they were crazy men in red capes who were trying to pry the Empire State building loose with crow bars. Now they were 10,000 scale models of my mother. I knew I had to respond. I couldn't ignore these questions any longer. I gathered all the electricity in my body into one small area just adjacent to my adam's apple; readied it, then wheeled and spat it out at the grim little figure who stood taunting me. I said, BUT WHY ARE THEY CANVASES? His mouth slammed shut. His hands slid off my shoulders weakly. I had caught him by surprise. I started to move forward. I had no idea why. But then I felt strong arms clutch me around the thighs. It was my female companion. She was straining to pull me away from the man.

I fought her hold, but her strength seemed not grounded in the solely physical. The harder I struggled, the harder she held. Then the man started laughing. YOU SEE, he shouted, YOU SEE. . . . THIS IS WHY THEY ARE CANVASES.

Please, please let me go, I pleaded, I have almost won. Let me go, you devilish shrew. Still she tugged at waist and legs. NOW SHE BEGAN TO SPEAK. The words shot out of her mouth like bullets from an aeroplane, strafing little chinese children in the newsreels. The words were sailing out of her mouth. They were material and concrete. Every now and then, one would strike my flesh and cause a small laceration. I began to weep. At first, I couldn't make out what she was saying, but then all the projectile-like syllables fell into place and became intelligible. YOU ARE CREATED IN GOD'S IMAGE AND THIS IS YOUR LIMITATION. . . . . . IF YOU DO NOT REALIZE THIS YOU WILL SURELY SUFFER THE FATE OF ALL FINITE THINGS ALL FINITE THINGS ALL FINITE THINGS DO YOU NOT REALIZE THE UNCERTAINTY OF THIS WORLD PLEASE TO NOT CHALLENGE THE INCORRIGIBLE MAD-NESS OF THINGS THAT ARE ETC. ETC. ETC. ETC. ETC. ETC. ETC. ETC. ETC. ETC. ETC. ETC. ETC. ETC. ETC. ETC. ETC. ETC. ETC. ETC. ETC. ETC. ETC. ETC. ETC. ETC. ETC. Then I got another brain-storm. I craned my head around until I could see the woman. I shouted at her, trying to make myself heard above her maddening gibberish. YOU SEE HIM TOO. ADMIT IT YOU SNOTTY LITTLE BITCH. YOU SEE HIM TOO. Suddenly, she was silent. She released me immediately, took a few backward steps and resumed the position she had affected when I first saw the man. She started to smile again. . . . and was mute.

He also (Maurice) stopped laughing, and was quiet. I approached him, bold and confident now. YOU SEE, IT'S ALL A JOKE. YOU CANNOT FOOL ME. I WON'T BE FOOLED BY ANY SHABBY TRICKS. A little grin tried to crawl out onto his cheek, but he supressed it successfully. The woman still stood motionless. WHAT IS IT YOU WANT TO SAY, the man asked. I began looking at the ground, trying to see if I could see my reflection in the pavement. WHAT IS IT YOU WANT TO SAY, he asked again a little louder. I shook my head slowly from side to side.

I am a canvas salesman, he said quietly.

I know, I shot in.

See that you remember that, he muttered.

I will, I grumbled, embarassed.

He started gathering up the canvases. Every now and then he would remove the tweed cap and wipe his forehead. The woman remained motionless. Soon, he had gathered all the canvases together and began tying them with a heavy cord. I watched rather dispassionately. The woman yawned. He got all the canvases tied, then hoisted them onto his shoulders. I was too embarassed to look at him. He began whistling again. The woman came towards me and grasped my hand tenderly. The man began to move away. She kissed me gently on the neck. He looked at me over his shoulder, out of the corner of his eye. She ran her tongue along the hollow of my throat. He turned the corner and was completely out of sight. She began to unzip my trousers with her other hand.

It was completely dark now. There weren't even any stars.

THE SYSTEM OF DANTE'S HELL

THE SYSTEM OF DANTE'S HELL

	Neutrals
	Circle 1. Virtuous Heathen
	Circle 2. Lascivious
Incontinent	Circle 3. Gluttons
	Circle 4. Avaricious and Prodigal
	Circle 5. Wrathful

Circle 6. Heretics*

		(1) Violent against others
Violent	Circle 7.	(2) Violent against self
		(3) Violent against God, nature, and art

		(1) Panderers and Seducers
		(2) Flatterers
		(3) Simonists
		(4) Diviners
Circle 8. Simply		(5) Barrators
Fraudulent		(6) Hypocrites
		(7) Thieves
		(8) Fraudulent Counsellors
		(9) Makers of discord
		(10) Falsifiers

	(1) to kindred
Circle 9. Treacherous	(2) to country and cause
	(3) to guests
	(4) to lords and benefactors

* I put The Heretics in the deepest part of hell, though Dante had them spared, on higher ground.

It is heresy, against one's own sources, running in terror, from one's deepest responses and insights . . . the denial of feeling . . . that I see as basest evil.

We are not talking merely about *beliefs*, which are later, after the fact of feeling. A flower, turning from moisture and sun would turn evil colors and die.

NEUTRALS: The Vestibule

But Dante's hell is heaven. Look at things in another light. Not always the smarting blue glare pressing through the glass. Another light, or darkness. Wherever we'd go to rest. By the simple rivers of our time. Dark cold water slapping long wooden logs jammed 10 yards down in the weird slime, 6 or 12 of them hold up a pier. Water, wherever we'd rest. And the first sun we see each other in. Long shadows down off the top where we were. Down thru grey morning shrubs and low cries of waked up animals.

Neutrals: The breakup of my sensibility. First the doors. The brown night rolling down bricks. Chipped stone stairs in the silence. Vegetables rotting in the neighbors' minds. Dogs wetting on the buildings in absolute content. Seeing the pitied. The minds of darkness. Not even sinister. Breaking out in tears along the sidewalks of the season. Grey leaves outside the junkshop. Sheridan Square blue men under thick quivering smoke. Trees, statues in a background of voices. Justice, Égalité. Horns break the fog with trucks full of dead chickens. Motors. Lotions.

The neutrals run jewelry shops & shit in silence under magazines. Women disappear into Canada. They painted & led interminable lives. They marched along the sides of our cars in the cold brown weather. They wore corduroy caps & listened to portables. The world was in their eyes. They wore rings & had stories about them. They walked halfway back from school with me. They were as tall as anyone else you knew. Some sulked, across the street out of sight, near the alley where the entrance to his home was. A fat mother. A fat father with a mustache. Both houses, and the irishman's near the playground. Balls went in our yards. Strong hitters went in Angel's. They all lived near everything.

                    A house painter named Ellic, The Dog, "Flash." Eddie, from across the street. Black shiny face, round hooked nose, beads for hair. A thin light sister with droopy socks. Smiling. Athletic. Slowed by bow legs. Hustler. Could be made angry. Snotty mouth. Hopeless.

The mind fastens past landscapes. Invisible agents. The secret trusts. My own elliptical. The trees' shadows broaden. The sky draws together darkening. Shadows beneath my fingers. Gloom grown under my flesh.

Or fasten across the lots, the grey garages, roofs suspended over cherry trees. The playground fence. Bleakly with guns in the still thin night. Shadows of companions drawn out along the ground. Newark Street green wood, chipped, newsstands. Dim stores in the winter. Thin brown owners of buicks.

And this not the first. Not beginnings. Smells of dreams. The pickles of the street's noise. Fire escapes of imagination. To fall off to death. Unavailable. Delayed into whispering under hurled leaves. Paper boxes roll down near the pool. From blue reflection, through the fence to the railroad. No trains. The walks there and back to where I was. Night queens in winter dusk. Drowning city of silence. Ishmael back, up through the thin winter smells. Conked hair, tweed coat, slightly bent at the coffee corner. Drugstore, hands turning the knob for constant variation. Music. For the different ideas of the world. We would turn slowly and look. Or continue eating near the juke box. Theories sketch each abstraction. Later in his old face ideas were ugly.

Or be wrong because of simple movement. Not emotion. From under all this. The weight of myself. Not even with you to think of. That settled. Without the slightest outside.

Stone on stone. Hard cobblestones, oil lamps, green house of the native. Natives down the street. All dead. All walking slowly towards their lives. Already, each Sunday forever. The man was a minister. His wife was light-skinned with freckles. Their church was tall brown brick and sophisticated. Bach was colored and lived in the church with Handel. Beckett was funeral director with brown folding chairs. On W. Market St. in winters the white stripe ran down the center of my thots on the tar street. The church sat just out of shadows and its sun slanted down on the barbershops.

Even inside the house, linoleums were cold. Divided in their vagueness. Each man his woman. Their histories die in the world. My own. To our children we are always and forever old. Grass grew up thru sidewalks. Mr. & Mrs. Puryear passed over it. Their gentle old minds knew my name. And I point out forever their green grass. Brown unopened books. The smell of the world. Just inside the dark bedroom. The world. Inside the sealed eyes of obscure relatives. The whole world. A continuous throb in the next room.

He raced out thru sunlight past their arms and crossed the goal. Or nights with only the moon and their flat laughter he peed under metal stairs and ran through the cold night grinning. Each man his own place. Each flower in its place. Each voice hung about me in this late evening. Each face will come to me now. Or what it was running through their flesh, all the wild people stalking their own winters.

The street was always silent. Green white thick bricks up past where we could see. An open gate to the brown hard gravel no one liked. Another day grew up through this. Crowds down the street. Sound in red waves waves over the slow cold day. To dusk. To black night of rusty legs. "These little girls would run after dark past my house, sometimes chased by the neighbor hoods." A long hill stuck against the blue glass. From there the woman, the whore, the dancer, the lesbian, the middleclass coloured girl spread her legs. Or so my father said. The dog Paulette was on fire, and I slipped out through the open window to the roof. Then shinnied down to the ground. I hid out all night with some italians.

HEATHEN: No. 1

1

You've done everything you said you wdn't. Everything you said you despised. A fat mind, lying to itself. Unmoving like some lump in front of a window. Wife, child, house, city, clawing at your gentlest parts. Romance become just sad tinny lies. And your head full of them. What do you want anymore? Nothing. Not poetry or that purity of feeling you had. Even that asceticism you pulled in under your breast that drunks & school-friends thought of as "sense of humor" . . . gone, erased, some subtle rot disposed in its place. Turning towards everything in your life. Whatever clarity left, a green rot, a mud, a stifling at the base of the skull. No air gets in.

* * *

The room sat quiet in the evening under one white bulb. He sat with a glass empty at his right hand. A cigarette burning the ugly dining-room table. Unanswered letters, half-thumbed magazines, old books he had to reread to remember. An empty fight against the sogginess that had already crept in thru his eyes. A bare bulb on a cluttered room. A dirty floor full of food particles and roaches. Lower middleclass poverty. In ten years merely to lose one's footing on a social scale. Everything else, that seriousness, past, passed. Almost forgotten. The wild feeling of first see-ing. Even a lost smell plagued the back of his mind. Coffee burning downtown when he paced the wet pavement trying to look intense. And that walked thru him like weather.

* * *

I feel sick and lost and have nothing to place my hands on. A piano with two wrong notes. Broken chinese chimes. An unfaithful wife. Or even one that was faithful a trudgen round me. Everything I despise some harsh testimonial of my life. The Buddhism to affront me. Ugly Karma. My thin bony hands. Eyes fading. Embarrassed at any seriousness in me. Left outside I lose it all. So quickly. My youth wasted on the bare period of my desires.

* * *

He lived on a small street with 8 trees. Two rooming houses at the end of the street full of Puerto Ricans. Rich white americans between him and them. Like a chronicle. He said to himself often, looking out the window, or simply lying in bed listening to the walls breathe. Or the child whimper under the foul air of cat leavings pushed up out of the yard by some wind. Nothing more to see under flesh but himself staring bewildered. At his hands, his voice, his simple benumbing life. Not even tragic. Can you raise tears at an unpainted floor. The simple incompetence of his writing. The white wall smeared with grease from hundreds of heads. All friends. Under his hands like domestic lice. The street hangs in front of the window & does not even breathe. Trucks go to New Jersey. The phone rings and it will be somebody he does not even understand. A dope addict who has written short stories. A thin working girl who tells jokes to his wife. A fat jew with strange diseases. A rich woman with paint on her slip. Hundreds of innocent voices honed to a razor-sharp distress by their imprecise lukewarm minds. Not important, if they moved in his head nothing would happen, he thought once. And then he stopped/embarrassed, egoistic. A cold wind on his neck from a smeared half-open window. The cigarette burned the table. The bubbles in the beer popped. He stared at his lip & tried to bite dried skin.

Nothing to interest me but myself. Disappeared, even the thin moan of ideas that once slipped through the pan of my head. The night is colder than the day. Two seconds lost in that observation. The same amount of time to stroke Nijinski's cheek. One quick soft move of my fingers on his face. That two seconds then that same two if they would if there were some way, would burn my soul to black ash. Scorch my thick veins.

I am myself. Insert the word disgust. A verb. Get rid of the "am." Break out. Kill it. Rip the thing to shreds. This thing, if you read it, will jam your face in my shit. Now say something intelligent!

2

I've loved about all the people I can. Frank, for oblique lust, his mind.
The satin light floating on his words. His life tinted and full of afternoons. My own a weird dawn. Hedges & that thin morning water covering
my skin. I had a hat on and wdn't sit down. Light was emptying the windows and someone else slept close to us, fouling the room with his
breath. That cdn't move. It killed itself. And opens stupidly now like a
time capsule. You don't rub your mouth on someone's back to be
accused. Move it or shut up!

(He was lovely and he sat surrounded by
paintings watching his friends die. The farmers went crazy and voted.
The FBI showed up to purchase condoms. Nothing interesting was done
for Negroes so they became stuck up and smelly.)

All the women I could put on a page have the same names. There was
a round bar where the bunch of us sat listening to the sea and a whore
suck her fingers. That white woman who counted in Spanish.

My wife
doesn't belong in this because she sits next to a ghost and talks to him as
if he played football for her college. He wd know if he sat in a bare bright
room talking his life away. If he sat, frozen to his lies, spitting his blood on
the floor. If he had no life but one he had to give continuously to others.
If he had to wait for Hussars to piss in his mouth before he had an
orgasm. If he could fly, or not fly, definitely. If something in his simple life
were really simple or at least understandable. If he were five inches taller
and weighed more. If he could kill anybody he wanted or sleep with statues of saints. Nothing is simpler than that. If there were a heaven he
understood or if he could talk to anyone without trying to find out how
much they knew about him. His capes. His knives. His lies. His houses.
His money. His yellow hats. His laughter. His immaculate harems for
heroes.

Still. The black Job. Mind gone. Head lost. Fingers stretch beyond his
flesh. Eyes. Their voices' black lust. The fog. Each to the other moves in
itself. He loves nothing he knows yet love is on him like a sickness. Your
hair. Your mouth. Your ideas (these others, these hundreds of others. Old
men you made love to in foreign cities have been given uniforms and sit

plotting your death in their sleep. All those people you've kissed. The lies you've told everyone. And you know there is a woman dying now because you will not murder her. Will not dive out of your darkness and smother her under your filth. She knows the old men.

The house is old and night smooths its fetters with screams. It rolls in the wind and the windows sit low above the river and anyone sitting at a table writing is visible even across to the other side. The shores are the same. A wet cigarette burns the brown table & the walls heave under their burden of silence.

HEATHEN: No. 2

1

The first sun is already lost. The house breathes slowly beside the river under a steel turn of bridge. Myself, again, looking out across at shapes formed in space. My face hangs out the window. Air scoops in my head. To form more objects, fashioned from my speech. Trees in the other state. More objects, room sags under light. My skin glistens like glass. Metal beads on the pavement. Eyes on mine. Slick young men with glass skin. Dogs.

He had survived the evilest time. A time alone, with all the ugliness set in front of his eyes. His own shallowness paraded like buglers across the dead indians. Some time, some space, to move.

All I want is to move. To be able to flex flat muscles. Tendons drag into place. My face, the girl said naked, is beautiful. Your face is beautiful, she had said, only this once in her dirty cotton dress. Bernice. Some lovely figure here in a space, a void. Completely unknown her stink. Dirty eyes slippery in dark halls. She lived under my grandmother and peed in the yard. Before the fire. And shouted in the movies under the threat of boredom and myself, who had not yet become beautiful.

Women are objects in space. This new sun, could define them, were they here, or sane, or given to logical things. The mind objects them. Sterile Diane. Not the red-haired thighs / and mad machine of come. Another beast in another wood. One who wore wings made of moths.

He sat and was sad at his sitting. The day grew around him like a beast. Large and vapid, with blue fur turned in the thick fall air. All those people were silent. Their voices grew thinner. Their heads shrank. Their shoes came untied. They had to tug up their stockings several times to make them stay. He was thinking about his enemies. The iron eyes they sucked in their sleep. His own image flayed & drowned mandala.

Innocent breathing. These lost beasts hated his mouth. They would kill him for it.

George was a child in blue bonnet. He stood naked against a window and begged for Oscar Williams. The piano struck notes at random. The wind did it. Naked he was smaller than his blue bonnet. His breasts were red sores, hard & indelicate, tasteless as the wet hour bleeding. The sun had come out. The rain had stopped. It was not yet dark.

All the other times I know form crusts under my tongue and hurt my speech. I slur my own name, I cannot remember anyone's name who I thought beautiful. Only indelicate furtive lust. Even intimacy dulled by some hacking silent blade. The knife of the lie. Lying to one's self. You are uglier than that. You are more beautiful. You have more sense than to kill yourself this way. You are invisible in my mouth & talk through my head like radios.

George would laugh & float 3 inches off the ground, in deference to the old man. Believing anything he told himself.

> You've done everything you
> despised. Flowers fall off trees, wind
> under low branches shoves them into
> quick chill of the river, the high
> leaves disappear over stone fences.

Frank in armor thrust out his sword. My flesh is stone but I scream and he cringes with grunts. He screamed when we were close and laughed at the night. Its wet insanity.

Diane disintegrated into black notes beneath my inelegant hands. She died. She died. She died. I walked out into the morning with her breathing on my face. I never came again.

More forms against the white sky. I remember each face, each finger, each dumb word against lips against my face. The words. The stink of insolence. Or even I backing away from the zone. The area of feeling. Where anyone can enter. Unawares, even the cautious sterile greeter.

Another man walked through me like hours. Not even closeness of flesh. Not against this blue ugly air. Not against you or myself. Not against the others, their unclosing eyes. The fat breasted fashionable slut of letters. Her blonde companion in the sulking dugouts of stupidity. She clasped my face in her bones & kissed silence into my mouth.

THE INCONTINENT: Lasciviousness

Petrus Borel is the lascivious man. Doubt yourself before you doubt me. To lie to anyone: white birds low over the house, over the roof. Me inside under the same roof. Night for the birds. And the light here burns all night. Burning away the air. Animal life will die. The plants later, when all is stone or the insane reflection of sun on stone. White rocks for the world. From water to low beach houses, expensive paintings to please that young elder.

Leather jacket, glasses, lost outside of purgatory. (Passd the neutrals into the first circle. And then the blue air blows in. Biting his thoughts. The man at the bar with fat trousers & filtered cigarettes. In his brain, white etch. Mouths without pictures.

But to the next level: Minds, faces collapse on the pavements outside of bars like these. Next to the traffic. The white wax casualness. Make up under the canopy. "You wouldn't be able to see those birds at night." To know the numbers inside darkness.

Your mouth, like the street, a cavern. Siren. Full moon hung low over wood. At the green cold streets. We were "downtown." Eclipse like metal, over the umbrellas, shrubs at high altitudes. And the doorman wd sit unconcerned in a white sport shirt.

Think to what you see. Even past, its origin in a dust we scrub ourselves of. A link to white and yellow spaces.

The idea of space. Eyes rub at night under alcohol. The distance to the ceiling. Crowds of lives, I could picture a man saying, between us and the ceiling. The river would roar underground. Ministers would walk by the windows. People would write poems. No one would be kissing me or talking seriously about my death.

It was a picture of a street. Six slim trees. Without animal life beneath the airplanes. Planets of justice. The white beard of God. All is suddenly not commonplace. Now it is again. Sinks. Laughter. Brooms. Language. You are empty of me. You could not recognize sidewalks without me. Lucre of the blood. The image is cold, without space, a dead talking of earth.

Lascivious is to meat. They take it into their mouths. Meat. Blood on the paper . . . or in Fielding's head on the sidewalk. A thrust. The walls of words, intimate gestures. The street took his feet. The dirt sung in night's hook. The moon again, in the cold.

A rung of the law. To thighs, because blood seeps from them. Flesh/ to pure air. Black smelly hair. Coarse, or softer than touch. Each to himself, as the pure image. Nothing remains with me . . . except myself to each, as to himself. The pure image. Nothing remains. a hallway of night. In a heavy season.

Anger is nothing. To me fear is much more. As if trees bled. The hour hung in my flesh. Pure act. The lie under streets stomping mist. The innocence of myself. Of you, under me. Of each finger dying. Egyptians, Praxiteles, Lester Young. Sources, implements under the ugly sea. Bright lips to colors seeping through the warm day. It could die. And the lust in the world fashioned into snow.

Gluttony

(It wd be present or forward, or as
each thing turns towards us, the
brown heavy past.)

City is gluttony. Mind you! The sparks hiss and sun drips on leaves.

This place is not another. Cold white sidewalks. Time, as intimate. To
myself, beautiful fingers. You stand so straight. The mob of buildings.
Their factories. Our incontinence.

She cd die on the street with her
stockings pulled up. Her letters, not to old men on the east side. Myself,
the young. Myself, again, under the spattering leaves. The west is a
bridge. We'll travel someplace wide open. Not that slow brown water. A
river. Another blue eye washing our land. Water to the east. We leave
under the heavy air. Still, and winter coming on.

Fog settles on the bricks
in the junkyard. The old cars smoking. In summer, smoke raised over the
cities, black in winters. The woman could die with her stockings pulled
up. Black bulbous eyes. Filthy sandwiches, if you can remember. A boy
named Thomas who drew well with perfect pencils.

Perfect, these paths.
Even on cement. We march well and head around the corner. A black
catholic girl had written my name on a trash can. I love you I love you I
love you. It was cold then, and I unwrapped my shiny badge. The birds'
peace officer. Skinny legs against the red buildings. Telephones against
the green braid rug. The warm radio. All their old voices.

That was a wide street where James Karolis lived. He died in a bathroom
of old age & segregation. His nose was stopped up and he could pee all
over anybody's floor. Mr. Van Ness wd stop by to shake my hand & soothe
his bohemians.

You cd be the leader of this weather. If you ran faster &

33

told those jokes again. 7 or eight boys slumped against the wall. Or under the jungle bars, the shadows wd get in your eyes. More faces. More leaves. A farm sits there for years.

What do you want now? The street disappears. Night breaks down. Dogs bark in blue mist.

The blossom, the flower, the magic. If my flesh is sweet, my mind is pure. I am awake in your cold world.

INCONTINENT: The Prodigal

On a porch that summer, in night, in my body's skin, drunk, sitting stiff-legged in a rocking chair. Vita Nuova. To begin. There. Where it all ends. Neon hotels, rotten black collars. To begin, aside from aesthetes, homosexuals, smart boys from Maryland.

The light fades, the last earthly blue, to night. To night. Dead in a chair in Newark. Black under irrelevant low stars.

On a hill night fades, behind the house. Silence. Unmessed earth. My feet, my eyes, my hands hung in the warm air. Foppish lovely lips. Allen wrote years later. A weeping wraith.

Hung in words, lying saints. The martyrs lose completely light. That slow feel of night. Industrial negroes with cold rusty fingers.

The steps of tears, or dust between tall shadowy buildings. Germans with bald heads. To go backwards, or cross over, into what you mean. What becomes realer than mere turning of hours. Shadows on long afternoons. Silent mouths

Break out. The turn. Bleaker. In the cold, my lips and hands turn hard. Peacock. Lone walker of mornings. Boxcars of fairies tilted into night. Jeliff Ave. Where Beverly lived and her father grew heavy mustaches. On that porch, on that air, words. To disappear, and leave the maid sad in her mother's gown.

A summer of dead names. Early twilight hoots of birds beyond the buildings. Each excess past. Now, this other, to be a beginning. A walk thru sun on stone. The train stations bracking a few blocks from where I walked.

He wore glasses and sold greeting cards. The buses went up Raymond Blvd. and turned left at Academy St. The O.D.B. (Office of Dependency Benefits) of the burning dogs. The red house with clubs. The white woman fondling me in a sand pit. The boy with his hand in my pocket. My watch. The lies. Snot. Wind blows smoke across tar. Chalked names. We jumped off the garage and I put my hand between our old friend's legs. Today the leaves clatter & the sun weights my fingers.

The old houses were slums except mine. Even that high apartment the french girl died in. Wallpaper, and bebop orchestras at the first sex. "Do anything you want to me . . . but don't hurt me. . . ." Wool for the cold. The old man sold his gas heaters and I kissed Lenore in the hall. She went back to the projects and had some baby. Leaves blew through the empty playground. The bigboys beat the little boys. The sun itself was grey.

We skipped together . . . in school. Her brothers (this other one), were failures. But she pressed close to me and stood that way for hours. My fingers loosened and I wished I had curly hair.

More than this is some other doing. Some other word. The man turned away cranes towards his beginning. Olson broke, Allen losing his hair. The faces seep together.

Or feathers of sun. Their noise. Steam from the streets. A long shadow of my body, tilted across the street. Danny Wilson's. A union organizer lived across the lot, Pooky, an italian with twin sisters. Or an accordionist, or the tiny television showing leaves. Augie's effeminate hands, my womanly mind. Voice, under their shrieks. Murray and Ora, hard and living. In light, they still sprawl in light. A thin bar of shadow on the stone. They live in light. The prodigal lives in darkness.

I have lost those clear days. Blue hoops, more days turning at the rust. The short throw across field. The pit. Noses. Rauscher. Old Black Rag picker.

And blind adventure, those fences, with the Germans & dotty faced Keneir. In summer that seems cold. A breath.

Did John Holmes really jump off the Warren St. bridge? But his legs healed and he watched us hump the big italian bitch in Sweeney's cloakroom.

Eliot, Pound, Cummings, Apollinaire were living across from Kresges. I was erudite and talked to light-skinned women.

Trains, parties, death in a chair. Come back or leave it. His heavy jaw fastened to yours, from unknown dustiness. Pure movement. Of which to place himself, as himself, in a wooden cell, looking down on blue fenced water and the statue of a colored man.

A black cloak of distance. A blue box of toys, or have it books and razors. Let blonde lips shatter on his face. Asleep under blue coats. Awake at night for any substance of lost day. Already past. Each second the blue air turns. Each invisible leaf. Each snowed down street. An impossible distance of shadows. Wool cloak of years. Not time, not ever time. Not to myself, a young fat-lipped corpse.

Tell your lies some other time. "Your parents still visit the child."

Wrathful

I had forgotten to run. But if you believed I'd cuss that girl out. Fuck you, he repeated in his chin. Behind his meat counter I think even later he admired me. The polack did, for what reasons my mother could tell you. We worked next to that hospital & worked for a fat old man that one summer in the garage with all those rotten potatoes. A long spinster. An ugly middleclass negro bitch laughing in the hot kitchen at my red wool shirt & new jeans. Because its "too hot." Liars. Gossips. Widows. Cooks. Lived in the basement & went around the corner to her inferior nephews.

A bucket of coal. She shouted that from her stairs. The Owl Club. My father's adultery. Bowling down Quitman Street. That old 3 finger man with the gas station. Andy. Is he still there? On Quitman St. Dolores, who sd to me behind her pimples. My brother is dumb, my mother is dumb, my father is drunk, but you're beautiful. Will you be a doctor & take me to the proctors. The movies. The ball games. & later we will watch television on our linoleum & throw apple cores out the window. A fat blind woman tipped me for bringing her cokes. I went home in the afternoon & fucked Beverly. She had a baby & hid its face in her lips. Her paintings. Her Vincent, not a white Frenchman but an old rag head from the south.

A belly rub, a christmas tree, a negro. Autumn, is correct always. In the dark instinct. They believed me, and told others. Their walks. Their love affairs. Their sun.

My substance dark & talked of now odd times when everybody's dressed up. Forgive me.

SEVEN (The Destruction Of America

                    The Dead,
are indians. White bones dust
in their jelly. Dead in the world, to
white dust bones.

                    And Riders,
                              coming towards us. The Gloom
lifting. Trees
blown back.
          Cold season,
                    of steel, colors,
                              cheap medicines.

I am, as you are, caught. Here,
is where we die.
          On this mountain,
                    Looking down.

We will die up here
in the cold.

White man white crushed stones. In the cold rattling. Small fires, from
drills. These hopis, pimps, rattlers, strolling in blue sun. Were killed or
tortured. Worked for the land. The sun, the wind Gods of our secret
ocean. Break out. Now, the boat rattles against soft mud. Its destination
printed in expensive inks, in the captain's pocket. That tall person
squeezing among shadows. These streets echo. The flag, so late, still
chiming on its pole. The cold draped above the buildings. No one there
to watch you. Dirt shows thru the grass. Dead trees rot in penthouses.
Dogs, mad at dust. The wind pounds white bones.

White man fedora smiles. Pink fingernails. Abstract death flowers. Color to live, he slunk. Away, the radio squalled & the weather got bad. She undressed and walked thru their ranks. A black feather like his teeth had clamps. Stuck out beyond his lips. My name, like Indians. Dead hard ground.

Violence

against others,

against one's self,

against

God, Nature and Art.

SEDUCERS

The cold light, even inside. Say Autumn. Say Railroad. Say leaves. Go back. After crossing the street. The tracks. Dark stones. Your own space, wherever. It was afternoon, when she died. Everyone lie. For Lillian. who never understood the seasons. My shadow against the marquees. The dark / and it clutched her. Lillian, so thin with my talk. Gifts against the cold. Her space, impossible to say. To define. That distance across the trees. Her park. Her friends.

   The sun had slept on grass in the south. The sun had marked its time. Lillian. Say love. Say slept. Say place your fingers here.

   There were, of course, parties. She came. I stayed in the metal halls, rifling the mailboxes. Grinning. Being popular. Dancing alone, or with those heavy fleshed men I forgot to tell most people abt. She would look out the window & identify us. Even in the shadows. Even from the roof, those myths, the beautiful naked speech.

   Go away & try to come back. Try to return here. Or wherever is softest, most beautiful. Go away, panderer. Liar. But come back, to it. Those high wire fences. The brown naked bodies. They turned or hurt or walked or pronounced my name. Does the word "foots" mean anything to you? She would say. Before she got skinny and died. Before that colored girl wept for her. Her false screams among the buffets, the dingy saturdays of her lovers.

   What is left. If you return? You deserve to find dead slums. Streets. Yellow houses near the tracks. Someone's mother still dying with an oil lamp. Hillside place.

They would know what to say. Even now. If they weren't afraid. Of myself. Of what I made myself. The blue and orange hills. Red buildings. He wd know, even in the hall, bent over money on the floor. Blues singer. Thin Jimmy with tugged up pegs. Headlight, does that word mean anything to you? Separate persons.

   Kenny got old. My sister. The street. The garbage.

Or the black walls & illiterate letters. To continue from that. Don't look. Don't go back there. You are myself's river. Blue speech. Kenny got old, I tell you. Don't go back. Look out the window. The television whines on their christmas. They thot I was rich. I thot the hall was dark. The light fixture shd have been fancier. I was not good to look at. smart tho. They thot I was smart, too. They expected something like this. These shadows.

Bubbles, does that mean anything. Artificial or not. Saturday or not. My birthday is Easter in church if I can get dressed up. Don't say it. That my suit will not be new this year. It'll be clean tho. It'll be grey covert cloth. It'll be pink & grey. It'll be short brimmed. It'll be a reservoir. A view of ourselves. Not as little boys. Men. Intelligences. Super Heterodyne Expensive radios. Zippers. Blue men like my father. Like those associations

The playground is old. Kenny is old. Headlight is old. I am not. I came back to see them. I am in a black room with my new shoes. The two women stare at me and the shoes. I am drunker than their world. They do not even hate me. They are amused. I am drunker than their seasons.

The Flatterers

.284, a good season. In the sun. In hell, my head
so much sun, and cold for this month. Cars too,
squealing at the clocks. Gone past. These hands,
the metal burning night / are pictures, dreams, cousins.

A good
season. Lost, the dust settling. On water, cobblestones, porches. We sat
there staring at the blue street. The restaurant. My lovers' drums. Heaps
of night. "You are a young man & soon will be off to college." They knew
then, and walked around me for it.

Tough fat poet hung in the custard
store. A marine. The silent brothers. Huge slick hands. They all had.
Except fat awkward William / eyes were flowers. Bellbottom pants. Slate
buildings.

"The woman that ran the place was a grouch, & you had to
stand up with the cold wind blowing on your back. Her husband, I
think, was a postman . . . like my father . . . but darker & more from the
south."

Down low for the dirt. For the hands touch. The backs of the
hands, dug in the dirt. Straight at you. On tar, in those low fences.
Murderers loose in the buildings. A severed head, bloody in the winter.
Near anthony's house & those other guys . . . The Buccaneers. But later,
summer, it bounced right & he swept it up, wheeling in the air to throw it
towards first. They were tough.

Or, the air, again, cold sun, wheeling, with
hands strained, sun full in the eyes, up & around, the ball leaving,
towards the squat shade homes, they yelled. They yelled, at me. The ball
rolling out. Amazed, they loved it. Even the weather. Our sweatshirts, and
Ginger strolling on the tar towards the jews. (Who got locked in the
bread box. With the cakes? The same place used to stink the windows up.
Frozen bums peeing through the windows. For cupcakes. Jelly donuts.
Adventure. We laughed about it.)

45

She looked at my legs. They had grease on them then, when I wasn't at the clock. The quick fingers & fear at cripple tommy, the hero of the projects. William cd beat me, for sure. In that big big gym I hid from my thighs. Too long. Strong gripping fingers.

What else. Lefty? You cd catch him in that park. More days strung out. Time & sun. He laughed about it himself, when those two bears waited outside the stadium. "Lenora sd that you were hers. Is that true?" Jo Anne. She got pregnant & somber. Like today, near father's hotel. Divine. The doctors lived near there & one of my dianes. Diana, really, & her tall dark mother & drunken aunts. That was like cellars. That smell, & big cars to boot. Her father was white & died old with a big mustache. She wanted to make it with him, & was afraid I did too. She wouldn't fix the phonograph where my picture was. What did that photo look like? (I think I had a german bush then. Not as large as that time in Orange watching the fags dance. His hair was red & mine stylish. My mother sat close to me watching my sister die. She really did later, when I was away. She sent me letters begging me to help her. Help her.

Beverly was my size & that started it. In the slums. Even we called them that, but all my later friends lived there. Behind those metal fences, for the playground. I never went there much, or only at night, to dance, & walk that fat girl home. They were all hip & beautiful. Even now, coming to strange things. Like this mist pushing off the day, Strange. These strangers, are beautiful. Be wary of them.

The woman liked me. Smart kid, she told everybody. I was fucking Beverly a little bit. The head of my dick went in, but I learned later to put my legs between hers, & that made it easier. She smiled when she found out. In that wet cellar.

Spots.
She never really was happy. Maybe / at the proctors with me because it was dark & she could laugh at stupid things. I killed her. She let me do anything because of it. Eat her years later when I learned. Too late then, she kept calling. Believed me dead or in "Porto Rico." I came back furious with her chimneys. Her father was right. After all.

Can you plunge into the woods? Lying by the stoop. Sell those gas heaters. Cook that food. Clean that building. Go to church.

Do you really think you were sane always. What about that powder-blue suit. Or dry-fucking Dolores Dean in your grandmother's house. Dolores Dean, and her less fortunate baby, Morgan. Big belly. Calvin Lewis did it.

He cdn't really play, I bet. I know pinball cdn't. Garmoney loved me. He got fat & forgot who I was. Hauling boxes. Bowling.

Playmaker. Strange for him to say it. At Robert Treat? The Boys' Club. Some obscure move with the hands. Across from Diane. Blacker, less desirable earlier. Grew huge in my eyes after all that killing. (Murdered my mother, father, sister, all the grandparents & uncles. Stepped out of their bloody flesh, a sinister shadow waiting for hardons.) She thought she could handle it, but it drove her crazy. She got educated & learned to make artificial birds. Another father for me, then. Blacker, too, less desirable. He walked her, on his wedding day, to the roof, & made her take off her skirt. He told me later drugged & dying.

"Anything you want Miss Sweeney. Big-eyed Miss Sweeney." "She Got Some bigass eyes." Ora Matthews. William Knowles (after he climbed the gas-pipes & began drumming like Elks on the desk), Murray Jackson. The Geeks. Miss Mawer, also, but better. Crippled lady. What wd she say now. Suck my pussy, hero. Eat me up.

You left that. But the cold is back. The hard gravel. Dorothy Bowman. Donald Pegram. Don't limit the world. It grows. It bulges. It is bleeding with your names, your soft fingers.

Who do you think you are on that couch with the lights off? Her father? Her porch? Her long street behind the railroad tracks? You are a train. Her father's noise in his sleep, of the south, from his eyes, under the weather, for you. Separate, again. These radios.

In the dark, she was soft. In the cellar. In the bedrooms. On the couch. Even with my mother's voice. My mother. My aunt frightened of the girl because they were both ugly. My aunt Gottlieb. Oh what an ugly church that ugly girl goes to. My grandfather had died in a warehouse full of election machines. Does that mean it was Autumn? Or that I wore badges or made it with Aubry at Belmar. Aubry who?

They all turn out good. I did. The way this is going. Who? Go back. Turn. The door will swing open into sun. Into Autumn. Into the cold. Into loud arguments at night with the door open. Small children die. I kill everything . . . I can. This is This. I am left only with my small words . . . against the day. Against you. Against. My self.

The corner is old. Headlight, bubbles. Now. Look for the lies. Them now. They go away, these lovers. For my running. Those soft flies over the shortstop's head. Please. Not as a dead man. Even Diane. A fair second baseman. You let him die. No. The lies. No.

(Have they moved out of the city? I mean her tall beautiful mother & no good boyfriend)

Good field

No Hit!

Simonists

Again, back. Dancing, again. The portions of the mountain under light and shade at noonday. Cf. *Purg.* iv. "When it is 3 P.M. in Italy, it is 6 P.M. at Jerusalem and 6 A.M. in Purgatory." Musicians crowd down the streets. Belmont Avenue, hung in front the hotdog store. The poet winds. Wine store, paint store. Buford & his brother. The National, more boldness.

Darkness. Shadows, the brown flags fold. Blue windows. Placards with large-lipped women. Lovers. You have a checkered swag, now cool it. Down the stairs. Pause on the stoop, to look both ways. The King of the Brewery tilted under night. A hill, for air, and my space. To Norfolk Street. The fag's boundary, they had a limit. Don't turn me over, please turn me over. Each his own area. of registration.
                                                    Beating them, in that bare light. He was humped over & his head bleeding. The lights bare, as his face. Bleeding. Simonist, thrown down from second story. They're dancing. The girl w/ wet clothes. A white girl in a rumba suit. A line of negroes waiting. To dance. Dis. The mirrors were blue, for her wedding, she slept on the roof. Jackie Bland & his band. Nat Phipps & his band. Magicians, falling from the heavens. Naked in the park. She had a blonde streak and weighed 5 stone. Lips. Hands. An alto saxophone. She walked into rooms. She knocked at yr door once you knew her. She drove a truck. Down the mountain.

Erselle sits there. Across, from you & the curled hair. He cd dance in that small room. A basement with sewing machines, and that was proper. His prognostication, in the shadows of the jungle gym was a leather jacket & lips swollen so bad he spit out yr name from the side of his mouth. Girls & hats. Those blue felts with grey bands. Bricks & garbage hands, across town. She stood there in the dark & waited for your fingers. My fingers. "Don't hurt me, please, just don't hurt me." Cross town. I cried, because we left. My overalls. My red shirt. My knickers. My picture like some wife years later in a coffee shop. Dressed in black. It was that easy

49

because he was a musician. To say "She looked like a little mouse." That was me, tho. He didn't say anything, he just shut right up & told people I lied. I believed him, standing in front of the Italians, & felt sad at the season.

Dancer. That was something too. Whistling. You want to be noticed. She asked you that question & made things come together. From whistling, things you danced to. Teddy & his golden boys. Spanish names. Their own women to line up, under that glaring light. The only light then. Dark, for them, now. They disappear. Under leaves? under words. Complete darkness, to penetrate. Your fingers are soft enough. But it's cold here & I keep my hands in my jacket.

Simoniacs, Simonists, Bolgia academic brown leaves. 3. The dancers. Mandrake, light suede shoes. Magic.

The Diviners

Gypsies lived here before me. Heads twisted backwards, out to the yards, stalks. Their brown garages, stocking caps, green Bird suits. Basil suits. 15 feet to the yard, closer from the smashed toilet. Year of The Hurricane. Year of The Plague. Year of The Dead Animals.

Existent. This is Orlando Davis, who with his curly hair & large ass, steps thru mists everywhere. They caught him stealing on his scooter. They, the cops(?), moralists dropped on him from the skies. The music: Rachmaninoff's 3rd piano glinting. Remarkable thick weather he moved thru. Not as a woman this time, a sultry male. He looked tired, or bewildered. And they mobbed him at the river's edge, yelling their faces at heaven.

John Wieners is Michael Scott, made blind by God. Tears for everything. The fruit of his days in the past. Is past, as from a tower, he fell. Simon, dead also. Under various thumbs, our suns will pass.

This is past. Ourselves, under the earth. She made to get away. Thru Lorber's window, we passed ourselves. They were, in all, with me: Arlotta, Strob, Starling(?) and someone else. At the same point, I leave to blaze in the elements. It was a labyrinth. Windows, broken glass in brown weeds. You kicked them as you walked, or rolled heavily if they threw you down.

Sitting across a river, they had fixed themselves with tender faces. Years later I place my fingers on their running skulls.

If anyone ever lived in a closet, it was me. There were tracks, streets, a diner, the dark, all got between me and their strings. "You're going crazy . . . in here with dark green glasses and the light off." It was a yellow bulb tho, and it all sat well on my shoulders. Vague wet air thrashed the stones. It sat well, without those faggots. Or ART, 5 steps up, in a wood house: a true arc.

That, and don't forget the canopied bed. The ugliest green

draperies dragged and hooked across the bed. Action as completeness. If I hung out the window, it was warm and people watched.

A guy named powell who is a lawyer. Air pushing. Straight stone streets. A guy named pinckney who is a teacher. (Place again, those fingers, on my strings. Walk in here smiling. Sit yourself down. Rearrange your synods, your corrections, your trees.

Dolores Morgan, who had an illegitimate child **** PROSPEROUS
    Calvin Lewis, who gave it to her **** PRIDE

Think about that: Michael at a beach, in the warm tide. The figures I saw *were* fucking. "Huge" shadows, sprawling open their cunts.

    Big Apple (myth says) knocked down a horse, split open a basketball player's skull.
For him, let us create a new world. Of Sex and cataclysm.

The rest, let them languish on their Sundays. Let them use shadows to sleep.

* * *

There was a pool hall I wondered about, an ugly snarled face, Jacqueline, money was no object for her probable Saturday walks. There were a few trees to circle, the pool hall, and slick Eddie. Also (because Eddie was only a later example) the first *Hipster.* Not Tom Perry in the chinese restaurant. Earlier(?) and in the sun. Saturday morning. It wd be cold & I was learning then to grow tired of the days. Special. I was layed out so flat, and lied, and loved anyone who'd cross my path. A few showed me unbelievable favor. A redhead maid with heavy lips. Worked for an exceptionally respectable faggot. Lived, with some ease, across from the beer barons,
    IT WAS HERE THAT THE GOLDEN BOYS FLED UP THE SREETS OF ROMANCE. HERE THAT THEY MADE THEIR HEROIC STAND AGAINST ME, ONLY TO SUCCUMB, LATER, TO MACHINATIONS DRAPED ACROSS THE WORLD. HERE, THEY THREW HANDS UP. AS IN CONQUEST, OR FINAL UGLY SUPPLICATION.
        REVERE THE

GOLDEN BOYS & ALSO LOS CASSEDORES. THEY TRIED.

* * *

You can never be sure of the hour. Someone stands there blocking the light. Someone has his head split open. Someone walks down Waverly Ave. Someone finds himself used.

This is high tragedy. I will be deformed in hell.

Or say this about people. "They breathed & wore plaid pedal pushers." Can you say from that, "I told you so. Look at him, A bebopper."

"Lefty is pretty hip," he said to get me in. To the fag's house. Blonde streak. The Proctors, all interchangeable in the fish truck. Myth shd be broad & rest easily in branch brook lake. It shd rest like the black trestle between Baxter Terrace & The Cavaliers. (Some slight people thot that we, The Cavaliers, were the same as The Caballeros. Some other nuts thot that we were their (The Caballeros) juniors. We came long before them, but they were older and knew all about sex (so they influenced the crowd). We were still mostly masturbators.

Charlie Davis married Dolores Davis. (He cd do a lot of things tolerably well. Third base. 12 pt. basketball game before he got replaced. That was a blow. Beau Furr was much better, but he came from the slums & I knew him very obliquely (except that time he threw me all those passes & Big John said I'd grow up fast & tricky & "be a bitch.") And some of it was wasted on Peggy Ann Davis, i.e., that long weave down the sidelines (abt 45 yards)

PAYDIRT IS THIS:

Ray Simmons, shy & bony, will work in commercial art houses & revere me all his life. (Enough of his missed layups!)

Sess Peoples (it got thru to him, somehow, he sd "Stoneface," "Emperor," "You little dictatorial fart") as dark as he was & embarrassed by what he smelled on my clothes, Give the World. Let him march thru it in September giggling thru his fingers.

(Advanced philosophy wd be more registrations. Get more in. Deep Blue Sea. I, myself, am the debil.

A RANKING OF THE CAVALIERS IN THE ORDER OF THEIR PRE-PONDERANCE: (Ray & Sess done formal, as they are, floating in for the easy dunk.)

Leon Webster (came later, after the decay. My head gone, in new grey flannel suit (Black wool a nigger called it). Away, so far away, wings melted. Rome, if you want metaphor. Use Rome, & Adams calls the turns. The Barbarians had come in. The cultivated & uncultivated alike. Sprawling thru the walls.) Suffice it to say he came from real slums & was as harsh as our enemies.

Morris Hines: As a compact, years ago under the shadows of those grey or brown buildings. Always heavier than his movement. Escape Bolgia in a buick. Left-handed first baseman: "Ingentes." Flatterer, even as whore Beatrice had her prediction, her Georges Sorel. We had our church. Sussex Ave. was rundown & all the negroes from the projects went there (the strivers after righteousness. American ideal, is not Cyrano's death on Lock Street. The poor went to Jemmy's church, but big Morris and his deacon father sat next to Joyce Smith's house every Sunday & their mother wd fan God. Malebolge (for the flatterers) for me, there is all you can imagine. Jehovah *me fecit*.

William Love: eyes are closed. (Was that Hudson St.? Warren?) He cd, after a fashion appear in Adams' class. He had short stubbed fingers he bit for his nerves. A butt. They called him (not our lovely names . . . these bastards like Ora, "Big Shot," called him "Bullet Head" or "Zakong.") I had fashioned something easier for his weakness but killers like Murray ground his face in the tar, & William wd chase him. Goof train. Rebound man, wheel'd & for a time, as to the properties of his life, dealed. I'm told (and so fell into disrepute. In hell the sky is black, all see what the other sees. Outside the dark is motionless & dead leaves beat the air.

CIRCLE 8 (Ditch 5)   Grafters (Barrators)

I am hidden from sight and guarded by demons. And
*   what?*
You find me here, as a street. A tree, under blue heaven.

The time, elapsed, as fingers cross the cold glass. Your
*   world*
has sunk in space, immersed in romance, like whatever in
*   my head*

fastens dreams upon my speech. Nothing makes a silence,
*   hands*
slow or picking dutch thin blooms, wind shatters lips.

It was fashion. In and out of those yellow slate homes. Beds there.
Italians. "The monk," outside the movies. You had forgotten about her
streets. And frenchman's creek. Critters, are foreigners. You had forgotten all their blackness. That tottering room you had only to open your
mouth he would have been in it, tottering. Like huge black figures circling the house. Lips, glasses & flags. Also like mad doctors, skinny with
acne. I slept several places, also with whores. But now now, this had done
it. Years before things moved slowly. You had poets to get to. And then,
some motions in the midwest. I traveled. From the Cavaliers, it was only
then to schools. Downtown, I went on a bus, or uptown with a horn. Not
the "gig" bag, but formal black peeling leather from the musky janitor's
room. He was a southerner and called some guy "Sam." Jr. Collins had
one, I thought, then. And someone looking like Dick Tracy (only, of
course, the nose wasn't as pointed.).

But that was where the rodeos got in
& Slick Andrew from the West. Dead Lillian called him Ungie, & he had
a faggot brother who is probably sucking a cock right this moment. On
Hillside Place or Waverly Ave. probably. Look him up, the next time
you're in that city (or state).

This leaves out Becky, who rode buses and carried a buzzard's cup. This thing she waved, as my wife will, but then on that bus it drove me into my room, where later my uncle moved and my mother argued at his weight. I learned to jerk off, because probably there were no windows there. I think now there were, because I heard the Orioles sing "It's Too Soon To Know" through them, the window(s)), also, some outside girl, Woman, Willa Fleming. She was 26 then, and I 13(?) no, probably 14 and 15.

There was a dance up those flights over the polish man (now I'd say "polack"). Lenora was there and we got tight. Stuck up later, tho. It didn't matter then. Beverly met me near the playground. A neighborhood house for underprivileged days. And we walked her home together. A whole crowd, including Frank the Liar. (A pitiful person. He too here, now, hid.

The Classical symphony. Second Ave., crossing the winter. Then, I walked, as if I grew old. Overcoats later, I still move that way. hands shoved deep in coat, in mind, what moves, as seldom the yard is green. Snow mounts invisible in the hours' air. Windows of slums chime with the cold.

This had past. This had come later. This moved, as sugar thru my fingers. As time, will. I prayed then, too. You can see it all from that street, like a grove of trees. Because it was quieter, even for them: we thot they were rich. And later, still her father had 2(3) jobs and all the clan moved in. Jews fled.

Ray moved in there later (that street) when it had run down, and the word had gotten out that Negroes were up the slopes. But Lennie was sweet too, and dark, and had a ruder humor. And Sess's brother Arnold too ugly and loud. Possessed of streets the moon missed.

You think you see? Famine there too. Driveways where the huge shadow of the King, his glass raised, rumbles under cars. All those houses went. Broome St. too. New myths? or fools die under the weight and cannot recognize their hands. New myth?

For Calvin, who has grown up thru the pavement. A homburg and huge cigar. Method Negro. Knives in our wealth, rape, that too thrown over. They scrambled towards the top. Summers mostly, to perform. I stayed at school and loved a girl named

Peaches. (Not really, all ploy, and a Ford, and true love the Queen herself employs. If I were Raleigh, A negress would walk up my back.

In Chicago
I kept making the queer scene. Under the "El" with a preacher. And later, in the rotogravure, his slick (this other, larger, man, like my father) hair, murrays grease probably. He had a grey suit with gold and blue threads and he held my head under the quilt. The first guy (he spoke to me grinning and I said my name was Stephen Dedalus. And I read Proust and mathematics and loved Eliot for his tears. Towers, like Yeats (I didn't know him then, or only a little because of the Second Coming & Leda). But Africans lived there and czechs. One more guy and it was over. On the train, I wrote all this down. A journal now sitting in a tray on top the closet, where I placed it today. The journal says "Am I like that?" "Those trysts with R?" And move slow thru red leaves.

You could be distant then because of the weather. Space, now those thin jews live there and my brusque cuckold friend. Another bond. You miss everything. Even pain.

Thin trees. There, it's so cold. Even downtown with pretty Negroes. Swimmers. Easter is past. So, I. The plan, to make it, On the Lam. You know. Me. These people never got thru. Once, in some rich spook's house, they played Rachmaninoff and I put it down. Not even recognizing what it was. The Isle of the Dead. Now, it can play and I can read, or pee, or think about my wife. It's gone, whatever smell rides in that air. Whatever time that was. However strong I was, who I thought I was.

A sideways time.

They fail tho. A woman now splits my face. Not what I am, who says that. Not what I am. My trips tho. Across town, or a few blocks away. Where I fell in final shame. At all of you. I don't recognize myself 10 seconds later. Who writes this will never read it.

IT IS FAILURE.
To love, if that were so. Look out the glass, at the yard changing. Trash blown across the fence. Disfigured voices.

You could be proper and know what to wear. You could look at shoes.

You could find things beautiful on a radio. You could eat rice and be calm on a bus going to New York. You could write those white women and know the world had opened and birds died in your fingers. Or later, an italian almost saw me weep.

YOU LOVE THESE DEMONS AND WILL NOT LEAVE THEM.

Tho they are evil, food smells up the house, outside is cold, drugs addle the brain, hands cut and bleeding. Flesh to flesh, the cold halls echo death. And it will not come.

I am myself after all. The dead are what move me. The various dead.

Hypocrite(s)

Is/fear.
  At noise (beneath
the floor. Streets.
      The very air.

You shout, or steal. The motion sure, the air, like sea pulled up. They'd cry in church so easy, so wooden & smelled up. Lemon oil, just behind the piano another room.

A door, just behind the last pew. The trustees filed in smiling. After they'd brought in the huge baskets of money. They'd smile & be important. Their grandsons would watch from the balcony (if you were middleclass baptists & had some women with pince-nez). Mrs. Peyton was one, but she stank & died skinny in a slum. They'd smile tho. Mr. Blanks. Mr. Russ. A dark man with a beautiful grey mustache. Also a weasely man (not the same one who'd announce things. Deacon Jones. The same as the song. The one who "threw the whisky in the well."

Bernice was a big usherette. Graves. They came in together and were beneath us. She smiled at me and wd have fucked at 13. Her mother watched me. Her mother was sly. Her mother was fat. Her mother liked that green statue of lincoln. Her mother gave me cookies and sd, "I married my first boyfriend." I wanted to know where the fuck he was. With lincoln, or working in the Adams' hat store. Easters they'd drag you in and make you buy pegs.

And black Betty. Stuck up, because she had "spanish" boyfriends (the golden boys, i.e., Teddy, Sonnyboy, Calvin, "and them") but the real reason I cdn't figure out. Her mother was burned and her sister stayed in the service. Shadows on those pavements. Boston Street, oil lamps, Orson Welles. A huge tailor.

They were all friends. Rufus the bootblack, low man on the totem pole. He had phone booths. Next to the florist. (The smart ones? I guess they thot that. Collier was the name. She was pretty at first but turned pale as wet wind. She disappeared one afternoon.

59

The old pimply-faced one went to some college and came back with bucks. His brother, younger, in the same high school as me and Jimmy. But he got out when it was plastic and Allen wore cardigans. He loved me because he knew I'd sucked his cousin off. (They were in league with the undertaker with the bad ear. Hayes. So, the hayeses, the colliers, Aubry, a woman with a child in the insurance projects. They were all connected. By blood, I guess. By ideas. By Jackie Robinson.

(There was also a spookier branch . . . included a pretty girl you'd see on shade calendars. The same ones they had in their florist shop. Roses and mixed daisies. Cheap flowers. Middleclass flowers.

Also, a mystery man who lived near the flower box. The refrigerator. I loitered there but he didn't respond. He knew about picnics and girls with rubber soles and good hair. He didn't tell me. He was Warren Slaten's style. Exposing me to softball in the suburbs and then showing up corny like that years later (in a nigger show) with a japanese pool cue and out of style clothes. A Square. And his mother worked in Klein's. Still, if you could say "South Munn Ave.," instead of Dey St. or Hillside Place or Belmont Ave., you had some note. You could watch ofays play tennis. You could come late to scout meetings and be made patrol leader of the flying eagles.

LeRoy was in it. Also Rudy. (Damn that he got in sideways, the Baxter Terrace mob. They had it going different. Not softball, not with the beautiful molded southern grass shiny money dear friend of sun walking smooth so far to talk quiet and knowing what it was to be something to live away and not know them. To not be me. To not know, finally, what it is that ran me. To come to this. To what you see here dying. To be that, and to be that, as I am, for you, for you all, for all space.

But he was slum (Rudy) that was the difference. That I knew that . . . & we had erected by whatever guise . . . forget Morris . . . how he did escape is worth knowing tho: Barry got out, but that's understandable. His temperament was like mine when I go abstract and people talk nonsense to me.

BUT NOT EVER FOR ANY OF US AGAIN THE LOVELY WORLD OF WARREN SLATEN OR THE REALLY BEAUTIFUL PETTIGREWS.

And Rudy's mother was ugly and looked up to my grandmother, so that made him lower. Place. Place each thing, each dot of life. Each person, will be PLACED. DISPOSED OF.

Rudy and LeRoy were a team. Also "Red." That must have dragged them. To live in Baxter Terrace yet be made to join the "fags" troop because they went to the same church.

So they tried to take over as far as athletics, &c. Only Rudy was any good tho . . . and still not much compared to Baxter or my friends. So we controlled that easy. And I outside, still, without touching any of them. A long walk home, & they used my name as if I was old and my wife had gone out "walking."

It took place in a sunday school. The declensions. The age. Tomson, his whole top head caved in like Martin's publisher. And his stepson big mouth teddy (the bastard was shorter than I and weak as a bitch. Mark, his real son, was mongoloid.) liked my sister. He and later his friend (the music teacher) Freddy. A "closet queen." They both hunted easter eggs in the churchyard, and even planned to fuck fred's sister so I cdn't.

Get in close with me. If you're in mountains. Or weird smells pack your head. Cereals. Cold water. "Gloom," Harvey called me. "Hi, Gloom." (If I knew what that meant. Or what became of him. His socks and shoes. His relatives. It wd be easy enough to predict the future. The past. The fireplaces and whores of the cemeteries of your linoleum.) This is tether. Push towards (SOME END.

It is static. It is constant. It is water. It is her lips. It is Aristotle's coughs in the tent all night in the snow. Why the old man lived to freeze us. His "reserve." Sandy, his name was. The same as the young wavy head jew I jabbed silly at camp. Also good body punches in the 2nd round brought down his guard. When he went down my first instinct was to run. But his brother congratulated me and thot he could kick my ass because he got a letter for band.

We did a lot of things, those years. Now, we do a lot of things. We drink water from streams. We walk down hoping to fuck mulattos when they bathe. We tell lies to keep from getting belted, and watch a faggot take a beating in the snow from our lie. Our fear.

Mutt the zipper. Mutt the zipper. Packed lunches, on Norfolk Street, beans, franks. The bus. Also a stone quarry. (That whole side I knew later, midnights, after work in a paint factory. You walk at night, fine. You show up. You sit. You alright. But you never be no doctor. (Hilary talking.)

Ora—Why you sit in the dark & fight me when I tickle?

Skippy—Boy, I'll beat your ass in Miss Powell's class, cause Johnnyboy and I are friends and "Jones" did that dopey funny book about guys robbing everybody. I live in a cloakroom. I live where you tried to get rid of those Ledgers.

Knowles—Baroom, Baroom, Baroom-Baroom-Baroom. Sho, I'll stop or climb. Or smile, or hit, or fuck (maybe, I guess, because the inkspots were popular and he had that correct trill). Miss Golden gave you a "D" in dependability and she hated something in you.

Murray—Nothing to it. Just be around and need a clean nose and hit people on the back of the head. Don't look for me now. It's too sociological and'd make you cry. You playground step. "Brains."

Becky—(Ha, Ha, with colored teeth and tightass girlfriend. That was cross town. The masonic temple she gave me hunter and coke and it tasted like it does now.) Spread my legs on the 9 Clifton. Let you in for somethings. A new building to incest. Hymn to later masturbation. You could have had me, if you'd come down. Gone Down.

Love—Ah bullshit.

Morris—(*Later*) Boy, this cat is something. Is my dead sister. The car crashed her huge eyes. My father's big buick. You rich running. Pigeon toes, you got us in to the Troops. (And those buildings, even tho Dolores, and the two crazy ones, football players and midgets) were crumbling. Were red, at the corner where my grandmother made "pageboys." Miss Still, was the lady she worked for. The other street, where Willie lived, continued to the lot and the women's detention home you could forget if you only looked at the tile store or the abandoned ice-house full of ammonia. Jr. Bell fell thru the floor. Jr. Bell died in the lake. Jr. Bell fucked Eunice before I did, or you. (In an alley behind the Zarros house, also crumbling grey behind Central . . . You pressed together.

Otis—We athletes. We bowlegged. We got crooked peckers. We see'd you get stuck in the ass in a tent. We wanted some and forgot later because you ran so fast and could twist past the line for 12. I still know Whatley and he still thinks you're a punk.

Gail—I'm fat, but Sammy likes it. Sammy and Wen Shi (& Tomson). They dig. because their heads are sawed off. I like Diane(a). Not her friends or spooky dead father. She's old fashioned. You like her, LeRoi? Huh? Marcelline ain't (whisper) shit.

Marcelline—I don't even know what the hell you mean. I had boyfriends and one even vomited in my mouth. New Years, you never understood it. Did you jock-strop bluejacket "foots"?

Sammy—I'm drafted and cool and wear an apron and we went to Coney last night.

Jackie Bland—You see me doing one thing (even tho you heard about me humping some chick in a condemned house) and you think you got something on me. Shit. I'm nigger stan kenton. I'm crazy. I got long arms and helped you whistle to juliet in the laundry (before they tore it down).

Nat P.—Intermission Riff. Is that what you know about Floyd Key and Allen Polite? You mean you never been to North Newark and met Scram and the cocksmen. Boy, we cool even tho we teach school now and disappeared in our powder-blue coats. (Billy can play better than you heard. You know Wayne? He played with us. You mean you never made the Los Ruedos? Wow. I ran track too, man, and waved my arms in sheer pinnacality.

JAN MANVILLE, MINNIE HAWKS, JUDSON, ALEX G.'S WIFE—Sylvia was part of our scene and you know she was hip. What about Holmes? He's a doctor now, and you know you admired him. He could run and liked to talk about sports. Caesar taught you to hurdle. He had great form. He's a doctor now too. All of us are somewhere. We own trees.

The Brantley Bros.—I'm a writer. I go to games. I knew you when. I was impressed. I'm weird in Newark. I limp like a tackle. I knew everybody. You wished a lot of times you could have talked with my sister. You know we don't understand what you mean by all this!

Yrs t.,
CAIAPHAS

Thieves

*(Was I to have made this far journey, only to find the very thing which I had fled?—*GAUGUIN*/ Noa Noa)*

Space is cheap salves. A trombone in a penthouse. Madness over the phone. Dispute, if the thief live. If he be climbing thru our smashed windows his voice dragged in silk stockings on the radio; Greasy Head? The metal can clunks in the head, the radio says "duh, duh, duh-duh." Soft, tho. As pure impression—pure distinction.

The three pigs. The three Suns. Three Blind mice. Three of a Kind. To make ready. witches. B. for five. wives. letters. strikes. bases. women. The Magi, are popular. Are broken glass. vases, crisp, some soft faggot voice drowning the night.

It was a hall. Jazz, is that vulgar. Hooks, in the air, like sun. Tuesday's blue metal adolescence. Mutt the zipper, again, the fireplaces. Guns on Christmas. Strange vanishing toys. The brown house. Registers (old new? a closet behind the red chair.

*   *   *

The room was deformed. A heavy jowl, smell, softer hands than streets. The moon is bitter. crushing the banister.

A girl named Lorraine who used to go as our cousin—and then her tits came. She was a tall "zaa-room" face. Zebra. Mattie McClean. Her blouse back was loose. She had another name. Thin glasses, like some oyster ostrich humping. A grey house, next to Lorraine's red johns manville. Her mother and she looked the same except her mother was quieter, but they had the same hair. Lorraine smiled nasty. And smelled up the pool. Even lied about the nature of dances. And fumbled excitement near the park. (Lies or ignorance) birds like tar smile.

This jumble of houses' collars. Shined shoes. Show biz. BILLY— "O.K.

vibe player, Blow!" ARNIE— Years later, the drain glows. Rhythms. Passports. We take our train to your astronomies. We evacuate sound. THE PAINTER— You Rat!

It could be run out. It could be yellow & black. It could have garages. It could be disinterested in its cement (or the years of cars that roll over my grandfather's grave.

PEGGY ANN— pigtails are for ugly girls. Snapshots, cotton dresses. To buy is to listen. To be had/caught/applauded in the smoke of our sound. In our Negro ulsters selling pot. In our language scared at the shadows of our crimes. DONALD— You're listening to the Symphony Sid Program.

But that, I told you musicians, the rooms we spoke of, that wind, Mere purity and light. This is sudden. Her red fingers. This is slanting here. To me (houses tilt down into my memory. Cars. Insides of mouths. I WANT YOU TO MEET MY FAMILY.

(rooms, aside, as this is. The door stands open. It did then and my fat uncle strides in. He is 6 ft 4" and knew these things in the spring of my thoughts.

Cardboard suitcases, essays. Walked in broke and humble. On Cornelia St. "She looks like a little mouse." Larry or I made that remark. The windows were dull. Cold slush in their mouths. Nothing got thru those clubs. The street would flow black, and a moon.

Trees wherever you are is irrelevant. TALLEY— Muscles, some biographies. Nobody knows nuthin. You got nuthin on me, but my upbringing.

Which in effect, is where we come in. To prefer phone calls, tassels on their shades (even from the street in Gramercy). Bohemians around too. Certainly she is beautiful, to be a lesbian, to be in stone, to be so close to my house.

Violence to my body. To my mind. Closed in. To begin at the limit. Work in to the core. Center. At which there is—nothing. The surface of thought. Pure undulation at the midyear, turned yellow as deserts, suns.

Cement room. stones, in place. Fell there, perfect. For echoes, murders. Blood looked strange on the street.

And there was that guy who wanted to fight my father about the game. Spencer, his name was. Tall & agile & dark. Skinny with long legs, low dangling hands on third base. I heard the language when I ran down to coach. Right near the fence, I could look across the street, and sometimes Danny would be out there, and I call him to the game. Usually the Davises (secret gypsies later making it as respectable shades). Algernon or Lonel(lionel), or pooky or fat (Jerome). Frank was the oldest, went away to Japan & got married. One girl, Evelyn, got fat and was transferred near the golf courses.

The woman, "Miss Davis" was the cruelest woman I know. Like Puerto Rican old women, the lower lip curls like dogs. Hatred or pure sight. Beast Fucci, wait like rachitic Algy for my baseball suit. Brown coarse gravel (if he thot my life was chrome. The orange house (Rev. Red's) large and not that first plunge into scum. Dead allies.

You defend them.
But it is not the alley, or Elaine Charles. (She backed down, in some kind of pit. "It's too big." And I thought from that that white women had small holes. Racing car drivers. Pooky had the correct helmet, and Orlando would threaten him with it. He (Orlando) led the outriders. But merely elements of the street's imagination. I was center. He had strength and hair that would lay flat under tonics. And he rages with his snakes. His dirtiness. His pretenses at fucking. "Board" (Bud) was his other name. And I called him board and found out only later it was his mother's twisted lips. Even after they caught him with that loot.

THE SECRET SEVEN: (met under our porch and gave parties—eating kits among the wet earth odors, rusted wet nails, footsteps.)
EDDIE
CLARK (cf. Vestibule) ALGERNON DAVIS (Board's brother) NORMAN SCOTT (cd run even with saddle head. Complete dust. Loosing, a slum in my own fingers. Earlier he made us laugh . . . "You mean those lidda mens?" Elks, we'd said. He was good w/ the little boys in Ringaleerio (as the whites say they sd different. Not our fays, they took their mark from us. Pooky wd say "rigaleerio" because his nose was stuffed. Dried snot on its edges. But Augie would say "ringy." Let's play ringy. He played w/ norfolk & Jay St. white factions as Keneir, Herbie Teufel, Johnny (who had strange staring fits the negroes were scared of), "White Norman" (to

differentiate between him and Scotty) & sometimes the Zarros Bros. Charlie Johnny William and Frank. Frank was little for a long time but suddenly grew up big. Up thru the silent pavements. His brother I always had to watch. Augie idolized him. He was tough & fast & silent. Charlie Zarros was a scary name then.

My sister Cassandra ELAINE. A confederate, lankier, bulging knees. Fast & that bitter decision to resist sweet life. Stale as death, her tears clog the hours.

The scar (a flab of cut skin like a halfmoon on her cheek. Like a photo a dead girl would clutch. Cry, those stale tears of time. An inch. A sudden light collapses around us. Illuminated we are "Dr. Caligari" or Orlando Davis. Beasts among reptiles. The huge flame of blasphemed God. Fucci screams from his lair, and we know, finally, his hurt name.

But she made good on all levels, except her lips were cold. And pouted— never like me, laughing wildly—or losing fights to J.D. in thick winter cold. (My father was ashamed that day. My hands were cold. "Frozen" Lois Jones screamed. Roy, his hands are frozen. Angel love him. Type. Move the blue file cabinets. She breaks down under pressure. Under this pressure (cool as blue steel in life and to the others, like Algy's—cruel. That power necessary—To Sustain Life. (Forever.

ORLANDO & ME. (Pre-conscious era. Bones of lost civilizations: the weird car I said I "built." Cd repair, from sheer radios. Listening to my lips chap. Wet patches on the paper factory. All the alleys back there. A maze. To disappear was what we wanted. To go out from here. Romantics. We wanted to split, the porch, even then. Beneath to caverns, slim romances.

The seventh person never came. Oh, of course, it was DANNY WILSON. (and his mother sad & cruel as italians. Hunted & hurt by perverted sons.)

LEROI, ELAINE, ORLANDO, NORMAN, EDDIE, ALGY & DANNY WILSON. (Fat afternoon saint. Eater of peanut butter & visitor at his sister's myriad "wettins."

THE EARLY PRE-DIASPORA CLAN (removed now from its beginnings. To the splints, slants, lies of later times. From that, e.g., KICK THE CAN. RED ROVER (the theme "Red Rover, Red

Rover, I dare you to come over") usually at night, the moon low, a telephone pole just in front of our steps. The Center. 19 Dey St. With a pole, right there, for Hi-Go-Seek.

HI-GO-SEEK. WAR. (i.e., not the cards, but the street game where you mark the streets into countries. MITCHELL 25921. (call me!) poor boy never had no phone till then. About the time the money vanished off the buffet & I sat weeping and peeing thru all the showings of THE FIGHTING SULLIVANS.) That's how Algy got my suit, my mother's wrath.

I * DECLARE * WAR * ON * ETHIOPIA! (cd be anybody. Peggy Davis even, when she played. They took names of anywhere. Augie wd take Italy sometimes. But everybody wanted to be America.)

MENU

14 packs of Kits
3 packages of Kool-Aid (grape or orange)
7 chocolate-covered graham crackers
7 Mary Janes

(these were staples. And the parties were well planned usually by Elaine, or Orlando who liked to eat. A few outsiders got invited.

Junior Bell— O.K., you got me! I'm dead & a black myth. Poems should be written about me. The myth of the cities Rise. (Black shadow against blue lake, floats face down in the eternity of condoms.)

RISE. against their dead bones. Restored to corridors, bus rides. The simple dark.

Eunice Reardon— Of course I know what happened. And I know that we weren't fucking (you & I) that night in Charlie's yard. We had on all our clothes. You pulled that stunt on your cousin. And used Jr.'s name as some "symbol" of all evil. The black arts.

NEWARK ST. (snakes writhe in the ditch, binding our arms. Our minds are strong. Our minds)

From one end to the other (Thos. Hardy begins, beneath chains, shaking off sun, appearing a huge pier where our brains are loaded.)
Its boundaries were Central Ave. To Sussex Ave. (1 block.) This is center I mean. Where it all, came on. The rest is suburb. The rest is outside this hole. Snakes die past this block. Flames subside.

(Add Sussex Ave. To Orange St. . . . because of Jim Jam & Ronnie & the cross-eyed girl who asked all new jersey to "do nasty."
                                                            (The slum LeRoy
lived there also. 3 other Leroys. Two Griffiths (who sd they were cousins. One, the tall dark one, had a brother Robert who went from wet cowardice—which never completely subsided—to hipster violence. THE GEEKS. As some liaison or at least someone who wdn't get done in. Like Murray. THE DUKES.

Where television and wine were invented. That strange wrecked house Carl (beautiful praxiteles) lived. Strange his life twisted. Charlie & he (& me too that warm summer we played & walked stiff legged). But they split up because he moved to a strange sad place. Made new friends. Treated us offhandedly. We never forgave him.
    Carl Howard, his brothers, one of whom played brilliant ball. The short one with the bullet head. And for the great BURRY'S CO. team. He pitched. Carl played 3rd base for us. But he fell in with the Robt. Treat Crowd.
    (Where they all teach now.)
In silence at the leaves. In deference to their mad forgotten lover.

                              * * *

JD STARLING, "STARING" JOHNNY, EUNICE & BILLY REARDON, JR. BELL, (old drunks 25, who still played on occasion & heroes to us, i.e., CHARLIE BOOZE & his brother, the slick head, Calvin. No, something else. A fabled pitcher, FRANK CUMMINGS (tucked his legs up but never made first string Central. Academic player for the playgrounds. I was faster & got more long gainers down the sides. "Comstu here" he said in "german" to impress us.
                    CHARLIE (and helen) PETERSEN. He was legendary black, but somehow made stupid awkward slow. Good natured but rusty. Disappeared when the new generation (Slanty eyes who had it

in for me & his sister Spotty Mae). Cambell their name was. Fast and southern.

THE ALDRIGES—Vivian (ubangi lips, later a tart, stupid whore. Rubber lips I called her also), Lawrence, the smart one. He probably works in the post office or collects debts for jews. Sammy (I hated. I wanted to blot out & kill when J.D. found out I was afraid of him (Sammy). Because the bigboys let me sit with them on the steps because I could insult anybody & win dozens constantly. "Your Mother's A Man." Separate, and sometimes abstruse. My symbols hung unblinked at. The surface appreciated, and I, sometimes, frustrated because the whole idea didn't get in . . . only the profanity.

And Lafayette, who set cats on fire.

That section of the street changed. Sociologists! Morons! Just past those cherry trees. Mary Ann Notare lived at the corner. & from there on Italians. Suddenly & without warning, they were all over. Those clean houses at the corner. How it slipped past me. What could they have said about me. Those old women sitting on the porch. The pizzeria on Sussex & Norfolk I never understood. (Until Morris moved there later.) The Armory was a block away from that bus stop. Years later I met Morris in his house after the summer cotillion. Respectable distance of years, educations. He had his finger cut off while I was in school. I saw him again crippled . . . wanting to know my new friend. Bumbling because he still wanted to play first base and by then we (the swag wearing middleclass spades of the town) were dancing. He (& Leon & Snooky & Love & Earl) had come into it late. They were around the early belly-rubbing days & only earl, because he bought a cadillac, could begin to understand our stance. Our new heads.

Ellipse. These sudden autumns.

THE EIGHTH DITCH (IS DRAMA

*(Your tongues are fire
& your stratagems hell
itself.)*

NARRATOR—Tent among tents. Inner tent, dark/blaring sounds from outside. Too dark for shadows. Tho the moon is heavy, large, upon the outside of the outside tents. A wood floor. Beds strewn about, beneath the inner tent. Cries outside. Deaf ears sleep, heavy ruffling sounds. Men asleep inside. Four men asleep.

This is the first scene. Tho it is the end. Show it first, to give it light. As it shd be seen (BEFORE) as some justification. Some mortal suffering; slant the scene towards its hero's life. His black trusts. Together, we look in.

FIRST SCENE: *Same as above only afternoon. Two men sit on bunks. One is reading, the other stares at the book from across the room. The flaps of the tent are up, & we are looking in, at the two.*

46—(*Young, smooth-faced turning pages slowly. Absently*) Brittle youth, they say, I am dead america. And they know the season's change. I am as I am. Young, from sidewalks of wind. I think nothing of you, or myself, who has not yet come out. We wait. (*Looks up*) You & I, somewhere, to hear!

64—Call me Herman. (*Now at reader*) What do you feel. Grass? Games? False muscles cut thru water, thru precious sanity. Your earth is round & sits outside the world. You have millions of words to read. And you will read them. (*Loudly*) So buy expensive clothes and become middleclass that summer after college. But don't sneak away! You can't. I'll never know you, as some adventurer, but only as chattel. Sheep. A "turkey," in our vernacular.

46—(*Puzzled, looking up*) Things are joys even cut off from our lives. This was a field. A rough wood, they cut off. For loot mostly, impersonal. Buses of young sinister shadows herded into summer. So much of this will get lost. These pictures, of what sadness?

Who are

you really?

64—The Street! Things around you. Even noises at night, or smells you are afraid of. I am a maelstrom of definitions. I can even fly. But as you must know, whatever, poorer than yrself. In hell, for it. If there is God. Or roofs where we lay under summer burning our minds. (64 *rises slowly, taking out cigarette, unbuttoning his shirt*)

46—You're not Grimsley. You don't shit under houses. I mean, you don't lie about who you are. I don't recognize you as anything. Just dust, as it must be thrown into the air. You'll disappear so fast. (*Sadly*) Can we talk about movies? What is it I shd talk about now? What shd I be thinking up? My uniform is pressed and ready. I sit, abstracted, suckling my thots. This is a siesta they told me.

64—(*Shirt open, crossing towards 46's bunk*) Forget your draperies. Your wallpaper. Television is not yet common. I love what is in me. These hours control our speech. You speak some other tongue. I understand your gestures. Your shadow on the pavement. Your strangeness.

46—What else can I give you? What else is as strong in me now. Bridges, smells. (*Pause, looking out the tent flap, smiling*) I delivered papers to some people like you. And got trapped in it; those streets. Their mouths stank of urine, black women with huge breasts lay naked in their beds. Filthy mounds of magazines, cakeboxes, children. I cd walk out of yr life as simply as I tossed newspapers down the sewer. It was Nassau St., mostly, and later the street where Skippy lived. Also Johnny Holmes. But that was cross town so I don't know if you know. I used to live in the insurance projects, right across from Tolchinskies pickle works. I almost killed myself twice around there. But we moved a couple of times since then. Even back here. Dey St. is where I live now & I control the Secret Seven.

64—Rarities. Elegance. Foppishness. Not really knowledge . . . tho I guess I wdn't know . . . actually. I take it as aggression . . . and hate you for it.

46—Do you think I'm rich?

64—It makes no difference. When you move to my neighborhood it'll be with a trumpet & school jacket. I have to make my move. I want to last, & this is the only way.

46—What do you mean? You want to last. How?

64—I want you to remember me . . . forever.

46—Remember you?? Why?

64—(*Smiles, now without shirt, and sitting on edge of cot*) I want you to remember me . . . so you can narrate the sorrow of my life. (*Laughs*) My inadequacies . . . and yr own. I want to sit inside yr head & scream obscenities into your speech. I want my life forever wrought up with yours!

46—You want immortality? Someone like you . . . You shd be happy you don't sleep forever in the vestibule. That you don't wipe your ass with newspapers or disappear into the marine corps. Damn. You know you cd turn up years later in a park studying *drama*. Thank whoever for that. You know it cd still happen!

64—I think not. Hah, even this much concentration has made my stock rise. Certainly these trees' shadows outside slant into my voice. That's enough to etch with certainty my fingers on yr lives. Your endless movings thru halls. (*Seriously*) But I want more. I will spread over you like heaven & push black clouds thru your eyes.

46—(*Turns on stomach reading the book again*) Perhaps, I am weak . . . but perhaps not.

64—(*Sitting on bunk begins to read book over 46's shoulder. As they are reading 64 places his hands on the other's shoulders, putting his face very close to the reader's*) What do you know? You sit right now on the surface of your life. I have, at least, all the black arts. The smell of deepest loneliness. (*Moves his fingers slowly on the other's shoulders*) I know things that will split your face & send you wild-eyed to your own meek thoughts!

46—Oh? I'm stronger than people think, I'm an athlete, and very quick witted. Ha, I'll bet you wdn't play the dozen with me. (*Looking up*)

64—No . . . I wdn't do that. You'd only make me mad and I'd have to kick yr ass. I want more than yr embarrassment! (*He sprawls his legs across the bunk, still holding the other's shoulders*) You still have to leave the country. You're not even out of high school yet. Paintings to see. Spend time in college. Spend money for abortions. Music to hear. Do you know about jazz yet?

46—Jazz? Hell yes. What's that got to do with anything?

64—You don't know yet, so why shd I bother. I don't know really. I never will quite understand.
                              But I do know you don't see anything at all clearly. Who's yr favorite jazz musician?

46—Jazz at the Philharmonic. Flip Phillips. Nat Cole.

64—Ha Ha . . . OK, sporty, you go on! Jazz at the Philharmonic, eh?

46—Yeh, that's right. I bet you like R & B & those quartets.

64—You goddam right . . . and I probably will all my life. But that's got nothing to do with anything. You'll know that when you narrate my life. I'll be a . . . . . foil! (*Slides down to where he is lying parallel to* 46, *hands still around his shoulders*)

46—Bellyrub parties too.

64—Yeh . . . I'm a bellyrub man! But that's my circle, now. I've reached my tether. I *am* static & reflect it meaningfully. But you, my man, are still in a wilderness. Ignorant & weak. You can be taken. It's 1947 and there are at least 13 years before anything falls right for you. If you live. (*Laughs*) I know names that control your life that you don't even know exist. Whole families of definitions. Memories. (*He moves his body onto the prone* 46)

NARRATOR—The mind is strange. Everything *must* make sense, must *mean* something some way. Whatever lie we fashion. Whatever sense we finally erect . . . no matter how far from what exists. Some link is made. Some blank gesture towards light.
This is 1947 and all of you (*out the flap*) have not been born. Not yrselves I look at now. These ears, hands, lips of righteousness. This is a foetus drama. Yr hero is a foetus. Or if we are to remain academic . . . he is a man dying.

46—You talk like a man with a paper ass. (*Turns page*)

64—Hah, that's all in your head, baby. I talk like Morton Street, Newark, where I live now. Three blocks down from Hillside Ave. I talk like a hippy dip negro with turned up shoes. I talk like where we are. My friend, my honorable poet, you hear, exclusively, what you want. (*Lying on top* 46, *begins moving his hips from side to side*)

46—Are you Aubry?

64—No . . . I told you to call me Herman. Herman Saunders, from Morton St. An underprivileged negro youth now in the boyscouts. You're what's known as a middleclass Negro youth, also in the boyscouts. You knew all that. (*He loosens his belt and slips his trousers halfway down*)

46—Well that's senseless enough. (*Continues to read, but every now & again peering halfway over his shoulder at* 64)

64—Oh, don't worry. Don't worry. Hucklebuck Steamshovel blues. I Got. Deadeye, redeye, mean man, blues. I Got. Don't worry. Just sit tight. (*Laughs*) Or no, you better not!

46—You talk alot!

64—Right, baby. Right, I do. I Got. Blues. Steamshovel blues. (*Begins loosening* 46's *belt, tugging gently at his trousers*) Blues. I Got. Abstract Expressionism blues. Existentialism blues. I Got. More blues, than you can shake your hiney at. (*Tugs harder at trousers*) Kierkegaard blues, boy are they here, a wringing and twisting. I even got newspaper blues. Or, fool, the blues blues. Not one thing escapes. All these blues are things you'll come into. I just got visions and words & shadows. I just got your life in my fingers. Everything you think sits here. Out thru that flap, the rest of your life. Hee hee, you don't know do you?

46—Oh shudup, shudup, willya, for christ's sakes keep your fat mouth quiet. (*Now tries to turn to get up from under* 64 *but the other has him secured and is pulling his pants down past his buttocks*)

64—You name it, I've got it. Pure description, thass me. Pure empathy for you, cocksucker.

46—What? What're you trying to do? I never sucked no cock!

64—You did . . . but you wdn't want to know now. Ask your grandmother. I mean about all those beaches and songs. Singing for your supper. Hah. You don't have any of the worries I got. I'm pure impression. Yeh. Got poetry blues all thru my shoes. I Got. Yeah, the po-E-try blues. And then there's little things like "The Modern Jazz Blues." Bigot Blues. Yourself, my man . . . your stone self. Talkin bout blues. There's a bunch. I mean, the 3 button suit blues. White buck blues (short short blues, go thru me like wind, I mean, pure wind). I'm pure expression. White friend blues. Adultery blues (comeon like you some dumb turkey, cool as you comeon to us, like a stone turkey they had you in the new world). Got what? Yeh, like love, baby, like love. I had the Kafka blues . . . and give it up. So much I give up. Chicago, Shreveport, puerto rico, lower east side, comeon like new days. Sun everywhere in your eyes. Blues, comeon, like yr beautiful self. (*Sinks down on boy, and* 46 *gives short sharp moan, head raising up quickly, then, looking over at* 64, *slumps head on elbows & closes eyes*)

Come on, man, wiggle a little. (46 *begins to move with the other, who is on top of him, pushing up and down as fast as he can*)

64—Oh, yeh, I came. I came in you. Yeh. (*Takes out penis and shows it to* 64) What's that make you think?

46—(*Still on stomach, looking blankly over his shoulder at* 64) I donno what it makes me think. Only thing is I guess I'll get pregnant.

64—(*Smiling*) Probably . . . so what?

46—How long will it take?

64—Not long, a few days.

46—(*Drops head on arms looking off outside tent*)

64—Now don't worry bout it too much. Take it slow.

(*Another youth comes into the clearing outside the tent. He goes to the tent and pushes the flaps back. Stands in doorway looking in*)

62—OTIS. Oh yeh! (46 *tries to pull up pants.* 64 *backs away slightly*) Yeh. I know what you guys were doing and I want some. (*He unzips his pants and takes out a short black crooked penis.* 46 *pulls up his trousers and sits up on edge of bunk*)

46—What the hell you talking about?

62—You know what I'm talking about. Comeon (*Waves penis around*)

64—Look Otis, why don't you be cool, huh? Make it.

62—Whaddayoumean? Make it? You goddam pig, you want all the ass for yrself, huh?

46—Look Otis, forget it will you. Leave me alone, for christ's sake! Will you just leave me alone.

62—Leave you alone? Oh, yeh . . . now huh? After that goddam Herman bangs the shit out of you! Bullshit. I want some too.

64—Go fuck yrself, you crooked dick muthafucka. Nobody want nonea your crooked ass peter. Go jerk off.

62—You bastard. (*Goes for 46 but 64 grabs him and they wrestle. 46 runs thru the flap*)

NARRATOR—It comes back. What you saw . . . of your own life. The past / is passd. But you come back & see for yourself.

FIRST SCENE AGAIN: *Inside the tent. Night heavy in it. Four shapes covered on the bunks. Deep slow breath of sleep. A figure rises from a bed, and the moon throws his shadow twisted on the canvas. He moves across the floor, stopping at one of the bunks.*

64—(*Whispering*) Psst, hey. (*Shaking 46*) Wake up. Hey. (*Looks over his shoulder at the other sleepers. 46 turns slow in sleep and 64 climbs into his bed*)

46—(*Waking half-frightened*) What? Who is it?

64—(*Grins . . . voice made low soothing*) It's me, Saunders. (*He moves close to 46 and pushes himself onto the other's hips*)

46—What do you want? (64 *doesn't answer, just leans back away from the other, taking off his shorts then pulling down the other's pajama bottoms*)

64—Shh, don't make so much noise. (*He lies prone on 46. He begins slowly moving his hips*) OOh, ooh, shit. (*Makes noises thru his teeth*)

46—Is this all there is?

64—Yes. And why do you let me do it?

46—Because you say it's all there is . . . I guess.

(*Now the other two figures under the tent rise from their bunks*)

Wattley—Hey what's going on!

Cookie—(*Peering thru dark*) Yeh, hell, what's happenin captain?

64—(*Begins laughing . . . now making loud sounds for the others' benefit*) OOOOh yeh, get it, sweet cakes. Throw that ol nasty ass. OooO.

Wattley—Oh, man . . . some free ass. I gotta get me some.

Cookie—Yeh, hell, yeh. Hurry up, Herman. We gotta get some too. Uh-huh.

64—(*Still moaning and whining*) Ok, Ok, don't rush me. This is just gettin good.

46—(*Barely looks up at the others, turns his head looking out the tent*) What other blues do you have, Herman? How many others?

64—(*Screaming with laughter*) Oh, yes, yes, yes. I got all kinds, baby. Yes, indeed, as you will soon see. All kinds. Ooooh, thass elegant.

(WATTLEY *and* COOKIE *crowd around the bed harassing* 64 *and screaming with anticipation*)

64—Goddamit don't make so much noise!

(*Tent flap is pushed back and* OTIS–62 *comes running in*)

62—Yeh, uhhuh, I knew it. I knew you'd be gettin off some more. Well, goddam it I'm gonna get somea this.

(*He rushes towards the others. There is a melee*)

46—But what kinds, Herman. What kinds?

64—Oooh, baby, just keep throwin it up like that. Just keep throwin it up.

THE NINTH DITCH: MAKERS OF DISCORD

The Christians

Next to nothing. Next to the street, from a window, under all the noise from radios, 9 Cliftons, slickheads in bunches wanting to beat punks up, cops whistling, my uncle coming in the room, changing his collars, putting on checkered coat & 3 pens in breast pocket. I'd be there shining one shoe, taking out the bellbottom "hip" suit (some girl at the Y, a Duke chick, first called it that. And my friends ridiculed it not realizing that I was moved away. Spirit hovered over the big king, the polacks, and Springfield Ave. I knew already how to dance, & hit Beacon St. a couple of times, late, when it was nice, and rubbed sweaty against unknown Negroes.

My sister wd be somewhere in shadows pouting, looking down 4 stories at the chinese restaurant, & hump hatted cool daddies idling past in the cold. Snow already past our window quiet on the street. Friday, cool snow, for everyone cd run out new swag coats & slouch towards their breathing lives. And I'd be getting ready, folding my handkerchief, turning around towards the mirror, getting out the green tyrolean with the peacock band. Cool.

I knew I'd be alone, or someone cd be picking me up in a car. (Later, or earlier, we'd crowd in Earl's cadillac & he'd squirm thinking years later how to be an engineer, and confront me at my bohemian lady (who'd turned by now to elevator operator for a church. It shows what happens. I never got to fuck her either, just slick stammerings abt the world & Dylan Thomas & never got the Baudelaire book back either. But that's over & not yet come to. A horizon to look both ways, when you stand straddling it.

Belmont wd be jammed. And even in the winter sound trucks slashed thru the snow yowling blues. The world had opened and I stood in it smelling masturbation fingers. Slower, faster, than my time.

The hill slanted & blind men came up cold, coming out of the valentine store pushing snuff under their lips. Guitars blistering, the three kegs liquor store sides pushed out, and red whores dangled out the windows.

The bus came finally. 9 Clifton (Becky, her friend, sometimes Garmoney . . . and all the loud drooping-sock romeos from Central).

Friday, it was mine tho. White people fleeing the ward (from where?). Parties I didn't care about, old slick-haired cats from the south with thin mustaches.

The bus stopped & I looked out the window, or counted buicks, or wondered about the sky sitting so heavy on the Krueger (pronounced Kreeger) factory. Down W. Kinney St., I knew I'd gotten out. Left all that. The Physical world. Under jews, for quarters, or whatever light got in. What talk I gave. My own ego, expanded like the street, ran under a bridge, to the river.

But after, loot against my leg, I'd move up the hill, thru Douglass, & finally up on the hill (unless I was late, taking meat out of Steve's window . . . then I'd pack into the Kinney).

  It was contrast, doing things both ways . . . & then thinking about it all shoved in my head, grinning at my lips, & hunting echoes of my thot.

  Central Ave., near my old neighborhood. (The Secret Seven, Nwk. St., The Boose Bros., Staring Johnny, Board, &c. yng pussies.)

From there, get out, rush across the street, the 24 or 44 wd come/wild flashes then with the frontier coming up. East Orange. Talk to anybody, but not now this was like Oregon. Or at least an airport now showing up loaded.

I barely drank tho, & it was the sharp air turned me on. Moving out, already. The project. But, again, alone.

No. Nwk. was where the party was. Cookie's place. (They were hip mostly because they were foreign, for that matter, myself too. No one knew who I was in the ward. A hero maybe, with foreign friends. Pretty cool. Some kind of athlete. So when I came to places like that (in time) I'd show up loose, rangy, very nice. Somedays wind swept thru my eyes and I'd stare off whistling. This Was An ATTRIBUTE.

Al came down from there to go to Barringer also Carl Hargraves, Jonesy, most of Nat's band & alot of freckle-faced negroes in Nwk.)

A balance could form then, could tear you up & set itself so soon before you. The snow increased. Made drifts and the wind was colder slammed snow against the streetlights.

The party was downstairs in a basement, impressive for me because of Warren & my father's real middleclass specters. Straight-haired lightskinned girls I met only at picnics. There were some here, & some reputations got to me peeling tenderness from my fingers.

Slanted lights, Ivory Joe Hunter at Yvette's earlier. But her people naturally I guess wd move in. Shadows were fascinating and I might have danced w/ some anonymous american sweating when I missed her feet. Stronger than I was. More sophisticated in that world, that dungeon of ignorance. Snow veiled the windows and the tin music squealed.

Barringer people, north newark hoods (there were such, & I was, like the reputations, amazed. I loved the middleclass & they wd thrust pikes at me thru my shadows. Everybody rubbed stomachs & I stood around and wished everyone knew my name.

The Dukes were killing people then. They were talked about like the State. Like flame against wood. They swooped in Attila & his huns. They made everything & had brown army jackets & humped hats like homburgs pulled down on their ears. One knew Garmoney well, one got killed i heard last month, one, a guy named rabbit who was lightweight golden gloves, loved my sister & turned up at my house for my father to scream at. We were rich I insist. (As Kenny or any of the hillside people cd tell you.)

No Cavaliers made these things, only, as I sd, occasionally Earl. All that had ended and I still didn't know. They envied me my interests and slunk outside the windows weeping.

So it was the end. Formal as a season.

Nine Chester Ave. Mahomet. The sick tribes of Aegina. Black skies of christendom, (the 44 pulled up near his house & I ran thru the snow right to the door. A blue light leaned up from the basement & high laughter & The Orioles). A world, we made then. Dead Columbus "its first victim." Spread out the world, split open our heads with what rattles in the cold. All sinners, placed against mute perfection.

They, the Dukes, came in like they did. Slow, with hands shoved deep in pockets. Laughing, respectable (like gunfighters of the west. When air stirred years later, and we rode out to the sea).

Now they spread out among us, & girls' eyes shifted from their men to the hulks sucking up the shadows. The Orioles were lovely anyway, & the snow increased whining against the glass.

SURE I WAS FRIGHTENED BUT MAN THERE WAS NOT A GODDAMNED THING TO DO. IN THIS CONCEPTION OF THE ENTIRE WORLD OF TECHNOLOGY WE TRACE EVERY-THING BACK TO MAN AND FINALLY DEMAND AN ETHICS SUIT-ABLE TO THE WORLD OF TECHNOLOGY, IF, INDEED, WE WISH TO CARRY THINGS THAT FAR.

They had taken up the practice of wearing berets. Along with the army jackets (& bellbottom pants which was natu-ral for people in that strange twist of ourselves, that civil strife our bodies screamed for . . . Now, too, you readers!).

So everyone, the others, knew them right away. Girls wdn't dance with them & that cd start it. Somebody trying to make a point or something. Or if they were really salty they'd just claim you stepped on their shoes. (Murray warned me once that I'd better cool it or I was gonna get my hat blocked. I was grateful, in a way, on W. Market Street: that orange restaurant where they had quar-ter sets.)

Tonight someone said something about the records. Whose property or the music wasn't right or some idea came up to spread them-selves. Like Jefferson wanting Louisiana, or Bertran deBorn given dignity in Hell. There was a scuffle & the Dukes won.

(That big fat clown, slick, the husky sinister person, bigeyed evil bastard . . . the one that didn't

like me had a weird name I can't think of and well-tailored "bells."
Rabbit, Oscar (a camp follower) and some other cowboys.) They pushed
the guy's face in and the light, hung on a chain, swung crazy back and
forth and the girls shot up the stairs. He, the n.nwk. cat, got out tho, up
the stairs & split cursing in the snow. Things settled down & the new
learning had come in. A New Order, & cookie clicked his tongue still
cool under it, & I sat down talking to a girl I knew was too ugly to attract
attention.

This wd be the second phase in our lives. Totalitarianism.
Sheep performing in silence.

He came back with six guys and a meat
cleaver. Rushed down the wooden stairs & made the whole place no
man's land. Dukes took off the tams & tried to shove back in the darkness. Ladies pushed back on the walls. Orioles still grinding for the snow.
"Where's that muthafucka." Lovely Dante at night under his flame taking
heaven. A place, a system, where all is dealt with . . . as is proper. "I'm
gonna kill that muthafucka." Waved the cleaver and I crept backwards
while his mob shuffled faces. "I'm gonna kill *some*body." Still I had my
coat & edged away from the center (as I always came on. There. In your
ditch, bleeding with you. Christians).

Now the blood turned & he licked
his lips seeing their faces suffering. "Kill anybody," his axe slid thru the
place throwing people on their stomachs, it grazed my face sending my
green hat up against the record player. I wanted it back, but war broke
out & I rushed around the bar. They tried to get up the stairs, the light
girls & n.nwk. people. All the cool men bolted. I crouched with my
mouth against the floor, till Cookie came hurdling over the bar &
crushed my back.

The Dukes fought the others. And were outnumbered (we wd suffer next
week . . .) Nixon punched them (& got his later in Baxter with a baseball
bat). And they finally disappeared up the stairs, all the fighters.

When we
came out & went slow upstairs the fat guy was spread out in the snow &
Nicks was slapping him in his face with the side of the cleaver. He bled
under the light on the grey snow & his men had left him there to die.

Personators (alchemists) Falsifiers

If I am a good man, godfearing, brought from the field to
myself, in music, this round eye of mind, Jesus' flesh is
world to me, in words, thoughts heavier than myself.

If I were myself, at last, brought back
                                        (the field turned
        round
so it chatters under wind like leaves wave the day
        back slowly.
Winter, for myself, the god man, the lover, who has
        neither, nor
will it help sprawling, like this, across.

They had to shake my belief in the seasons. (If they could, coming in
here like that, drunk, cracks in the street, tar taste. I could walk under
those signs looking for their loves, or run out, like later, and bleed to
death of old age. I could come back around those corners, down those
hills (not saturday bright money, or the red-haired ladies of the consul.)
But bullets, and the aroma of Negroes, finally. All of them in that movie,
or living silently in pink houses.

* * *

So what becomes of me if Joe Louis and Roosevelt are caught here? As
the leaves lay flat on the grey ground. As they will, each time I look. Wind
in trash, moves. If they stand with me, as death will. As you can, lying flat
and alone without me. As your love could, were it made of softer breath.

They are our life. As Gods, or the signal raised over the city. The bright planes, and smokes of the summer. The ball's descent, splendid, bouncing if I picked it up and made the proper move. So, smells sit around us, seducing our years.

*   *   *

Those 12 years of God, all strength followed (and the walks into halls, and their dusty windows. They would quote something, or remember who was who. Who was placed, made to enter the pure world of system. As our lives slip through the fingers of giants. Their voices ruling the radios. (Notes there dissolving. As prayers will. Now his mouth is shut. He will not pray again.

Fat, or how they moved. Sullen, lies about them later. To push it in. All, all, what he tasted in his bottoms. At his soul's hurt, days would crawl in place. Each thing at the top of buildings looking down, across to where he died. Years later this was.

But God should be here. Should have his station, his final way of speech. More powerful than our dim halls, or the white mustache of the polack.

Hand could barely reach him. They'd scrape his chest / he pulled it back. Dancing away, left hand down. Shuffling. This God, on an orange porch, they listened with their sticks. Their travels out of hell, hells of the eastern city. Our country grew, its savages were given jobs. So it should, she wd laugh you to pieces, laugh you drunkenly at your hope.

He moved, and was with us in our shops. Our old men listened to the arms chop the air. Across the various yards, black gravel and white slat fences of the rich, who know nothing. Who are not jewish, even now they live where they do, with things around them grown to words. Their hands miss me. Their eyes twisted, packed with slender days.

The 12 years of God, are the last night. The Twelfth, that same thick evening air, summers, or when the last of the men got in. Winter, near christmas, they pulled in, swung down off their mounts. Shakespeare rattled drunkenly in the fog, folksingers, a thin Negro lying to his white girlfriend. Near parks, sitting cold in the scaly light like an empty room birds walk thru. Birds walk thru.

(And who was it drunk had told me unconvinced? His mother's rules. The groups walking with their trees. To make our proof . . . that there were Gods, whose world sat wet in the morning with our own.)

"So, I went for it. What the hell. Buncha drunks pissing on the corner. Plainclothes cat leaning out his black car window whistling. We move back towards the stoop. Turning both ways for Dukes." (Earlier or later, the cars would move away from the curb towards our lives. We had made it so far. This other group, my lieutenants, admirals, dentists.)

And they came thru it. Knew the punch, the stories, and how the doors sat open, and adults were ashamed to be so old they could not cry. They looked, if they would, or do now at what shows up saturdays needing a guide to place his life, his soul in their huge dark hands.

THE LATER GROUP

(if we die for the two big men. Satyr play shd move next! Change the scenery. Get the faggot off, and try to sober him up. Chrissakes. Clank (Airthefugginplaceout)

. . . WAS TP (Hollywood Ted & Co.) Everyone alive is a contemporary. As the man who beat Louis, or the Georgia heat where Roosevelt's head split. We know them together as part of our time.

And TP fit there. A Friend of The Family, really (as you people are now. Knowing so much). But I envied them, tony, sonny-boy, the rest. And it's so easy to cross them now. They've failed. Suppliants. Their dancing saved them those early times. Their coats. But it changed. The sun moved . . . our Gods, I said, had died. We weren't ready for anarchy . . . but it walked into us like morning.

So, look, for the first time at Anonymous Negroes and Harry S. Truman. (How's that grab you?) yall?) Anarchy, for a time.

Lucky, at first the war held. And we could think in that. I had a gun. But we didn't realize except what bled. And it had for youth. That when God is Killed, talking to oneself is a sign of nuttiness. (Our grandparents suffered.

And I watched them dance knowing that God was dead . . . and now, what it meant. I bought a checkered coat, green hat, kept alone, late, nights, till finally in a restaurant I met another man, and he stayed with me till my life was public.

* *

      This lousy vaudeville group. (Historically, only a later development of The Golden Boys and Los Cassedores.) But the net had been drawn tighter. And new loves grew out of stone.

    (A Story Of The New Group   THE RAPE

CIRCLE 9: Bolgia 1—Treachery To Kindred

THE RAPE

I'd moved outside to sit. And sitting brought the others out. (The NEW group, I thot about them with that name then.) The New Group. What had been my distance. Looking across the crowd at the motion and smoke they raised. Jackie's listless band, exciting, in it. Junkies humped over their borrowed horns and sending beams of cock up niggers' clothes.

Now I'd move past. They had come too. To see me. Or see what the great "sharp" world cd do. Their white teeth and mulatto brains to face the ofay houses of history. THE BEAUTIFUL MIDDLECLASS HAD FORMED AND I WAS TO BE A GREAT FIGURE, A GIANT AMONG THEM. THEY FOLLOWED WITH THEIR EYES, OR LISTENED TO SOFT MOUTHS SPILL MY STORY OUT TO GIVE THEIR WIVES. The fabric split. Silk patterns run in the rain. What thots the God had for us, I trampled, lost my way. Ran on what I was, to kill the arc, the lovely pattern of our lives.

Summers, during college, we all were celebrities. East Orange parties, people gave us lifts and sd our names to their friends. (What was left of the Golden Boys, Los Ruedos, splinter groups, and only me from the Cavaliers.) We'd made our move. They had on suits, and in my suit, names had run me down. Stymied me with pure voids of heat, moon, placing fingers on books.

Now, the party moved for us. And we made all kinds. This one was hippest for our time. East Orange, light-skinned girls, cars pulling in, smart clothes our fathers' masters wore. But this was the way. The movement. Our heads turned open for it. And light, pure warm light, flowed in.

I sat on a stoop. One of the white stoops of the rich (the Negro rich were lovely in their nonimportance in the world).

93

Still, I sat and thot why they moved past me, the ladies, or why questions seemed to ride me down. The world itself, so easy to solve . . . and get rid of. Why did they want it? What pulled them in, that passed me by. I cd have wept each night of my life.

* *

A muggy dust sat on us. And they made jokes and looked at me crooked, feasting on my eyes. Wondering why they liked me.

Sanchez, one of Leon's men, came out, whistled at the crowd of Lords, got his drink, and listened to a funny lie I told. He got in easy.

School came up, my own stupid trials they took as axioms for their lives. Any awkwardness, what they loved, and told their mothers of my intelligence. Still it sprung on them, from sitting in the trees. Silent with the silence; delighted in itself for thinking brutal concrete moves.

They Could Not Come To Me. It would be a thrust, or leave it home! Move the bastards out! A New Order (?) what came later returning to New York, to see Art, outside my head for the first time, and 200 year old symphonies I'd written only a few months earlier.

* *

A drunken girl, woman, slut, moved thru the trees. Weaving. I folded my arms and watched the trees, green almost under the porch lamp paste her in. They turned to me to see what noises I was making. Stupid things I'd thought I heard.

Foot slid down steps: up. Marking time, lime. Pulling at my tie, I watched and none of our girls was out. The party pushed noise into the dark. Only the cellar lights in the house spread out, light brown parents pushed their faces into pillows and hoped the party made their son popular.

She was skinny, dark and drunk. Nothing I'd want, without what pushed inside. They sd that to themselves, and to each other. What a desperate sick creature she was, and what she wanted here in their paradise.

And it took hold of me then. Who she was. Why I moved myself. Who she was,

and what wd be the weight her face wd make. So I looked at them and crossed my eyes so they would think, for an instant, what I thought.
                                                                                            The
chick was drunk. And probably some dumb whore slept to the end of the Kinney line. From the 3rd ward, she found herself with us. Trees. And the grey homes of the city, the other city, starting to fade on the hill.
                                                                                            She
came to me. Direct. Even slit eyes gave me away. She moved straight. And paused to pat her coat. (Sanchez gave her a Lucky Strike.) She asked me with the fire making a shadow on her forehead where was Jones St.

We all knew that was Newark. And I had got the thing stirring.

* *

But how long till the logic of our lives runs us down? Destroys the face the wind sees. The long beautiful fingers numbed in slow summer waves of darkness?
                    Never. Never. The waves run in. Blue. (Our citizens are languid as music. And their hearts are slow motion lives. Dead histories I drag thru the streets of another time. Never.

* *

Five, with me. And the woman. Huge red lips, like they were turned inside out. Heavy breath, almost with veins. Her life bleeding slow in the soft summer. And not passion pushed her to me. Not any I could sit with magazines in the white toilet wishing love was some gruesome sunday thing still alive and fishy in my clothes. Still, smelling, that single tone, registered in our heads, as dirt paths where we lay the other ladies naked, and naked bulbs shown squarely on their different flesh.

I said, "Jones St." and that held over the street like drums of insects. Like some new morning with weird weather swam into our faces. The meanings, we gave. I gave. (Because it sat alone with me . . . and I raised it. Made it some purely bodily suck. The way my voice would not go down. A tone, to set some fire in dry wood. An inferno. Where flame is words, or lives, or the simple elegance of death.)
                    Sanchez showed his teeth (I think, he stood sideways looking at the car. Jingling the keys at the tone of my words.) The others moved. "We'll take you there." I almost fell, so

moved that what I could drag into the world would stay. That others could see its shape and make it something in their brittle lives. "I'll take you there."

* *

Calvin, Donald, Sanchez, Leon, Joe & Me.
The Woman.

* *

They made to laugh. They made to get into the car. They made not to be responsible. All with me. (Tho this is new, I tell you now because, somehow, it all is right, whatever. For what sin you find me here. It's mine. My own irreconcilable life. My blood. My footsteps towards the black car smeared softly in the slow shadows of leaves.) The houses shone like naked bulbs. Thin laughter from the party trailed us up the street.

Sanchez threw the car in the wrong gear, nervous. It made that noise, and Donald (the dumb but handsome almost athlete jumped 10 feet . . . the others laughed and I chewed skin quickly off my thumb . . .) the woman talked directions at the floor.

Donald was at the woman's left, I at her right. The others packed in the front. Looking at us, across the seat. (Sanchez thru the mirror.) The whole night tightened, and it seemed our car rumbled on a cliff knocking huge rocks down a thousand feet. The thunderous tires roared. And roared.

The laugh got thinner. And the woman had trouble with her head. It flopped against her chest. Or her short brittle hair wd jam against my face, pushing that monstrous smell of old wood into my life. Old wood and wine. What there is of a slum. Of dead minds, dead fingers flapping empty in inhuman cold.

I winced (because I thot myself elegant. A fop, I'd become, and made a sign to Calvin in the mirror that the woman smelled. He grinned and rubbed his hands to steady them.

Hideous magician! The car rolled its banging stones against the dark. Ugly fiend screaming in the fire boiling your bones. Your cock, cunt, whatever in your head you think to be, is burning. Tied against a rock, straw packed tight into your eyes. POUR GASOLINE, SPREAD IT ON HIS TONGUE. NOW LIGHT THE STINKING MESS.

*   *   *

Shadow of a man. (Tied in a ditch, my own flesh burning in my nostrils. My body goes, simple death, but what of my mind? Who created me to this pain?)

Oh, the barns of lead are gold. You have abandoned God.

Now, he abandons you! Your brain runs like liquid in the grass.

*   *   *

I began to act. First hands dropped on the wino's knee. And she flopped her head spreading that rancid breath. So I pulled her head back against the seat, and moved my fingers hard against her flesh. Tugged at the wool skirt and pushed my hand between the stocking and the bumps upon her skin. Her mouth opened and she sounded like humming. Also, a shiver, like winter, went thru her/ and I almost took my hands away.

Donald saw me, and when I looked across at him he felt her too. The others in front gabbled & kept informed by craning in their seats.

I moved my fingers harder, pushing the cloth up high until I saw what I thot was her underwear. Some other color than pink, with dark stains around the part that fit against her crotch.

Her head slumped forward but the eyes had opened, and there was a look in them made me look out the window. But I never moved my hands. (Someone giggled up front.)

The car moved at a steady rate. The dim lights on. Up out of East Orange and into dark Montclair. With larger whiter homes. Some dirt along the way, which meant to us, who knew only cement, some kind of tortured wealth. We wd all live up here some way. Big dogs barked at the car from driveways and Sanchez looked over his shoulder at me to get his signals straight.

Donald said something to me across the woman and she raised her head, glaring at Calvin's back.

"What the hells goin on?" Calvin laughed. I

moved my fingers swifter straining for the top of the pants. Donald simply rolled her stockings down. And the woman grabbed his hand, quietly at first. But when she sensed that we would pile on her in the car shoving our tender unwashed selves in her eyes and mouth, she squeezed Donald's hand so hard it hurt.

"Bitch!"

"What're you boys tryina do?" No answer from us. The front riders sat tight in their seats, watching the big houses, and wishing probably it was now, when they are sitting prying the dark with staler eyes.

(In those same houses, waiting until I die when they can tell all these things with proper reverence to my widow.)

* *

The woman changed her mind. (She saw what was happening and stared at me for seconds before she spoke again. She braced herself against the seat and made a weeping sound.)

"Oh my life is so fucked up. So wasted and shitty. You boys don't know. How life is. How it takes you down. You don't know . . . Those ties and shirts . . . Shit . . . how hard a woman's life can be."

Her voice got softer or she thot she'd make it tender. It came out almost bleaker than a whine. . . .

"I'm sick too. A long time. The kind of thing makes men hate you. Those sores on my self."

(She meant her vagina.)

This was news to everyone. "I'm sick," she moaned again, making her voice almost loud. "And you boys can ketch it . . . everyone'a you, get it, and scratch these bleeding sores."

Donald moved his hand away. The woman screeched now, not loud, but dragging in her breath.

Apprehension now. As if the wall was almost down but the enemy's hero arrived to pour boiling oil in my warriors' eyes. I wdn't have that easy copout. Fuck that . . . goddamit, no pleas.

I made Donald put his hands back. I scowled the way I can with one side of my mouth, the other pushing the woman back. "Shit, I don't believe that bullshit! Prove it, baby, lemme see! I wanna see the sores . . . see what they look like!"

New life now. Reinforced, the others laughed. I pushed again. "O.K., mama, runout them sores . . . lemme suck'em till they get well." Another score: but how long, we were deep in Montclair, and some car full of negroes up there wd be spotted by the police . . . that swung thru my mind and I looked up quickly thru my window. Even rolled it down to hear.

"I'm sick . . . and you boys ketch what I got you'll never have no kids. Nobody'll marry you. That's why I'ma drunk whore fallin in the streets."

Marriage, children. What else could she burn? Donald fell away again. The rest swallowed, or moved their hands. Only Calvin ran to my aid. He grabbed a huge hunting knife still in its scabbard and twisted suddenly in his seat waving it in the woman's face. But the absurdity of it killed the move completely and we broke running down the slope:

                                                   "Shutup bitch"
(Calvin) "Shutup . . . I'm a goddam policemen (sic) and we're (sic) lookin for people like you to lock'umup!"

                              He waved the knife and Leon even laughed at him. It was over. The woman probably knew but took it further. She screamed as loud as she could. She screamed, and screamed, her voice almost shearing off our tender heads. The scream of an actual damned soul. The actual prisoner of the world.

          "SHEEEEEET, YOU BASTARDS LEMME GO.
          SHEEEET. HAALP. AGGGHEEE"

Donald reached across the whore and pushed the door open. The car still moving about 20 miles an hour and the sudden air opened my eyes in the smoke. The bitch screamed and we all knew Montclair was like a beautifully furnished room and someone would hear and we would die in jail, dead niggers who couldn't be invited to parties.

                                        Calvin   reached across the seat, and shouted in my face. "Kick the bitch out!" I couldn't move. My fingers were still on her knee. The plan still fixed in my mind. But the physical world rushed thru like dirty thundering water thru a dam. They ran on me.

"Throw this dumb bitch out." Calvin grabbed her by the arm and Donald heaved against her ass. The woman tumbled over my knees and rolled, I thought, slow motion out the car. She smashed against the pavement and wobbled on her stomach hard against the curb.

The door still swung open and I moved almost without knowing thru it to bring the woman back. The smoke had blown away. I saw her body like on a white porcelain table dead with eyes rolled back. I had to get her.

I dove for the door, even as Sanchez made the car speed up, and slammed right into the flopping steel. It hit me in the head and Leon wrenched me back against the seat. Calvin closed the door.

I could see the woman squatting in the street, under the fake gasoline lamp as we turned the corner, everybody screaming in the car, some insane allegiance to me.

6. The Heretics

"The whole of lower Hell is surrounded by a great wall, which is defended by rebel angels and immediately within which are punished the arch-heretics and their followers."

And then, the city of Dis, "the stronghold of Satan, named after him, . . . the deeper Hell of willful sin."

Blonde summer in our south. Always it floats down & hooks in the broad leaves of those unnamed sinister southern trees. Blonde. Yellow, a narrow sluggish water full of lives. Desires. The crimson heavy blood of a race, concealed in those absolute black nights. As if, each tiny tragedy had its own universe / or God to strike it down.

* *

Faceless slow movement. It was warm & this other guy had his sleeves rolled up. (You cd go to jail for that without any trouble. But we were loose, & maybe drunk. And I turned away & doubled up like rubber or black figure sliding at the bottom of any ocean. Thomas, Joyce, Eliot, Pound, all gone by & I thot agony at how beautiful I was. And sat sad many times in latrines fingering my joint.

But it was dusty. And time sat where it could, covered me dead, like under a stone for years, and my life was already over. A dead man stretched & a rock rolled over . . . till a light struck me straight on & I entered some madness, some hideous elegance . . . "A Patrician I wrote to him. Am I a Patrician?"

* *

We both wore wings. My hat dipped & shoes maybe shined. This other guy was what cd happen in this country. Black & his silver wings & tilted blue cap made up for his mother's hundred bogus kids. Lynchings. And he waved his own flag in this mosquito air, and walked straight & beauty was fine, and so easy.

He didn't know who I was, or even what. The light,

then (what george spoke of in his letters . . . "a soft intense light") was spread thin over the whole element of my world.

Two flyers, is what we thot people had to say. (I was a gunner, the other guy, some kind of airborne medic.) The bright wings & starched uniform. Plus, 24 dollars in my wallet.

That air rides you down, gets inside & leaves you weightless, sweating & longing for cool evening. The smells there wide & blue like eyes. And like kids, or the radio calling saturdays of the world of simple adventure. Made me weep with excitement. Heart pumping: not at all towards where we were. But the general sweep of my blood brought whole existences fresh and tingling into those images of romance had trapped me years ago.

* *

The place used me. Its softness, and in a way, indirect warmth, coming from the same twisting streets we walked. (After the bus, into the main fashion of the city: Shreveport, Louisiana. And it all erected itself for whoever . . . me, I supposed then, "it's here, and of course, the air, for my own weakness. Books fell by. But open yr eyes, nose, speak to whom you want to. Are you contemporary?")

And it seemed a world for aztecs lost on the bone side of mountains. A world, even strange, sat in that leavening light & we had come in raw from the elements. From the cardboard moonless world of ourselves . . . to whatever. To grasp at straws. (If indeed we wd confront us with those wiser selves . . . But that was blocked. The weather held. No rain. That smell wrapped me up finally & sent me off to seek its source. And men stopped us. Split our melting fingers. The sun moved till it stopped at the edge of the city. The south stretched past any eye. Outside any peculiar thot. Itself, whatever it becomes, is lost to what formal selves we have. Lust, a condition of the weather. The air, lascivious. Men die from anything . . . and this portion of my life was carefully examining the rules. How to die? How to die?

*

The place, they told us, we'd have to go to "ball" was called by them *Bottom*. The Bottom; where the colored lived. There, in whatever wordless energies your lives cd be taken up. Step back: to the edge, soothed the wind drops. Fingers are cool. Air sweeps. Trees one hundred feet down, smoothed over, the wind sways.

And

they tell me there is one place/

for me to be. Where
it all
comes down. &
you take up
your sorrowful
life. There/
with us all. To
whatever death

*

The Bottom lay like a man under a huge mountain. You cd see it slow in some mist, miles off. On the bus, the other guy craned & pulled my arm from the backseats at the mile descent we'd make to get the juice. The night had it. Air like mild seasons and come. That simple elegance of semen on the single buds of air. As if the night were feathers . . . and they settled solid on my speech . . . and preached sinister love for the sun.

The day . . . where had it gone? It had moved away as we wound down into the mass of trees and broken lives.

The bus stopped finally a third of the way down the slope. The last whites had gotten off a mile back & 6 or seven negroes and we two flyers had the bus. The driver smiled his considerate paternal smile in the mirror at our heads as we popped off. Whole civilization considered, considered. "They live in blackness. No thought runs out. They kill each other & hate the sun. They have no God save who they are. Their black selves. Their lust. Their insensible animal eyes."

"Hey, son, 'dyou pay for him?" He asked me because I hopped off last. He meant not my friend, the other pilot, but some slick head coon in yellow pants cooling it at top speed into the grass. & knowing no bus driver was running in after no 8 cents.

"Man, the knives
flash. Souls
are spittle

on black earth. Metal
dug in flesh chipping
at the bone."
I turned completely around to look at the bus driver. I saw a knife in him
hacking chunks of bone. He stared, & smiled at the thin mob rolling
down the hill. Friday night. Nigguhs is Nigguhs. I agreed. & smiled, he
liked the wings, had a son who flew. "You gon pay for that ol coon?"

"No," I said, "No. Fuck, man, I hate coons." He laughed. I saw the night
around his head warped with blood. The bus, moon & trees floated heavily in blood. It washed down the side of the hill & the negroes ran from it.

I turned towards my friend who was loping down the hill shouting at
me & ran towards him & what we saw at the foot of the hill. The man
backed the bus up & turned around / pretending he was a mystic.

* * *

I caught Don(?) and walked beside him laughing. And the trees passed
& some lights and houses sat just in front of us. We trailed the rest of the
crowd & they spread out soon & disappeared into their lives.

The Bottom was like Spruce & Belmont(the ward) in Nwk. A culture of
violence and foodsmells. There, for me. Again. And it stood strange when
I thot finally how much irony. I had gotten so elegant (that was college /
a new order of foppery). But then the army came & I was dragged into a
kind of stillness. Everything I learned stacked up and the bones of love
shattered in my face. And I never smiled again at anything. Everything
casual in my life (except that life itself) was gone. Those naked shadows
of men against the ruined walls. Penis, testicles. All there (and I sat
burned like wire, w/ farmers, thinking of what I had myself. When I peed
I thot that. "Look. Look what you're using to do this. A dick. And two
balls, one a little lower than the other. The first thing warped & crooked
when it hardened." But it meant nothing. The books meant nothing. My
idea was to be loved. What I accused John of. And it meant going into
that huge city melting. And the first face I saw I went to and we went
home and he shoved his old empty sack of self against my frozen skin.

* *

Shadows, phantoms, recalled by that night. Its heavy moon. A turning
slow and dug in the flesh and wet spots grew under my khaki arms. Alive

to mystery. And the horror in my eyes made them large and the moon came in. The moon and the quiet southern night.

* *

We passed white shut houses. It seemed misty or smoky. Things settled dumbly in the fog and we passed, our lives spinning off in simple anonymous laughter.

We were walking single file because of the dirt road. Not wanting to get in the road where drunk niggers roared by in dead autos stabbing each others' laughter in some grey abandon of suffering. That they suffered and cdn't know it. Knew that somehow, forever. Each dead nigger stinking his same suffering thru us. Each word of blues some dead face melting. Some life drained off in silence. Under some grey night of smoke. They roared thru this night screaming. Heritage of hysteria and madness, the old meat smells and silent grey sidewalks of the North. Each father, smiling mother, walked thru these nights frightened of their children. Of the white sun scalding their nights. Of each hollow loud footstep in whatever abstruse hall.

* * *

THE JOINT

(a letter was broken and I can't remember. The other guy laughed, at the name. And patted his. I took it literal and looked thru my wallet as not to get inflamed and sink on that man screaming of my new loves. My cold sin in the cities. My fear of my own death's insanity, and an actual longing for men that brooded in each finger of my memory.

He laughed at the sign. And we stood, for the moment (he made me warm with his laughing), huge white men who knew the world (our wings) and would give it to whoever showed as beautiful or in our sad lone smiles, at least willing to love us.

He pointed, like Odysseus wd. Like Virgil, the weary shade, at some circle. For Dante, me, the yng wild virgin of the universe to look. To see what terror. What illusion. What sudden shame, the world is made. Of what death and lust I fondled and thot to make beautiful or escape, at least, into some other light, where each death was abstract & intimate.

* * * *

There were, I think, 4 women standing across the street. The neon winked, and the place seemed mad to be squatted in this actual wilderness. "For Madmen Only." Mozart's Ornithology and yellow greasy fags moaning german jazz. Already, outside. The passage, I sensed in those women. And black space yawned. Damned and burning souls. What has been your sin? Your ugliness?

And they waved. Calling us natural names. "Hey, ol bigeye sweet nigger . . com'ere." "Littl ol' skeeter dick . . . don't you want none?" And to each other giggling at their centuries, "Um, that big nigger look sweet" . . . "Yeh, that little one look sweet too." The four walls of some awesome city. Once past you knew that your life had ended. That roads took up the other side, and wound into thicker dusk. Darker, more insane, nights.

And Don shouted back, convinced of his hugeness, his grace . . . my wisdom. I shuddered at their eyes and tried to draw back into the shadows. He grabbed my arm, and laughed at my dry lips.
    Of the 4, the pretty one was Della and the fat one, Peaches. 17 year old whores strapped to negro weekends. To the black thick earth and smoke it made to hide their maudlin sins. I stared and was silent and they, the girls and Don, the white man, laughed at my whispering and sudden midnight world.
Frightened of myself, of the night's talk, and not of them. Of myself.
    The other two girls fell away hissing at their poverty. And the two who had caught us exchanged strange jokes. Told us of themselves thru the other's mouth. Don already clutching the thin beautiful Della. A small tender flower she seemed. Covered with the pollen of desire. Ignorance. Fear of what she was. At her 17th birthday she had told us she wept, in the department store, at her death. That the years wd make her old and her dresses wd get bigger. She laughed and felt my arm, and laughed, Don pulling her closer. And ugly negroes passed close to us frowning at the uniforms and my shy clipped speech which they called "norf."
                                                                                So
Peaches was mine. Fat with short baked hair split at the ends. Pregnant empty stomach. Thin shrieky voice like knives against a blackboard. Speeded up records. Big feet in white, shiny polished shoes. Fat tiny hands full of rings. A purple dress with wrinkles across the stomach. And

perspiring flesh that made my khakis wet.

The four of us went in the joint and the girls made noise to show this world their craft. The two rich boys from the castle. (Don looked at me to know how much cash I had and shouted and shook his head and called "18, man," patting his ass.)

The place was filled with shades. Ghosts. And the huge ugly hands of actual spooks. Standing around the bar, spilling wine on greasy shirts. Yelling at a fat yellow spliv who talked about all their mothers, pulling out their drinks. Laughing with wet cigarettes and the paper stuck to fat lips. Crazy as anything in the world, and sad because of it. Yelling as not to hear the sad breathing world. Turning all music up. Screaming all lyrics. Tough black men . . . weak black men. Filthy drunk women whose perfume was cheap unnatural flowers. Quiet thin ladies whose lives had ended and whose teeth hung stupidly in their silent mouths . . rotted by thousands of nickel wines. A smell of despair and drunkenness. Silence and laughter, and the sounds of their movement under it. Their frightening lives.

*   *

Of course the men didn't dig the two imitation white boys come in on their leisure. And when I spoke someone wd turn and stare, or laugh, and point me out. The quick new jersey speech, full of italian idiom, and the invention of the jews. Quick to describe. Quicker to condemn. And when we finally got a seat in the back of the place, where the dance floor was, the whole place had turned a little to look. And the girls ate it all up, laughing as loud as their vanity permitted. Other whores grimaced and talked almost as loud . . . putting us all down.

10 feet up on the wall, in a kind of balcony, a jew sat, with thick glasses and a cap, in front of a table. He had checks and money at the table & where the winding steps went up to him a line of shouting woogies waved their pay & waited for that bogus christ to give them the currency of that place. Two tremendous muthafuckers with stale white teeth grinned in back of the jew and sat with baseball bats to protect the western world.

On the dance floor people hung on each other. Clutched their separate flesh and thought, my god, their separate thots. They stunk. They screamed. They moved hard against each other. They pushed. And wiggled to keep the music on.

Two juke boxes blasting from each corner, and four guys on a bandstand who had taken off their stocking caps and come to the place with guitars. One with a saxophone. All that screaming came together with the smells and the music, the people bumped their asses and squeezed their eyes shut.

Don ordered a bottle of schenley's which cost 6 dollars for a pint after hours. And Peaches grabbed my arm and led me to the floor.

The dancing like a rite no one knew, or had use for outside their secret lives. The flesh they felt when they moved, or I felt all their flesh and was happy and drunk and looked at the black faces knowing all the world thot they were my own, and lusted at that anonymous America I broke out of, and long for it now, where I am.

We danced, this face and I, close so I had her sweat in my mouth, her flesh the only sound my brain could use. Stinking, and the music over us like a sky, choked any other movement off. I danced. And my history was there, had passed no further. Where it ended, here, the light white talking jig, died in the arms of some sentry of Africa. Some short-haired witch out of my mother's most hideous dreams. I was nobody now, mama. Nobody. Another secret nigger. No one the white world wanted or would look at. (My mother shot herself. My father killed by a white tree fell on him. The sun, now, smothered. Dead.

* * *

Don and his property had gone when we finished. 3 or 4 dances later. My uniform dripping and soggy on my skin. My hands wet. My eyes turned up to darkness. Only my nerves sat naked and my ears were stuffed with gleaming horns. No one face sat alone, just that image of myself, forever screaming. Chiding me. And the girl, peaches, laughed louder than the crowd. And wearily I pushed her hand from my fly and looked for a chair.

We sat at the table and I looked around the room for my brother, and only shapes of black men moved by. Their noise and smell. Their narrow paths to death. I wanted to panic, but the dancing and gin had me calm, almost cruel in what I saw.

Peaches talked. She talked at what she thought she saw. I slumped on the table and we emptied another pint. My stomach turning rapidly and the room moved without me. And I slapped my hands on the table laughing at myself. Peaches laughed, peed, thinking me crazy, returned, laughed again. I was silent now, and felt the drunk and knew I'd go out soon. I got up feeling my legs, staring at the fat guard with me, and made to leave. I mumbled at her. Something ugly. She laughed and held me up. Holding me from the door. I smiled casual, said, "Well, honey, I gotta split . . I'm fucked up." She grinned the same casual, said, "You can't go now, big eye, we jist gittin into sumpum."

"Yeh, yeh, I know . . . but I can't make it." My head was shaking on my chest, fingers stabbed in my pockets. I staggered like an acrobat towards the stars and trees I saw at one end of the hall. "UhUh . . . baby where you goin?"

"Gotta split, gotta split . . . really, baby, I'm fucked . . up." And I twisted my arm away, moving faster as I knew I should towards the vague smell of air. Peaches was laughing and tugging a little at my sleeve. She came around and rubbed my tiny pecker with her fingers. And still I moved away. She had my elbow when I reached the road, head still slumped, and feet pushing for a space to go down solid on. When I got outside she moved in front of me. Her other girls had moved in too, to see what was going on. Why Peaches had to relinquish her share so soon. I saw the look she gave me and wanted somehow to protest, say, "I'm sorry. I'm fucked up. My mind, is screwy, I don't know why. I can't think. I'm sick. I've been fucked in the ass. I love books and smells and my own voice. You don't want me. Please, Please, don't want me."

But she didn't see. She heard, I guess, her own blood. Her own whore's bones telling her what to do. And I twisted away from her, headed across the road and into the dark. Out of, I hoped, Bottom, towards what I thot was light. And I could hear the girls laughing at me, at Peaches, at whatever thing I'd brought to them to see.

So the fat bitch grabbed my hat. A blue "overseas cap" they called it in the service. A cunt cap the white boys called it. Peaches had it and was laughing like kids in the playground doing the same thing to some unfortunate fag. I knew the second she got it, and stared crazily at her, and my look softened to fear and I grinned, I think. "You ain't going back without dis cap, big eye nigger," tossing it over my arms to her screaming friends. They tossed it back to her. I stood in the center staring at the lights. Listening to my own head. The things I wanted. Who I thot I was. What was it? Why was this going on? Who was involved? I screamed for the hat. And they shot up the street, 4 whores, Peaches last in her fat, shouting at them to throw the hat to her. I stood for awhile and then tried to run after them. I cdn't go back to my base without that cap. Go to jail, drunken nigger! Throw him in the stockade! You're out of uniform, shine! When I got close to them, the other three ran off, and only Peaches stood at the top of the hill waving the hat at me, cackling at her wealth. And she screamed at the world, that she'd won some small niche in it. And did a dance, throwing her big hips at me, cursing and spitting . . . laughing at the drunk who had sat down on the curb and started to weep and plead at her for some cheap piece of cloth.

And I was mumbling under the tears. "My hat, please, my hat. I gotta get back, please." But she came over to me and leaned on my shoulder, brushing the cap in my face. "You gonna buy me another drink . . . just one more?"

* * *

She'd put the cap in her brassiere, and told me about the Cotton Club. Another place at the outskirts of Bottom. And we went there, she was bouncing and had my hand, like a limp cloth. She talked of her life. Her husband, in the service too. Her family. Her friends. And predicted I would be a lawyer or something else rich.

The Cotton Club, was in a kind of ditch. Or valley. Or three flights down. Or someplace removed from where we stood. Like movies, or things you think up abstractly. Poles, where the moon was. Signs, for streets, beers, pancakes. Out front. No one moved outside, it was too late. Only whores and ignorant punks were out.

The place when we got in was all light. A bar. Smaller than the joint, with less people and quieter. Tables were strewn around and there was a bar with a fat white man sitting on a stool behind it. His elbows rested on the bar and he chewed a cigar spitting the flakes on the floor. He smiled at Peaches, knowing her, leaning from his talk. Four or five stood at the bar. White and black, moaning and drunk. And I wondered how it was they got in. The both colors? And I saw a white stripe up the center of the floor, and taped to the bar, going clear up, over the counter. And the black man who talked, stood at one side, the left, of the tape, furtherest from the door. And the white man, on the right, closest to the door. They talked, and were old friends, touching each other, and screaming with laughter at what they said.

We got vodka. And my head slumped, but I looked around to see, what place this was. Why they moved. Who was dead. What faces came. What moved. And they sat in their various skins and stared at me.

Empty man. Walk thru shadows. All lives the same. They give you wishes. The old people at the window. Dead man. Rised, come gory to their side. Wish to be lovely, to be some other self. Even here, without you. Some other soul, than the filth I feel. Have in me. Guilt, like something of God's. Some separate suffering self.

Locked in a lightless shaft. Light at the top, pure white sun. And shadows twist my voice. Iron clothes to suffer. To pull down, what had grown so huge. My life wrested away. The old wood. Eyes of the damned uncomprehending. Who it was. Old slack nigger. Drunk punk. Fag. Get up. Where's your home? Your mother. Rich nigger. Porch sitter. It comes down. So cute, huh? Yellow thing. Think you cute.

And suffer so slight, in the world. The world? Literate? Brown skinned. Stuck in the ass. Suffering from what? Can you read? Who is T. S. Eliot? So what? A cross. You've got to like girls. Weirdo. Break, Roi, break. Now come back, do it again. Get down, hard. Come up. Keep your legs high, crouch hard when you get the ball . . . churn, churn, churn. A blue jacket, and alone. Where? A chinese restaurant. Talk to me. Goddamnit. Say something. You never talk, just sit there, impossible to love. Say something. Alone, there, under those buildings. Your shadows. Your selfish tongue. Move. Frightened bastard. Frightened scared sissy motherfucker.

* * *

I felt my head go down. And I moved my hand to keep it up. Peaches laughed again. The white man turned and clicked his tongue at her wagging his hand. I sucked my thin mustache, scratched my chest, held my sore head dreamily. Peaches laughed. 2 bottles more of vodka she drank (half pints at 3.00 each) & led me out the back thru some dark alley down steps and thru a dark low hall to where she lived.

She was dragging me, I tried to walk and couldn't and stuck my hands in my pockets to keep them out of her way. Her house, a room painted blue and pink with Rheingold women glued to the wall. Calendars. The

Rotogravure. The picture of her husband? Who she thot was some officer, and he was grinning like watermelon photos with a big white apron
on and uncle jemima white hat and should've had a skillet. I slumped on
the bed, and she made me get up and sit in a chair and she took my hat
out of her clothes and threw it across the room. Coffee, she said, you
want coffee. She brought it anyway, and I got some in my mouth. Like
winter inside me. I coughed and she laughed. I turned my head away
from the bare bulb. And she went in a closet and got out a thin yellow
cardboard shade and stuck it on the light trying to push the burned part
away from the huge white bulb.

Willful sin. in your toilets jerking off. You refused God. All frauds, the
cold mosques glitter winters. "Morsh-Americans." Infidels fat niggers at
the gates. What you want. What you are now. Liar. All sins, against your
God. Your own flesh. TALK. TALK.

And I still slumped and she pushed my head back against the greasy
seat and sat on my lap grinning in my ear, asking me to say words that
made her laugh. Orange. Probably. Girl. Newark. Peaches. Talk like a
white man, she laughed. From up north (she made the "th" an "f").

And sleep seemed good to me. Something my mother would say. My
grandmother, all those heads of heaven. To get me in. Roi, go to sleep,
You need sleep, and eat more. You're too skinny. But this fat bitch
pinched my neck and my eyes would shoot open and my hands dropped
touching the linoleum and I watched roaches, trying to count them getting up to 5, and slumped again. She pinched me. And I made some
move and pushed myself up standing and went to the sink and stuck my
head in cold water an inch above the pile of stale egg dishes floating in
brown she used to wash the eggs off.

I shook my head. Took out my handkerchief to dry my hands, leaving
my face wet and cold, for a few seconds. But the heat came back, and I
kept pulling my shirt away from my body and smelled under my arms, trying to laugh with Peaches, who was laughing again.

I wanted to talk now. What to say. About my life. My thots. What
I'd found out, and tried to use. Who I was. For her. This lady, with me.

She pushed me backwards on the bed and said you're sleepy I'll get in with you. and I rolled on my side trying to push up on the bed and couldn't, and she pulled one of my shoes off and put it in her closet. I turned on my back and groaned at my head told her again I had to go. I was awol or something. I had to explain awol and she knew what it meant when I finished. Everybody that she knew was that. She was laughing again. O, God, I wanted to shout and it was groaned. Oh, God.

She had my pants in her fingers pulling them over my one shoe. I was going to pull them back up and they slipped from my hands and I tried to raise up and she pushed me back. "Look, Ol nigger, I ain't even gonna charge you. I like you." And my head was turning, flopping straight back on the chenille, and the white ladies on the wall did tricks and grinned and pissed on the floor. "Baby, look. Baby," I was sad because I fell. From where it was I'd come to. My silence. The streets I used for books. All come in. Lost. Burned. And soothing she rubbed her hard hair on my stomach and I meant to look to see if grease was there it was something funny I meant to say, but my head twisted to the side and I bit the chenille and figured there would be a war or the walls would collapse and I would have to take the black girl out, a hero. And my mother would grin and tell her friends and my father would call me "mcgee" and want me to tell about it.

When I had only my shorts on she pulled her purple dress over her head. It was all she had, except a grey brassiere with black wet moons where her arms went down. She kept it on.

Some light got in from a window. And one white shadow sat on a half-naked woman on the wall. Nothing else moved. I drew my legs up tight & shivered. Her hands pulled me to her.

*

It was Chicago. The fags & winter. Sick thin boy, come out of those els. Ask about the books. Thin mathematics and soup. Not the black Beverly, but here for the first time I'd seen it. Been pushed in. What was flesh I hadn't used till then. To go back. To sit lonely. Need to be used, touched, and see for the first time how it moved. Why the world moved on it. Not a childish sun. A secret fruit. But hard things between their legs. And lives governed under it. So here, it can sit now, as evil. As demanding, for me, to have come thru and found it again. I hate it. I hate to touch you. To feel myself go soft and want some person not myself. And here, it had moved outside. Left my wet fingers and was not something I fixed. But dropped on me and sucked me inside. That I walked the streets hunting for warmth. To be pushed under a quilt, and call it love. To shit water for days and say I've been loved. Been warm. A real thing in the world. See my shadow. My reflection. I'm here, alive. Touch me. Please. Please, touch me.

* * *

She rolled on me and after my pants were off pulled me on her thick stomach. I dropped between her legs and she felt between my cheeks to touch my balls. Her fingers were warm and she grabbed everything in her palm and wanted them harder. She pulled to get them harder and it hurt me. My head hurt me. My life. And she pulled, breathing spit on my chest. "Comeon, Baby, Comeon . . . Get hard." It was like being slapped. And she did it that way, trying to laugh. "Get hard . . . Get hard." And nothing happened or the light changed and I couldn't see the paper woman.

And she slapped me now, with her hand. A short hard punch and my head spun. She cursed. & she pulled as hard as she could. I was going to be silent but she punched again and I wanted to laugh . . . it was another groan. "Young peachtree," she had her mouth at my ear lobe. "You don't like women, huh?" "No wonder you so pretty . . . ol bigeye faggot." My head was turned from that side to the other side turned to the other side turned again and had things in it bouncing.

"How'd you ever get in them airplanes, peaches (her name she called me)? Why they let fairies in there now? (She was pulling too hard now & I thot everything would give and a hole in my stomach would let out words and tears.)Goddam punk, you gonna fuck me tonight or I'm gonna pull your fuckin dick aloose."

How to be in this world. How to be here, not a shadow, but thick bone and meat. Real flesh under real sun. And real tears falling on black sweet earth.

I was crying now. Hot hot tears and trying to sing. Or say to Peaches. "Please, you don't know me. Not what's in my head. I'm beautiful. Stephen Dedalus. A mind, here where there is only steel. Nothing else. Young pharaoh under trees. Young pharaoh, romantic, liar. Feel my face, how tender. My eyes. My soul is white, pure white, and soars. Is the God himself. This world and all others.

And I thot of a black man under the el who took me home in the cold. And I remembered telling him all these things. And how he listened and showed me his new suit. And I crawled out of bed morning and walked thru the park for my train. Loved. Afraid. Huger than any world. And the hot tears wet Peaches and her bed and she slapped me for pissing.

I rolled hard on her and stuck my soft self between her thighs. And ground until I felt it slip into her stomach. And it got harder in her spreading the meat. Her arms around my hips pulled down hard and legs locked me and she started yelling. Faggot. Faggot. Sissy Motherfucker. And I pumped myself. Straining. Threw my hips at her. And she yelled, for me to fuck her. Fuck her. Fuck me, you lousy fag. And I twisted, spitting tears, and hitting my hips on hers, pounding flesh in her, hearing myself weep.

* * * * * * * *

Later, I slipped out into Bottom. Without my hat or tie, shoes loose and pants wrinkled and filthy. No one was on the streets now. Not even the whores. I walked not knowing where I was or was headed for. I wanted to get out. To see my parents, or be silent for the rest of my life. Huge moon was my light. Black straight trees the moon showed. And the dirt roads and scattered wreck houses. I still had money and I.D., and a pack of cigarettes. I trotted, then stopped, then trotted, and talked outloud to myself. And laughed a few times. The place was so still, so black and full of violence. I felt myself.

At one road, there were several houses. Larger than alot of them. Porches, yards. All of them sat on cinder blocks so the vermin would have trouble getting in. Someone called to me. I thought it was in my head and kept moving, but slower. They called again. "Hey, psst. Hey comere." A whisper, but loud. "Comere, baby." All the sides of the houses were lit up but underneath, the space the cinder blocks made was black. And the moon made a head shadow on the ground, and I could see an arm in the same light. Someone kneeling under one of the houses, or an arm and the shadow of a head. I stood straight, and stiff, and tried to see right thru the dark. The voice came back, chiding like. Something you want. Whoever wants. That we do and I wondered who it was kneeling in the dark, at the end of the world, and I heard breathing when I did move, hard and closed.

I bent towards the space to see who it was. Why they had called. And I saw it was a man. Round red-rimmed eyes, sand-colored jew hair, and teeth for a face. He had been completely under the house but when I came he crawled out and I saw his dripping smile and yellow soggy skin full of red freckles. He said, "Come on here. Comere a second." I moved to turn away. The face like a dull engine. Eyes blinking. When I turned he reached for my arm grazing my shirt and the voice could be flushed down a toilet. He grinned and wanted to panic seeing me move. "Lemme suck yo dick, honey. Huh?" I was backing away like from the hyena cage to see the rest of them. Baboons? Or stop at the hot-dog stand and read a comic book. He came up off all fours and sat on his knees and toes, shaking his head and hips. "Comeon baby, comeon now." As I moved back he began to scream at me. All lust, all panic, all silence and sorrow, and finally when I had moved and was trotting down the road, I looked around and he was standing up with his hands cupped to his mouth yelling into the darkness in complete hatred of what was only some wraith. Irreligious spirit pushing thru shadows, frustrating and confusing the flesh. He screamed behind me and when the moon sunk for minutes behind the clouds or trees his scream was like some animal's, some hurt ugly thing dying alone.

* * * *

It was good to run. I would jump every few steps like hurdling, and shoot my arm out straight to take it right, landing on my right heel, snapping the left leg turned and flat, bent for the next piece. 3 steps between 180 yard lows, 7 or 9 between the 220's. The 180's I thought the most beautiful. After the first one, hard on the heel and springing up. Like music; a scale. Hit, 1–23. UP (straight right leg, down low just above the wood. Left turned at the angle, flat, tucked. Head low to the knee, arms reaching for the right toe, pulling the left leg to snap it down. HIT (right foot). Snap left HIT (left). Stride. The big one. 1–23. UP. STRETCH. My stride was long enough for the 3 step move. Stretching and hopping almost but in perfect scale. And I moved ahead of Wang and held it, the jew boy pooping at the last wood. I hit hard and threw my chest out, pulling the knees high, under my chin. Arms pushing. The last ten yards I picked up 3 and won by that, head back wrong (Nap said) and galloping like a horse (wrong again Nap said) but winning in new time and leaping in the air like I saw heroes do in flicks.

* * * *

I got back to where I thought the Joint would be, and there were city-like houses and it was there somewhere. From there, I thought I could walk out, get back to the world. It was getting blue again. Sky lightening blue and grey trees and buildings black against it. And a few lights going on in some wood houses. A few going off. There were alleys now. And high wood fences with slats missing. Dogs walked across the road. Cats sat on the fences watching. Dead cars sulked. Old newspapers torn in half pushed against fire hydrants or stoops and made tiny noises flapping if the wind came up.

I had my hands in my pockets, relaxed. The anonymous seer again. Looking slowly at things. Touching wood rails so years later I would remember I had touched wood rails in Louisiana when no one watched. Swinging my leg at cans, talking to the cats, doing made up dance steps or shadow boxing. And I came to a corner & saw some big black soldier stretched in the road with blood falling out of his head and stomach. I thot first it was Don. But this guy was too big and was in the infantry. I saw a paratrooper patch on his cap which was an inch away from his chopped up face, but the blue and silver badge had been taken off his shirt.

He was groaning quiet, talking to himself. Not dead, but almost. And I bent over him to ask what happened. He couldn't open his eyes and didn't hear me anyway. Just moaned and moaned losing his life on the ground. I stood up and wondered what to do. And looked at the guy and saw myself and looked over my shoulder when I heard some-one move behind me. A tall black skinny woman hustled out of the shadows and looking back at me disappeared into a hallway. I shouted after her. And stepped in the street to see the door she'd gone in.

I turned to go back to the soldier and there was a car pulling up the road. A red swiveling light on top and cops inside. One had his head hung out the window and yelled towards me. "Hey, you, Nigger, What's goin on?" That would be it. AWOL. Out of uniform (with a norfern accent). Now murder too. "30 days for nigger killing." I spun and moved. Down the road & they started to turn. I hit the fence, swinging up and dove into the black yard beyond. Fell on my hands and knees & staggered, got up, tripped on garbage, got up, swinging my hands, head down and charged off in the darkness.

The crackers were yelling on the other side of the fence and I could hear one trying to scale it. There was another fence beyond, and I took it the same as the first. Swinging down into another yard. And turned right and went over another fence, ripping my shirt. Huge cats leaped out of my path and lights went on in some houses. I saw the old woman who'd been hiding near the soldier just as I got to the top of one fence. She was standing in a hallway that led out in that yard, and she ducked back laughing when she saw me. I started to go after her, but I just heaved a big rock in her direction and hit another fence.

I got back to where the city houses left off, and there were the porches and cinder blocks again. I wondered if "sweet peter eater" would show up. (He'd told me his name.) And I ran up the roads hoping it wdn't get light until I found Peaches again.

At the Cotton Club I went down the steps, thru the alley, rested in the black hall, and tapped on Peaches' door. I bounced against it with my ass, resting between bumps, and fell backwards when she opened the door to shove her greasy eyes in the hall.

"You back again? What you want, honey? Know you don't want no pussy. Doyuh?"

I told her I had to stay there. That I wanted to stay there, with her. That I'd come back and wanted to sleep. And if she wanted money I'd give her some. And she grabbed my wrist and pulled me in, still bare-assed except for the filthy brassiere.

She loved me, she said. Or liked me alot. She wanted me to stay, with her. We could live together and she would show me how to fuck. How to do it good. And we could start as soon as she took a pee. And to undress, and get in bed and wait for her, unless I wanted some coffee, which she brought back anyway and sat on the edge of the bed reading a book about Linda Darnell.

"Oh, we can have some good times baby. Movies, all them juke joints. You live here with me and I'll be good to you. Wallace (her husband) ain't due back in two years. We can raise hell waiting for him." She put the book down and scratched the inside of her thighs, then under one arm. Her hair was standing up and she went to a round mirror over the sink and brushed it. And turned around and shook her big hips at me, then pumped the air to suggest our mission. She came back and we talked about our lives: then she pushed back the sheets, helped me undress again, got me hard and pulled me into her. I came too quick and she had to twist her hips a few minutes longer to come herself. "Uhauh, good even on a sof. But I still got to teach you."

* * * * * *

I woke up about 1 the next afternoon. The sun, thru that one window, full in my face. Hot, dust in it. But the smell was good. A daytime smell. And I heard daytime voices thru the window up and fat with optimism. I pulled my hands under my head and looked for Peaches, who was out of bed. She was at the kitchen end of the room cutting open a watermelon. She had on a slip, and no shoes, but her hair was down flat and greased so it made a thousand slippery waves ending in slick feathers at the top of her ears.

"Hello, sweet," she turned and had a huge slice of melon on a plate for me. It was bright in the room now & she'd swept and straightened most of the shabby furniture in her tiny room. And the door sat open so more light, and air could come in. And her radio up on a shelf above the bed was on low with heavy blues and twangy guitar. She sat the melon on the "end table" and moved it near the bed. She had another large piece, dark red and spilling seeds in her hand and had already started. "This is good. Watermelon's a good breakfast. Peps you up."

And I felt myself smiling, and it seemed that things had come to an order. Peaches sitting on the edge of the bed, just beginning to perspire around her forehead, eating the melon in both hands, and mine on a plate, with a fork (since I was "smart" and could be a lawyer, maybe). It seemed settled. That she was to talk softly in her vague american, and I was to listen and nod, or remark on the heat or the sweetness of the melon. And that the sun was to be hot on our faces and the day smell come in with dry smells of knuckles or greens or peas cooking somewhere. Things moving naturally for us. At what bliss we took. At our words. And slumped together in anonymous houses I thought of black men sitting on their beds this saturday of my life listening quietly to their wives' soft talk. And felt the world grow together as I hadn't known it. All lies before, I thought. All fraud and sickness. This was the world. It leaned under its own suns, and people moved on it. A real world. of flesh, of smells, of soft black harmonies and color. The dead maelstrom of my head, a sickness. The sun so warm and lovely on my face, the melon sweet going down. Peaches' music and her radio's. I cursed chicago, and softened at the world. "You look so sweet," she was saying. "Like you're real rested."

* * * * *

I dozed again even before I finished the melon and Peaches had taken it and put it in the icebox when I woke up. The greens were cooking in our house now. The knuckles on top simmering. And biscuits were cooking, and chicken. "How you feel, baby," she watched me stretch. I yawned loud and scratched my back getting up to look at what the stove was doing. "We gonna eat a good lunch before we go to the movies. You so skinny, you could use a good meal. Don't you eat nuthin?" And she put down her cooking fork and hugged me to her, the smell of her, heavy, traditional, secret.

"Now you get dressed, and go get me some tomatoes . . . so we can eat." And it was good that there was something I could do for her. And go out into that world too. Now I knew it was there. And flesh.

I put on the stained khakis & she gave me my hat. "You'll get picked up without yo cap. We have to get you some clothes so you can throw that stuff away. The army don't need you no way." She laughed. "Leastways not as much as I does. Old Henry at the joint'll give you a job. You kin count money as good as that ol' jew I bet."

And I put the tie on, making some joke, and went out shopping for my wife.

* * * * * * *

Into that sun. The day was bright and people walked by me smiling. And waved "Hey" (a greeting) and they all knew I was Peaches' man.

I got to
the store and stood talking to the man about the weather about airplanes
and a little bit about new jersey. He waved at me when I left "O.K . . . you
take it easy now." "O.K., I'll see you," I said. I had the tomatoes and some
plums and peaches I bought too. I took a tomato out of the bag and bit
the sweet flesh. Pushed my hat on the back of my head and strutted up
the road towards the house.

It was a cloud I think came up. Something
touched me. "That color which cowardice brought out in me." Fire burns
around the tombs. Closed from the earth. A despair came down. Alien
grace. Lost to myself, I'd come back. To that ugliness sat inside me waiting. And the mere sky greying could do it. Sky spread thin out away from
this place. Over other heads. Beautiful unknowns. And my marriage a
heavy iron to this tomb. "Show us your countenance." Your light.

It was a
light clap of thunder. No lightning. And the sky greyed. Introitus. That
word came in. And the yellow light burning in my rooms. To come to see
the world, and yet lose it. And find sweet grace alone.

It was this or what I thought, made me turn and drop the tomatoes on
Peaches' porch. Her window was open and I wondered what she was
thinking. How my face looked in her head. I turned and looked at the
sad bag of tomatoes. The peaches, some rolling down one stair. And a
light rain came down. I walked away from the house. Up the road, to go
out of Bottom.

* * * *

The rain wet my face and I wanted to cry because I thot of the huge black
girl watching her biscuits get cold. And her radio playing without me.
The rain was hard for a second, drenching me. And then it stopped, and
just as quick the sun came out. Heavy bright hot. I trotted for awhile then
walked slow, measuring my steps. I stank of sweat and the uniform was a
joke.

I asked some pople how to get out and they pointed up the road
where 10 minutes walking had me at the bottom of the hill the bus came
down. A wet wind blew up soft full of sun and I began to calm. To see
what had happened. Who I was and what I thought my life should be.

What people called "experience." Young male. My hands in my pockets, and the grimy silver wings still hanging gravely on my filthy shirt. The feeling in my legs was to run up the rest of the hill but I just took long strides and stretched myself and wondered if I'd have K.P. or some army chastisement for being 2 days gone.

3 tall guys were coming down the hill I didn't see until they got close enough to speak to me. One laughed (at the way I looked). Tall strong black boys with plenty of teeth and pegged rayon pants. I just looked and nodded and kept on. One guy, with an imitation tattersall vest with no shirt, told the others I was in the Joint last night "playin cool." Slick city nigger, one said. I was going to pass close to them and the guy with the vest put up his hand and asked me where I was coming from. One with suspenders and a belt asked me what the wings stood for. I told him something. The third fellow just grinned. I moved to walk around them and the fellow with the vest asked could he borrow fifty cents. I only had a dollar in my pocket and told him that. There was no place to get change. He said to give him the dollar. I couldnt do that and get back to my base I told him and wanted to walk away. And one of the guys had gotten around in back of me and kneeled down and the guy with the vest pushed me backwards so I fell over the other's back. I fell backwards into the dust, and my hat fell off, and I didn't think I was mad but I still said something stupid like "What'd you do that for."

"I wanna borrow a dollar, Mr. Half-white muthafucka. And that's that." I sidestepped the one with the vest and took a running step but the grinning one tripped me, and I fell tumbling head forward back in the dust. This time when they laughed I got up and spun around and hit the guy who tripped me in the face. His nose was bleeding and he was cursing while the guy with the suspenders grabbed my shoulders and held me so the hurt one could punch me back. The guy with the vest punched too. And I got in one good kick into his groin, and stomped hard on one of their feet. The tears were coming again and I was cursing, now when they hit me, completely crazy. The dark one with the suspenders punched me in my stomach and I felt sick and the guy with the vest, the last one I saw, kicked me in my hip. The guy still held on for awhile then he pushed me at one of the others and they hit me as I fell. I got picked up and was screaming at them to let me go. "Bastards, you filthy stupid bastards, let me go." Crazy out of my head. Stars were out. And there were no fists just dull distant jolts that spun my head. It was in a cave this went on. With music and whores danced on the tables. I sat reading from a book aloud and they danced to my reading. When I finished reading I got up from the table and for some reason, fell forward weeping on the floor. The negroes danced around my body and spilled whisky on my clothes. I woke up 2 days later, with white men, screaming for God to help me.

════════════════════

SOUND AND IMAGE

What is hell? Your definitions.

I am and was and will be a social animal. Hell is definable only in those terms. I can get no place else; it wdn't exist.

Hell in this book which moves from sound and image ("association complexes") into fast narrative is what vision I had of it around 1960–61 and that fix on my life, and my interpretation of my earlier life.

Hell in the head.

The torture of being the unseen object, and, the constantly observed subject.

The flame of social dichotomy. Split open down the center, which is the early legacy of the black man unfocused on blackness. The dichotomy of what is seen and taught and desired opposed to what is felt. Finally, God, is simply a white man, a white "idea," in this society, unless we have made some other image which is stronger, and can deliver us from the salvation of our enemies.

For instance, if we can bring back on ourselves, the absolute pain our people must have felt when they came onto this shore, we are more ourselves again, and can begin to put history back in our menu, and forget the propaganda of devils that they are not devils.

* * * *

Hell is actual, and people with hell in their heads. But the pastoral moments in a man's life will also mean a great deal as far as his emotional references. One thinks of home, or the other "homes" we have had. And we remember w/love those things bathed in soft black light. The struggles away or towards this peace is Hell's function. (Wars of consciousness. Antithetical definitions of feeling(s).

Once, as a child, I would weep for compassion and understanding. And Hell was the inferno of my frustration. But the world is clearer to me now, and many of its features, more easily definable.

1965

TALES

A Chase (Alighieri's Dream)

Place broken: their faces sat and broke each other. As suns, Sons gone tired in the heart and left the south. The North, years later she'd wept for him drunk and a man finally they must have thought. In the dark, he was even darker. Wooden fingers running. Wind so sweet it drank him.

Faces broke. Charts of age. Worn thru, to see black years. Bones in iron faces. Steel bones. Cages of decay. Cobblestones are wet near the army stores. Beer smells, Saturday. To now, they have passed so few lovely things.

Newsreel chickens. Browned in the street. I was carrying groceries back across the manicured past. Back, in a coat. Sunk, screaming at my fingers. Faces broken, hair waved, simple false elegance. I must tell someone I love you. Them. In line near the fence. She sucked my tongue. Red, actual red, but colored hair. Soft thin voice, and red freckles. A servant.

You should be ashamed. Your fingers are trembling. You lied in the garage. You lied yesterday. Get out of the dance, down the back stairs, the street, and across in the car. Run past it, around the high building. Court Street, past the Y, harder, buttoning a cardigan, to Morton Street. Duck down, behind the car. Let Apple pass; a few others. Now take off back down Court, the small guys couldn't run. Cross High, near Graychun's, the Alumni House, donald the fag's, the jews, to Kinney. Up one block, crooked old jews die softly under the moon. Past them. Past them. Their tombs and bones. Wet dollars blown against the fence. Past them, mattie's Dr., waltine, turn at Quitman. You can slow some, but not too much. Through the Owl Club, Frankie, Dee's dumb brother, turn, wave at them. Down the back steps, to dirt, then stone. The poolroom, eddie smiles, points at his hat, pars his car keys, phone numbers. Somerset and the projects. To Montgomery and twist at Barclay. Light people stare. Parties, relationships forming to be explained later. Casual strangers' faces known better than any now. Wood jaws sit open, their halls reek, his fingers tug at yellow cotton pants and slip inside. One finger her eyes open and close—her mouth opens moaning deep agitated darkly.

In the middle of the street, straight at the moon. Don't get close to the buildings. Too many exits, doors, parks. Straight at the moon, up Barclay. Green tyrolean, grey bells, bucks. The smoking lights at Spruce. Hip charles curtis. But turn before Herman or Wattley. They pace in wool jails, wool chains, years below the earth. Dead cocks crawling, eyes turned up in space. Near diane's house and the trees cradling her hidden flesh. Her fingers, her mouth, her eyes were all I had. And she screams now through soft wrinkles for me to take her. A Nun.

Wheeling now, back on the sidewalk, Saturday drunks spinning by, fish stores yawned, sprawled niggers dying without matches. Friends, enemies, strangers, fags, screaming louder than all sound. Young boys in hallways touching. Bulldaggers hiding their pussies. Black dead faces slowly ground to dust.

Headlight, Bubbles, Kennie, Rogie, Junie Boy, T. Bone, Rudy (All Hillside Place) or Sess, Ray, Lillian, Ungie, Ginger, Shirley, Cedie Abrams. Past them, displaced, blood seeps on the pavement under marquees. Lynn Hope marches on Belmont Ave. with us all. The Three Musketeers at the National. (Waverly Projects.) Past that. Their arms waving from the stands. Sun and gravel or the 3 hole opens and it's more beautiful than Satie. A hip, change speeds, head fake, stop, cut back, a hip, head fake . . . then only one man coming from the side . . . it went thru my head a million times, the years it took, seeing him there, with a good angle, shooting in, with 3 yards to the sidelines, about 10 home. I watched him all my life close in, and thot to cut, stop or bear down and pray I had speed. Answers shot up, but my head was full of blood and it moved me without talk. I stopped still the ball held almost like a basketball, wheeled and moved in to score untouched.

* * *

A long stretch from Waverly to Spruce (going the other way near Hillside). A long stretch, and steeper, straight up Spruce. And that street moved downtown. They all passed by, going down. And I was burning by, up the hill, toward The Foxes and the milk bar. Change clothes on the street to a black suit. Black wool.

4 corners, the entire world visible from there. Even to the lower regions.

The Alternative

This may not seem like much, but it makes a difference. And then there are those who prefer to look their fate in the eyes.

Between Yes and No
—Camus

The leader sits straddling the bed, and the night, tho innocent, blinds him. (Who is our flesh. Our lover, marched here from where we sit now sweating and remembering. Old man. Old man, find me, who am your only blood.)

Sits straddling the bed under a heavy velvet canopy. Homemade. The door opened for a breeze, which will not come through the other heavy velvet hung at the opening. (Each thread a face, or smell, rubbed against himself with yellow glasses and fear at their exposure. Death. Death. They (the younger students) run by screaming. Tho impromptu. Tho dead, themselves.

The leader, at his bed, stuck with 130 lbs. black meat sewed to failing bone. A head with big red eyes turning senselessly. Five toes on each foot. Each foot needing washing. And hands that dangle to the floor, tho the boy himself is thin small washed out, he needs huge bleak hands that drag the floor. And a head full of walls and flowers. Blinking lights. He is speaking.

"Yeh?" The walls are empty, heat at the ceiling. Tho one wall is painted with a lady. (Her name now. In large relief, a faked rag stuck between the chalk marks of her sex. Finley. Teddy's Doris. There sprawled where the wind fiddled with the drying cloth. Leon came in and laughed. Carl came in and hid his mouth, but he laughed. Teddy said, "Aw, Man."

"Come on, Hollywood. You can't beat that. Not with your years. Man, you're a schoolteacher 10 years after weeping for this old stinking bitch. And hit with a aspirin bottle (myth says)."

The leader, is

sprawled, dying. His retinue walks into their comfortable cells. "I have duraw-ings," says Leon, whimpering now in the buses from Chicago. Dead in a bottle. Floats out of sight, until the Africans arrive with love and prestige. "Niggers." They say. "Niggers." Be happy your ancestors are recognized in this burg. Martyrs. Dead in an automat, because the boys had left. Lost in New York, frightened of the burned lady, they fled into those streets and sang their homage to the Radio City.

The Leader sits watching the window. The dried orange glass etched with the fading wind. (How many there then? 13 Rue Madeleine. The Boys Club. They give, what he has given them. Names. And the black cloth hung on the door swings back and forth. One pork chop on the hot plate. And how many there. Here, now. Just the shadow, waving its arms. The eyes tearing or staring blindly at the dead street. These same who loved me all my life. These same I find my senses in. Their flesh a wagon of dust, a mind conceived from all minds. A country, of thought. Where I am, will go, have never left. A love, of love. And the silence the question posed each second. "Is this my mind, my feeling. Is this voice something heavy in the locked streets of the universe. Dead ends. Where their talk (these nouns) is bitter vegetable." That is, the suitable question rings against the walls. Higher learning. That is, the moon through the window clearly visible. The leader in seersucker, reading his books. An astronomer of sorts. "Will you look at that? I mean, really, now, fellows. Cats!" (Which was Smitty from the City's entree. And him the smoothest of you American types. Said, "Cats. Cats. What's goin' on?" The debate.

The leader's job (he keeps it still, above the streets, summers of low smoke, early evening drunk and wobbling thru the world. He keeps it, baby. You dig?) was absolute. "I have the abstract position of watching these halls. Walking up the stairs giggling. Hurt under the cement steps, weeping . . . is my only task. Tho I play hockey with the broom & wine bottles. And am the sole martyr of this cause. A.B., Young Rick, T.P., Carl, Hambrick, Li'l' Cholley, Phil. O.K All their knowledge "Flait! More! Way!" The leader's job . . . to make attention for the place. Sit along the sides of the water or lay quietly back under his own shooting vomit, happy to die in a new grey suit. Yes. "And what not."

How many here now? Danny. (brilliant dirty curly Dan, the m.d.) Later, now, where you off to, my man. The tall skinny farmers, lucky to find sales and shiny white shoes. Now made it socially against the temples. This "hotspot" Darien drunk teacher blues . . . "and she tried to come on like she didn't even like to fuck. I mean, you know the kind. . . ." The hand extended, palm upward. I place my own in yours. That cross, of feeling. Willie, in his grinning grave, has it all. The place, of all souls, in their greasy significance. An armour, like the smells drifting slowly up Georgia. The bridge players change clothes, and descend. Carrying home the rolls.

Jimmy Lassiter, first looie. A vector. What is the angle made if a straight line is drawn from the chapel, across to Jimmy, and connected there, to me, and back up the hill again? The angle of progress. "I was talkin' to ol' Mordecai yesterday in a dream, and it's me sayin' 'dig baby, why don't you come off it?' You know."

The line, for Jimmy's sad and useless horn. And they tell me (via phone, letter, accidental meetings in the Village. "Oh he's in med school and married and lost to you, hombre." Ha. They don't dig completely where I'm at. I have him now, complete. Though it is a vicious sadness cripples my fingers. Those blue and empty afternoons I saw him walking at my side. Criminals in that world. Complete heroes of our time. (add Allen to complete an early splinter group. Muslim heroes with flapping pants. Raincoats. Trolley car romances.)

And it's me making a portrait of them all. That was the leader's job. Alone with them. (Without them. Except beautiful faces shoved out the window, sunny days, I ran to meet my darkest girl. Ol' Doll. "Man, that bitch got a goddamn new car." And what not. And it's me sayin' to her, Baby, knock me a kiss.

Tonight the leader is faced with decision. Brown had found him drunk and weeping among the dirty clothes. Some guy with a crippled arm had reported to the farmers (a boppin' gang gone social. Sociologists, artistic arbiters of our times). This one an athlete of mouse-like proportions. "You know," he said, his withered arm hung stupidly in the rayon suit, "That cat's nuts. He was sittin' up in that room last night with dark glasses on . . . with a yellow bulb . . . pretendin' to read some abstract shit." (Damn, even the color wrong. Where are you now, hippy, under this abstract shit. Not even defense. That you remain forever in that world. No light. Under my fingers. That you exist alone, as I make you. Your sin, a final ugliness to you. For the leopards, all thumbs jerked toward the sand.) "Man, we do not need cats like that in the frat." (Agreed.)

Tom comes in with two big bottles of wine. For the contest. An outing. "Hugh Herbert and W.C. Fields will now indian wrestle for ownership of this here country!" (Agreed.) The leader loses . . . but is still the leader because he said some words no one had heard of before. (That was after the loss.)

Yng Rick has fucked someone else. Let's listen. "Oh, man, you cats don't know what's happenin'." (You're too much, Rick. Much too much. Like Larry Darnell in them ol' italian schools. Much too much.) "Babes" he called them (a poor project across from the convents. Baxter Terrace. Home of the enemy. We stood them off. We Cavaliers. And then, even tho Johnny Boy was his hero. Another midget placed on the purple. Early leader, like myself. The fight of gigantic proportions to settle all those ancient property disputes would have been between us. Both weighing close to 125. But I avoided that like the plague, and managed three times to drive past him with good hooks without incident. Whew, I said to Love, Whew. And Rick, had gone away from them, to school. Like myself. And now, strangely, for the Gods are white our teachers said, he found himself with me. And all the gold and diamonds of the crown I wore he hated. Though, the new wine settled, and his social graces kept him far enough away to ease the hurt of serving a hated master. Hence "babes," and the constant reference to his wiggling flesh. Listen.

"Yeh. Me and Chris had these D.C. babes at their cribs." (Does a dance step with the suggestive flair.) "Oooooo, that was some good box."

Tom knew immediately where that bit was at. And he pulled Rick into virtual madness . . . lies at least. "Yeh, Rick. Yeh? You mean you got a little Jones, huh? Was it good?" (Tom pulls on Rick's sleeve like Laurel and Rick swings.)

"Man, Tom, you don't have to believe it, baby. It's in here now!" (points to his stomach.)

The leader stirs. "Hmm, that's a funny way to fuck." Rick will give a boxing demonstration in a second.

Dick Smith smiles, "Wow, Rick you're way," extending his hand, palm upward. "And what not," Dick adds, for us to laugh. "O.K., you're bad." (At R's crooked jab.) "Huh, this cat always wants to bust somebody up, and what not. Hey, baby, you must be frustrated or something. How come you don't use up all that energy on your babes . . . and what not?"

The rest there, floating empty nouns. Under the sheets. The same death as the crippled fag. Lost with no defense. Except they sit now, for this portrait . . . in which they will be portrayed as losers. Only the leader wins. Tell him that.

Some guys playing cards. Some talking about culture, i.e., the leader had a new side. (Modesty denies. They sit around, in real light. The leader in his green glasses, fidgeting with his joint. Carl, in a brown fedora, trims his toes and nails. Spars with Rick. Smells his foot and smiles. Brady reads, in his silence, a crumpled black dispatch. Shorter's liver smells the hall and Leon slams the door, waiting for the single chop, the leader might have to share. The door opens, two farmers come in, sharp in orange suits. The hippies laugh, and hide their youthful lies. "Man, I was always hip. I mean, I knew about Brooks Brothers when I was 10." (So sad we never know the truth. About that world, until the bones dry in our heads. Young blond governors with their "dads" hip at the age of 2. That way. Which, now, I sit in judgment of. What I wanted those days with the covers of books turned toward the audience. The first nighters. Or dragging my two forwards to the Music Box to see Elliot Nugent. They would say, these dead men, laughing at us, "The natives are restless," stroking their gouty feet. Gimme culture, culture, culture, and Romeo and Juliet over the emerson.

How many there now? Make it 9. Phil's cracking the books. Jimmy Jones and Pud, two D.C. boys, famous and funny, study "zo" at the top of their voices. "Hemiptera," says Pud. "Homoptera," says Jimmy. "Weak as a bitch," says Phil, "Both your knowledges are flait."

More than 9. Mazique, Enty, operating now in silence. Right hands flashing down the cards. "Uhh!" In love with someone, and money from home. Both perfect, with curly hair. "Uhh! Shit, Enty, hearts is trumps."

"What? Ohh, shit!"

"Uhh!", their beautiful hands flashing under the single bulb.

Hambrick comes with liquor. (A box of fifths, purchased with the fantastic wealth of his father's six shrimp shops.) "You cats caint have all this goddam booze. Brown and I got dates, that's why and we need some for the babes."

Brown has hot dogs for five. Franks, he says. "Damn, Cholley, you only get a half of frank . . . and you take the whole motherfucking thing."

"Aww, man, I'll pay you back." And the room, each inch, is packed with lives. Make it 12 . . . all heroes, or dead. Indian chiefs, the ones not waging their wars, like Clark, in the legal mist of Baltimore. A judge. Old Clark. You remember when we got drunk together and you fell down the stairs. Or that time you fell in the punch bowl puking, and let that sweet yellow ass get away? Boy, I'll never forget that, as long as I live. (Having died seconds later, he talks thru his rot.) Yeh, boy, you were always a card. (White man talk. A card. Who the hell says that, except that branch office with no culture. Piles of bullion, and casual violence. To the mind. Nights they kick you against the buildings. Communist homosexual nigger. "Aw man, I'm married and got two kids."

What could be happening? Some uproar. "FUCK YOU, YOU FUNNY LOOKING SUNAFABITCH."

"Me? Funny-looking? Oh, wow. Will you listen to this little pointy head bastard calling *me* funny looking. Hey, Everett. Hey Everett! Who's the funniest looking . . . me or Keyes?"

"Aww, both you cats need some work. Man, I'm trying to read."

"Read? What? You gettin' into them books, huh? Barnes is whippin' your ass, huh? I told you not to take Organic . . . as light as you are."

"Shit. I'm not even thinking about Barnes. Barnes can kiss my ass."

"Shit. You better start thinking about him, or you'll punch right out. They don't need lightweights down in the valley. Ask Ugly Wilson."

"Look, Tom, I wasn't bothering you."

"Bothering me? Wha's the matter with you ol' Jimmy. Commere boy, lemme rub your head."

"Man, you better get the hell outta here."

"What? . . . Why? What you gonna do? You can't fight, you little funny looking buzzard."

"Hey, Tom, why you always bothering ol' Jimmy Wilson. He's a good man."

"Oh, oh, here's that little light ass Dan sticking up for Ugly again. Why you like him, huh? Cause he's the only cat uglier than you? Huh?"

"Tom's the worst looking cat on campus calling me ugly."

"Well, you are. Wait, lemme bring you this mirror so you can see yourself. Now, what you think. You can't think anything else."

"Aww, man, blow, will you?"

The pork chop is cooked and little charlie is trying to cut a piece off before the leader can stop him. "Ow, goddam."

"Well, who told you to try to steal it, jive ass."

"Hey, man, I gotta get somea that chop."

"Gimme some, Ray."

"Why don't you cats go buy something to eat. I didn't ask anybody for any of those hot dogs. So get away from my grease. Hungry ass spooks."

"Wait a minute, fella. I know you don't mean Young Rick."

"Go ask one of those D.C. babes for something to eat. I know they must have something you could sink your teeth into."

Pud and Jimmy Jones are wrestling under Phil's desk.

A.B. is playin' the dozen with Leon and Teddy. "Teddy are your momma's legs as crooked as yours?"

"This cat always wants to talk about people's mothers! Country bastard."

Tom is pinching Jimmy Wilson. Dan is laughing at them.

Enty and Mazique are playing bridge with the farmers. "Uhh! Beat that, jew boy!"

"What the fuck is trumps?"

The leader is defending his pork chop from Cholley, Rick, Brady, Brown, Hambrick, Carl, Dick Smith, (S from the City has gone out catting.

"Who is it?"

A muffled voice, under the uproar, "It's Mister Bush."

"Bush? Hey, Ray . . . Ray."

"Who is it?"

Plainer. "Mister Bush." (Each syllable pronounced and correct as a soft southern american can.) Innocent VIII in his bedroom shoes. Gregory at Canossa, raging softly in his dignity and power. "Mister Bush."

"Ohh, shit. Get that liquor somewhere. O.K., Mr. Bush, just a second. . . . Not there, asshole, in the drawer."

"Mr. McGhee, will you kindly open the door."

"Ohh, shit, the hot plate. I got it." The leader turns a wastepaper basket upside-down on top of the chop. Swings open the door. "Oh, Hello

Mister Bush. How are you this evening?" About 15 boots sit smiling toward the door. Come in, Boniface. What news of Luther? In unison, now.

"Hi . . . Hello . . . How are you, Mister Bush?"

"Uh, huh."

He stares around the room, grinding his eyes into their various hearts. An unhealthy atmosphere, this America. "Mr. McGhee, why is it if there's noise in this dormitory it always comes from this room?" Aww, he knows. He wrote me years later in the air force that he knew, even then.

"What are you running here, a boys' club?" (That's it.) He could narrow his eyes even in that affluence. Put his hands on his hips. Shove that stomach at you as proof he was an authority of the social grace . . . a western man, no matter the color of his skin. How To? He was saying, this is not the way. Don't act like that word. Don't fail us. We've waited for all you handsome boys too long. Erect a new world, of lies and stocking caps. Silence, and a reluctance of memory. Forget the slow grasses, and flame, flame in the valley. Feet bound, dumb eyes begging for darkness. The bodies moved with the secret movement of the air. Swinging. My beautiful grandmother kneels in the shadow weeping. Flame, flame in the valley. Where is it there is light? Where, this music rakes my talk?

"Why is it, Mr. McGhee, when there's some disturbance in this building, it always comes from here?" (Aww, you said that . . .)

"And what are all you other gentlemen doing in here? Good night, there must be twenty of you here! Really, gentlemen, don't any of you have anything to do?" He made to smile, Ha, I know some of you who'd better be in your rooms right now hitting those books . . . or you might not be with us next semester. Ha.

"O.K., who is that under that sheet?" (It was Enty, a student dormitory director, hiding under the sheets, flat on the leader's bed.) "You, sir, whoever you are, come out of there, hiding won't do you any good. Come out!" (We watched the sheet, and it quivered. Innocent raised his finger.) "Come out, sir!" (The sheet pushed slowly back. Enty's head appeared. And Bush more embarrassed than he.) "Mr. Enty! My assistant dormitory director, good night. A man of responsibility. Go-od night! Are there any more hiding in here, Mr. McGhee?"

"Not that I know of."

"Alright, Mr.

Enty, you come with me. And the rest of you had better go to your rooms and try to make some better grades. Mr. McGhee, I'll talk to you tomorrow morning in my office."

The leader smiles, "Yes." (Jive ass.)

Bush turns to go, Enty following sadly. "My God, what's that terrible odor . . . something burning." (The leader's chop, and the wastepaper, under the basket, starting to smoke.) "Mr. McGhee, what's that smell?"

"Uhhh," (comeon, baby) "Oh, it's Strothers' kneepads on the radiator! (Yass) They're drying."

"Well, Jesus, I hope they dry soon. Whew! And don't forget, tomorrow morning, Mr. McGhee, and you other gentlemen had better retire, it's 2 in the morning!" The door slams. Charlie sits where Enty was. The bottles come out. The basket is turned right-side up. Chop and most of the papers smoking. The leader pours water onto the mess and sinks to his bed.

"Damn. Now I have to go hungry. Shit."

"That was pretty slick, ugly, the kneepads! Why don't you eat them they look pretty done."

The talk is to that. That elegance of performance. The rite of lust, or self-extinction. Preservation. Some leave, and a softer uproar descends. Jimmy Jones and Pud wrestle quietly on the bed. Phil quotes the *Post*'s sport section on Willie Mays. Hambrick and Brown go for franks. Charlies scrapes the "burn" off the chop and eats it alone. Tom, Dan, Ted and the leader drink and manufacture lives for each person they know. We know. Even you. Tom, the lawyer. Dan, the lawyer. Ted, the high-school teacher. All their proper ways. And the leader, without cause or place. Except talk, feeling, guilt. Again, only those areas of the world make sense. Talk. We are doing that now. Feeling: that too. Guilt. That inch of wisdom, forever. Except he sits reading in green glasses. As, "No, no, the utmost share/Of my desire shall be/Only to kiss that air/That lately kissèd thee."

"Uhh! What's trumps, dammit!"

As, "Tell me not, Sweet, I am unkind,/That from the nunnery/Of thy chaste breast and quiet mind/To war and arms I fly."

"You talking about a lightweight mammy-tapper, boy, you really king."

Oh, Lucasta, find me here on the bed, with hard pecker and dirty feet. Oh, I suffer, in my green glasses, under the canopy of my loves. Oh, I am drunk and vomity in my room, with only Charley Ventura to understand my grace. As, "Hardly are those words out when a vast image out of *Spiritus Mundi*/Troubles my sight: somewhere in sands of the desert/A shape with lion body and the head of a man/A gaze blank and pitiless as the sun,/Is moving its slow thighs, while all about it/Reel shadows of the indignant desert birds."

Primers for dogs who are learning to read. Tinkle of European teacups. All longing, speed, suffering. All adventure, sadness, stink and wisdom. All feeling, silence, light. As, "Crush, O sea the cities with their catacomb-like corridors/And crush eternally the vile people,/The idiots, and the abstemious, and mow down, mow down/With a single stroke the bent backs of the shrunken harvest!"

"Damn, Charlie, We brought back a frank for everybody . . . now you want two. Wrong sunafabitch!"

"Verde que te quiero verde./Verde viento. Verdes ramas./El barco sobre la mar/y el caballo en la montaña."

"Hey, man, I saw that ol' fagit Bobby Hutchens down in the lobby with a real D.C. queer. I mean a real way-type sissy."

"Huh, man he's just another *actor* . . . hooo."

"That cat still wearing them funny lookin' pants?"

"Yeh, and orange glasses. Plus, the cat always needs a haircut, and what not."

"Hey, man you cats better cool it . . . you talkin' about Ray's main man. You dig?"

"Yeh. I see this cat easin' around corners with the cat all the time. I mean, talkin' some off the wall shit, too, baby."

"Yeh. Yeh. Why don't you cats go fuck yourselves or something hip like that, huh?"

"O.K., ugly Tom, you better quit inferring that shit about Ray. What you trying to say, ol' pointy head is funny or something?"

"*Funny . . . how the sound of your voice . . . thri-ills me. Strange . . .*" (the last à la King Cole.)

"Fuck you cats and your funny looking families too."

A wall. With light

at the top, perhaps. No, there is light. Seen from both sides, a gesture of life. But always more than is given. An abstract infinitive. To love. To lie. To want. And that always . . . to want. Always, more than is given. The dead scramble up each side . . . words or drunkenness. Praise, to the flesh. Rousseau, Hobbes, and their betters. All move, from flesh to love. From love to flesh. At that point under the static light. It could be Shostakovich in Charleston, South Carolina. Or in the dull windows of Chicago, an unread volume of Joyce. Some black woman who will never hear the word *Negress* or remember your name. Or a thin preacher who thinks your name is Stephen. A wall. Oh, Lucasta.

           "Man, you cats don't know anything about Hutchens. I don't see why you talk about the cat and don't know the first thing about him."

           "Shit. If he ain't funny . . . Skippy's a punk."

"How come you don't say that to Skippy?"

"Our Own Boy, Skippy Weatherson. All-coon fullback for 12 years."

"You tell him that!"

"Man, don't try to change the subject. This cat's trying to keep us from talking about his boy, Hutchens."

"Yeh, mammy-rammer. What's happenin' McGhee, ol' man?"

"Hooo. Yeh. They call this cat Dick Brown. Hoooo!"

Rick moves to the offensive. The leader in his book, or laughs, "Aww, man, that cat ain't my boy. I just don't think you cats ought to talk about people you don't know anything about! Plus, that cat probably gets more ass than any of you silly-ass mother fuckers."

"Hee. That Ray sure can pronounce that word. I mean he don't say mutha' like most folks . . . he always pronounces the mother *and* the fucker, so proper. And it sure makes it sound nasty." (A texas millionaire talking.)

"Hutchens teachin' the cat how to talk . . . that's what's happening. Ha. In exchange for services rendered!"

"Wait, Tom. Is it you saying that Hutchens and my man here are into some funny shit?"

"No, man. It's you saying that. It was me just inferring, you dig?"

"Hey, why don't you cats just get drunk in silence, huh?"

"Hey, Bricks, what was Hutchens doin' downstairs with that cat?"

"Well, they were just coming in the dormitory, I guess. Hutchens was signing in that's all."

"Hey, you dig . . . I bet he's takin' that cat up to his crib."

"Yeh, I wonder what they into by now. Huh! Probably suckin' the shit out of each other."

"Aww, man, cool it, willya . . . Damn!"

"What's the matter, Ray, you don't dig love?"

"Hey, it's young Rick saying, that we oughta go up and dig what's happenin' up there?"

"Square mother fucker!"

"Votre mere!"

"Votre mere noir!"

"Boy, these cats in French One think they hip!"

"Yeh, let's go up and see what those cats are doing."

"Tecch, aww, shit. Damn, you some square cats, wow! Cats got nothing better to do than fuck with people. Damn!"

Wall. Even to move, impossible. I sit, now, forever where I am. No further. No farther. Father, who am I to hide myself? And brew a world of soft lies.

Again. "Verde que te quiero verde." Green. Read it again Il Duce. Make it build some light here . . . where there is only darkness. Tell them "Verde, que te quiero verde." I want you Green. Leader, the paratroopers will come for you at noon. A helicopter low over the monastery. To get you out.

But my country. My people. These dead souls, I call my people. Flesh of my flesh.

At noon, Il Duce. Make them all etceteras. Extras. The soft strings behind the final horns.

"Hey, Ray, you comin' with us?"

"Fuck you cats. I got other things to do."

"Damn, now the cat's trying to pretend he can read Spanish."

"Yeh . . . well let's go see what's happening cats."

"Cats, Cats, Cats . . . What's happenin'?"

"Hey, Smitty! We going upstairs to peep that ol' sissy Hutchens. He's got some big time D.C. faggot in there with him. You know, we figured it'd be better than 3-D."

"Yeh? That's pretty hip. You not coming, Ray?"

"No, man . . . I'm sure you cats can peep in a keyhole without me."

"Bobby's his main man, that's all."

"Yeh, mine and your daddy's."

Noise. Shouts, and Rick begs them to be softer. For the circus. Up the creaking stairs, except Carl and Leon who go to the freshman dorm to play ping-pong . . . and Ted who is behind in his math.

The 3rd floor of Park Hall, an old 19th-century philanthropy, gone to seed. The missionaries' words dead & hung useless in the air. "Be clean, thrifty, and responsible. Show the anti-Christs you're ready for freedom and God's true word." Peasants among the mulattoes, and the postman's son squats in his glasses shivering at his crimes.

"Hey, which room is his?"

"Three Oh Five."

"Hey, Tom, how you know the cat's room so good? This cat must be sneaking too."

"Huhh, yeh!"

"O.K. Rick, just keep walking."

"Here it is."

"Be cool, bastard. Shut up."

They stood and grinned. And punched each other. Two bulbs in the hall. A window at each end. One facing the reservoir, the other, the fine-arts building where Professor Gorsun sits angry at jazz. "Goddamnit none of that nigger music in my new building. Culture. Goddamnit, ladies and gentlemen, line up and be baptized. This pose will take the hurt away. We are white and featureless under this roof. Praise God, from whom all blessings flow!"

"Bobby. Bobby, baby."

"Huh?"

"Don't go blank on me like that, baby. I was saying something."

"Oh, I'm sorry . . . I guess I'm just tired or something."

"I was saying, how can you live in a place like this. I mean, really, baby, this place is nowhere. Whew. It's like a jail or something eviler."

"Yes, I know."

"Well, why don't you leave it then. You're much too sensitive for a place like this. I don't see why you stay in this damn school. You know, you're really talented."

"Yeh, well, I figured I have to

get a degree, you know. Teach or something, I suppose. There's not really much work around for spliv actors."

"Oh, Bobby, you ought to stop being so conscious of being coloured. It really is not fashionable. Ummm. You know you have beautiful eyes."

"You want another drink, Lyle?"

"Ugg. Oh, that cheap bourbon. You know I have some beautiful wines at home. You should try drinking some good stuff for a change. Damn, Bob, why don't you just leave this dump and move into my place? There's certainly enough room. And we certainly get along. Ummm. Such beautiful eyes and hair too."

"Hah. How much rent would I have to pay out there. I don't have penny the first!"

"Rent? No, no . . . you don't have to worry about that. I'll take care of all that. I've got one of those gooood jobs, honey. U.S. guvment."

"Oh? Where do you work?"

"The P.O. with the rest of the fellas. But it's enough for what I want to do. And you wouldn't be an expense. Hmmp. Or would you? You know you have the kind of strong masculine hands I love. Like you could crush anything you wanted. Lucky I'm on your good side. Hmmp."

"Well, maybe at the end of this semester I could leave. If the offer still holds then."

"Still holds? Well why not? We'll still be friends then, I'm certain. Ummm. Say, why don't we shut off that light."

"Umm. Let me do it. There. . . . You know I loved you in Jimmy's play, but the rest of those people are really just kids. You were the only person who really understood what was going on. You have a strong maturity that comes through right away. How old are you, Bobby?"

"Nineteen."

"O baby . . . that's why your skin is so soft. Yes. Say, why wait until the end of the semester . . . that's two months away. I might be dead before that, you know. Umm."

The wind moves thru the leader's room, and he sits alone, under the drooping velvet, repeating words he does not understand. The yellow light burns. He turns it off. Smokes. Masturbates. Turns it on. Verde, verde. Te quiero. Smokes. And then to his other source. "Yma's brother," Tom said when he saw it. "Yma Sumac, Albert Camus. Man, nobody wants to go by their right names no more. And a cat told me that chick ain't really from Peru. She was born in Brooklyn man, and her name's Camus too. Amy Camus. This cat's name is probably Trebla Sumac, and he ain't French he's from Brooklyn too. Yeh. Ha!"

In the dark the words are anything. "If it is true that the only paradise is that which one has lost, I know what name to give that something tender and inhuman which dwells within me today."

"Oh, shit, fuck it. Fuck it." He slams the book against the wall, and empties Hambrick's bottle. "I mean, why?" Empties bottle. "Shiiit."

When he swings the door open the hall above is screams. Screams. All their voices, even now right here. The yellow glasses falling on the stairs, and broken. In his bare feet. "Shiit. Dumb ass cats!"

"Rick, Rick, what's the cat doing now?"

"Man, be cool. Ha, the cat's kissin' Hutchens on the face, man. Um-uh-mm. Yeh, baby. Damn, he's puttin' his hands all over the cat. Aww, rotten motherfuckers!"

"What's happening?"

"Bastards shut out the lights!"

"Damn."

"Gaw-uhd damn!"

"Hey, let's break open the door."

"Yeh, HEY, YOU CATS, WHAT'S HAPPENING IN THERE, HUH?"

"Yeh. Hee, hee. OPEN UP, FAGGOTS!"

"Wheee! HEY LET US IN, GIRLS!"

Ricky and Jimmy run against the door, the others screaming and jumping, doors opening all along the hall. They all come out, screaming as well. "LET US IN. HEY, WHAT'S HAPPENIN', BABY!" Rick and Jimmy run against the door, and the door is breaking.

"Who is it? What do you want?" Bobby turns the light on, and his friend, a balding queer of 40 is hugged against the sink.

"Who are they, Bobby? What do they want?"

"Bastards. Damn if I know. GET OUTTA HERE, AND MIND YOUR OWN DAMN BUSINESS, YOU CREEPS. Creeps. Damn. Put on your clothes, Lyle!"

"God, they're trying to break the door down, Bobby. What they want? Why are they screaming like that?"

"GET THE HELL AWAY FROM THIS DOOR, GODDAMNIT!"

"YEH, YEH. WE SAW WHAT YOU WAS DOIN' HUTCHENS. OPEN THE DOOR AND LET US GET IN ON IT."

"WHEEEEEE! HIT THE FUCKING DOOR, RICK! HIT IT!"

And at the top of the stairs the leader stops, the whole hall full of citizens. Doctors, judges, first negro directors of welfare chain, morticians, chemists, ad men, fighters for civil rights, all admirable, useful men. "BREAK THE FUCKIN' DOOR OPEN, RICK! YEH!"

A wall. Against it, from where you stand, the sea stretches smooth for miles out. Their voices distant thuds of meat against the sand. Murmurs of insects. Hideous singers against your pillow every night of your life. They are there now, screaming at you.

"Ray, Ray, comeon man help us break this faggot's door!"

"Yeh, Ray, comeon!"

"Man, you cats are fools. Evil stupid fools!"

"What? Man, will you listen to this cat."

"Listen, hell, let's get this door. One more smash and it's in. Comeon, Brady, lets break the fuckin' thing."

"Yeh, comeon you cats, don't stand there listenin' to that pointy head clown, he just don't want us to pop his ol' lady!"

"YEH, YEH. LET'S GET IN THERE. HIT IT HIT IT!"

"Goddamnit. Goddamnit, get the fuck out of here. Get outta here. Damnit Rick, you sunafabitch, get the hell outtahere. Leave the cat alone!"

"Man, don't push me like that, you lil' skinny ass. I'll bust your jaw for you."

"Yeh? Yeh? Yeh? Well you come on, you lyin' ass. This cat's always talking about all his 'babes' and all he's got to do is sneak around peeping in keyholes. You big lying asshole . . . all you know how to do is bullshit and jerk off!"

"Fuck you, Ray."

"Your ugly ass mama."

"Shiit. You wanna go round with me, baby?"

"Comeon. Comeon, big time cocksman, comeon!"

Rick hits the leader full in the face, and he falls backwards across the hall. The crowd follows screaming at this new feature.

"Aww, man, somebody stop this shit. Rick'll kill Ray!"

"Well, you stop it, man."

"O.K., O.K., cut it out. Cut it out, Rick. You win man. Leave the cat alone. Leave him alone."

"Bad Rick . . . Bad Rick, Bad ass Rick!"

"Well, man, you saw the cat fuckin' with me. He started the shit!"

"Yeh . . . tough cat!"

"Get up Ray."

And then the door does open and Bobby Hutchens stands in the half light in his shower shoes, a broom in his hands. The boys scream and turn their attention back to Love. Bald Lyle is in the closet. More noise. More lies. More prints in the sand, away, or toward some name. I am a poet. I am a rich famous butcher. I am the man who paints the gold balls on the tops of flagpoles. I am, no matter, more beautiful than anyone else. And I have come a long way to say this. Here. In the long hall, shadows across my hands. My face pushed hard against the floor. And the wood, old, and protestant. And their voices, all these other selves screaming for blood. For blood, or whatever it is fills their noble lives.

The Largest Ocean in the World

for Larry Wallrich

Toppled. Cold dark stone, spread thru the darker night. And night.
Again he would come down. Come thru it settling fast, without breathing,
as disguised as the day itself had become. Sun dead. The bright instincts.
Hurdled, years before, after, all had formed. Settled, the ripples of
weather, darkness, flesh, among the torn stones.

He came down the stairs with motors crippling his face. Where the
brain sagged, and ran into deeper colors. They spread. The walks ran
together. Voices of the students. Voices of the preachers. Voices of the
simple past. Kept toward missions. All repose, response, dulled. At last to
a single dripping cock. It sat inside his heart. And hardened at what the
moon proposed. What the night meant to have breathing around, and so
quiet, and so sure, and without the madness turned him inside, killed
him, made him, what you called, "a murderer."

The street was dark, without their hands. They slept. So, the street
would not.

Whistling. He had his hands in the back pockets.

A thin man. A small boy. A naked thing for any who looked. For any
would stick their mouths to his. Or watch him breathe. This man, boy,
self, had not come here to see you. (Where you live now.) Had not asked
you for your life, or proposed a vile connection, i.e., "I Love You": "Come
With Me," or simpler, "Listen, Please, Listen To Me." But you had not
lived then. Or come from where the things set up dark words in you.

This is an old song. Where the street, a wide avenue, turns and is lost as
it approaches the river. Not knowing himself, or the town. Just what
pushed him. He could move. He could move, himself. And scream,
scream, it to him. You, not some other, are like this. Were of this flesh.
You, talk to him, pass him by, hold up a hand to see what he will say. Run,
from you. (From me, who came back, now, in some fit, to play God.)

No one passed him on the street. Then someone did. Then a car went
by. And one with a kissing couple slowed at a light, then pulled quickly
toward the park. (Is it meaningful to speak of form, and say, there is a

form love takes. As meaningful as the woman slumped in the hallway, weeping, under those coarse lights, weeping, for all her hurts, my own.)

How many worlds; for blood infests our minds. The eye is its own creation. The fingers. There are men who live in themselves so they think their minds will create a different place of ecstasy. That it will love them.

A ridge of trees. Tall thin lights, lighting only the tops of leaves. Soft as it reached us. Harsh at the top, making shadows that moved without flesh.

A long sloping walk. His head had bent, was bent, always. (They will say that you are abstracted. That you are funny. That you are not what you seem, but evil. And fall out drunk and sick and shed that skin. Shed it now. To this. An "X", on the graph, where you paused.)

Up near the theaters, where the city changed. Was softer, grew wilder, and green even beneath the darkness. A drugstore at an intersection with the full white moon pressed under the glass. A tree at its edges, folding slowly. The dead fill the streets. And their dead thoughts. I do not know this place.

Seeing no one. Not wanting any one. But you all. I want now to have all your minds. Want now, to be them. To feel all you feel. Think, your hundred thoughts. Sink down on your lover, and tell about myself. Yourself. (The thin boy at the corner, under the blurred lights, green tops and wires under the moon.) Seeing no one, and wanting, no one. Wanting. He could press himself against the darkness and suck it into himself. He could sit down here and weep. He could die. He could grow older, and find himself calmer, more detached, disposed to sit and talk with us about himself. He could find himself lying about his life, and see back across blood, to the blank marquee and quiet intersection of his discovery. Balboa. You have made your move. The waters move softly here. Blue clear warm water, barely moving. And smooth sand for miles. No one here. Or where you came from. (We will give a date for your madness, stretched at the sea's edge screaming at the new sun as it came up. We will say, of you, that you were always "alone.")

To move again. Let it sink in. (Let the waters turn, the ocean, mount. Huge waves, strike down trees. So far down beneath where you sprawled and watched the light change the water's pigment.)

Bells thread the night. He is twisting his hips like a young girl, hands in his hair. He is walking quietly, with his lips pinched and cheeks drawn to kiss someone. (He kisses his own hands, and smells their palms.) He is putting his hands on his flanks to feel them jerk, as he sways gently through his night. He is a soft young girl, running his hands over his own body. The bells shake the darkness. The waves draw up over all the land. But there was no one else. The girl is pulled under, and as the waters die she drifts face down and quiet. It was getting light. More cars moved up the streets, and he waved at one.

Uncle Tom's Cabin: Alternate Ending

"6½" *was* the answer. But it seemed to irritate Miss Orbach. Maybe not the answer—the figure itself, but the fact it should be there, and in such loose possession.

"OH who is he to know such a thing? That's really improper to set up such liberations. And moreso."

What came into her head next she could hardly understand. A breath of cold. She did shudder, and her fingers clawed at the tiny watch she wore hidden in the lace of the blouse her grandmother had given her when she graduated teacher's college.

Ellen, Eileen, Evelyn . . . Orbach. She could be any of them. Her personality was one of theirs. As specific and as vague. The kindly menace of leading a life in whose balance evil was a constant intrigue but grew uglier and more remote as it grew stronger. She would have loved to do something really dirty. But nothing she had ever heard of was dirty enough. So she contented herself with good, i.e., purity, as a refuge from mediocrity. But being unconscious, or largely remote from her own sources, she would only admit to the possibility of grace. Not God. She would not be trapped into *wanting* even God.

So remorse took her easily. For any reason. A reflection in a shop window, of a man looking in vain for her ankles. (Which she covered with heavy colorless woolen.) A sudden gust of warm damp air around her legs or face. Long dull rains that turned her from her books. Or, as was the case this morning, some completely uncalled-for shaking of her silent doctrinaire routines.

"6½" had wrenched her unwillingly to exactly where she was. Teaching the 5th grade, in a grim industrial complex of northeastern America; about 1942. And how the social doth pain the anchorite.

Nothing made much sense in such a context. People moved around, and disliked each other for no reason. Also, and worse, they said they loved each other, and usually for less reason, Miss Orbach thought. Or would have if she did.

And in this class sat 30 dreary sons and daughters of such circumstance.

Specifically, the thriving children of the thriving urban lower middle classes. Postmen's sons and factory-worker debutantes. Making a great run for America, now prosperity and the war had silenced for a time the intelligent cackle of tradition. Like a huge grey bubbling vat the country, in its apocalyptic version of history and the future, sought now, in its equally apocalyptic profile of itself as it had urged swiftly its own death since the Civil War. To promise. Promise. And that to be that all who had ever dared to live here would die when the people and interests who had been its rulers died. The intelligent poor now were being admitted. And with them a great many Negroes . . . who would die when the rest of the dream died not even understanding that they, like Ishmael, should have been the sole survivors. But now they were being tricked. "6½" the boy said. After the fidgeting and awkward silence. One little black boy, raised his hand, and looking at the tip of Miss Orbach's nose said 6½. And then he smiled, very embarrassed and very sure of being wrong.

I would have said "No, boy, shut up and sit down. You are wrong. You don't know anything. Get out of here and be very quick. Have you no idea what you're getting involved in? My God . . . you nigger, get out of here and save yourself, while there's time. Now beat it." But those people had already been convinced. Read Booker T. Washington one day, when there's time. What that led to. The 6½'s moved for power . . . and there seemed no other way.

So three elegant Negroes in light grey suits grin and throw me through the window. They are happy and I am sad. It is an ample test of an idea. And besides "6½" is the right answer to the woman's question.

[The psychological and the social. The spiritual and the practical. Keep them together and you profit, maybe, someday, come out on top. Separate them, and you go along the road to the commonest of Hells. The one we westerners love to try to make art out of.]

The woman looked at the little brown boy. He blinked at her, trying again not to smile. She tightened her eyes, but her lips flew open. She tightened her lips, and her eyes blinked like the boy's. She said, "How do you get that answer?" The boy told her. "Well, it's right," she said, and the boy fell limp, straining even harder to look sorry. The negro in back of the answerer pinched him, and the boy shuddered. A little white girl next to him touched his hand, and he tried to pull his own hand away with his brain.

"Well, that's right, class. That's exactly right. You may sit down now Mr. McGhee."

Later on in the day, after it had started exaggeratedly to rain very hard and very stupidly against the windows and soul of her 5th-grade class, Miss Orbach became convinced that the little boy's eyes were too large. And in fact they did bulge almost grotesquely white and huge against his bony heavy-veined skull. Also, his head was much too large for the rest of the scrawny body. And he talked too much, and caused too many disturbances. He also stared out the window when Miss Orbach herself would drift off into her sanctuary of light and hygiene even though her voice carried the inanities of arithmetic seemingly without delay. When she came back to the petty social demands of 20th-century humanism the boy would be watching something walk across the playground. OH, it just would not work.

She wrote a note to Miss Janone, the school nurse, and gave it to the boy, McGhee, to take to her. The note read: "Are the large eyes a sign of————?"

Little McGhee, of course, could read, and read the note. But he didn't of course understand the last large word which was misspelled anyway. But he tried to memorize the note, repeating to himself over and over again its contents . . . sounding the last long word out in his head, as best he could.

Miss Janone wiped her big nose and sat the boy down, reading the note. She looked at him when she finished, then read the note again, crumpling it on her desk.

She looked in her medical book and found out what Miss Orbach meant. Then she said to the little Negro, Dr. Robard will be here in 5 minutes. He'll look at you. Then she began doing something to her eyes and fingernails.

When the doctor arrived he looked closely at McGhee and said to Miss Janone, "Miss Orbach is confused."

McGhee's mother thought that too. Though by the time little McGhee had gotten home he had forgotten the "long word" at the end of the note.

"Is Miss Orbach the woman who told you to say sangwich instead of sammich," Louise McGhee giggled.

"No, that was Miss Columbe."

"Sangwich, my christ. That's worse than sammich. Though you better not let me hear you saying sammich either . . . like those Davises."

"I don't say sammich, mamma."

"What's the word then?"

"Sandwich."

"That's right. And don't let anyone tell you anything else. Teacher or otherwise. Now I wonder what that word could've been?"

"I donno. It was very long. I forgot it."

Eddie McGhee Sr. didn't have much of an idea what the word could be either. But he had never been to college like his wife. It was one of the most conspicuously dealt with factors of their marriage.

So the next morning Louise McGhee, after calling her office, the Child Welfare Bureau, and telling them she would be a little late, took a trip to the school, which was on the same block as the house where the McGhees lived, to speak to Miss Orbach about the long word which she suspected might be injurious to her son and maybe to Negroes In General. This suspicion had been bolstered a great deal by what Eddie Jr. had told her about Miss Orbach, and also equally by what Eddie Sr. had long maintained about the nature of White People In General. "Oh well," Louise McGhee sighed, "I guess I better straighten this sister out." And that is exactly what she intended.

When the two McGhees reached the Center Street school the next morning Mrs. McGhee took Eddie along with her to the principal's office, where she would request that she be allowed to see Eddie's teacher.

Miss Day, the old, lady principal, would then send Eddie to his class with a note for his teacher, and talk to Louise McGhee, while she was waiting, on general problems of the neighborhood. Miss Day was a very old woman who had despised Calvin Coolidge. She was also, in one sense, exotically liberal. One time she had forbidden old man Seidman to wear his pince-nez anymore, as they looked too snooty. Center Street sold more war stamps than any other grammar school in the area, and had a fairly good track team.

Miss Orbach was going to say something about Eddie McGhee's being late, but he immediately produced Miss Day's note. Then Miss Orbach looked at Eddie again, as she had when she had written her own note the day before.

She made Mary Ann Fantano the monitor and stalked off down the dim halls. The class had a merry time of it when she left, and Eddie won an extra 2 Nabisco graham crackers by kissing Mary Ann while she sat at Miss Orbach's desk.

When Miss Orbach got to the principal's office and pushed open the door she looked directly into Louise McGhee's large brown eyes, and fell deeply and hopelessly in love.

The Death of Horatio Alger

The cold red building burned my eyes. The bricks hung together, like the city, the nation, under the dubious cement of rationalism and need. A need so controlled, it only erupted out of the used-car lots, or sat parked, Saturdays, in front of our orange house, for Orlando, or Algernon, or Danny, or J.D. to polish. There was silence, or summers, noise. But this was a few days after Christmas, and the ice melted from the roofs and the almost frozen water knocked lethargically against windows, tar roofs and slow dogs moping through the yards. The building was Central Avenue School. And its tired red sat on the corner of Central Avenue and Dey (pronounced *die* by the natives, *day* by the teachers, or any non-resident whites) Street. Then, on Dey, halfway up the block, the playground took over. A tarred-over yard, though once there had been gravel, surrounded by cement and a wire metal fence.

The snow was dirty as it sat dull and melting near the Greek restaurants, and the dimly lit "grocey" stores of the Negroes. The rich boys had metal wagons, the poor rode in. The poor made up games, the rich played them. The poor won the games, or as an emergency measure, the fights. No one thought of the snow except Mr. Feld, the playground director, who was in charge of it, or Miss Martin, the husky gym teacher Matthew Stodges had pushed into the cloakroom, who had no chains on her car. Grey slush ran over the curbs, and our dogs drank it out of boredom, shaking their heads and snorting.

I had said something about J.D.'s father, as to who he was, or had he ever been. And J., usually a confederate, and private strong arm, broke bad because Augie, Norman, and white Johnny were there, and laughed, misunderstanding simple "dozens" with ugly insult, in that curious scholarship the white man affects when he suspects a stronger link than sociology, or the tired cultural lies of Harcourt, Brace sixth-grade histories. And under their naïveté he grabbed my shirt and pushed me in the snow. I got up, brushing dead ice from my ears, and he pushed me down again, this time dumping a couple pounds of cold dirty slush down my neck, calmly hysterical at his act.

J. moved away and stood on an icy garbage hamper, sullenly throwing wet snow at the trucks on Central Avenue. I pushed myself into a sitting position, shaking my head. Tears full in my eyes, and the cold slicing minutes from my life. I wasn't making a sound. I wasn't thinking any thought I could make someone else understand. Just the rush of young fear and anger and disgust. I could have murdered God, in that simple practical way we kick dogs off the bottom step.

Augie (my best white friend), fat Norman, whose hook shots usually hit the rim, and were good for easy tip-ins by our big men, and useless white Johnny who had some weird disease that made him stare, even in the middle of a game, he'd freeze, and sometimes line drives almost knocked his head off while he shuddered slightly, cracking and recracking his huge knuckles. They were howling and hopping, they thought it was so funny that J. and I had come to blows. And especially, I guess, that I had got my lumps. "Hey, wiseass, somebody's gonna break your nose!" fat Norman would say over and over whenever I did something to him. Hold his pants when he tried his jump shot; spike him sliding into home (he was a lousy catcher); talk about his brother who hung out under the El and got naked in alleyways.

* * *

(The clucks of Autumn could have, right at that moment, easily seduced me. Away, and into school. To masquerade as a half-rich nigra with shiny feet. Back through the clean station, and up the street. Stopping to talk on the way. One beer gets you drunk and you stand in an empty corridor, lined with Italian paintings, talking about the glamours of sodomy.)

Rise and Slay.

I hurt so bad, and inside without bleeding I realized the filthy grey scratches my blood would carry to my heart. John walked off staring, and Augie and Norman disappeared, so easily there in the snow. And J.D. too, my first love, drifted against the easy sky. Weeping at what he'd done. No one there but me. THE SHORT SKINNY BOY WITH THE BUBBLE EYES.

Could leap up and slay them. Could hammer my fist and misery through their faces. Could strangle and bake them in the crude jungle of my feeling. Could stuff them in the sewie hole with the collected garbage of children's guilt. Could elevate them into heroic images of my own despair. A righteous messenger from the wrong side of the tracks. Gym teachers, cutthroats, aging pickets, ease by in the cold. The same lyric chart, exchange of particulars, that held me in my minutes, the time "Brownie" rammed the glass door down and ate up my suit. Even my mother, in a desperate fit of rhythm, was not equal to the task. Which was simple economics. I.e., a white man's dog cannot bite your son if he has been taught that something very ugly will happen to him if he does. He might pace stupidly in his ugly fur, but he will never never bite.

But what really stays to be found completely out, except stupid enterprises like art? The word on the page, the paint on the canvas (Marzette dragging in used-up canvases to revive their hopeless correspondence with the times), stone clinging to air, as if it were real. Or something a Deacon would admit was beautiful. The conscience rules against ideas. The point was to be where you wanted to, and do what you wanted to. After all is "said and done," what is left but those sheepish constructions. "I've got to go to the toilet" is no less pressing than the Puritans taking off for Massachusetts, and dragging their devils with them. (There is in those parts, even now, the peculiar smell of roasted sex organs. And when a good New Englander leaves his house in the earnestly moral sub-towns to go into the smoking hells of soon to be destroyed Yankee Gomorrahs, you watch him pull very firmly at his tie, or strapping on very tightly his evil watch.) The penitence there. The masochism. So complete and conscious a phenomenon. Like a standard of beauty; for instance, the bespectacled, softbreasted, gently pigeon-toed maidens of America. Neither rich nor poor, with intelligent smiles and straight lovely noses. No one would think of them as beautiful but these mysterious scions of the puritans. They value health and devotion, and their good women, the lefty power of all our nation, are unpresuming subtle beauties, who could even live with poets (if they are from the right stock), if pushed to that. But mostly they are where they should be, reading good books and opening windows to air out their bedrooms. And it is a useful memory here, because such things as these were the vague images that had even so early, helped shape me. Light freckles, sandy hair, narrow clean bodies. Though none lived where I lived then. And I don't remember a direct look at them even, with clear knowledge of my desire, until one afternoon I gave a speech at East Orange High, as sports editor of our high school paper, which should have been printed in Italian, and I saw there, in the auditorium, young American girls, for the first time. And have loved them as flesh things emanating from real life, that is, in contrast to my own, a scraping and floating through the last three red and blue stripes of the flag, that settles the hash of the lower middle class. So that even sprawled there in the snow, with my blood and pompous isolation, I vaguely knew of a glamorous world and was mistaken into thinking it could be gotten from books. Negroes and Italians beat and shaped me, and my allegiance is there. But the triumph of romanticism was parquet floors, yellow dresses, gardens and sandy hair. I must have felt the loss and could not rise against a cardboard world of dark hair and linoleum. Reality was something I was convinced I could not have.

And thus to be flogged or put to the rack. For all our secret energies. The first leap over the barrier: when the victim finds he can no longer stomach his own "group." Politics whinnies, but is still correct, and asleep in a windy barn. The beautiful statue of victory, whose arms were called duty. And they curdle in her snatch thrust there by angry minorities, along with their own consciences. Poets climb, briefly, off their motorcycles, to find out who owns their words. We are named by all the things we will never understand. Whether we can fight or not, or even at the moment of our hugest triumph we stare off into space remembering the snow melting in our cuts, and all the pimps of reason who've ever conquered us. It is the harshest form of love.

* * *

I could not see when I "chased" Norman and Augie. Chased in quotes because, they really did not have to run. They could have turned, and myth aside, calmly whipped my ass. But they ran, laughing and keeping warm. And J.D. kicked snow from around a fire hydrant flatly into the gutter. Smiling and broken, with his head hung just slanted towards the yellow dog ice running down a hole. I took six or seven long running steps and tripped. I couldn't have been less interested, but the whole project had gotten out of hand. I was crying, and my hands were freezing, and the two white boys leaned against the pointed metal fence and laughed and slapped their knees. I threw snow stupidly in their direction. It fell short and was not even noticed as it dropped.

(All of it rings in your ears for a long time. But the payback . . . in simple terms against such actual sin as supposing quite confidently that the big sweating purple whore staring from her peed up hall very casually at your whipping has *never* been loved . . . is hard. We used to say.)

Then I pushed to my knees and could only see J. leaning there against the hydrant looking just over my head. I called to him, for help really. But the words rang full of dead venom. I screamed his mother a purple nigger with alligator titties. His father a bilious white man with sores on his jowls. I was screaming for help in my hatred and loss, and only the hatred would show. And he came over shouting for me to shut up. Shut Up skinny bastard. I'll break your ass if you don't. Norman had both hands on his stomach, his laugh was getting so violent, and he danced awkwardly toward us howling to agitate J. to beat me some more. But J. whirled on him perfectly and rapped him hard under his second chin. Norman was going to say, "Hey me-an," in that hated twist of our speech, and J. hit him again, between his shoulder and chest, and almost dropped him to his knees. Augie cooled his howl to a giggle of concern and backed up until Norman turned and they both went shouting up the street.

I got to my feet, wiping my freezing hands on my jacket. J. was looking at me hard, like country boys do, when their language, or the new tone they need to take on once they come to this cold climate (1940's New Jersey) fails, and they are left with only the old Southern tongue, which cruel farts like me used to deride their lack of interest in America. I turned to walk away. Both my eyes were nothing but water, though it held at their rims, stoically refusing to blink and thus begin to sob uncontrollably. And to keep from breaking down I wheeled and hid the weeping by screaming at that boy. You nigger without a father. You eat your mother's pussy. And he wheeled me around and started to hit me again.

Someone called my house and my mother and father and grandmother and sister were strung along Dey street, in some odd order. (They couldn't have come out of the house "together.") And I was conscious first of my father saying, "Go on Mickey, hit him. Fight back." And for a few seconds, under the weight of that plea for my dignity, I tried. I feinted and danced, but I couldn't even roll up my fists. The whole street was blurred and hot as my eyes. I swung and swung, but J.D. bashed me when he wanted to.

My mother stopped the fight finally, shuddering at the thing she'd made. "His hands are frozen, Michael. His hands are frozen." And my father looks at me even now, wondering if they'll ever thaw.

Going Down Slow

Ah, miserable, thou, to whom Truth, in her first tides, bears nothing but wrecks
—Melville

In his mind Lew Crosby was already at Mauro's loft. But the soft neon rain and long wet city streets caused the separation. The logical affront of reason, or imagination staled into thinking of itself as reality, or "a reality." As mediocre neo-freudians always say in bars, leaning on one arm, half to themselves, "that's your reality."

But Crosby was no neo-freudian, so he measured a real distance on top of his fantasy, and continued very swiftly to walk. If he was a neo-anything, and this was his own thinking, he was a neo-shithead, a neo-dope. He opened his mouth pretending to talk to himself so the curiously refreshing drizzle would spray onto his tongue. He pretended talking to himself, like a Genet heroine pretending he is a woman. The more fully Crosby knew he was pretending to talk, and that no real sound was issuing from his lips, the more he felt that he was actually in conversation with himself. And it made him move even faster through the rain; knowing that he was a comfort to himself, and could make interesting conversation, entertain himself, even against the ugliest situations.

He said, "Ugly," and only once. He meant it about the weather, the tone of the sky. And not, oh shit no, about whatever was running him through the streets. At quarter to three Saturday morning.

The long street grew shorter as he approached the avenue that intersected it, and divided it from another seemingly endless crosstown city block. The rain stopped, and a light wind slowly whirled shallow puddles off the few awnings of stores and apartment buildings. A car would go by occasionally. A whore. One time a policeman watched Crosby from a doorway, lighting a cigarette. And probably wondered why this skinny little man was crying and shaking his head, working his jaws like speech, almost bulling up the deserted street. Crosby did break into a run occasionally, and usually when he did he would actually say some things. Usually he said, "Shit," or "Goddamn Goddamnit," clenching his teeth at the sound, his hands ripping away his jacket pockets, they were driven in so hard.

He had come, at 2:30 A.M. from a woman's house. A woman he had slept with many times. He had slept with her that night again. And when they had finished the action part of his visit, and the woman pulled his narrow body tightly against her own, he looked at his watch, which he hadn't taken off, and thought with a little start and maybe relief that he ought to be starting home. "It's two o'clock," he said to the woman. And she held him a little tighter, burying her face in his throat. "Leah, I've got to make it now."

The woman let him go suddenly, stretching one arm with its hand so they both hung awkwardly off the couch. That's where Crosby and Leah Purcell had been, for maybe an hour. Turning and grabbing on a narrow day-bed couch. Tearing each other's clothes, panting and pulling, till they both lay naked, or nearly naked, and now a little wasted, still shoved against each other so as not to fall off the narrow cot.

"You wouldn't stay all night?" Leah, on the outside, stretched one of her legs trying to get it solidly on the rug.

"I wouldn't. How could I?" Crosby pushed himself up on his hands. "How could I stay here all night?"

"I don't think you want to."

"No?"

"No. And besides your wife wouldn't mind." The girl rolled completely away from him, putting both her feet on the floor. She ran her hand over a mound of clothes, trying to find her pants.

"No?"

"Hey, Lew." She got the pants and then the brassiere. "Would you mind if Rachel were staying with somebody? No, I mean seeing somebody . . . like you do?"

Crosby pulled himself onto the floor and started to get his clothes together. He could do it more quickly than the girl, because even in the most fearful throes of passion he still knew exactly where he had thrown, or placed, his clothes. He started with his socks, and then his underwear. "What do you mean, seeing somebody?" His shirt, then the pants, fastening the belt. He took his tie out of the jacket.

Leah was still in her underwear. She stood now more in the center of the room, pulling her long hair together. "Suppose Rachel was seeing someone—sleeping with them—just like you and I sleep together, have been sleeping together, about twice a week for the last two months. Would it bother you?"

Lew smiled. He had his jacket on, and ran his hands through the pockets searching for cigarettes. When he got one in his mouth and knew that his speech would be muffled he half-shrugged half-didn't say some kind of affirmative answer. It meant yes though. And he even repeated it.

Leah stopped pulling her hair and bent down toward the floor to retrieve her large reddish comb. As she bent Lew squinted in the almost darkness, grimacing self-consciously at the woman's large self-conscious behind.

"It would, huh? It would really bother you . . . even though you do the same thing?"

"Uh huh." Lew took a step in the direction of the hall.

"What kind of thinking is that?"

"Mine." There was a book Lew came in with that he missed now, and he stooped to feel along the floor.

"Lew, don't go now. Stay for a while . . . let me make some tea. I've got some brandy too."

He got the book, and threw his raincoat over his shoulder. "Uh uh, I've got to make it."

"Oh, come on Lew, you don't have to go. Rachel won't mind. She's not even home."

A hot laugh dug through Lew Crosby's feelings, coming in through the nostrils and eyes. A good punch line. He was in the street and looking for money for a cab. But by the time it occurred to him to get a cab he had run almost thirteen blocks. A bunch of dominoes spilled over. Flap, flap, flap, etc., the white dots blinding him like monster street lights. Flap, flap, flap. All kinds of recent history, in cold images ate at the white hot screaming in his skin. The screaming he watched float up out of his stomach and scratch his eyeballs sideways. Now what? Now what? Now what? Or flap, flap flap, his steps, and legs, stretching out along the pavement. And his fiction still beat wet against his leg . . . flap flap flap.

At the house he stood a long time on the front step looking at the two front windows. It was dark inside. For sure For sure. And he had to put his head between his knees to cool the blood and nausea pumping at it from the inside. He put his hands on his hips, holding his head between his knees. Like a hurdler or half-miler. A bent wire squeezed together among the pictures. The stone tablets of conversation and act. He got days mixed up and dates, and stories. Fantasies replaced each other. Fantasies replaced realities. Realities did not replace anything. They were the least of anybody's worries. Even when he got inside and there was no one there. Or only the baby, sleeping very quietly in her crib, and an old college friend who had been staying at the house over the last few weeks.

Crosby walked up and down the long narrow apartment as if he were looking for clues. Even though he had gone through all the really vulgar Sherlock Holmes shit quite a while ago. He came to the front then walked to the back. He did it again. And on the fourth trip to the front he shook Mickey Lasker on the couch, and spoke very rapidly to him at the moment Mickey opened his eyes. "Is Rachel at Mauro's house?"

Because Mickey was not quite awake he answered immediately. "Yes . . . Yes . . . that's where she is." When he realized exactly what was happening, Lasker's eyes flew open and his hands fell and tightened at his sides. "Lew . . ." but Crosby had turned and run out of the house.

There was a light in Mauro's window. Or Lew figured at three o'clock it was probably the only window lighted. The loft was only a few blocks, about five, from the Crosby's apartment. And the flaps then, thinking about the distance, fit a picture of something. For instance, "I'm going for a walk, Lew. I'll be back in a little while." Meaning, only five blocks, and not that brand of all-night magic. Finish *my* business while you read. And not with the cruelty it is to leave someone lying awake early mornings shuffling through faces.

Or "dance class," and a quick drink after, or stop in to hear some music, but home early, from jiving with the girls. (One of whom, "the girls," Lew found out, the wife of Crosby's closest friend, was fucking Mickey Lasker every chance she got. Mostly Thursdays . . . "dance" night.) "Oh, baby, it's Brook Farm." One of the things Lew pretended to say when the rain ran in his mouth.

But Rachel looked so quietly guilty, and it canceled what Lew thought when she came in on time from her screwing. Oh, come on asshole, don't make liars out of everybody. Or something, mixed with the slanting light on his book. The open bottle. His glass so handy, and plenty of good ideas. So fixed and necessary; that each thing remain understood. How can you read *Pierre* if you think your wife's doing something weird? Then you got to take time out to think about *her*. Oh boy . . . and then what? How much time can you waste like that? A poem? An honesty, like watching the rain from a doorway. Any simple but really complex way of feeling can be distorted by all these people. These conversations and rationales. Opinions, posturings, lies. Just to pass the time. From one dismal minute to the next. A bad painter sweeping his brush like counting. Talk, talk, talk, (in a foreign accent). I don't want to say what I mean. But shutup anyway, I don't want to hear about you. Just live your life and shutup! Railing like that. Wasting everything. After it had taken so long to get it together. I am Lew Crosby, a writer. I want to write what I'm about, which is profound shit. Don't ask me anything. Just sit there if you want to. No, I'm not thinking. I'm just sitting. Don't try to involve yourself with me.

"Lew, Lew, answer me. Lew? Say, don't you ever listen to what I'm saying?"

Now it wanted to rain again, just as Crosby opened the downstairs door. The loft was on the third floor. When he got outside the door he could hear low music and conversation. He banged on the door, almost as hard as he could. There was only more conversation, a little louder, but much the same as before. He didn't knock again, but the door swung open and he could see his wife sitting at a table just behind the short husky Japanese who opened the door.

"Hello, Lew," Mauro said, pulling the door wider. Crosby walked over to the table.

"Get your coat, Rachel." He wanted his voice to be soft and it almost was. "Get your coat and come on." His wife got halfway up from the table and looked over her shoulder.

"Lew," the painter said, "Lew, sit down and have a drink. We civilized people."

Crosby got hold of his wife's arm and pulled her out of the chair. He shoved her toward the door. The Japanese touched Crosby's arm.

"Lew, have a drink. We civilized people." Lew, of course, wanted to turn and hit Mauro in the face. Then he wanted to kick him in the face. But Mauro used to teach him, Lew, judo. Lew figured this clown just wanted to throw him on his ass. Wow. Brook Farm.

Lew got his wife's coat and pushed her through the door. She began to cry when they got to the bottom of the stairs. Lew wouldn't say anything. He walked a little in front of her. No rain now, only a damp sluggish wind off the river . . . and the spilling puddles. "Lew," Rachel was still crying, and louder. "Lew . . . Lew!" He walked faster, beginning to cross the wide avenue closest to their apartment. "Lew," Crosby's wife called very loudly, and he walked very quickly up the front steps.

He left the front door and the apartment door open. Rachel closed them as she passed. When she got inside the final door, Lew was standing in the middle of the room. Mickey Lasker brushed them both on the way out, tucking in his shirt. "Rachel," he just about whispered as he passed her.

"Lew," Rachel walked very close to her husband. The room was half-lit by a street light through a window, but also the sky was turning a little grey.

"You fucking whore. You goddamn fucking whore," Lew was looking out the window at the light. But he kept calling Rachel a fucking whore. She cried again, calling his name over and over. And he kept looking out the window repeating his thing. When Rachel touched his arm he spun around and swung at her hand. But then he started talking. "Why with that bastard? If you wanted to fuck somebody, why pick a complete dope? A stupid asshole like that? For chris'sake, for chris'sake. You know what? It follows all along . . . you just don't have any goddamn taste. A goddamn mediocrity. You were that when I first met you and goddamn you still are. A middle-class wreck. Christ, Christ . . . why don't you go the hell back where you came from? Christ. God!"

Her husband's stream of useless profanity cleared Rachel Crosby's head. She blew her nose while he shouted. And wiped her eyes. Lew went on shouting, but when he paused for a second Rachel said, as if she were holding a normal conversation, "What about you? What about you? I know you've been sleeping with Leah Purcell for the last few months. Nine o'clock in the morning. For God sakes! Lew, don't come on like that. How can you be so angry when you've been screwing around with that girl like you have? Leaving me here all the time. God, Lew . . . what did you expect?"

"I never slept with Leah Purcell." Lew was screaming now. Then he would shut up. Then he would call his wife a whore. Then he would call her mediocre, then he would say she needed a fool like Mauro because she was a fool. He wanted to call the Japanese a bad painter, but he figured that would be dumb. Even if it was true. "You're a dumb whore. A stupid mediocre bitch. Go away dumb whore. Go away."

He thrashed his arms, spit on the floor. Kicked tables and threw chairs against the wall. Smashed cheap glasses and pushed some flowers on the couch. Rachel started to scream now. All the things she'd said before. But now she screamed. And she hit her husband, on the chest and arms, till he stopped calling her a dumb whore, and began to grab at her arms. "I'll slap the hell out of you." He was trying to scream as loud as she was. She was saying go ahead . . . go ahead, and he slapped her once, across her face, and caught her before she fell. Then they stood holding each other for about thirty minutes.

* * *

When Lew pulled gently away from his wife it was even lighter in the room. He looked toward the front of the house and started walking toward the door. His wife said Lew again. But he left without speaking.

He almost retraced his steps. Not wobbling so much, but quickly, and only moving his mouth when he had something to say. When he got to the loft the light was dimmer but there was still a light. But now the downstairs door was locked. Lew brought up his hand stiffly and shoved it noisily through one of the door's small windows. Turning the knob from the inside he pushed the door open with his knee. There were three or four medium cuts on both sides of his hand, and they bled freely until Lew tied the hand in his handkerchief.

Once in the hall he leaped up the stairs, but as quietly as he could, landing on each step on his toes. When he got to Mauro's door his hand itched in the handkerchief and he remembered that the painter could probably wipe up the loft with him. So Crosby went back down one flight of stairs and rummaged through a pile of wood he remembered. But he took a metal pipe out of the pile and stuck it in his pocket with the cut-up hand.

When the door swung open this time Lew drew the pipe out and up and very hard down on Mauro's forehead. The next blow struck Rachel's lover near his ear. He fell quickly, with only a trifling wheeze. Blood was covering his head before he hit the floor.

Crosby looked at the man on the floor and still took a step into the room. He looked at the table with two separate crowds of beer cans. Then came in and looked at the unmade bed. He kneeled and smelled the wrinkled sheets. When he straightened up he tossed the pipe over his shoulder toward the painting area. Then he walked quickly through the door running down the stairs.

When the air hit him in the face, Lew got everything pretty straight. He even wondered whether the guy was dead. But he started, now, running in the street as fast as he could, twisting his hand up under a street light to see how badly it was hurt. He was running toward Leah Purcell's house.

* * *

About fifteen minutes later, running, walking, holding his hand at the wrist, or swinging it in wide arcs trying to stop it from stinging, Lew moved past the narrow tenement where Leah lived, and kept pushing down the street.

Seven o'clock he got to Bob Long's house, and some people were already hitting the street. Mostly Puerto Ricans, in sad vectors toward whatever ugly trick "Charlie" had put them in.

Another loft, with long shallow stairs. Bob lived at the top in a huge double studio with democratic antiques and his paintings. Blue girls, black girls, yellow and green girls. And in the background always some strange voyeur in a top hat riding a slow horse. Most of the paintings were that, or should have been that. Green people, orange people, magenta people. And they were always working out. Kama Sutra fashion. They made it from behind. Standing on horses. All ways. Girls and girls, men and horses. Girls and horses. And violent violet landscapes.

Inside, early early in the morning, Bob and two bohemians were getting ready to bolster the economy by sticking old needles in their arms. They greeted Lew, who was bleeding very badly, but only Bob got up to look at his hand. While he cleaned his hand Lew told Bob everything that had happened that night. Very quickly, like stage directions. Bob looked at him without saying anything. Letting Lew finish. They bandaged the hand. "Mauro, huh?" was all Bob would say. "Wow! Mauro, huh?"

"Yeh. I just left the cat. With his head caved in. I don't know if he's dead or not. I thought I'd sit around here for a while . . . you know."

"Yeh, man, yeh. Just sit." And then a soft benevolence came into Bob's voice. "Come on and get high with us. We got enough. And one of them turkeys can go get some more if we have to."

"What is it, horse?"

"Uh huh." Bob looked in the mirror at a mole on his chin. He ran some water in the sink and dabbed at the mole uselessly.

"I didn't know you did that."

"Oh, man, sure. Groovy stuff."

They went back to the nodding bohemians. Both of whom had taken as much out of the bag as they possibly could without making it too noticeable that they had gotten some of Bob's. Before he even looked at the bag Bob said, "O.K., which one of you faggots burned me?" Both of the bohemians laughed. "Eddie, you gonna have to make the run." Bob picked up the bag, shaking it and holding it up to the light. "Yeh, faggot, you better get on your horse."

Bob showed Lew what to do. And even put the needle into his arm. It was warm and dead in Lew's stomach throat and head. He sat so far away from anything you can name. Inside a deadness that kept so much uselessness away. Slow greedy pictures of dominoes.

Lew volunteered Eddie five dollars to make the run. Sitting with his knees hugged up under his chin; trying not to vomit, but harder and straighter anyway. And just out of everybody's reach.

Heroes Are Gang Leaders

My concerns are not centered on people. But in reflection, people cause the ironic tone they take. If I think through theories of government or prose, the words are sound, the feelings real, but useless unless people can carry them. Attack them, or celebrate them. Useless in the world, at least. Though to my own way of moving, it makes no ultimate difference. I'll do pretty much what I would have done. Even though people change me: sometimes bring me out of myself, to confront them, or embrace them. I spit in a man's face once in a bar who had just taught me something very significant about the socio-cultural structure of America, and the West. But the act of teaching is usually casual. That is, you can pick up God knows what from God knows who.

Sitting in a hospital bed on First Avenue trying to read, and being fanned by stifling breezes off the dirty river. Ford Madox Ford was telling me something, and this a formal act of teaching. The didactic tone of *No More Parades*. Teaching. Telling. Pointing out. And very fine and real in its delineations, but causing finally a kind of super-sophisticated hero worship. So we move from Tarzan to Christopher Tietjens, but the concerns are still heroism. And what to do to make the wildest, brightest, dispersal of our energies. In our not really brief flight into darkness. Either it is done against the heavens, sky flyers, or against the earth. And the story of man is divided brusquely between those who know the sky, and those who know only the earth. And the various dictators, artists, murderers and ministers, can come from either side. Each Left and Right, go right up to the sky, and the division is within their own territory. Lindberghs and Hemingways, Nat Turners and Robespierres. What they do is gold, and skyward, from whatever angle, they fly and return to an earth of mistakes. So Christopher Tietjens being made a cuckold, and trying vainly to see through mist and shadows down to Sylvia's earth. She called so furiously for him to fall. My friend, Johnny Morris, fighting off the Ku Klux Klan only to return from those heights to the silent hallway of some very real shack and watch some fool wrestle with his wife. Various scenes complete each other with desperate precision.

Sitting there being talked to by an old Tory, fixed and diseased by my only life. And surrounded, fortunately enough, by men like myself, who are not even able to think. Wood alcohol drinkers, dragged in from the Bowery, with their lungs and bellies on fire. Raving logicians who know empirically that Christianity can only take its place among the other less publicized concerns of men.

Sixty-year-old niggers who sit on their beds scratching their knees. Polacks who have to gurgle for the rest of their lives. Completely anonymous (Scotch-Irish?) Americans with dark ratty hair, and red scars on their stomachs. They might be homosexuals watching me read Thomas Me-an, and smelling the mystery woman's flowers. Puerto Ricans with shiny hair and old-fashioned underwear shirts, eating their dinner out of Mason jars.

And we are all alive at the same time. Contemporaries in that sense. (Though I still think myself a young man, and am still in love with things I can do.) Of the same time and source. Inheritors of so many things we will never understand. But weighted with very different allegiances, though if I am silent for a long time I hope we all believe in a similar reality. That I am not merely writing poems for Joel Oppenheimer or Paul Blackburn . . . but everything alive. Which is not true. Which is simply not true. Our heroisms and their claims are fictitious. But if we are not serious, if we do not make up a body of philosophy out of which to work we are simply hedonists, and I am stretching the word so that it includes even martyrs. Flame freaks.

In the bed next to mine was a man, Kowalski, a very tall Polish man with a bony hairless skull, covered with welts and scratches. He had drunk paint remover and orange juice. He was the man who gurgled now, though he kept trying to curl his lips and smile. But I was hoping he would find out soon what a hopeless gesture that was, and stop it. I wanted to say to him, "Why don't you quit fucking around like that? It's certainly too late to be anybody else's man now. Just cut that shit out." With his weird colored teeth hanging below his lip, cutting the smile into strips of anguish.

He would eat my fruit when I offered it, or the nuts a rich lady gave me. Since I was not merely a "poor man" or a derelict, but a writer. That is, there was a glamorous reason I was in this derelict's ward. Look at my beard, and all the books on the table. I'm not like the rest of these guys. They're just tramps. But I'm a tramp with connections.

He would talk too, if I didn't watch him. He would gurgle these wild things he found in the tabloids. And point out murders and rapes to me, or robberies where everybody got away clean. He described the Bowery to me like it was a college, or the Village, or an artist's colony. An identical reality, with the same used up references . . . the same dishonesties and misplaced loyalties. The same ambition, naturally. Usually petty and ravaging. Another cold segment of American enterprise, and for this reason having nothing at all to do with their European counterparts, beggars . . . whom I suppose are academic and stuffy in comparison. Bums have the same qualifications as any of us to run for president, and it is the measure of a society that they refuse to. And this is not romanticism, but simple cultural observation. Bums know at least as much about the world as Senator Fulbright. You better believe it.

But one day two men came into our ward. A tall red-faced man, like from his neck up he had been painted by Soutine, or some other nut. The other man, was lost in his gabardine suit, like somebody who was not even smart enough to be rich. When I looked up from my book at them, I thought immediately what a stupid thing to think about people that they were cops. Although, of course, that is just what they were: cops. Or detectives, since they were in "plain" clothes, which is as hip as putting an alligator in a tuxedo. Very few people would make a mistake, except say those who would say it was a crocodile. That is, zoology majors.

The alligators came right down the aisle to Kowalski's bed; the little baggy one carrying a yellow pad on a writing board. They had been talking to each other very calmly and happily about something. Probably about man-eating tigers or the possibility of whores on Mars. But their faces quickly changed and reset when they got to the end of the row, and stood before my derelict's bed. "Hey," the red-faced man said, "Hey," at Kowalski who was sleeping or by now pretending to sleep, "Hey, you Kowalski?" He shook the old man's shoulder, getting him to turn over. Kowalski shook his head in imitation of sleep, frowned and tried to yawn. But he was still frightened. Probably confused too, since I'm sure he'd never expected to see cops in a place the Geneva Convention states very specifically is cool. In fact he wiped his eyes convinced, I'm certain, that the two police officers were only bad fairies, or at worst, products of a very casual case of delirium tremens. But, for sure, the two men persisted, past any idea of giggling fantasy.

"Hey. You Kowalski?"

The old man finally shook his head slowly yes, very very slowly, yes. Pulling his sheets up around his neck like a woman or an inventive fag, in a fit of badly feigned modesty. The cops looked on their list and back at Kowalski, the tall one already talking. "Where'd you get the stuff, Kowalski? Huh?" The derelict shrugged his shoulders and looked cautiously toward the window. "We wanna know where you got the stuff, Kowalski, huh?" Finally, it must have dawned on the derelict that his voice was gone. That he really couldn't answer the questions, whether he wanted to or not, and he gurgled for the men, and touched his throat apologetically. The red cop said, "Where'd you get the stuff, Kowalski, huh? Come on speak up." And he put his head closer to the bum's, at the same time shaking his shoulder and finally, confronted by more gurgles, took the derelict's pajama shirt in his fingers and lifted the man a few inches off the bed. The little toady man was alternately watching and listening, and making checks on his yellow pad. He said, "Comeon," once, but not very viciously; he looked at me and rubbed his eyes. "Comeon, fella."

The large cop raised his voice as he raised Kowalski off the bed, and shook him awkwardly from side to side, now only repeating the last part of the question, "Huh? Huh? Huh?" And the old bum gurgled, and began to slobber on himself, his face turning as red as the policeman's, and his eyes wide and full of a domesticated terror. He kept trying to touch his throat, but his arms were bent under his body, or maybe it was that he was too weak to raise them from where they hung uselessly at his side. But he gurgled and turned redder.

And here is the essay part of the story. Like they say, my *point of view.* I had the book, *No More Parades,* all about the pursuit of heroism. About the death and execution of a sky-man, or at least the execution, and the airless social compromise that keeps us alive past any use to ourselves. Chewing on some rich lady's candy, holding on to my ego, there among the elves, for dear god given sanctified life. Big Man In The Derelict Ward. The book held up in front of my eyes, to shield what was going on from slopping over into my life. Though, goddamn, it was there already. The response. The image. The total hold I had, and made. Crisscrossed and redirected for my own use (which now sits between the covers of a book to be misunderstood as *literature.* Like neon crosses should only be used to advertise pain. Which is total and final, and never really brief. It was all I had. Like Joe Friday, or César Vallejo, in a hopeless confusion of wills and intents. To be judged like Tietjens was or my friend in the hallway watching his wife or breaking his fingers against an automobile window. There is no reasonable attitude behind anything. Nuns, passion killers, poets, we should all go out and get falling down drunk, and forget all the rules that make our lives so hopeless. Fuck you Kowalski! Really, I really mean it. St. Peter doing his crossword puzzle while they wasted another hopeless fanatic. It fits, and is more logical than any other act. Ugly Polish tramp).

Till finally I said, "That man can't speak. His voice is gone."

And the tall man, without even looking, wheezed, "And who the fuck asked you?"

It is the measure of my dwindling life that I returned to the book to rub out their image, and studied very closely another doomed man's life.

The Screamers

Lynn Hope adjusts his turban under the swishing red green yellow shadow lights. Dots. Suede heaven raining, windows yawning cool summer air, and his musicians watch him grinning, quietly, or high with wine blotches on four-dollar shirts. A yellow girl will not dance with me, nor will Teddy's people, in line to the left of the stage, readying their *Routines*. Haroldeen, the most beautiful, in her pitiful dead sweater. Make it yellow, wish it whole. Lights. Teddy, Sonny Boy, Kenny & Calvin, Scram, a few of Nat's boys jamming long washed handkerchiefs in breast pockets, pushing shirts into homemade cummer-bunds, shuffling lightly for any audience.

"The Cross-Over," Deen laughing at us all. And they perform in solemn unison a social tract of love. (With no music till Lynn finishes "macking" with any biglipped Esther screws across the stage. White and green plaid jackets his men wear, and that twisted badge, black turban/on red string conked hair. (OPPRESSORS!) A greasy hip-ness, down-ness, nobody in our camp believed (having social-worker mothers and postman fathers; or living squeezed in lightskinned projects with adulterers and proud skinny ladies with soft voices). The theory, the spectrum, this sound baked inside their heads, and still rub sweaty against those lesser lights. Those niggers. Laundromat workers, beauticians, pregnant short-haired jail bait separated all ways from "us," but in this vat we sweated gladly for each other. And rubbed. And Lynn could be a common hero, from whatever side we saw him. Knowing that energy, and its response. That drained silence we had to make with our hands, leaving actual love to Nat or Al or Scram.

He stomped his foot, and waved one hand. The other hung loosely on his horn. And their turbans wove in among those shadows. Lynn's tighter, neater, and bright gorgeous yellow stuck with a green stone. Also, those green sparkling cubes dancing off his pinkies. A-boomp bahba bahba, A-boomp bahba bahba, A-boomp bahba bahba, A-boomp bahba bahba, the turbans sway behind him. And he grins before he lifts the horn, at Deen or drunk Becky, and we search the dark for girls.

Who would I get? (Not anyone who would understand this.) Some light girl who had fallen into bad times and ill-repute for dating Bubbles. And he fixed her later with his child, now she walks Orange St. wiping chocolate from its face. A disgraced white girl who learned to calypso in vocational school. Hence, behind halting speech, a humanity as paltry as her cotton dress. (And the big hats made a line behind her, stroking their erections, hoping for photographs to take down south.) Lynn would oblige. He would make the most perverted hopes sensual and possible. Chanting at that dark crowd. Or some girl, a wino's daughter, with carefully vaselined bow legs would drape her filthy angora against the cardboard corinthian, eying past any greediness a white man knows, my soft tyrolean hat, pressed corduroy suit, and "B" sweater. Whatever they meant, finally, to her, valuable shadows barely visible.

Some stuck-up boy with "good" hair. And as a naked display of America, for I meant to her that same oppression. A stunted head of greased glass feathers, orange lips, brown pasted edge to the collar of her dying blouse. The secret perfume of poverty and ignorant desire. Arrogant too, at my disorder, which calls her smile mysterious. Turning to be eaten by the crowd. That mingled foliage of sweat and shadows: *Night Train* was what they swayed to. And smelled each other in The Grind, The Rub, The Slow Drag. From side to side, slow or jerked staccato as their wedding dictated. Big hats bent tight skirts, and some light girls' hair swept the resin on the floor. Respectable ladies put stiff arms on your waist to keep some light between, looking nervously at an ugly friend forever at the music's edge.

I wanted girls like Erselle, whose father sang on television, but my hair was not straight enough, and my father never learned how to drink. Our house sat lonely and large on a half-Italian street, filled with important Negroes. (Though it is rumored they had a son, thin with big eyes, they killed because he was crazy.) Surrounded by the haughty daughters of depressed economic groups. They plotted in their projects for mediocrity, and the neighborhood smelled of their despair. And only the wild or the very poor thrived in Graham's or could be roused by Lynn's histories and rhythms. America had choked the rest, who could sit still for hours under popular songs, or be readied for citizenship by slightly bohemian social workers. They rivaled pure emotion with wind-up record players that pumped Jo Stafford into Home Economics rooms. And these carefully scrubbed children of my parents' friends fattened on their rhythms until they could join the Urban League or Household Finance and hound the poor for their honesty.

I was too quiet to become a murderer, and too used to extravagance for their skinny lyrics. They mentioned neither cocaine nor Bach, which was my reading, and the flaw of that society. I disappeared into the slums, and fell in love with violence, and invented for myself a mysterious economy of need. Hence, I shambled anonymously thru Lloyd's, The Nitecap, The Hi-Spot, and Graham's desiring everything I felt. In a new English overcoat and green hat, scouring that town for my peers. And they were old pinch-faced whores full of snuff and weak dope, celebrity fags with radio programs, mute bass players who loved me, and built the myth of my intelligence. You see, I left America on the first fast boat.

This was Sunday night, and the Baptists were still praying in their "faboulous" churches. Though my father sat listening to the radio, or reading pulp cowboy magazines, which I take in part to be the truest legacy of my spirit. God never had a chance. And I would be walking slowly toward The Graham, not even knowing how to smoke. Willing for any experience, any image, any further separation from where my good grades were sure to lead. Frightened of post offices, lawyer's offices, doctor's cars, the deaths of clean politicians. Or of the imaginary fat man, advertising cemeteries to his "good colored friends." Lynn's screams erased them all, and I thought myself intrepid white commando from the West. Plunged into noise and flesh, and their form become an ethic.

Now Lynn wheeled and hunched himself for another tune. Fast dancers fanned themselves. Couples who practiced during the week talked over their steps. Deen and her dancing clubs readied *avant-garde* routines. Now it was *Harlem Nocturne*, which I whistled loudly one Saturday in a laundromat, and the girl who stuffed in my khakis and stiff underwear asked was I a musician. I met her at Graham's that night and we waved, and I suppose she knew I loved her.

Nocturne was slow and heavy and the serious dancers loosened their ties. The slowly twisting lights made specks of human shadows, the darkness seemed to float around the hall. Any meat you clung to was yours those few minutes without interruption. The length of the music was the only form. And the idea was to press against each other hard, to rub, to shove the hips tight, and gasp at whatever passion. Professionals wore jocks against embarrassment. Amateurs, like myself, after the music stopped, put our hands quickly into our pockets, and retreated into the shadows. It was as meaningful as anything else we knew.

All extremes were popular with that crowd. The singers shouted, the musicians stomped and howled. The dancers ground each other past passion or moved so fast it blurred intelligence. We hated the popular song, and any freedman could tell you if you asked that white people danced jerkily, and were slower than our champions. One style, which developed as Italians showed up with pegs, and our own grace moved toward bell-bottom pants to further complicate the cipher, was the honk. The repeated rhythmic figure, a screamed riff, pushed in its insistence past music. It was hatred and frustration, secrecy and despair. It spurted out of the diphthong culture, and reinforced the black cults of emotion. There was no compromise, no dreary sophistication, only the elegance of something that is too ugly to be described, and is diluted only at the agent's peril. All the saxophonists of that world were honkers, Illinois, Gator, Big Jay, Jug, the great sounds of our day. Ethnic historians, actors, priests of the unconscious. That stance spread like fire thru the cabarets and joints of the black cities, so that the sound itself became a basis for thought, and the innovators searched for uglier modes. Illinois would leap and twist his head, scream when he wasn't playing. Gator would strut up and down the stage, dancing for emphasis, shaking his long gassed hair in his face and coolly mopping it back. Jug, the beautiful horn, would wave back and forth so high we all envied him his connection, or he'd stomp softly to the edge of the stage whispering those raucous threats. Jay first turned the mark around, opened the way further for the completely nihilistic act. McNeeley, the first Dada coon of the age, jumped and stomped and yowled and finally sensed the only other space that form allowed. He fell first on his knees, never releasing the horn, and walked that way across the stage. We hunched together drowning any sound, relying on Jay's contorted face for evidence that there was still music, though none of us needed it now. And then he fell backwards, flat on his back, with both feet stuck up high in the air, and he kicked and thrashed and the horn spat enraged sociologies.

That was the night Hip Charlie, the Baxter Terrace Romeo, got wasted right in front of the place. Snake and four friends mashed him up and left him for the ofays to identify. Also the night I had the grey bells and sat in the Chinese restaurant all night to show them off. Jay had set a social form for the poor, just as Bird and Dizzy proposed it for the middle class. On his back screaming was the Mona Lisa with the mustache, as crude and simple. Jo Stafford could not do it. Bird took the language, and we woke up one Saturday whispering *Ornithology*. Blank verse.

And Newark always had a bad reputation, I mean, everybody could pop their fingers. Was hip. Had walks. Knew all about The Apple. So I suppose when the word got to Lynn what Big Jay had done, he knew all the little down cats were waiting to see him in this town. He knew he had to cook. And he blasted all night, crawled and leaped, then stood at the side of the stand, and watched us while he fixed his sky, wiped his face. Watched us to see how far he'd gone, but he was tired and we weren't, which was not where it was. The girls rocked slowly against the silence of the horns, and big hats pushed each other or made plans for murder. We had not completely come. All sufficiently eaten by Jay's memory, "on his back, kicking his feet in the air, Go-ud Damn!" So he moved cautiously to the edge of the stage, and the gritty Muslims he played with gathered close. It was some mean honking blues, and he made no attempt to hide his intentions. He was breaking bad. "Okay, baby," we all thought, "Go for yourself." I was standing at the back of the hall with one arm behind my back, so the overcoat could hang over in that casual gesture of fashion. Lynn was moving, and the camel walkers were moving in the corners. The fast dancers and practicers making the whole hall dangerous. "Off my suedes, motherfucker." Lynn was trying to move us, and even I did the one step I knew, safe at the back of the hall. The hippies ran for girls. Ugly girls danced with each other. Skippy, who ran the lights, made them move faster in that circle on the ceiling, and darkness raced around the hall. Then Lynn got his riff, that rhythmic figure we knew he would repeat, the honked note that would be his personal evaluation of the world. And he screamed it so the veins in his face stood out like neon. "Uhh, yeh, Uhh, yeh, Uhh, yeh," we all screamed to push him further. So he opened his eyes for a second, and really made his move. He looked over his shoulder at the other turbans, then marched in time with his riff, on his toes across the stage. They followed; he marched across to the other side, repeated, then finally he descended, still screaming, into the crowd, and as the sidemen followed, we made a path for them around the hall. They were strutting, and all their horns held very high, and they were only playing that one scary note. They moved near the back of the hall, chanting and swaying, and passed right in front of me. I had a little cup full of wine a murderer friend of mine made me drink, so I drank it and tossed the cup in the air, then fell in line behind the last wild horn man, strutting like the rest of them. Bubbles and Rogie followed me, and four-eyed Moselle Boyd. And we strutted back and forth pumping our arms, repeating with Lynn Hope, "Yeh, Uhh, Yeh, Uhh." Then everybody fell in behind us, yelling still. There was confusion and stumbling, but there were no real fights. The thing they wanted was right there and easily accessible. No one could stop you from getting in that line. "It's too crowded. It's too many people on the line!" some people yelled. So Lynn thought further, and made to destroy the ghetto. We went out into the lobby and in perfect rhythm down the marble steps. Some musicians laughed, but Lynn and some others kept the note, till the others fell back in. Five or six hundred hopped-up woogies tumbled out into Belmont Avenue. Lynn marched right in the center of the street. Sunday night traffic stopped, and honked. Big Red yelled at a bus driver, "Hey, baby, honk that horn in time or shut it off!" The bus driver cooled it. We screamed and screamed at the clear image of ourselves as we should always be. Ecstatic, completed, involved in a secret communal expression. It would be the form of the sweetest revolution, to huckle-buck into the fallen capital, and let the oppressors lindy hop out. We marched all the way to Spruce, weaving among the stalled cars, laughing at the dazed white men who sat behind the wheels. Then Lynn turned and we strutted back toward the hall. The late show at the National was turning out, and all the big hats there jumped right in our line.

Then the Nabs came, and with them, the fire engines. What was it, a labor riot? Anarchists? A nigger strike? The paddy wagons and cruisers pulled in from both sides, and sticks and billies started flying, heavy streams of water splattering the marchers up and down the street. America's responsible immigrants were doing her light work again. The knives came out, the razors, all the Biggers who would not be bent, counterattacked or came up behind the civil servants smashing at them with coke bottles and aerials. Belmont writhed under the dead economy and splivs floated in the gutters, disappearing under cars. But for a while, before the war had reached its peak, Lynn and his musicians, a few other fools, and I, still marched, screaming thru the maddened crowd. Onto the sidewalk, into the lobby, halfway up the stairs, then we all broke our different ways, to save whatever it was each of us thought we loved.

Salute

It started when I was coming up North Gun Road on my way from the flight line back to my barracks. Bright and hot afternoon, in Puerto Rico. The heavy engines scraping the heat down heavier. Overhead the big planes pulled their noses up, or dipped them coming across the flat blue water, clearing thick palms, the town of San Locas, the long high metal fence, then down, if the pilot was good on most of the wheels, down onto the long flat runway, the engines churning and spinning metallic light across the tar and cement. When planes left or came in, you'd turn your head, no matter how many times, just to watch. Maybe only a few seconds. But watch, till the thing disappeared on the ground, to be wheeled close to a hangar by the grease balls, or off and up, like into the sun, out across the motionless sky.

I was walking slowly, or pretty slowly, in shabby two-piece fatigues, the kind with the color washed out. My fatigue hat was the same color, the brim frayed and bent so the edges fit down tight around my eyes. My stripes . . . there were two of them . . . bent at the edges away from the cloth of the fatigues, old soldier style, though I was only maybe a year and a half in, with another year and a half to go.

The air force was where I did all my reading, or a great deal of it. At least it was where I started coming on like a fullup intellectual, and got silent and cagey with most of the troops, and stayed in my room most nights piling through *Ulysses* or Eliot or something else like that. Sometimes writing shreds of literature myself, most times about things of which I had very little knowledge at all. Death or Eternity or Love or something like that, weeping sometimes at my fate, hitched like a common fool (I'd come up with the word Plebeian a few days before, and used it to insult my duty sergeant who just retorted by doubling my duties. And he didn't even know what the hell I was saying . . . though he asked one lieutenant later in the day, who told him . . . and of course the man felt more than justified piling it on me, who was, besides being an insufferable silent snob, a loose-mouth nigger . . . both at the same time) to the air force of the united states. Weep was what I did then, not even

really, those long nights, being actually hurt. I was bugged maybe, but
the thought of weeping was what animated me. It was deep and got me
into a zone of feeling I'd only guessed existed before. Once really in college I walked up Georgia Avenue pretending to be a faggot, feeling alone
and weeping in my hands. That was for effect. No it was a dull night in
the dormitory, and the hopelessness of the thing, the circumstance,
maybe, of being locked off the streets, by the foreignness of the city,
Washington, D.C., and the inequitable foreignness of my own changing
insides, drove me out, even against my will, onto those streets which
revolved slowly in the fog like moors. But those were solid beginnings, or
maybe the affair was older than that anyway, there are hundreds of
halfway houses to any revelation, and the simplest fact of vision needs
probably hundreds of seeings.

Tears then were harder because the social context was more normal,
that is, outwardly, college feeling, the twists of late adolescence, are everywhere advertised as American phenomena anyone should understand.
The army thing is too though, through the endless happiness of a Sad
Sack or Marion Hargrove, or the Jewish soldier, Sam Levene and the
good strong cowboy, who are bosom buddies and whichever survives will
in fact weep himself, over his friend's body, hugging the dead flesh to his
face, with the shells and enemy bursting all around this suddenly understandable passion. I remember seeing even a few intellectuals, shambling
stupidly through their agonizing paces, the meaninglessness and essential cowardice of thought being everywhere evident at least to anyone
who watched the thin four-eyed dope who covered the real world with
words that impressed the producer's mother.

But this real army life was, like any reality, duller, less flashy than any
kind of fancy, and finally a lot grimmer. So the quality of response, and
observation. I'd read all day when I could, or walk down near the
beaches. I'd read all night if nobody came in to talk or with an open jug
of rum, and similar sad nostalgias. (These from my few friends, other
fledgling thinkers and lost geniuses of feeling.) In those days we were
finding out things wholesale, there was so much we didn't know that
could be picked up even from the Sunday Times, the air mail copy of
which cost seventy-five cents, since it was flown down from the States
Saturday night to keep all the colonists happy. I made lists of my reading,
with critical comments that grew more pompous with each new volume,
even my handwriting changed and developed a kind of fluency and arch-

ness that wanted to present itself as sophistication. I made my own fric-
tions. I sent my own brain out into any voids I imagined I could handle.
Actual trips into San Locas for whores and all-night drunks were kept to
a minimum, since the projection of any despair I felt to be my own
responsibility, and wanted such revelation orderly, or at least completely
at my beck and call. I wanted to cry when I wanted to cry, in this sense,
like any big businessman, loving only those accidents that I could use pos-
itively. So the urge to walk around dark waterfronts or hang out with
ancient sex deviates or share the whore's bed with two other soldiers, I
kept to as few requests as possible. And just one deathly trip through the
off limits venereal disease capital of the island, hotly pursued by pimps
and their hunchbacked wives, who waved their knives and cursed what
they thought was an America I loved, would suffice for weeks . . . since I
felt then for the first time in my life, that words were equally as dangerous, or at least I knew they could set the blood flowing in my face as
quickly as the stale breath of any Puerto Rican.

But the only real thing reading does for anyone is to shut them up for
a few hours, and let the other senses function as usefully as the mouth.
Quiet already, a young man will grow sullen. Sullen, he will grow into
stone. But any "normal" most times noisy city half-slick young college type
hipster will close his mouth for all times, so ugly will have been the nature
of his re-evaluation of the world, and his life.

So the service became my first arena. The ideas that were coming in so
quickly (in Chicago a few months earlier I had made a vow to myself that
every day I would learn something . . . that afternoon I began to read
Ulysses) I tried to implement immediately, although most times, I was so
unsure as to what they were exactly, as life things, that I must have carried
a very heavy frustration around with me like a gun. Side streets were tunnels into myself, on all those cold days. Nights would open me up, or twist
my insides out, so that the blood of my desire flowed on sidewalks and
even, naturally enough, into gutters. Chicago was the town I went
through the most changes in. I slept with a couple of old women . . . or
maybe only one of them was really, old. She had some name that suggested the church to me. (Remembering, now, Lorca, and his understanding of the sexual basis to the Spanish Catholic church: Martyrs
staggering toward that specifically Spanish heaven, the bodies full of
arrows, blood shining, because of the painter's mind, and the sun drawn
with wide yellow staffs to portray it as divine. Spanish wars too, thick with

deep greens and purples, popeyed diers strangling on their horses, death everywhere, beautiful laceration of the world.) And that was more guilt, if that's really what it is that holds me so firmly to the world. At any rate I thought then, even so young, and still maintain that it is simple guilt that makes me move at all. Only feeling comes to me, and did then, plain and unexplainable.

Without a thought, then, I walked around that desert, and held my screams in check. Most times in reverie like dilettante *petit mal.* There were holes in the world. Holes everywhere. I filled them with whatever I could find. My pain, or laughter, secret learnings, and staring hours at my face, picking shaving bumps, in the mirror.

But now there was a thin blond man standing directly in front of me. He didn't know me. He'd never even seen me, before. (Maybe his mother got fucked by an escaped mad coon sex deviate who resembled the perspiration of my ideas. Or the father? I mean, there could have been some wild connection . . . did his wife buy a broom in my grandfather's grocery store? No. In the South or the North? Ahhh. No she never been there.

But now there was a thin blond man standing directly in front of me. He didn't know me. He'd never even seen me, before. (Maybe . . . but he recognized the clothes I wore, though he didn't like their style. He wdn't now, with what I've got on this minute, yellow corduroy pants, and a beard, so no progress finally.

He recognized I was in the service same as him, only he was thin blond stupidly stern, and he required a service of me. A duty. He watched me I suppose move past him, with story wind blinding me. I didn't see the cat, really. Or maybe I did, and figured I'd dreamed him, and wanted to dissolve him to get back to the part of the bit where I go down on the tall black girl in the swamps.

"You in a hurry, Airman?" I heard. He recited the Magna Charta and Bill of Rights before I turned without moving to see him as he rode in with the afternoon, hot and alien. "You in a hurry?" What hurry, would I be in. I had, I think I said, another year and a half in this shit. Where would I be going? I didn't know. I wondered did this cat really have something important to say. But he was a lieutenant. First or second, and maybe from Baltimore or Wilmington. A place nobody has to think about, except for the ugly edge of South in his speech.

"What's the matter with you?" I heard. He tried to remember Joe

Dimaggio's consecutive game streak, his mother's face, the key to his happiness, with fifty bucks a minute in a clean town near the Gulf. Shit, he was a human being too.

"Don't you know you're supposed to salute officers?" I heard. He might almost have grinned if I hadn't looked so evil. But that's the way I look all the time. Check my fan club pictures and see. All autographed "With Emotional Prestige . . . All Best . . . Ray Robinson." But I cdn't tell him that then. I thought he wdn't understand . . . that's the kind of prick I was.

When the focus returned. (Mine) I don't know what that means. Focus, returned. . . that's not precise enough. Uh . . . I meant, when I could finally say something to this guy . . . I didn't have anything to say. But I knew that in the first place. I said, "Yes sir, I know all about it." No, I didn't say any such shit as that. I sd, "Well, if the airplanes blow up, Chinese with huge habits will drop out of the sky, riding motorized niggers." You know I didn't say that. But I said something, you know, the kind of shit you'd say, you know.

Words

Now that the old world has crashed around me, and it's raining in early summer. I live in Harlem with a baby shrew and suffer for my decadence which kept me away so long. When I walk in the streets, the streets don't yet claim me, and people look at me, knowing the strangeness of my manner, and the objective stance from which I attempt to "love" them. It was always predicted this way. This is what my body told me always. When the child leaves, and the window goes on looking out on empty walls, you will sit and dream of old things, and things that could never happen. You will be alone, and ponder on your learning. You will think of old facts, and sudden seeings which made you more than you had bargained for, yet a coward on the earth, unless you claim it, unless you step upon it with your heavy feet, and feel actual hardness.

Last night in a bar a plump black girl sd, "O.K., be intellectual, go write some more of them jivey books," and it could have been anywhere, a thousand years ago, she sd "Why're you so cold," and I wasn't even thinking coldness. Just tired and a little weary of myself. Not even wanting to hear me thinking up things to say.

But the attention. To be always looking, and thinking. To be always under so many things' gaze, the pressure of such attention. I wanted something, want it now. But don't know what it is, except words. I cd say anything. But what would be left, what would I have made? Who would love me for it? Nothing. No one. Alone, I will sit and watch the sun die, the moon fly out in space, the earth wither, and dead men stand in line, to rot away and never exist.

Finally, to have passed away, and be an old hermit in love with silence. To have the thing I left, and found. To be older than I am, and with the young animals marching through the trees. To want what is natural, and strong.

Today is more of the same. In the closed circle I have fashioned. In the alien language of another tribe. I make these documents for some heart who will recognize me truthfully. Who will know what I am and what I wanted beneath the maze of meanings and attitudes that shape the reality of everything. Beneath the necessity of talking or the necessity for being angry or beneath the actual core of life we make reference to digging deep into some young woman, and listening to her come.

Selves fly away in madness. Liquid self shoots out of the joint. Lives which are salty and sticky. Why does everyone live in a closet, and hope no one will understand how badly they need to grow? How many errors they canonize or justify, or kill behind? I need to be an old monk and not feel sorry or happy for people. I need to be a billion years old with a white beard and all of ASIA to walk around.

The purpose of myself, has not yet been fulfilled. Perhaps it will never be. Just these stammerings and poses. Just this need to reach into myself, and feel something wince and love to be touched.

The dialogue exists. Magic and ghosts are a dialogue, and the body bodies of material, invisible sound vibrations, humming in emptyness, and ideas less than humming, humming, images collide in empty ness, and we build our emotions into blank invisible structures which never exist, and are not there, and are illusion and pain and madness. Dead whiteness.

We turn white when we are afraid.

We are going to try to be happy.

We do not need to be fucked with.

We can be quiet and think and love the silence.

We need to look at trees more closely.

We need to listen.

Harlem 1965

New-Sense

Nothing changed in the passage. The same world. The same decisions. Only the role is altered, the "facing up." Shadows stalk the same. Sounds hang. The hand on the face, knees bent to sit, quiet a fitful thing, and the honest people somehow cowed because they want to say so much filth on themselves, they cannot focus on the filth of their enemies.

I lived in a small town, and grew up in a small town. I lived in large cities, and was small-town in the midst of them. I lived in big mansions that were small shacks huddled against the screams of the poor. I lived fantasies in the center of ugly reality. And reality was the feeling I wanted, and escaped to, from a fantasy world, where I cd have everything. Where I cd be everything.

O.K., let it focus on women. My typing and thinking are slow after so long a layoff my fingers and the fingers of this skyscraper I carry around on my neck. But who can be involved in anything like screaming passion. Except your dick gets hard, and you want to hug somebody to it. You want some warmth. You want to lay back and look at the ceiling, and smoke grass and relax away from yr tedious ambitions.

Grey romance. On and on. It comes again. Like after the sudden summer, being jammed up in a room talking shakespeare at night w/ a white girl, and then going for that for the difference it made. The slight difference, which is no slightness, but a narrow turning that pushed on, means you have arrived at a different place. A different world.

But there was no burning screaming menace involved. No passion. Except the pushing and wondering if this was really the way beautiful things happened. The logic and rationales we posited. The sucking and licking. The turning and lying. The need to have each other, and be different for that.

But essentially you find yrself w/ someone and that's that. Unless some heavy thing can shake you. Or you're just an ambling hunk of swine and bone, just poking along, rejecting this vegetable, or eating all of them, making thick layers of dead rot, we must call our kindest memories. Our sentiment.

But unless you think about it, focus on it, romance is dream. And what is with you is grey dull heavy. Tho it can lead to the deepest flash connection. And the spiritual value of looking up in the dim quiet and seeing the same face is an umbrella of God. Why we feel so deeply things might possibly be "organized."

You can either sit and think about what you're doing, which is then nothing at all. Or move, and faster, and faster, and zooooom, not even maybe get the chance to feel what's happening. Nothing in private, nothing to think about, since it's all presented, and there, and present to be talked about, and murdered over. No reflection.

Dull romance. What life can finally be. What you sit and remember, and what you do, the really scorching part of everything, so fast it goes without you, though it has you in it.

What we produce leads back to ourselves. Input-transducer-Output. And from the last we know something of the machine that produced it. All accident and passion, or the black man in black or the white man in white, feeding variables into a known piece of machinery.

(O world I want to change you, and these fantasies are sundays in the wet silence, gathering my strength about me, clear and free, for a hard thing. Which must be done, and gotten, in order that peace come, and be free, and unconditional.)

* * *

We would be in love now. I could go make love to somebody right now, instead of hacking at this machine. Right now, lost second, I could. And pull them close to me, and be said to find and be in, LOVE. But there's a kind of raw thin quality to it. A slotting. That I'm reacting to. A fixity and predictability to myself, in that context that holds me away. Even tho the context itself, can never be predicted. (Unless yr abstract white man sitting with sequined beasts.

Their teeth. Their smiling. Shit it turns yr stomach.)

That close thing is always valuable. And only sick people want to speculate about it. Want to see it. When you can't see it. Nothing to see, except the voyeur bullshit, a kind of distorted diseased intellectualism.

But it's the same thing. Wanting to understand what's

going on, rather than just getting in it moving. Like Jake and Ray in my man's book. Jake moved straight and hard and survived with a fox in Chicago, probably, where he'd come home tired and drunk at nights after work and work this happiness over (her name was Felice). And Ray, a name I'd already saved for my self, sailing around the stupid seas with a "wistful" little brown girl waiting for him while he masturbated among pirates . . . dying from his education. Shit. It's too stupid to go into.

Can we make a world and do actual work in it? Can we find actual love in it? Everything. What provides the slim inch of satisfaction in life?

(But that's the point, "Satisfaction." What is that? Hulme spoke of "Canons of Satisfaction." He meant a hierarchy of what grooves you.

And what we try to do. Not try. The thinkers try. The extremists, Confucius says, shooting past the mark. But the straight ahead people, who think when that's what's called for, who don't when they don't have to. Not the Hamlet burden, which is white bullshit, to always be weighing and measuring and analyzing, and reflecting. The reflective vs. the expressive. Mahler vs. Martha and The Vandellas. It's not even an interesting battle.

Except we black people caught up in Western values. So deeply. Having understood the most noble attempts of white men to make admirable sense of the world, now, reject them, along with any of them. And the mozarts are as childish as the hitlers.

Because reflect never did shit for any of us. Express would. Express. NOW NOW NOW NOW NOW NOW.

Blood Everywhere.
And heroes march thru
smiling.

Unfinished

Coming into Jocks in Harlem, with friends and the inside redlit up middle-class faggots (no, homosexuals) scattered discreetly around, sharp in their new shit.

Summer evening, with friends, I said. Their faces float around, and their names. Love, talk, expectation, the leading on. The close light that separates the tribes of life. Where is the spectacular, and the handling of it, and the love of it, and the reward for its being alive and screaming? The love of everything.

Which is calm enough. These faces hanging in the calm, and the low talk and occasional soft ha-ha of a fag.

Then you sprawl and talk about what happened that day, that wild summer 65 uptown, when a lot new blood came in, and there were a lot of closer questioners of day to day making-it in America.

The atmosphere is important. Very important. The tales people will tell even to this day, of shit that simply did not happen. Feet walked by above us. You cd see some through a window. Few people made up biographies for them.

There were snakes and panthers in the town. Tho a lot of funny shit happened. A lot of fools got exposed. A lot of cowards. A lot of maniacs. Reality syndrome. Black people piled in the street. Negroes piled in certain nigger coolout stations.

WHITE PHILANTHROPY RUNS AMUCK AGAIN

Sit in a useless evening not even getting drunk. Just with people and make some remarks. Maybe these dancers were there that night, and there was nothing to talk about because you can't talk to dancers about academic shit like what the world is. So you can suck-sipping ale out the end of a glass, listen to some vague shit about somebody who told somebody else off, and not even be there. You could be in southcarolina murdering the governor, by strangling him with a wide belt, and your knee cocked in the small of his back.

People are going about their business. Somebody else comes in the bar, everybody looks up, the fags respond or disrespond, or if it's somebody somebody knows, there is a little more racket, before the half-white juke box takes over again. And maybe some lightskinned lady with streaks in her hair will wander in mission unknown.

All settled in time and space, another nothing to add to hundreds of others. The various freaks up and down the streets. Like black blondes or niggers with good jobs. Maybe junkies from southcarolina who came up north to get deadhooked forever, in the evil smells of dying blackness. But they, at least, are real. These dead junkies. In their weird outside world. But then another colored man will stop in the hallways of some shaky white philanthropy and talk to you like he was practicing to be a traitor.

A multiplicity of failures. But everybody, shit, can claim something. To have made it! Whatever. From whatever to where ever the wind blows enough dollars to cool out bad conscience. Facing us, on the street each day, thousands of fools and cowards.

So they all join hands and make a fool/coward cartel that controls the minds of ordinary men. And it is this cartel we work against, to kill them. Drown them in their blood, so that the mind might again soar to its completion and a new brightness begin.

We could sit and joke, or if with heavier friends, philosophize about the day, Malcolm's death, the number of faggots in The Big Apple, being careful not to offend anybody sitting in our immediate party.

And simple bullshit incidents lend a personal form to time. And all the facts we want are carried back with the specific context of their happening.

Red bar faces. The room tilted under the ground, just a few steps down. The gaiety of pretension. These creeps won't even get like in the Harlem Club, and tear the windows out. These are cool Knee Grows who have a few pesos in their pockets (earned by letting whitey pass gas in their noses). There is a cruel frustration drifts through places like that . . . places filled with young & old black boushies. . . . And you could think about white invisible things being dragged back and forth across the ceiling. Maybe they are talismans of white magic, secret, hideous, ofay mojos, their god waves back and forth over black people's heads, making them long to be white men. It's too horrible to think about shit like that.

This kind of thing can be entertaining or no. But it's always intimidating.

A guy came into this bar, probably just stopped raining outside. Very light sprinkle. And this guy comes in hooked up in these weird kind of metal crutches, where they have metal straps around the legs. A kind of big brown cat, bulky even strapped and crippled up like he was. He was making some kind of noise when he came into the place. Or it was some kind of rumble accompanied him in, limping like he was on those metal rods. He must been at the bar 10 seconds before he pulls himself over near our table. Metal niggers slid out of his way. I was not even looking.

But it wasn't me anyway. I'm here writing, this never happened to this person. It was somebody else.

At the table sitting watching him approach the friends of the world, all happy at being that. No, these shitty dancers, with lyrical eyelashes, and little tiny walks if they're technically male, just barely women. The women, the same, only it's not as spectacular to be women invert like it is for men. The burden of balls.

Oh the weird smiles that exist in life. Too much. To think about right now, but if you ever get a chance think about that shit. How many different kinds of smiles there are, and what they infer or imply or telegraph.

When the cripple cat came up to the table he says some shit, to one of the guys. Like he had seen him the other night on television. And the guy who had been congratulated for being on television gave a sort of pseudo-humble hero smile (which is not a rare variety actually).

Yes, yes, yes, (addressing the people in invisible dreams) Yes, yes, that is my work, yes, oh wow, groove somebody recognized he and set up the guillotine trap. A long terrorized scream, and the blade, bloody already comed whistling down. Trying to smile at people is experimentation or cliché. I have a standard good natural tooth viewer I use most times in such occasions. But was that me at the table. The one who speaks now. The heart that feeds me my life.

But this is a story now. There are facts in it anyway, for the careful.

This was a funny looking guy, he needed to stop

smiling so you could get a good look at his face. But that's probably why he kept smiling . . . a really fucking sinister smile . . . now that I think about it. Or maybe not sinister, but insinuating, dangerous by default.

And keeps talking and talking, ordering drinks. He began doing this the minute he got up to the table. And fairly loud getting louder with each click of my machine. He was very loud by now. And laughing. But the laughter was decoration for something colder than you ever ran into.

Yeh I saw you on television, and you gave em hell boy. L the minute I saw that program I wanted to call up the station and tell them crackers how much I agreed with what you were saying. Hand. Hand. Pats–shakes. Smiles. Crackers. Hunkies. All the words. I was watching. L was watching like he does, close up and steady, big deep eyes to see. And seeing, can you act my man, the question hung in the world hot as sun. But sunshine is cool, ain't it? It grows the shit from in my heart. It makes the earth magic start. It's cool, and beauty, ba-by. Ba-by. Everything is all right. Up tight. Out of sight. Went on and on, warm lights glows walk box walk. Be lady fair sister sliding down bars, Through Wars, and smoke of dead niggers, negroes, coons, woogies, etcetera, killing each other. Killing Each Other. Selves. Selves. Killing Each Other.

> I heard your thing,
> can you dig mine. You
> a success in the West,
> aint that a mess. Up in
> your ches' Polluted
> Stream. Dead fish,
> animals still to evolve.
> A fluke, like black and
> white together in the
> same head or bed, it
> makes no never mind.

He came at me, H had tied my hands behind me, got me in the face. It was bad, and blood came out.

> Where. TimeGap
> keys. Senseless
> Strung Gulls low
> over the sea. That

was another
incident in the
spanish lowlands
with Hannibal's
mulattoes, still
passing for White.
But yall cain'
fight.

Correction. The above is bullshit twisted from another time.

What happened. He was bleeding his twisted love. Like the story, and the image of piles of dead fish being broken in half by a jew to feed niggers at the seashore. Shure Rastus. We miss understand, by 3 and one half inches.

Bleed is it bleed bleed bleed. Love, they want white love and there's nothing like that in the world. There's no white peace either (Oh you mis understand . . . we sd *Peach* . . . simple colored monarch. "Arrest Him For Sodomy . . . He Fucked Melville." I'm in jail listening to the cripple now. He moaning inside he loves you so. Stand up L. He wants to touch you his mouth is close, with Vat 69 breath stinging your pause. He got pause thass why he teach moles to shit outta airplanes.

He was going to hit L. He loved him so much. He was going to hit. Him. Why he was screaming inside. Inside. Where the true song rages forever like the very sun. Inside he was screaming it was me not you you just said it but it was me I live and am hurt by the motherfucking world so deeply, much deeper than you what the fuck do you know what the moth-erfucking shit do you know frail ass motherfucker i'm a cripple hurt motherfucker you ever feel 10 thousand passion tender notes eat your face for time.

He raged now, dropping his crutches on the floor. Inside flowed on out. It was out fire down below, all in the street, fags look out, the cripple, a giant of a man, a motherfucker. . . . WATCH OUT L. . . . WATCH
                              And L, cool, said brother, what you
in to?

The cat came back from outside. He had another drink he came back over. Aw I aint into shit man. I used to sing my ass off though. He began singing. Something about love naturally. A song faggotass Tony Bennett used to sing. But this cat was singing about an actual kingdom, of kings and queens. And he disappeared smiling into the night.

New Spirit

I sprung my face and the brains fell out. I saw this little girl. I was sitting thinking about the time the plumber came, I paid him and he didn't do anything. I was in the basement, looking up at cold morning. My face was leaking, the furnace fire grumbled and I wanted to remember this story, a tale, to tell you, miss, before you left to ride the invisible flesh of the world.

They were sitting talking about you Bumi. About stuff they wanted you to be, and think, about an image they had of eating potato salad and going to the girlfriends. A cross around your neck. My face was covered with hot brains. They made a talk-noise, and the people thought it was me. Hello, Bumi, you still there, still hear me??

They wanted to be angry. Your mother frowned and murmured Christia like it was something she knew about knew, in fact, a christ-jew a beatnik in sandals with a psychedelic twitch. He seed stuff.

We beat drums through the talk. We beat drums. We chanted to you, baby, wanted you back. Nothing. But they said god was white and you could see him in the chapel of the unity funeral home, waiting for funerals. The undertaker was a stereotype nigger faggunder, taker. He was taking me, baby. Caskets start at . . . he went on picking his soul's nose.

Your mother knew that thinking killed you. It made you worry. She had no use for it. She probably right, baby. The shit I put on you. But not no wooden cross to carry. I wanted a woman. I needed the shelter of someone's arms, and there you were. My friend Jr. Walker put it thus.

Then the next day they wanted to know whether or not I was going to steal the baby clothes. The furnace of flowers around you. The silent bed. Your sandals. Your stepping rhythms pulling my skin apart, they wanted to know, if I was going to give your clothes back.

See that's what makes you paranoid, people saying shit like that. And being right among logs, and letters, toads never changing, the mist around that birth spot, where they settle into mud, returned, wait you can't unebolve (v don't exist for us) but there they go, back in the water.

Ceremony: Middleclass negroes
            Yoruba temple
            Nationalists
            Inch of Hippy
            Where was I? Why didn't I go?

I was there, love, listening to these people in the front room discuss the night in the hospital when they discussed the night in the front room. Serj can verify this. The night she came to me, in front of a burning building, and we invaded the starroads. And the other woman. And the other woman. And the long black sister she took. The other woman. We weep together. She is not asking me the same questions. She is floating against the sides of the room, being looked at, deciding, whether she wants to be a colored woman. You didn't have the choice baby, the way you came in, straight off the warm streets, straight into the future.

Now I'm getting something together to say. to them. to yr people, all of them. I want you when you want me again. We'll get together, hang out or something. Even your shadow has split. Nothing here but dumb shit, and me.

You want to talk to this cat called me from newyork with the white wife, no, i mean with somebody else's white wife?? No. You want to speak to Sandy or Linda or Moosey or Bobby, or JB or that fat little girl with the big behind? The peace lady? O.K., I'll tell them what you sd.

In the hospital the people didn't seem disturbed, they told jokes. We just don't realize how many people die. (You cd ride a bicycle O.K., you cd swim, you think this rational shit is easy. I shd cry or scream you cd dance like a mutherfucka', excuse the language, who'm I talking to peaceful dignified spirit, you still know me don't you saying mother fucka to everything and trying to find something, spirit help me love me don't leave me.

The flower wasn't dying by the window when i screamed at your mother. They hadn't sung in the afternoon then. They hadn't gotten lost trying to find the cemetery. The other tale hadn't been told, the one about the cat with two wives who lost again hands down to his own grim life. You know that story.

I hadn't looked down at this dead girl then. With hands folded, and smile-pouting. Her lips stuck out more in death, not mad, but damn there was so much she hadn't done or seen, which makes the shallowness of life that angels blank on so much, finally you know the shit's not even worthy of pulsating perfection. Oh love.

But people stood outside in the rain waiting to get in to see this dead girl. And the priest chanted, and the people thought and felt and acted, some wept. Some demanded an investigation of death. Some wanted to sue. Some wrote poems. Some got drunk. Some fucked women in the dark then, not knowing you watched.

I looked at the newspaper. I took a walk. I thought about a lot of things. I wanted a story, a tale, to tell you. Something you could remember of me, and yrself, to take with you long journey; you were born on the 12th, the second fifth, the reach, at the fifth round, into new humanity. I'm at 7. A first knowing. The realizing, that when I die, if this is last I'll come no more to these shitty towns. This little girl that dances, don't be jealous of her spirit, she's in a box out somewhere in newjersey. Somebody's gonna build a bench nearby, out of stone. I might come out some late afternoons or mornings, very early, still wet and cold.

It's about love, yes it is. And about feeling, and who we are, who we really are alone joined up together with so many hearts to the beginning of the human epic. (I told you these people slid down the rock, plop, back to the one-celled, they thought it was hip, to be so positive.)

We'll be alone without you creative child. My youth. My tenderness. My warm creature with the big ass and lips. What we knew turns to dust, at this very moment. How fast you can travel. Baby. How much speed and jive with you, so much, so beautiful, I can't quite understand. What can I educate you to now, you know so much more than any body. You left it. The dumb part of what I remember. Not even a story. And I know this doesn't make sense.

No Body   No Place

The shapes in the darkness had histories. Falling out of windows failing to become mayor of their mothers' universes. We must work together, put on the right brightness. The clothes. Our robes and gowns. Stop killing each other, wheel to face the actual Killers.

I wanted to do this and wheel. And wheel. And wheel. And be. And couldn't. Monkees walked on my fingers. People misunderstood. In such a short space, to rise. To float. To be the other. Above the skin. Bones tossed, left. A will in the left of the desk, in a brown envelope. Do not dispute what is there. Of light and despair.

To keep from thinking, which is evil. Sky does not think. Nor trees. To stand at the edge of that feeling because I couldn't use it. Instead I'd be in Alabama with the fire. In the shadow thrown dancing by the cracker's ego. And them. They'd get their shit together and try to leave. They'd try to throw it all out. They'd try to start again. And grown children, who one day will be faced with the same prerogatives, the same alternatives. The same lies, and crisscross. Trying to grow. Trying to be good people. God people. God men. and Women of the earth and sky.

* * *

The telephone rings and it is a friend of mine. Who talks smoothly and softly about things I am interested in. To back and take away your yes from, your eyes from, the event. The torture and manhoodmaking. The final step with hands open, and eyes open, to embrace whatever. I could not get angry at the tortured. I could only hate myself. And love them beyond their knowledge, and they rise anyway. They reach anyway. They make their moves, as I make mine. But at the level of each his separate adjustment to being God. To being owners of all that there is.

* * *

Many years ago I wanted to be myself. And still I walk that same line. This

209

man whose life I watched. Whose soul is mine, and another's. This child beaten for his love and his stupidity. In the earth fire wind of the era of our captivity. When we dressed like beasts and walked into enclaves of suffering like cowboys. Hair glued separately, identifying the part of the world we'd been oppressed in. Dirt and dust, and torn pants. And big eyes blacked and tossed dumbly to the ground, and held by our friends from the final killing and disappearance into the woods of life. Where the sweet fruit and inner adventure is. My lovely woman with me, in long green and softness. She stands there smiling, with me, now, forever, as something turns colors and sweetens the forest itself.

But in a stark black and white tube. With my brothers and sisters on benches for sale. And the beasts themselves darting in and out inside, in their capes and revenge. The machines. The rumbling insides of the robots. Inside her "chest" the motors whirr. . . . "NUrse NURSE," the name she responds to, stumble-walking toward us, rotting Kate Smith, hands outstretched the mummy a missionary to help us, to cover us over with dirt, again, but we rise through, flowers, in bright colors, even trampled we rise and hug the sun and sky and are strong, believe me, strong.

My brother stands there beat and bleary eyes. His friends with him shambling, a rude group, a motion, a place in the universe. "We demand to be loved. We demand to be alive. We demand to be looked at like human beings. We demand that we are always so beautiful. And dirty. And bent. And drunk. And ignorant. And praying to mover of universe. To the east or the west or the south or the north or the pointless no place in space world of loves and adventure. All place are us and God, and we demand in the death shadow of the yellowow world, something for ourselves. Our friend here is hurt. Is injured. Help him, lady."

And he stands there with his opening of the sweater, and his droopy pants, and shows the stab wounds. The blood and tearing gap. His heart just beneath it, throwing the blood to the top.

* * *

in the sticks in the sticks in the flying thin money for somebody dirt a lot of us lived together through this. You read the newspapers? Have you seen that statue of Lincoln? How it's turned green? You walk down there near the jew with the busted head. In the army navy store. And the pimps in sam johnson hoods bending so cool. Fulla punks of the universe in exactly the same order as we.

There were the neighbors and whoever lived here. With us. Whoever passed through in sinister laments. Pointing the shadows, conducting their own adventures. They'd hurt, and look in the mirrors of our silence with big shoes, stomping the music book a blue stamp a final agony for the soul gone weak in the seas.

He was a man who'd glued himself to that life. His hat, and rolly girth, a speech like that, and himself flying toward a basket, not sure of the shot, but the power was definitely, hip. We are the zigzags of our own design. Is it secret? Are they walking the streets each night with hands in their pockets to see God? Or what? I mean why are we here, if you don't know, sit down, be calm, zippppppppp.

I couldn't be but sitting here seeing and hearing. Like phones and pointed grimaces. white dudes answering the no for our lives. I couldn't walk stupid or unfeeling or in hip germany, forever. It was my own life. I looked at it. Watched it in other people's eyes. It was nothing to me but real.

So what can I say to remember. The smooth thing, you think you want. You want to label me. Describe me finally for an elk.? "Why yes, you fool."

* * *

I saw (that) man. The drifts of his life. In sequence. A dance a masquerade of effects who which were will who plys the place, moving. Exact any trip. Back. Exact any trip. The same. And no fooling no lying to the lord the god of ooooooooooo his own foreverforce. . . .

I thought I was talking to a schoolteacher and wanted to explain something for him to teach. When someone asks me to react. When I do. It's not for real. It's lower than that. Tilted somehow, black people. I know what I want to see, am the only one. . . . but he passed, he passed. he's slow his taught his is a moving being of the one thought the one the one.

This is an exact crevice. This is a sunrise like seeing the logic of the white castle. The hamburgers and gauze hats and little cups of coffee and orange drink. the slavery. I know these girls want something to fill them up. they can't long so need so much leap out of themselves to grab at the essence of life. They are always.

The gas talks. Water. solids. Animals. Understand the total meaning of the world. Understand what men are for. What they will be. If he could crawl up the street waving his arms and drunk with the idea of loss, drag himself up, and think about the giants he warred against, and and what and crack it, oh god what have i done?

This is the silhouette of the man. The flashes of light. Signals from the future evolutions, the future worlds that we will be there. What we make and are, we long for our strength, as a completion of the energy we project.

Now and Then

This musician and his brother always talked about spirits. They were good musicians, talking about spirits, and they had them, the spirits, and soared with them, when they played. The music would climb, and bombard everything, destroying whole civilizations, it seemed. And then I suppose, while they played, whole civilizations, actually *were* destroyed. Leveled. The nuns whimpered with church spears through their heads. Blind blond babies bled and bled. Dogs ate their mothers and television was extinct except the image burned in it forever, in the future soft museums of our surviving civilization. A black way. A black life. From the ways and roads of the black man living, surviving, being strong.

But when they stopped, the brothers, they were not that strong. Like any of us, the music, their perfection, was their perfect projection of themselves, past any bullshit walking around tied up unspiritual shit. They could be caught with white girls, and talk unintelligibly, or sometimes around one's glasses a little sliver of white fear would idle, and he'd laugh it away, and talk about his music, shadowboxing, practicing his survival and perfection.

Mostly their peters slammed them, and brought them lower than themselves, or the need to live, like to have money, and be whole in the tincan halfassed sense the white man's way, which he put on us, and is still so much a part of all our lives. (A man on the radio explaining blackpower.)

I mean they could only talk when they were not playing. As I can only talk, or feel the frustration of needing too. Of not sitting in the circle of circumscribed light. Reeling. Passing. (Like my dead lovely girl, passed, passed, passed, gone.) Getting into the next level of vision. Seeing and being. I want to go. I want to fly. Lift me spirit. Help me. Just talk. That's all. With the tongue in the roof of my mouth. Just spirit. Nothing but. I hurt. I want. I need. All these endless flesh frustration categories. Which are only that. This is a saint. No place. This is a god. No where. This is a feeling. Me. I am all feeling. Here by the wet window burned in its tone. I am all the not being that my limit has set, not knowing yet my whole. Yet

I do and can not speak with my entire spirit. Can not fly. Though I understand the need. The way. I do not can not be do are. Walls. Walls. Lie in the death of the almighty. Wishing.

Like I write to keep from talking, and try by that to see clear to where I must go. Chakra. Enlightenment. The seven lives. The many planetary adventures. Air fire water. Scale. Hung in the balance to see the deaths. Tell them horns. Tell them words. Tell them example of a man little man with big eyes went away came back grew loved made things died without point, in the history of no world and the world passed, the continent sank, and nothing but nothing was ever accomplished since everything was already done, and what more could be done.

The brothers cast shadows in the world, and tales were told about them. They told tales about themselves. One was short and one was tall. They scared a lot of people because they were new. They *were* spiritual. But not like Norman. Black Norman short brother brought to my house one afternoon, he was looking like the passer, like he knew more, than any of us. "You think it's about personalities." He said that. "About personalities," and the door swung open sunlight, no, nothing, came in, to the force of, to the heart of, my self. I cdn't speak. You think it's about personalities. You think it's about your self. Whew. was in the air. I see him years later standing in a doorway on 125th street, the ways of men. Further out, gone, than any of us. Even now, with the wind of God blows through me. "Come on faggot," his face turned on 130th street in that stance of hard ashy elbows, and read the deep cowardice of a wd be killer. All of the would be killers, cowards, and dancers with high fists, killing the village white killers. And the killer, JM, the soldier, subsided. To darkness of more fears, and another road he had to find, having seen the fire in Black Norman rage into heavens we know nothing of.

Black Norman, was not always Black Norman either. He was weaker too. He was not always in the rain on the street in the doorway communing with God. He wanted money. He wanted his flesh. He *thought* he was strong sometimes (though in his weakest moments). God of Norman of God of where I touch. Feel this, and pass. All you dudes. Feel this, and pass.

But they, the brothers were pals of mine. Good friends, in a world of alligators and shitheads, lunatics, happy liars, cowards, white people. There was warmth. There was something done, in our inch. But God knows. God chooses whom he will. (Your prerogative, ol man, to call

such, knowing the blue eyes of the will, of the days, of the number passing, all, such, and me, and the. . . . heart stopped, girl, please, I want to
know, where's the door I came in yestiddy, where??? I cdn't, don't, and
they look at me, I want, ... stop it, stoooopidt!)

My pals and me, against everything. It seemed. They made music like
heaven's bowels. I loved them in the sound. They loved women tho. Like
Amos and Andy in the Harem of the Butchers. It was a conquest they
thought about winning shit. Like boys. The tall one was all boy, a kid,
really. Raw, like they say, of new kinda gunfighters type. The other rooted
in a cleaner rhythm than the world around him, though he created the
things that could weaken him. Responded. There are invisible allegiances
in our bones. Things we must look at. Why? The smoke of smells. The
web of things we've touched or seen. Womb-earth.

People can be corny at the same time they're not. Can reach that?
(Children line up against the wall and select your failure machine. He's
going down, wind, scarf badarf waves, hello clancey jackson sits on the
steps looking at the girl, can grow, the g clef vibrates hairs pussies, con-
glomerates of afternoon triumphs, evening walks across the floor, as
beautiful. They want to be Gods. We must desire god and his ism.

(I can describe one guy tall with a large adam's apple. With wirerim
glasses and sneaky smile. Sneaky high up there, pardner? Har to breaf???

The other more flash gordon without the popsicle. Maybe a joint
sometime. Whenever. And a white tuft of sparks thrust out his lower jaw.

This is the scandal of a small town that all the stupid people are the
same as in a big town, so they seem, stupider. Dig?? So the lovers, seem,
S-O-M-E-H-O-W, loveier (is that a category of human espresso??)

Sometimes they looked like Batgroup unemployed. No place, like, to
hover. (In all honesty, this is a one-way street, come back, the shit's
changed. Evolver, which is different from revolver, which has long hair
and kills. Even in song.)

"Black People We Must Take Over This Planet As The Prime Possessors
Of Natural Energies." Red Hook always wanted them to write a song with
that as the title, but they didn't when I was "knowin'dem" (a description
of bat-street, in back of the sixteenth dead president, in bronze and the
key to the city in the future brain of the tall basketball players dodging
father divine's hustlers on the street. You cannot ask for more than
immaculation????? (I cdn't wish no worse on you.) Except we need each
other. Red Hook would lecture like Sun-Ra sometimes, when Ra is talking

to certain corny niggers about selling out black people. Bat-group would leave for the midwest at night, zooming, and blowing, and come back hooked up, literate, in dey shit, fresh.

Or trailing chicks around, they'd go get the energy to do that. Here. One's wife was somewhere and somewhere else. One was a pole. Like wood. Wresting a killer humility. A egogod, telling the shadow of what you claim you never had. Or left, the older ones claim to have gained knowledge through error. And how much of that is really true. Guess?? And they'd follow, or one would, Red Hook, or the source. Maybe rubbed on Hook's coat or African shirt. A dazzle, a stink glow of the source, the possibility of being kings and loved men of a strong people.

They wanted a show. A place. It was good and bad. There too was too much slack for bad wind. They schemed, and darted. Made shit, and you think, didn't realize it? Think about yrself. You do the same shit. People watch. They watch from across the street through the window with their linoleums drying in late afternoons. They chart your life. They know you walk on glass splinters running shit, like on the radio. Murray the K type shit. "We've all seen what you can do, man." JB talking.

So they'd make both scenes like on a bridge, going to Europe with the Snowmen, then coming back with the key to the invasion of the warm countries by the barbarians, the coldbeasts. And snuggled up with one, a lady, MY God WHAT WOULD THEY TELL THEM BITCHES LOCKED UP IN COPENHAGEN? WITH ICE BLOWING AGAINST THE WINDOWS. AND SOME SHIT HAPPENING IN NEW YORK OR CLEVELAND DIDN'T INVOLVE YOU? YOU DIDN'T KNOW??? WHAT??? and come back to Atomic Bomb shit.

"You shure yo' shit strong enough, my man??"

Ornette in a hindu Edwardian sack of jewish bass stealers.

But it is in an age of The Miracles. Which must be put to work for us. All our energy. Even the brothers must finally be used for the lot. To raise u. To fly us all into the grace we seek. Which is, without light what they mean then by, Power. Amen.

The night I want to talk about they had gone to this girl's house I know. (She was sort of an unofficial city limit hostess in them parts. And she had a sickness then, covered people, turn them into different parts of a whole. You want I should characterize that whole? You want I shd patch my wings or retreat to the cellar to brood? It was spread so clean and cool tight got mucho everything-o actually, everybody had some of the shit inem. People stood around. Music was playing. Slick thin insect pee pees were uncovered. Screens full of air. And the aspirations of all the neighbors, in that particular part of the earth, they had rent to pay, get up next day for hip jobs, meet head on with the white unicorn unfortunately being ignorant and blowing bugles on the top of the baptist churches (UNCONSCIOUSLY, MOTHERFUCKER, ALRIGHT!!!???) to warn Cary Grant's boys that eastboots were about to slay them.

Is this the scene yr *avant-garde* shit degravitates?? In-habitates?? Ya Wohl, marches out the plank splashes into the little rich lady section of universal attention. A vibration in the yellow pages. Pussy for sale!

Aww crisscross shit. Crisscross shiiiiiit, yeh. Reall crisscross shit. People opening and closing doors. Telephones. Creep business being done. Yeh. Singing chicks. Chick wd stand there like some mediocre white lady with one-strap gown and janis paige button and lion eatin her ass, really swingingk.)

The husband was calling for the muslim woman. She was devout and weird to the poorer americans. "ALLAH WAS VERY HIP." That's a photomontage of success. "Yesh I was righteous before Bud or Elijah." Meanwhile, there is a trumpet player fuggingkher. He's hip. He's a spiritual beingk. He's spooky. He knows about ghoses. He's a strongbean like John Carradine of duh good guise. He's fuggingkher, riley, really. You goddam catholic pay attention to the meter!

"You mean. . . . What . . . naw . . . really no kidding. Really?"

Yeh it's the tall brother . . . yeh, goes in the room with the broad, then she gets a call from whatsaname, the hostess, that this muslim dude is comin. Like her husbain. Yeh.

Was he playing earlier that evening . . . tall brother? (Nobody here to ask, children playing in the streets. Gentle movement of the earth.) But anyway around that same time he walked water legends with his sound and grew into something he'd never be except in that thrust of his own invisible energy.

Chick hears this and panics. Everybody in the joint did. Hostess. Lil brother. Lil bro's woman, who's really pinhead priest's chick, stopped making it with funkybutt the organiz for a minute, took up with higher math cats. Maybe bealbelly the mystic ex-photographer saxophone player who has speakers inserted in the stones. They blah. They blah. They blah.

Cat comes in finally, the muslim. Tall brother splits to the bedroom lays on the bed under the cover, stiff as wood pole. (Remember I described him befoe??) Hostess pins him almost faints. Muslim chick, OPuretwat the black beauty, pulls it all off, except for a second she fades into the bedroom for a suck off a burning joint. Frozen for a second, in tableau,

the shit is run successfully
muslim chick and her husband
leave

another frozen moment (EXCEPT THE RUSH OF ALL THINGS IS THE RUSH OF ALL THINGS AND ON IS STILL EVER WAS AND IS NOW OMMMMMMMMMMMMMMMMMMMMMMMMMMMMMM THE END-LESS)

Then everybody unfreezes and a loud cackle of success in America rises up from this not really humble abode. Lil brother is happy, and puts on his newest record. Hostess titters walks around touching her guests on the arm. Tall brother finally comes out of the bedroom sez, "Shit, that cat cdn't seen me anyway, even if he'd come in there. I was really a ghost."

Exactly before the laughter

Answers in Progress

Can you die in airraid jiggle
torn arms flung through candystores
Touch the edge of answer. The waves of nausea
as change sweeps the frame of breath and meat.

"Stick a knife through his throat,"
        he slid
          in the blood
            got up running toward
              the blind newsdealer. He screamed
           about "Cassius Clay," and slain there in the
        street, the whipped figure of jesus, head opened
      eyes flailing against his nose. They beat him to
    pulpy answers. We wrote Muhammad Ali across his
face and chest, like a newspaper of bleeding meat.

The next day the spaceships landed. Art Blakey records was what they
were looking for. We gave them Buttercorn Lady and they threw it back at
us. They wanted to know what happened to The Jazz Messengers. And
right in the middle, playing the Sun-Ra tape, the blanks staggered out of
the department store. Omar had missed finishing the job, and they staggered out, falling in the snow, red all over the face chest, the stab wounds
in one in the top of a Adam hat.

The space men thought that's what was really happening. One beeped
(Ali mentioned this in the newspapers) that this was evolution. Could we
dig it? Shit, yeh. We were laughing. Some blanks rounded one corner, Yaa
and Dodua were behind them, to take them to the Center. Nationalized
on the spot.

The space men could dig everything. They wanted to take one of us to
a spot and lay for a minute, to dig what they were in to. Their culture and
shit. Whistles Newark was broke up in one section. The dead mayor and
other wops carried by in black trucks. Wingo, Rodney and them waving at

us. They stopped the first truck and Cyril wanted to know about them thin cats hopping around us. He's always very fast finger.

Space men wanted to know what happened after Blakey. They'd watched but couldn't get close enough to dig exactly what was happening. Albert Ayler they dug immediately from Russell's mouth imitation. That's later. Red spam cans in their throats with the voices, and one of them started to scat. It wigged me. Bamberger's burning down, dead blancos all over and a cat from Sigma Veda, and his brothers, hopping up and down asking us what was happening.

We left Rachel and Lefty there to keep explaining. Me and Pinball had to go back to headquarters, and report Market Street Broad Street rundown. But we told them we'd talk to them. I swear one of those cats had a hip walk. Even thought they was hoppin and bopadoppin up and down, like they had to pee. Still this one cat had a stiff tentacle, when he walked. Yeh; long blue winggly cats, with soft liquid sounds out of their throats for voices. Like, "You know where Art Blakey, Buhainia, is working?" We fell out.

*   *   *

Walk through life
beautiful more than anything
stand in the sunlight
walk through life
love all the things
that make you strong, be lovers, be anything
for all the people of
earth.

You have brothers
you love each other, change up
and look at the world
now, it's
ours, take it slow
we've long time, a long way
to go,

we have
each other, and the
world,
dont be sorry
walk on out through sunlight life, and know
we're on the go
for love
to open
our lives
to walk
tasting the sunshine
of life.

Boulevards played songs like that and we rounded up blanks where we had to. Space men were on the south side laying in some of the open houses. Some brothers came in from the west, Chicago, they had a bad thing going out there. Fires were still high as the buildings, but Ram sent a couple of them out to us, to dig what was happening. One of them we sent to the blue cats, to take that message, back. Could W dig what was happening with them? We sent our own evaluation back, and when I finished the report me and Pinball started weaving through the dead cars and furniture. Waving at the brothers, listening to the sounds, we had piped through the streets.

Smokey Robinson was on now. But straight up fast and winging. No more unrequited love. Damn Smokey got his thing together too. No more tracks or mirages. Just the beauty of the whole. I hope they play Sun-Ra for them blue cats, so they can dig where we at.

Magic City played later. By time we got to the courthouse. The whole top of that was out. Like you could look inside from fourth or fifth floor of the Hall of Records. Cats were all over that joint. Ogun wanted the records intact.

Past the playgrounds and all them blanks in the cold standing out there or laying on the ground crying. The rich ones really were funny. This ol cat me an Pinball recognized still had a fag thing going for him. In a fur coat, he was some kind of magistrate. Bobby and Moosie were questioning him about some silver he was supposed to have stashed. He was a silver freak. The dude was actually weeping. Crying big sobs; the women crowded away from him. I guess they really couldn't feel sorry for him because he was crying about money.

By the time we got to Weequahic Avenue where the space men and out-of-town brothers were laying I was tired as a dog. We went in there and wanted to smoke some bush, but these blue dudes had something better. Taste like carrots. It was a cool that took you. You thought something was mildly amusing and everything seemed interesting.

I talked with Pinball and the blue leader about Ben Caldwell's paintings . . . the one where the guy is smoking the reefer. We thought about the changing reference, of our new world. As it stood already in the old ruins. And we all felt like Bird. The old altosaxophonist . . . but the limits opened out into the pure lyric tone of powerful beings. But when the Sun-Ra tape came on this blue dude really opened up. He dug the hell out of it. Perfect harmony these cats had too. Boooooo—Iiiiiiiiioooooooooooooo . . . daaaaa ahhhhhhhh aaaaahhhhhh . . . booooo OOOOOOOOOOOOO ooooooooooaaaaaaaaaooooaaaaa

Claude McKay I started quoting. Four o'clock in the morning to a blue dude gettin cooled out on carrots. We didn't have no duty until ten o'clock the next day, and me and Lorenzo and Ish had to question a bunch of prisoners and stuff for the TV news. Chazee had a play to put on that next afternoon about the Chicago stuff. Ray talked to him. And the name of the play was Big Fat Fire.

Man I was tired. We had taped the Sigma. They were already infested with Buddhas there, and we spoke very quietly about how we knew it was our turn. I had burned my hand somewhere and this blue cat looked at it hard and cooled it out. White came in with the design for a flag he'd been working on. Black heads, black hearts, and blue fiery space in the background. Love was heavy in the atmosphere. Ball wanted to know what the blue chicks looked like. But I didn't. Cause I knew after tomorrow's duty, I had a day off, and I knew somebody waitin for me at my house, and some kids, and some fried fish, and those carrots, and wow.

That's the way the fifth day ended.

March 1967

God and Machine

The present, like the past, is laughter and hills, where from to listen. Understand if you can, blood. The all—the every. The solitary is the unitary—development. Of everything.

We were sitting at the edge of civilization. The missing teeth & split heads of our fossils were not yet in place in weightless metal blocks. Or dark spots on rubbery granite smoke. Magnetic sounds intoned behind and above, wherein the supplicants, not a precise word—rather the *applicants*—could apply themselves, and expand their capacity because of the ancient energy, and how it told a story and built a future. Progressive perfection.

The earth could be bare and silent. Husbands and wives all gone. The single unit of energy heralded the perfection. An emerald eye—a pyramidal jewel of smoke. All voices and music lunged at high consciousness through and amidst. Tied together like flesh or metal. And lived. And lived. And changed, again.

Because true civilization would come even after the worship of men by machines. The great computers linked together through space in hymned rhythms, actually worshiped man. The species of ape yet with "hair," and uncivilized ways. But the beacon of energy, the fire nucleus, persists. Like the stare of sunlight creates life itself. There is a hotter brighter huger great immenser sun. Invisible to baby species, but father mother pregnant cause to itselfs endless reproduction throughout space.

All the knowledge & experience was put into machines to code & store & ultimately *grade*. The machines became judges & final scientific arbiters of life and evolution. And they themselves evolved and passed from artifact to organi-fact to mental self projecting communalized intelligences.

The ancient men gave themselves to the machines with the obsession of finding a purity impossible among themselves. They, the last cycle of the visible, having survived the presocial warmakers, conceived of what the beasts meant, and what they would do was perfect a distorted arithmetic. Their own and the beasts. The great cities rose from filthy infested hovel gatherings. The primitive "individualists" were slain in the streets & power released to circulate throughout a new system.

Cosmogenesis brought the moving cities, the intermingled earth sky water experience, where communal intelligences the ancients called cities or nations (the latter "the most creative unit," hence the largest) came into being, which energized & transmuted by collective will formed into single mobile units, which themselves moved, changed forms, grew mated and created.

The early nation-giants, primitive cosmogenetic forms, literally melted and entered the cell magnetism & created the giant. The consciousness of the person(al) cells expanded with additive melting & cross-entering.

The sole planet experience had been replaced by multi-planetary experience. The seas were explored & settled. And the great cosmogenetic "lovers" moved in harnassed collective consciousness into whatever elemental context they decided. They moved from plain to planet to sea to be planets, systems themselves. The philosophy was the lifestyle & life span. Great beautiful machines of the cosmos.

But the continued worship of man would be like ancient presocial warmakers regarding their corpuscles with special awe. The term "man" fell into disrepute or disuse.

This particular tune, a cellular primer, will form the basis for larger music dealing with the creation of visible soul. (We must be near where probably other forms preceded our mwalimu.) It is necessary to "whistle these jams" so that the mental passes rapidly to the spiritual. (These were once even lower forms. The presocial miniature forms dealt primarily with them. Called physical-intellectual. An expansion cycle stretching the short period from ice to space ages.)

It is the great machine music form of visible soul commune that indirectly preceded ours. The lost vestige of "specialization" or later personification. The invisible became visible.

All this developed while great machines roamed through space & water, and beneath the planets. The energy intelligence asserting nuclear predominance. The great machines were Gods to men and men were their Gods. The exchanging of forms from solid to gas from human soul to spirit—a still continuing process—left languages written in the wind.

It was the first revelation the humanized communal computers had. Their *creation,* developed in a leap away from their creators, that moved them great distance beyond and above the simple hymning of ancient, tho evolutionary, information.

The spiritual revelation of the Ujamaa computers. Sea air planet subplanetary experiences arranged in the tonal points or "Gods." (Dig the ancient mss of Sun-Ra.) Expressed simultaneously by *all* the great machine-Gods, created the new era in which we now live. Everything, as it was, disappeared. The "invisible music," exchanging cultural forms, in constant revelationary consciousness, "appeared" without appearing in lower seen. (It is difficult to express *seen,* except it was not as hip. Seen placed whatever in some *special* hence not general context and limited experience. Unseen developed, first as "theory" then known, tho it always, like all forms, "existed.") Until, as now, it predominated. The unseen communal computers were our direct ancestors. Which brings us almost to the present age. The age of desired completeness, I would suppose we'd call it. We have called it that already havent we? The total unit magnetism draws us. All this is memory bop. Blood. To carry the new right home.

Organic nation factories roaming invisibly closer to one another. Each huge and loving. Are we finally atoms or men or suns. We are Gods and machines. And the magnetism lessens the machine of us. It is the magnetism that is the music structure, the sound, the life, the flow, the intelligence, the cosmogenetic factor, itself. Our name is magnetism. As the unity forms our name is the single intelligence. It is the music itself. It is all that is created, the creator the force the single all everything 0000000000000000000000000000000

Imamu
14 Aug 1970
wa mwaka ya Dabuka-Gaidi

6 PERSONS

A Longish Poem About a Dude

An Introduction to *6 Persons*
by Henry C. Lacey

In 1974 Amiri Baraka completed a highly autobiographical fictional work entitled *6 Persons*. According to Baraka, this work was an effort to record his artistic and political progression from his New York experiences—both Lower East Side and Harlem—to the early days of his return to Newark. Although it was originally commissioned by Putnam's, the author noted in a 1991 interview with Charlie Reilly in *Conversations with Amiri Baraka* (University Press of Mississippi, 1992) that the publisher expressed dissatisfaction with the final work and reneged on the agreement.

The long-ignored manuscript of *6 Persons* presented a number of problems. It consisted of 229 pages of primitive photocopy with frequently indistinguishable punctuation; missing words; occasionally indecipherable handwritten additions, corrections, and abbreviations; and orthographic inconsistencies. Moreover, there was, on occasion, evidence of missing text.

Upon receipt from Lawrence Hill Books of a newly typeset manuscript, and assurance of Mr. Baraka's sympathy with the proposed work, I began in earnest the task of editing *6 Persons*. This work was additionally facilitated by my receipt of a Scholar-in-Residence appointment from the Faculty Resource Network of New York University, which afforded me the opportunity to immerse myself in the editing of the manuscript and to confer in person with Mr. Baraka in Newark. The exchanges resulted in agreement on the standardization of those aforementioned problematic areas as well as the general revising and critiquing of the overall manuscript. Generally speaking, Mr. Baraka resisted any effort to bring "political correctness" to the document, preferring instead to have the novel be an honest reflection of where he was—both politically and artistically—at the time of the writing.

With the exception of the opening section, "I," which appeared in *Selected Plays and Prose of Amiri Baraka/LeRoi Jones* (Morrow, 1979), the novel is heretofore unpublished. In a number of ways, it is Baraka's most sustained and ambitious work of fiction. Completed in 1974, it, like *The System of Dante's Hell* and the stories of *Tales*, is based on the author's life. Unlike the earlier works, however, *6 Persons* moves "straight ahead" from the streets of Newark to Howard University, the U.S. Air Force, Greenwich Village, Harlem, and back to Newark (called Finland Station in the novel). This in no way suggests that *6 Persons* is the conventional bildungsroman. Although clearly the fictionalized rendering of the author's "furious passage," it is presented through a shifting narrative presence or point of view and without a dominating protagonist after the first three chapters. The latter sections of the novel are, indeed, notable for several key figures, each of whom bears some striking similarity to the author.

Comprised of seven chapters ("I," "You," "He," "They," "You [plural]," "We," and "We & All"), the story is told from several points of view. The opening chapter ("I") is a first-person rendering of the self-absorbed world of the preadolescent, blissfully unaware, for the most part, of the harsher realities of a racist society. The second chapter ("You") is an interior monologue wherein the central character revisits the influences and experiences of his formative years—family, friends, popular culture idols, preparatory schools, churches, colleges, and so on. In essence, this chapter is presented also by the "I" narrator. It is tempered, however, by a deepening cynicism. The third, fourth, and fifth chapters seem to be related by a street-wise, urban griot who follows "LJ" and/or "Bro" from his Air Force days to the feverish, "blacker-than-thou" milieu of the cultural nationalists in Finland Station. The sixth and seventh chapters ("We," "We & All") are presented, first, from the point of view of the disillusioned cultural nationalist and, finally, the embryonic Marxist.

A reading of *The Autobiography of LeRoi Jones* (both the 1984 and 1997 versions) evidences detailed treatment of many of the experiences noted in *6 Persons*. In this fictionalized handling, however, the evocation of the era is impressionistic. The lyrical, suggestive, and private ruminations of the various narrative voices present not so much a novel as "a longish poem about a dude," to use the words of the speaker of the "He" chapter. In contrast to the *Autobiography*, *6 Persons* is not meant to be analytical or "archival," as noted by Baraka in an interview with this writer.

As noted earlier, in the latter chapters, *6 Persons* does not focus definitively on a central figure. Instead of the sharply drawn "LJ" or "Bro," we see a plethora of characters playing the changes on what we have come to know as Amiri Baraka's lifesong. We follow their exploits through the narrator's use of the all-inclusive and accusatory pronouns "they" (invoked primarily in reference to the Beat coterie) and "you," "yall," and "ya" (referring to the uncompromising and angry cultural nationalists). This tendency is evidenced also in the final chapters, not only by the speaker's use of "we," but also by the presence of such characters as Burt Corliss, Mickey, and Barney, all of whom reflect, in a markedly cubist manner, pronounced facets of the real-life Amiri Baraka. The novel's resolution is suggested via the final chapter, wherein the experiences of the (1) reluctant scion of the black middle class, (2) budding intellectual/soldier, (3) Beat writer/ivory tower aesthete, (4) angry race warrior/socially committed artist, (5) idealistic cultural nationalist, and (6) budding Marxist (i.e., the six persons) all come together. In chapter seven ("We & All"), the author acknowledges the necessity of these various passages in his movement to authentic selfhood: "Endless series of selves resolve, and at each pt [sic] of progress, we are whoever we must be to develop and reunderstand reality."

With the publication of *6 Persons*, we are given access to yet another vital and defining piece from one of the most influential American writers of our times. In this work, we see also the powerful handling of those ideas and stylistic characteristics that we have come to expect from Amiri Baraka. The crackling street idiom as heard by his unfailing ear, the unapologetic love and thorough knowledge of black music, the frequently scathing humor—all are present in abundance in *6 Persons*.

I

Who can speak of their birth? Years later someone can testify as to its alleged meaning, heaping on years of subsequent rhythms, edging it toward whatever ideal has come to please them. I am not who was born, nor even less who was thought up. We are all projections of some one, some great being, some be-ing, a verbal process ongoing even today the window presses its sunny-rainy presence, young bloods laugh fight hug day to them. On-going. Be-ing. So I, is a process, a be-ing. Flash back to the beginning, you are adrift in speed faster than light.

I thought sometimes I was here as Jesus to stunt and be crucified. I thought on Dey Street all these people here know I'm Jesus, and they just makin' believe they don't. Blankin' on divinity like that. And I'd try to whip around and catch them staring. Almost caught 'em that time. Mattie McClean I definitely suspected of digging the actual and not wanting to give it away. Lorraine, some others. I wasn't sure the Davis family knew it. But some people on that street, and environs, I was sure knew, and were just being creepy about it.

Was this the way it went down. Jesus in Newark on Dey Street trying to figure out why no one wd just come right out with it. But that's absolutely weird now. It ain't really, but it is to everybody hearing it I guess. The sickness I was weighted with, if it was, and it was, and is. The Jesus Nigger, I guess because I knew no one else had all the shit that was going thru my head and feelings going thru theirs. But that must be simple abstracting of the world. Simple capitalism. Imperialism. The greed of the "I," so removed, totally, from every other be-ing that its process allegedly goes on singularly, unrelatedly, totally in isolation, great Horse Testicles! Its goldern legend reaching, its beam a fold of sun around the devil's haid. He on a calendar, cool, and detached. I dug them flicks of Jesus on the calendar. Like Ron O'Neal in *Superfly*. The hairdo, but he was less hysterical than sfly, never imaged as pushing cocaine, had his own thing he pushed. Marx defined it as dope tho?

Why I wanna been J.C.? The schizophrenia of the African slave then a yng colored boy in new-erk, bashed by weird stuff.

I thought later about expiring in the electric chair for some reason. That was *Gangbusters* Saturday nights that produced that. Strapped in a chair with hoofbeats mashin' up the hall. Somehow that whole projection left me unsettled. I thought it cd get me, even being Jesus. God-Devil that came on Sundays, and the Jesus thing too. Warden Swartzkopf, black head, was the keeper of the gangbusters, and he sounded like he could get to me.

I wanted to be everything I ever thought of. At 12 years old, I remember that if I'd been born in 1933 I'd have been 13. That was on Dey Street near Sussex Avenue. Near Joyce's fence, and Mattie's house. But all of this is simply to introduce the I. The basis of struggle and weight of absolute craziness. (Not madness, but craziness. Like it just wasn't anything real to me. Nothing. Everything was a figment of my imagination. I created it. Thought it up. It wasn't real. And since then my straight and difficult task has been to convince myself that I am actually in the world, and not vice versa.)

But if I wanted to make a strict chronicle of I. And not be rent and twisted by the weighted flashes booming in, the cackles and silences. The simple shut doors and screams inside my head. It wd be difficult. To make such a straightforward document of my life. Because in fact sometimes I yet cannot face understanding that my life has been a roll of minutes. A series of absolutely connected images, being born and passing almost at the same time. I think my life an incredible maze and blotch of shadows, circuses, dives, and floats. Much sadness. Much happiness. Mostly expectation and desire. And yet it is all here in me to be rerevealed reunderstood.

1934 October Kinney Memorial Hospital

I don't know what happened. That's not real, just reported to me. Kindergarten in the wind. Kindergarten at central, a room, with children whispering in their hands, coats on a table.

Later I got sick and went to the hospital and learned to read. While with measles and chicken pox and whooping cough, which I went to straighten out first, the others came. Kissing a little girl at night in the next crib, we padded out the crib and exchanged diseases. So Ho hospital. When I got back from kissing Meta in the isolation hospital I knew how to read. It was experience that did it. The diseases, the isolation, the little ol' girl and me in the nighttime in the hars-pital. And then Target comics, and the Targeteers. That was easy then, coming beneath such heavy experimentation with life. Yeh. Alone in the hospital, miles and miles away, that void of warmth was filled with words. And Meta(?) at night, the necessary Black adventure. All real and unreal. But existent in me, an everywhere song covering my breath and be-ing. Rising laughter at a tide of happiness, hope, blue feeling. I knew how to read good when I got back, in kindergarten . . . kinny garden . . . Targeteers, in the little chairs. It be cold as whatnot outside and I was readin', jim. And everybody cd dig it!

I's hung to a ribbon of multidimensional minutes. Amen.

Was it the city that made I so crazy? The total environment, of personal history. The history of ah race. Nothing so grandiose, yet precisely that. I carried and carry in me, always probing the maximum consciousness of existence. I could read. I could walk in the halls. And in me then, and now, to some extent. A knowing urge controlled my daylight giving eyes. In a dark hallway my eyes wd light it up, wheeling around like meat lighthouses. Taking in every inch of every existence. Climbing a fence, a spotlight, twin spotlights, wd bathe the yard. Bloods in the house pull the curtain, squinting. Smile or ball up they fist. Some, momentarily blinded, would listen to Lionel Hampton's "Flying Home," in 1940's spook-america, happy, hapeeeee!

I didn't like to fight. The spooky room I carried with me, on my neck, or sometimes like a vacuum chamber, the world squeezed in. Stared at endlessly. I tasted it, felt it, was beat by it. Sat up at night, hearing weird sounds. I looked at shadows, saw old mysterious men with filled bags of questions. I talked to old drunk wino ladies across the street. (Miss Ator.) She was hunched over, spitting. Men went in and out. Old dudes with tore down bulky skies. In an old shaky house leaning to one side. Eddie Clark was in there running in an' out, grinning. Mysteries mysteries mysteries. Yet somehow interpreted as mysteries and understood simply as that, mysteries. I had the consciousness of myself as anything. Sometimes good looking. I'd keep that one afternoon. I wanted my hair to look a certain way. Like combed kinda round, and wavy. My skin wd be shiny. I'd have on some kind of shirt, or maybe moccasins. And you know be clean. I'd like that, being handsome. Then sometimes, I had a pimple and'd be ugly, and sorry to be ugly. Or my mother (another eye) would have some jive on me. Some short suit, or funny lookin' tie or something. I'd be in church, or with her with some people patting my head or hand telling me I looked like my father. Of course I did, and my sun, look like me. Over and over again, tho that wasn't bad, being told that, it was just repetitious. Everybody, said that. Everybody. Oh, he look just like his father. Ain't he the spittin' image of Roy? Who else I suppose to look like? Thank god I dont look like you.

I had a dog name Paulette and the hurricane came and blew a tree down on the dog's house. I think that's what happened to Paulette. That hurricane came and blew a tree down on our bathroom, busted in the roof. Nature was right on our case over there. Another time, it snowed the day after xmas, 5 feet deep, or something, and we had to go help dig the school out. One time Roosevelt was giving out money for killing Japanese beetles. And they was everywhere. We had bottles full of beetles.

Also we had tomatoes in the back yard and a fig tree. Across the street some white people lived in a red and white house. They had cherries and peaches in their back yard. And we were always over there raiding. They had a brick stoop. There were white people in that block. Angel Cordasco, Angel Domenica Cordasco lived on one side of us. On the other side a vacant lot, and driveway to our back yard. They had a big hill we used to play on. Was a house there once. And next to the hill, Old Man Doyle. My grandfather used to call him Ol' Man Doyle. Old red-faced white man, and faded wife. The white folks with the cherries directly across the street, and next to them some poorer crackers jammed up in a brown and yellow house. A dude named Dominick, a crazy dude always running around talking some stuff. He was an ice man. A little ice man with a ice pick in his belt. Then next to him the Days. About 11ty 11 niggas in a alley, in the worselooking house on the block. Algernon, Lonel, Board, Fat, Rookie, Evelyn, Will, Frank . . . Mrs. Badass Day, like a lady Joe Louis wearin' them niggas out daily. A buncha others. But that's all I remember right now, other names'll come. Then another cleaned up white folks house, little nasty snotty nose italian also named Rookie. With little ugly twin sisters tied together in a harness crying. That was the center of the block, on both sides of the street. The center. And under my house, under the stoop, was where our famous club, the Secret Seven, met and ate kits and drank kool-aid and plotted to fly.

Around this center, to one side across the street, a vacant lot next to the cherry and peach yard, with its white fence. An old gravel yard, with something at the back I never understood. Then Miss Ator, with Eddie

Clark in there. Lorraine who went for my cousin next to him, Mattie, then Joyce's fence and yard, and around the corner New Hope, where some folks still singing praises to the creator of everything!

Going toward Central Avenue, on that same side after Board's house, then Rookie's house, then cement, for a parking lot for a factory, then Dannie Wilson's house, and his grandmother whippin' him. His funny brother, and even funnier cousin Clarence, who switched his whatname from the time he came into the world, sucking his thumb. He immediately got more ambitious. On my side, after Doyle, the playground, then Central Avenue School, and the corner and cold big-time Central Avenue. With white folks offices and auto parts and other stuff I cdn't use and so wasn't really inerested in. After Clarence's house on the other side, silent brown houses church folks lived in and a restaurant, white enamel outside where schoolchildren ate lunch and office and factory workers ate. Past Angel's house going that way, nothing but a big factory where they took stuff in and out, off a loading dock, it stretched to the corner.

Sociologists do yr mangy thing! Analyze this neighborhood. Negroes and Italians. And an ol' oirishmen! See but there's more jimmy! Around the corner on Nwk St. Jammed up with bloods, po' as spit. But that weird neighborhood with even an old tenement in it, among the two story houses, which we really thought was way out, all them ol' po' niggers stuck up in that building like that. Dam, they all in there? It sprinkled with Italians too, and their house generally better than ours. And at the corner Mary Ann Notare, at Sussex and Nwk Street. But across there, same street going to Orange jim jam and them and a hallway smell like pee. That little cross-eyed girl. Plus "The Frenchman" Lafayette, and his sick brother Sammy. He is the one who set dogs and cats on fire. Plus Lawrence and Vivian, J.D., J.B., Ralph, Pearly Mae, Shirley the present wife of the State Assembly man whose ass we getting ready to kick, Frank Cox, The Boose Brothers, also Augie Delappi, Staring Johnny with the strange disease, Norman. Newark Street that was, just a zoomed up version of Dey Street. Integrated neighborhood. One way, you look up a jail, with big stone walls, a subway. Mhisani, lived up at the corner over the subway with Himaya, Harold and Jackie, then. Plus Bad Edna Fields who won all fights, legendary in her time. We went up to Irvington to battle the Italians for her just last year. Go another way through Lock Street where Karolis, a really ugly, snotgreennose stupid cracker, a Greek, I fictionalized for a play for some reason. That was the goofiest doofiest most backward cracker in school. We used to take tech on him. Even I took tech on him. Or at least messed him over every day I saw him. Hey Karolis you dumb bunny!

Why I later then tried to sanctify him in fiction???? Who knows? Ora used to beat him everytime he laid eyes on him. Maybe I felt sorry for him. Big Shot wd punch him knock him down, kick him. But Karolis he just acted goofy. Lock Street Black Norman who said of the Elks that they were "them lidda mens." Leroy Griffith, Leroy Griffin lived on Nwk Street, and they were related. Lock Street was worse than Nwk Street with even poorer Italians and Greeks. And we ran together and apart. We played and fought. And we always won around there because we dominated. Across Lock was Baxter Terrace which in those days was segregated, blacks on one side whites mostly Italians I guess, on the other. Anthony Arlotta was one dude I hung with in school at least and a dude named Thomas Ravell who's probably in some advertising agency cutting his competitors' throat. But the Days—Norman Danny Eddie—were my young out-in-the-street running buddies. Were these the very beginnings?? What is that? The very beginnings the very end, of the I. Exactly that, and nothing else, but this material throbbing substance—readily "identified"—I've followed yr work, it is a policeman talking through a bullhorn. "I'VE FOLLOWED YR WORK!" Is it a threat, the demeaning I, so surrounded by exact limitations?

My beginnings in the dust of the thundering herd of Egyptian sky deities. In the sperm riding slippery tracks to fertilize me mutter. I AM. I AM MMMMMMMMMMMMMMM one hollow ring, a billion fleshy rings, around the universal egg.

My beginned in Community Hospital, called then Kinney Memorial, after a light-skinned Negro who rose to the top of the bloods. Like they say they named buildings after him, but also a street, W. Kinney Street. From there we lived across the street from the pickle factory in the Prudential Projects. To get hit in the head with a rock, by some dude, for a major trauma. To get hit by a car in front of the house, major trauma. (I don't even remember this, it's been told to me . . . the rock I remember. The throw of it, out there under a hard brick light. A brick side the knot. The why of that is no longer in my mind, tho the seeds of it are what grew up big perhaps the reasons people still do that are probably still existent. I called the rock out?? Awww. As goofy as that sounds, it's probably demonstrable.)

Same place, this earliest of memories, where I was abandoned by my self on a fire escape. This story has been told often, it's probably being told now somewhere. I was on a fire escape by myself. A yng dude out there, just a little ways from the opening to the ground! But I didn't go for it, to write this, I edged back and sat looking at the unconscious streets. Cars & stuff. I think I remember that. Having heard it a number of times. Where a man came to teach us ghetto yoots how to play tennis. Nobody learnd. Maybe they did . . . I didn't. But there are dudes from the same neighborhood that did learn, whether they learned it from Bro Francis (the wdbe teacher's name) or not, I'm not hip.

Where I saw girls walk and could not claim them. And so made up fantasy lives in which we were together some way. Then and later than then and later than then, and later . . .

I had a life in which I wd show up at dances alone, and look at people dance. In which I wd fantasize about being able to dance, but could actually dance. If I wd only dance, I wd put under the fantasy, knowing I cd if I only wd. Have dared to open up the whole self construct to anything that was interested, except on paper years later, knowing everything, being omnipotent. How impotent, actually, when it is the world in which life is and where it must be lived, not on paper, as westernized folk wd have us believe, it is only life which is important or valuable. Only life and its projections are but it's displaced or reflected.

But I also had a life, in which I wd later show up with friends, and a sense of community appeared and we circulated to watch the few down dudes among us get down, and wd comment like we do, wishing we was the ones. Eyes still, flashing. Whole nations come into being. Old historian rail on. I was a young black child in a hostile world, yet the hostility of that world only slashed in at moments. For instance when this cracker at the Bronx Zoo, an attendant, answered when I held my nose and asked how he could stand it working in the elephant house, said, he lived in Harlem, he could stand anything. And that was a splinter of hate went completely through me. I did not bleed so complete and swift, underhanded even. The little bigeyed boy, brown skinned, roundfaced, off checking closer than most, who walked and laughed with the group. Miss Powell, the only black teacher in Central Avenue School, had taken us on a trip to the zoo. She was the only teacher that ever took her classes anywhere. You dig? Like the African Free School being started as the first free education for black or white in America, because of our needs. And

the poor whites, the longed for working class they show their revolutionary zeal by hammering at black children with putrid distortions of the
world . . . that hurt and shape, but they will get it all back, hard as the
hardest known element in creation, revolution.

Eyes, I, bigeyed boy. Popeye, they used to say, trying to put me down.
Hey popeye. Hey that dude look like a Martian. Hey you little Martian.
Hey pop. Hey Eyes! (I's, over and over, and over and under, the water and
the land, the years and the faces, I sought through the eyes to find yet my
self intact, and waiting to begin.) Is it that they called me omnivisioned
spectacularly endowed, in the seein' dept., or just funny looking . . .
maybe schizophrenic. Hey I's! This man can definitely SEE! Which meant
I was, on a very low level, a seer.

But with such physical see-ability, how come the world came down in
fragments and splinters. In flashes and rhythmic thuds, rather than whole
and initialed, considered like history, real and usable. We need a whole
story to see whole, to be really and truly holy. Meaning in tune with every
thing. All the reality, its multiple addresses, and parallel appearances.
Awash in a see of others. Yet the others (I will talk about those eyes as I's
as others, as theys, after . . .) many times have a thing, a bigger more positive (active in touch with reality) self. An I. A presence, an ego, put
together in stone and steel. In charter and theory. In law and society that
will inundate yr splinter truthed eye. Will cover over like the famous quivering blob, yr lonely loving I.

I–W. Kinney St.

I–Douglass-Harrison

I–Boston Street

I–Dey St.

I–8th Avenue (after McKinley Jr. High experience, moving from black
domination in integrated hoax to white domination and black subjugation. I, I, I, I sd, I did, I went, I thought, I felt, I wanted, I didn't, I wdn't.
Yes, it was me. All these parts to the same I).

I–Belmont Ave.

I–Hillside Ave.

I–Eckert Ave.

I–7 Morton St.

I–402 W. 20th St.

I–324 E. 14th St.

I–(Somewhere on 17th Street)

I–27 Cooper Sq.

I–4424 7th Ave. (109 W. 130th St.) (This is questionable, to hold yrself up to ridicule. It's not sympathy I want. To kill this I, but change. Transformation. Not death and transfiguration. But life and transformation.

All all this shd have been the milk I drank, bigeyed in my carriage. Across from Tolchinsky's pickle works I'm saying I shd've been told about Tolchinsky and all the Tolchinskies of the world. Maybe I cd've helped the bastid. But then I's can only help I's and then not much. But maybe I cd've helped myself? No chance?? But you shd tell me what the world is. Tell me what it is, and who I am in it. Instruct the I to see. Tell it all the things your eye has seen these twenty million years on earth. As the ships the engines the ideologies are ready for the great I to rise from this planet.

I lived with a brown family named Jones and they were family to I. I slept in the house with them I and my sister Elaine slept there. I slept and went to school. I climbed out of windows and back into them. Shot off guns in the playground, watched dogs set on fire, back and forth up the street to school. Being born, moving every few years, like we do, back and across, the town. I cd say it was unfeeling, yet joy and rapture unforeseen, linked our hurts, our black eyes together, and made a strength I knew but didn't realize till much later . . . caught in the death urge of the oppressors.

Trace that growingup, through the streets, and to the gaslight in Boston Street, where a yellow light allowed my grandmother to pick glass from my slashedup knee. Like an operation with the midnight oillamp flickering. Busted my head open befoe, you know. Broke my collar bone falling off the stoop. Broke my hand. Measles, chicken pox, whooping cough, mumps, one summer they thought it was meningitis. Plus I got hoarse every summer. And still growing, growing up, growing to what? In the years of turns and twists, still confused, turned around. Splinters and slivers of everything, flying in, upside which way. Strained through red glass, strained thru silent eyes turned to the ground when they shd have been locked deep in mine. Explain the world. Clear up this twisting darkness not my self. This blank explosion draws my tongue and eye and ear toward simple silence. Nothing. Explain the world. Let this I come into it. Growing, to what. Flash Gordon. Governor Roosevelt of the Uncle Don world. Wash white. Kato. Tonto. Who? Explain the world, singers, preachers, walkers, outrageous loud talking brother who ever, sliding in the dust sidewalks.

Always walking toward my own face. (And who?? Then next category to rise. I'm watching . . . who?? Next bub, bud, bloom, fancy dan, riding o country port wine bottles turned up night cold summer IIIIIIII seeing this. IIIII, in love with it all. It's real. Not even that. It's there. I can see it. I even smell stuff. Yeh. I I I I I I I, explain the world. Please. Never stop however. I see me changing forms. From midget, to midget. Of all I survey. I stand, and let it roll in. I take it all in, drink deep of all around me.

Barclay Street, Boston Street, West Market Street, Rufus Spa near our church, and a little yard to play in, like Obalaji, I'd run around and play, my man, play for all I was worth. West Market Street in them days was pretty fly, Julius' big grocery store, like what a super market wd mean today, and my grandfather was in tight with Julius, and we got stuff on credit and they delivered, and the place smelled boss . . . right up the street from Bethany.

West Market Street, so much of my life spent near there. The Grand Hotel, Bro Russell, big time no. man clean as daylight. Don Newcombe, Monte Irvin, Leon Harvey, Pat Patterson, Leon Ruffing, Larry Doby, Lennie Pearson, all hang out in there. Tough life. With my father watching the Newark Eagles win the black world series, the Negro World Series, I'm sorry. Very Sorry! A no-hitter opening day, raring back then, and all the bloods' moufs fly open . . . jim. Too much. A no-hitter, opening day. Tell me a cracker did that?? Of course (we) . . . all the I's threw the cushions out on the field. And the cracker never let I^{100} have them again. Who needed them seats?

W/ Rheingold and Vat 69. Schenley's and whatnot. I was a heavy hot dog man. Get me a hot dog and some root beer, jim, and it was me, in paradise city, digging the purity and body and flavor of the world. With my old man who knew about all that. He told me about that. He filled that I complete. Dudes wd say, Hey, Roy, this must be you. Look just like you man. You mighty mf-in' right, my man!

The Negro National League was perfect, and so Jackie Robinson was constructed in a small laboratory in the California Hills. Although they never perfected his speech. The way he talked was a dead giveaway. I knew the minute I heard him he wasn't no authentic blood. You cd hear rubber valves contracting when he said "guys," or "jackie robinson." He

really sd, jeckee rawbinsun. I cd spot that right away. A plastic man to
break up the Negro National Leagues for Branch Rickey and unnamed
white millionaires.

But then some I's end up going for the blanks. Negro-Blanco coopera-
tion. Sleek white cadillac, and under the hood 360 niggers in tennis
shoes. Yeh. Man. Yeh Boy. 360 niggers, a nigger for each degree. Some o'
them niggers got degrees, and they under the hood too. In Ko-rea,
Vitnam, some bloods spilled they blood in Salerno, Cherbourg,
Bougainville, Tarawa, yeh, gotta a good thing goin', a goods thing, still
still goin'. And I's goin' for it. Goin' goin' for it.

Can you remember the Negro National League? I do. And the world
champion Newark Eagles, down 'eck at Ruppert Stadium. All the wild
pretty bloods be there sunday afternoon. After church, and that madness
dealt with. Goin' through the turnstile wit' my fadda. It was beautiful,
beautiful. Colored society blasting . . . till Effa Manley, the light skinned
lady what runned the team, told Bizz Mackey about the coming of corporate capitalism. Bizz was the fat manager what had to get another gig after
the going of his world champions to the crackers . . . since Doby, Irwin,
Harvey, Ruffin, Pearson the heart of the squad split. Into the big time.
Just like you bloods fount out about integration down south, since you
was screaming for it. Some eyes screamin', marchin' in d.c. Wit' Rabbi
Prinz and Walter Reuther, drum majors for JFK. And then this old blood
principal look up in Waltavista, SC and he the janitor in the integration.
Groovy groovy. Very groovy. You got a good thing goin' for you DuPont-o-
Gulf. The straight man for mephisto. I can't believe in no devil no more,
he got too much power. Can't even let the cracker be no devil, no super-
natural shit. Just natural shit. Natural shit what got to be cleaned up. I got
that devil shit from P. John Rome's slow s&m man. Squeeze yo' peenie in
a minie.

This was a whole thing we went for in the '40s . . . artificial light. Nigger
turn the corner looking for Jua/Panga, get Westinghouse and G.E. Be
Maaaad! We shall overcome, true enough. But what, to do what. And how
the I get to be all that heavy?

All this time I had been posing for photographs in various parts of the
universe. Turning my self into another me, to yet turn, and be returned.
All the way round. That whole 360 degrees of niglews, be my self
whistling hey like with a chain. Most times an invisible chain, singin hey
bar ba re bop! But I didn't pose like no Louie Jordan tho I cd dig "Joey,

Joey, Joey-Joey-Joey . . . Joey, Joey, Joey, Joey-Joey . . . Moe and Joe had a candy store, sellin' numbers behind the door. Cops come in and Joe run out. Brother Moe begin to shout. Run Joe! Hey the man at the door. Run, Joe, and he won't let me go." I cd dig that. Still do. Cd dig Louie and his tympani five. Caledonia. What make yr big head so hard? He stone cold dead in the market man. I kill nobody but me husbin.

But I never pose like that. I always pose like a little colored boy. Smilin'. With bald head and gapped teeth. In funny little suits. Sometimes with my sister, who cdn't smile. Sometimes I posed alone, with a ball, on Belmar Beach lookin like Amiri . . . anyway. Or in a tub, looking like Ras Jua. Or in a coat and hat at the World's Fair lookin like Obalaji. I's, and big eyes staring into the future. Hoping somebody wd tell me the truth. Tell me what all this is.

This is my story. I. I tell it like I want to. Follow the eye, and you'll see.

This is my story. The story of I who was born in north east america. An African youth, hid under cotton futures. Hid under slavery, oppression. Hid under my people tryin' to make it, tryin' to raise me. Tryin' to put all slavery oppression behind them, when it was on them, in them, in front of them. And mid '60s bloods still saying we shall over come. And how the I get that heavy.

This is my story. The story of an I. A Black I, growin' to pieces puzzlin' them pieces together. The slivers and slants. The fake magic, the pure political subjugation of the little boy. The little sweet roundfaced big I'd boy. In the crib. On the fire escape. In the street hit in the head by a car. In the park hit in the head by a stone. In camp watchin' niggers do it to each other. Watchin' lil homosexual Max go from tent to tent, tryin' to get in the present tense. An I to see the various pieces of life in america. Because that's what this was and is.

This is my story. The story about an I who was raised in urban America, in a middle class laboratory, a middleclass negro laboratory, resting in the blood community. Where you went in off blood street, and entered the magic land of confusion and aspiration. Of grand fathers and small fathers and big uncles and sweet grandmothers and pretty mothers. I swore my mother was the most beautiful woman I'd ever seen.

In those laboratories, connected by tunnels to Bethany Baptist Church, to dance classes, to events at which the Negro National Anthem was sung, and shivers of unknown delight wd buzz my brain, to wake me up micrometers to say, yeh, yeh, dig it, a Negro National Anthem.

This is the eye story. The story of a brown I. Growin' in spite of all the delusion, and mixmatched values. Struggling with radio, and movies and my mother and father's hallucinations. I cd lie my can off. Yeh. Lie. Make up stuff. Create. Yeh. Look, POOF, this is a whole 'nother thing here. Can you dig it??

But an I that lived in a brown house with a porch, and hung out underneath the porch plotting the coming Revolution. I had sent a letter to Roosevelt with a detailed drawing of a moving-fort, on wheels. Roosevelt never answered. I never understood that. Nobody mentioned it being in the papers, or on the radio. Hop Harrigan never mentioned it. Roosevelt simply *never* answered. (Obalaji writes to Nyerere!)

An I so confused. At Robt Treat (now Garvey). Central Ave. McKinley Jr Hi. Barringer Hi (Highwopdistrict), Nwk Rutgers (when the only building they had was down on Rector and near the library. And the only other bloods was a long headed dude with glasses named Conrad). This one cracker, an old snuffy smith dude with tobacco, wd always make cracks about the woogies, and we I guessed just grinned and took it. But never grinned nowhere near a grin under the skin, nor am I sure I grinned on top, just finger the tuba, tryin' to be Miles Davis. Did that cracker know about Miles Davis?? Cracker are you alive anywhere, no. You ain' alive. Yr dust ain' alive, it cnt fertilize a nut. At Howard. Confuse. At FSU. At New School. At Columbia.

Speed of light take the I. From a little boy at Douglass Harrison, to watchin' my son run up the street with an orange in his hand.

I lived in various houses. Went to various schools. Played various games. Liked baseball (infield, but poor arm, cd always get on base, and run. Slide head first into home. Later pitched (!!!) that's weird, how cd I pitch with a weak arm, cdn't make the throw from shortstop or 3rd base, I cd play 2nd. Football, swift running back. Scatback. Run back punts, weave along the sidelines, throw them fakes, and tuck it in. Cross the line. Yeh. Cd do that. And catch. Cd go up and catch and play good defense, intercept, tuck it in, and get down, cross the line. Cd even play line. And make the tags. But light in the behind. Played good playground ball, with all the highschool pros.

Loved football. Went also with my ol' man to see the NY Giants. But that was big-time white stuff, and it sat off away from the heart, but still the roar of that, the bigness of that, the wildness of that, tho impersonal, cd transport the little me. And I had Em Tunnell, the defensive genius, to pick off passes, and do the blood number duck and dodge all the way in. That was real and direct and like the monopolists cd dig, straight for the nigger's heart.

I dug football.

Red Rover.

Ringaleerio.

Higoseek.

War.

Running around chasin' each other. Climin' fences. Explorin'. Goin' weird places in the neighborhood, like new worlds, up over the used car roof, where there was gravel, and you might cd find stuff.

Everything was more dangerous and less dangerous, at the same time. Getting busted for stealing out of white folks' cars on Central Avenue was terrifying, being taken down to the station, to talk to the white man sittin' at his desk, with my parents standing behind me, lit me up, in terms of cold fear and trembling. But also it was so way out only the fear not the reality took me. And doing it, trying to get in those cars, taking that paltry rubbish was for us only taking stuff that was static, it wasn't active or being claimed. Sitting there for our adventure.

It seemed I was always at the pit end of some adventure. Faced with lies backfiring or tricks that didn't take. Effects from dubious causes. For instance why take that money from the buffet shelf and go to see *The Fighting Sullivans*? No logic to that, cd I dig I'd get caught. And how up tight my parents must've been, not because of the dough, a few measly quarters, but I stayed to see that flick 4 or 5 times, all day. From early in the morning until late at night, about these 5 Irish brothers that got killed in the War. Wiped out this entire family of Irish character actors. On a ship, a flaming carrier, and drunk Thomas Mitchell weeping. I wept a few times, peed on myself, and my head started hurting I was so hungry. Trying to go home, from the Proctors over to Dey Street, I felt sick, and so rested, laid out flat, on a garbage hamper, hands under my head, and rested, I had to walk that Central Avenue hill from Broad Street all the way. A dude stopped his car, and came over, a white man, and asked me if I was all right. I sd ok, I was waiting for a bus. Then got up and trudged wearily, my wet pants sticking to my leg, back to the house, where blood parents leaped with 44 foots.

What made you do that?

Answer yr mother, McGhee.

What made you do that?

The devil.

What?

The devil.

That must have been a high comic dialogue. I sd the devil I guess believing that. Why not. If it's wrong, and that dude is in charge of wrong stuff, then you need to get on him. I got beat with a toaster cord, beat half to death. But not clear to sanity!

I stole from my mother even. Why? I wanted the dust. And I didn't feel it was "stealing," just that was where the dough beed. So I was unbee-in' it.

I really don't know. What's to know. Just I thought I needed the change, and used to take it. One time, in the South, my mother caught me going in her pocket book which was left in the car. Again, some kind of weird strap. Plus fists, smacks, grunts, cries. So infuriated was my mother. I was scared because my mother never hit me with her fists, usually just a strap. Which hurt, and brought fear. But fists, was like some extrafamilial attack. It unnverved me, but only temporarily restored my sanity.

"Yr mother and I have decided to stay behind you," my father sd, when I got thru lookin' down at the white man's desk, while he bullshitted me about right and wrong.

But what they taught me, my parents, and the others who created this I so perfectly, in its staggering imperfection. They made me too "polite," in one sense. Too removed from the rush and crush of blood. Realities, screams disappear into the tunnel now replaced in my head-heart. My heart pumps words, and concepts. Papers and decisions. Screaming death like a black airplane dived down murdering off a building! Walk the real streets feel the warm blood turn. Say, hey, bro, what's to it. What you into, and whatnot. They pushed me back of a shadowy stair, and there to wait, breathlessly for my self to return, with all the feeling and soul I lost, looking for what??

I was taught all this madness, or had it placed around me, and me around it. The radio sat in the "front room," much sickness got in there. I looked at the *Daily News* everyday, because my father read the sports. Ol' man Krotzer, with his dimwitted self sd to me, "Why do you read that horrible paper?" And for the first time I saw a shadow . . . why indeed, for the sports, I answered. Those sports that sit at Churchill Downs in silk cravats and wager lives for their pleasure.

I was taught good hair and bad hair. Lightskinnd folks in moccasins at picnics was hip. Bethany Baptist was the home of lightskinned folks but I didn't find that out till many years later, although I knew it, or was in it, brown skinnd. I didn't even really understand the "war" between my brown grandmother and the cold white boney Miss Banks of the flower committee till years later, although I knew that too. (Coming of the class struggle peeped in right there, in its bubbling bubbling, in its slow accumulation, of lightskinned negro advantage, brown skin negro frustration . . . till 1971 suddenly a qualitative leap, and eureka we has the makin' of a fullfledged class, goblin, whass that mystical mumbler, well a class Jethro is some throwed together group a' studs with the same interests, who defense them together, in 1971 eureka Kingfish Fatso is de boy, what come to show how its done, and suddenly there they be all them middle-classniggas from so long ago diggin', like the Bamberger Boys, them lightskinndfolks what used to run the Bamberger elevators and dress in tuxedoes, and none a' you brown niggas cd be in that . . . but color ain't the whole carrot, Oxface, niggas throwd around so tough revolution can be made by some lightskinned and for sure some niggas black as god want to be capitalist freaks and suck the life outta babies.) But eureka from lightskinned Miss Banks of the flower committee hoardin' a way to whitey, and the preacher he looked like Cecil B. deMille's version of our father who art in heaven—white hair white skin green eyes—yeh, bubba, singin' them ol' Mozart tunes with a fag with a croquignole setting up there wavin' at them wommens like he was directin' something, he was just tryin' to point his hiney at some protein projectile. . . . But the class struggle yeh, then suddenly in 1971, and 2, and 3, fat gibber lip skunky funky declare the opening of the nigro pseudobourgeois hot foots. And other niggers' jaws begin to get tighter and tighter! Yeh it's called a "qualitative leap." In the rhythm of any organism's internal dynamism oba-padow—salt peanuts salt peanuts.

Pressed into me, this I, filled with the ignoble sentiments of slave labor. I wore a stocking cap, like my father, and used Nunile. Of course! What you youse, Mulligan?? Tryin' a get them waves, honey. A rumple-rumple-rumple—lean and clean and intelligent, but greasy jim, very greasy. That was a serious breach in the bourgeois' cover story. Is white peepas greasy?? (You better believe it Sambo, very greasy veddy veddy greasy, indeed!) Look in them ol' yearbooks waves and waves, some sitting up halfways like water leaping at a ship, fish in that mammy jammy too (but that's a different group, but all groups the same group in the world, as they unfurl like flags identifying the level of their development).

Petty bourgeois bloods of america, this is most of our storee. The I is fashioned, by the Charlie McCarthy machine. Tho we ain't exactly Charlie because we have the choice that Amilcar Cabral explained. We can commit class suicide, and move at one with the masses of our people, and that will be the warmth to heat up our heads into hearts, and turn the paper language into concrete acts of revolution!

The formation of the I. From the old Nile to Nunile. The creation of plasticnigrew. Who is really made to sip the lesser shit of americus. How we I's grew in school, and on the street. How we I's were not the strict crazy niggers of *Ebony* fantasies, but the niggers the fantasies were supposed to trick into being worshipers and followers of the pseudobooshies. Humbled in the glow of yaller skin or brown dust.

But these I's we is ran too far and too wide. Or the potential is in us other than this personal I, to have made a move, and got the trick exposed. As the negro pulled the rabbit out the hat, "you" (I'll deal with this category later) dug, it wasink no rabbick but a cracker's nasty foot! I mean I cd not dig bein' The Spiro's bodyguard nor The Agnew's bodyguard (two beasts, Bro, Ish points out)—which is a big unwashed foot Pseudo pull out the hat drippin' in ol' dookie he say is magic. Ain't magic, 'tis tragic. I cdn't be no nigger in charge a' no republican shenanigans on the whole west coast. Republican nigger shenanigans. What this pseudo say to Reagan. Hellaw Raeg, I checked yr last 40 pitchers, dry as a mertherferker! Cdn't say thet. Ain't in 'em to say it. Cda been inem. Ain't now.

All drained out. By these processes I document. By this tragic path, stares like an open mouth dripping corny music. And (we) are told to follow beasts or hallowed savages who stand forever dead on the walls of churches and colored lodges, amen.

Finally, and despite the gigantic institutionalized lie into which we are suspended without a history or a personality, there is a realization that this is not total or final. Unless we can drive white brougham cadillacs into concentration camps. When President Brooke (James Earl Jones)—for real! Signs the paper saying yall worshipers ain't worshiping hard enough, all who ain't get on the train take ya to them camps and whatnot.

You

You are always finding yrself, hooking up, and vanishing. I mean, it must seem that way, to the blind. You always looking, craning yr head, to see something, there, off in the distance. Yeh. You do that. You look. Your eyes blow up huge—your children's too. You know you can identify all your children, like you cd identify yrself—the eyes.

But then you didn't, haven't, actually vanished. Maybe vanished from one spot, one situation. But that's not vanishin'. There's no magic to walking, to going where you going. Do you know, by the way, where that is? Going. In and out of yrself. Collect, to project.

You remember the 12th birthday, and then, all the slants and jousts. But do you remember being 16, being at Rutgers, checking out a Princeton student sitting next and in front of you, in the chemistry class, with the Princeton cut and striped shirt, or blue, button-down? And the sneakers. And khakis. You thought that was superhip. You had just got off the wagon out of the ghetto north to Barringer, in Italian lands, fascist rule in high school. Where yng detectives, football players, community relationsmen, politicians, gangsters (the failures), executives, plainamericans, got their line cohered.

You had a black wool suit. Like a grey flannel suit, but it had bloodtown bells. 22 inch bottoms and a vest. Very hip. You remember in the Jones Street Y, just a block away from where you sit today, a "chick" said, hey, that suit is very hip. One of the best days of yr young clarifying life. Those were the precracker bells, of Duke days. But still big hats and very very cool, you mean, yes, cool, very cool. In them days. We would stand some evenings, the real cool, on South Orange Avenue, near Jones Street and discuss the world of music, my man, sounds. Discuss sounds, with my brother, who is now fat and given to checkered seersucker, and panama stingys. You wd say, "Hey Gene, what's happening?" And hear that, what was and was and yet was, and still to be. What Miles was doing. Miles is cool, I didn't dig at the time that Miles was so hooked up with white people. Miles had you whistling "Venus de Milo," "Budo," "Godchild," "Move," "Jeru," "Boplicity." The titles were deep, the orchestration, with

251

tubas, frenchhorns, and Miles, niggercool, was startling, there on High Street, with groceries on my shoulder. You was going to high school, soon to go to Rutgers, and then to stand with Genie, my man Genie, and say, "Yah, Miles is cool, man. You dig Miles?" You, SSid, wd say, "That was George Wallington's 'Godchild,' featuring Miles Davis." If you was really in yr hip, you'd say, "Miles Dewey Davis." And you, L J, you'd be trying to find out what "cognoscenti" meant. Miles. Bird. Charlie Parker. Bird is fantastic. You need to come over to The Silver Saddle, man. Dig Bird. Charlie Parker. You heard Bird, Charlie Parker. "Bloomdido." OOOOcoolya dooooo. Bird, Charlie Parker. In the night you, Gene. You. You, Garm, did stand and whistle, did hum, and lilt in wiggling rhythm, you Pinball, did come on like the life force, like the deities.

You had a band on Malcolm X Shabazz Blvd. Belmont then. Good mountain. The Hill. Simmons alto, Dallas, tubs, you on tpt, sideways near the corner of the lips, to simulate the coolth. The coolth. The stealth of growth to see. To see. You dig Charlie Parker, Bird?? Blee-doolya, beeeeee??? That was running through our streets, through our air, and minds, in my fingers, packing groceries for steve at the l&m supermarket carrying them Saturdays down this same High Street. Tho in them days, zee-dooool-ya, it was filled with old and baby Zionists, having not yet made they move. Tips in quarters, them was weird houses, clean in a twi-light way. Smelled like other stuff. Some other stuff, bro, you dig? Old dying Jews sat lined up across the street, behind a fence, where they'd been put, by their kinfolk, to split in exile. They was round the corner, where now sits fishfry joints and soul city. Black folks piled up 16 stories. The final comedown stirring on the block, with turned up jeephats.

You came from that, you still in that, you are all that, you are love and the final revenge of the Afrikan upon the colonizer. The welding stare of music turned to fire and knives. You got the technology to kill these bug-gers, or you just gonna talk? You just gon talk, and get somebody killed. Them days, later on, that's all you did. But how'd you get that way, young man? Was you like that on High Street with that trumpet case?

What filled you with so much hate? (Are you filled with hate??)

What turned you from whistling and trying to hit that note? (As you turned, you went to New York, and bought records. You wore a beret and empty glasses.) "To Be or Not To Bop." You played "Opus de Bop," Max Roach BeBop Boys. The ReBop Boys. Leo Parker. Lee Konitz (weirdoes). Later Brubeck (getting whiter, jim) Dug Desmond—? (What? Yeh, you want the real history or a story? Give your story, turkey go head.) Jazz at Oberlin (very white), the fool hanging banging banging . . . deedeedeedeedee banging and the other totling tootling whee whee, like marbles bled through a tube (very white). How you get that white?? From where. Not from Bird. (Bird hung with white women.) They paraphrased his solo on "Buzzy," "Better Get Yourself a White Girl." Miles hung with white women. Jeffries hung with white women, but that bitch cut his throat. (All them dudes. Wd say in some reverent way they had a white bitch.) Jazz got white. Cool sounds was white boys. Was Europe making its move. The left wing of sound. Louie Jordan wasn't white. Amos Milburn wasn't white. "Caledonia." Larry Darnell, my man, he said, "You're right up on top now, you want to be free. You're afraid to be seen with someone like me. You're afraid to present me to the friends of yr set, oh well, I guess, it's best for us to forgive and forget. . . . Why you fool, you poor sad worthless foolish fool, do you think yr money cd pay for the times. . . . ? I'll cry when you leave me, my only sin was that I loved you much too much."

Larry Darnell, he definitely wasn't white. Little Jimmy Scott wasn't white. But Larry Darnell was playing at the Orange Armory with Stan Getz, and Stan Getz was playing "The Lady in Red" and "Long Island Sound," and we got hooked on Stan Getz. The cultural aggression of that. To get hooked on Stan Getz, and Dexter Gordon roamed the streets making God a noise. Pres sd cool can be funky. Yeh, Pres blasted by cold American dead wit. Eyes. You got eyes? Yeh, you got eyes, huge eyes, to see. Journey to See-ing. But go on how'd you get so white, with Larry Darnell, Louie Jordan? You cd walk around reciting Larry Darnell, "You're right up on top now . . . ," even to them chicks in the bus. That wasn't white.

You cd got to Lloyd's Manor, and do the stone funky mambo, Wed. night, and check out Little Esther. Lil' Esther sd, "Job out in the forest." Naw that was Johnny Otis, her man, sd that. "Job out there in the forest, fighting a big ol' grizzly bear, how come you ain't out in the forest?" Then Esther got in it, "I'm a lady." Johnny Otis say, "They got lady bears out there!" Can you dig it??? Hope so.

You went to Barringer with them Italians. That had something to do with it. To McKinley before that. Whited you right up. And the deadly plan of the bourgeois blood, to make it if you can. Yo mama had the Tuskegee plan, the Fisk plan, from granddaddy, and from yo' ol' man's school teachers. And then to funky Rutgers, checkin' out Princeton dropouts (who now say you're the cia—). German professor down on Rector street sd, "You vant to learn cherman, eh?" And he cd dig it, you know. "You vant to learn cherman, eh?" Ol' bad-head dude. He probly was, in the movies, like a German professor, or mad doktor. Doktor Mengele, perhaps. Perhaps. Mishaps. No haps, bro. Remember, you used to say that? "What's happening captain?" "No haps, my man. Ain't nothin' shakin' but the bacon, and that don't matter cause that's in the platter." "Duh vord fur vater iss vasser."

Across the street, right down now where they run another nigger coolout station. Wasser. Across the street, our first drunk, Evereet. Drunk. Drunk. Drunk maybe 13 glasses of beer. Got wasted. Crawled home to Hillside Place. By then, stretched out on the porch and your mama cried, oh what's to become of him, drunk. She hit you in the head, what's become of you . . . you . . . on the porch, drunk, tryin' to learn cherman, getting whiter, whiter.

That's why you cd sit copyin' ee cummings meticulously out of some absolutely ununderstood text. Tho you must have understood, something. Something of what beyond the instant lesson, it "meant." It was the facade of a culture. The facade of madness that you brought, and finally consumed, letting it almost consume you, in the process. It is always thus, what you eat, gets a chance to eat you. From the inside!

Look at this, this was me to my parents. I don't know what this means. I wrote it. You were practicing? What'd you say Anna Lois, Coyt, to that? So you could sit, even after getting raised out of Rutgers. So foreign was it. A dustbowl, nothing to feel. All they said blew by me. You know? The chem class was almost over in the summer, and I didn't even know the abbreviations. I was sittin' there making up abbreviations. You mean we had that in class? Yeh, LJ, you had that. You was in here wen they went over it.

So then, before you left, you had a whole lot of reality. The waves of it passed through life objects, social disguises. In growth, hung on the same line, from appearance to disappearance. So you make many appearances and disappearances, simulating the ultimate, who knows? Signifying change, multiformed, multipurposed, as if to reveal, to who's asking, the purpose of all and every. Except you don't know that, tiresome to consider. You think that there's more to this than the producing of objects, that there's more to your life, to peoples' lives, than the producing of

objects. The ultimate produced phenomenon is consciousness! And are
these states of consciousness, the appearances, and disappearances. Even
screaming in your mama's crib. WAAAAAAAHH! Consciousness. And wd
you, in your infinite capacity to compromise, call that an object?

You say that to say, you had been turned white before going off to
Colored School. Colored School beckoned to save you from the cold
internment in alabaster forever, amen. At Luger U. the coldness of that,
except for the prof who was hysterical about T.S. Eliot. So hysterical, it
made you actually, sometime later, read that bugger. To yr ultimate horror, and seduction to madness of tombs and dead flies. Old men in tennis
shoes, fanning their nonexistent peters, crosses, moronic emotional
states. It produced a feeling for death, for deathliness, eeriness, empti-
ness, vacancy and blankness. This little devil named Marks preached and
preached (he was only 5 foot, 1 inch and stood on his tip toes), growing
angry that these sons and daughters of urban lower middling poverty wd
sit and not be swept immediately into the vacuum of servility to the far
right. He was the only passioned object on the scene, hence you checked
him, and actually checked out what he was talkin' about, the texts. "April
is the cruelest month," absolute madness, whiteness, run on you, in your
bellbottoms. Coming from Belmont avenue on a bus, to hear this madness. And beguiled by it, edging deeper, dug a dude in a button-down
shirt and seersucker pants, still the absolute coolness, tomblike, stay-away-
from-life quality forced you to duff, LJ, to cut out, split. It's death there.
I cant dig this. Can't dig it. Got to split.

They wd let you be a big athlete, and you knew that was garbage, compared to simple respectability in speed in the neighborhood, to becoming an instant flash. These dudes is just punks. You won 100, 200, ½ mile,
and finished second in the mile, the same day, in some intraschool races.
Ahh, these dudes is just punks. You didn't even show that to no dudes on
Hillside Avenue or the Cavaliers, fading as all that was, by you driving
deep into cracker land. Still all yall knew that was corny.

But that is how it's s'posed to work. How it later, in another term, and
context (the same effect bro, tho). Thass how it's s'posed to go down.
You the one and the only. You the chief thief and midget genius here-
abouts. Stay inside the gate and stretch out, because here is the irony.
This is the real world. The real world. Power world. You can and could
pass through and behind those alabaster doors and be celebrated. Call it
44 thou a year and some other slick stuff. You cd talk different. Dress the

way that dude with the button-down did when he got clean. Be all the stuff *The New Yorker* says be, implies the aristocrat of actuality. Be the blue nose Roman (before that meant Italian). Go to plays in the early evening after the school football game, in some freckle face sunny suburb, rah rah, and have a tie with stripes and jacket and corduroy pants and heavy-soled shoes. But see that stuff on one level cd be dealt with in Colored School without becoming a total corpse. An actual mummy in the service of the dead. At Colored School, black stuff cd get in, rhythms and stuff wd inch in, and we was Colored Kids, rah rah, and had a nother, brother, another other thing going down, was down, was way . . . (way too much) and whatnot. Yes, and whatnot, my man, my main man, we could be aristocratic niggers instead of aristocratic white people. And you, LJ, had the sense to go for that, as warmer, yes, finally, and what not, than that straight-out ghost worship.

But see, the surrogate is committed at another level to the master. The master's cause is his cause as his life. The master has mastership as his cause in his life. But how much cleaner for the master to be the master, while the surrogate is the master, for the master, and is nobody for himself. Colored School is for the surrogates, who are allowed to keep their superficial colored selfs, but in actuality, they have given the inside up to worship of the master. The white boy with the button-down animates them, in a secret worship, colored for the school. But the bloods in the White School are strings of whiteness simple, and acknowledge it totally. In Colored School, it's crueler because it works internally and the worship is the life. A group of colored people, colored for the master. In White School We Were All White, and dead. In Colored School, we paaaaarrrrty, get down, stay high, crack them books, all in the service of the master. And you are a follower, each single self, a devoted monk, of the cause. And your crowd, these secret service men, cia agents, housin' authority officials, antipoverty whips, insurance executives, airline pilots, board members, responsible professionals (the party is the ritual, the rite of absolute submission, for here is where all energy that seems to relate to the surrogate's self is used, in the party). The party is the only example of a nigger on the loose. And so all the political economic social fire borne in us, to finally roast this mammyjammy up is let out, in slobber kissing, butt wiggling, pot smoking, wine sipping, whisky guzzling, crazy talking, singing, flinging, getting into yr thingsing, at the party. Yeh. The Set. "You goin' to any sets, man?" (JBHighHiney used to ax) "You goin' to any sets, bro?" YOU'd nix this dude as corny, "Naw man." "Ah come on J, you know all about the sets, man. You the hip one. Everybody know you know all sets, look at that vine you got on. You the hip one. You the clean-ny." (Knowin' all the time, he wasn't hip at all, in his mammymade, throwntogether jive, and this dude old man had funny money. It's just the dude was corny, even with that money, corny. So we put him on. You put him on. We, as surrogates, lord, in your service, put him on.) "Naw, don't know no sets, Benny."

You know how you cd tell you speak for the petty bourgeois because you was always hungry in school, in Colored School. Eatin' Nabs and orange sodas, or Al's hotdogs. Al always had the earthangels running in the store. Old Al, he laid back, 'cept at night, when he figured the real hardheads might try to cop some stuff, he'd be there with them thick round glasses and mashed-in face. Jiving the public. Them 12 cent hotdogs, left you before you got across the street. Best to get them, take them back to the dormitory, so you could at least have a memory of eatin' before you went to sleep. Light pink hotdogs, first poot, they had cut out. A belch wd cut 'em in two.

Always looking for dust. Coins. Geetas. Bux. Chobles. Green. "Hey man, you got any paper?" "What, Parks, you better get outta here, man. You got the rich-ass doctor father. Don't come over here with no tired stuff like that. What happened to yr money, turkey?" (Parks might get ½ serious, trying to trick a gofer.) "Ah man, I don't get no money. No man, my ol' man don't like me. He don't send me no money. I'm just down here makin' it, like everybody else."

"Don't bug us with that. Go get some of them freshmen with that noise."

"Yeh, Bennie, lay out for the next 3 billion choruses."

"Hey LJ, is choruses really the plural of chorus?"

"Hey, AB, why don't you split with Parks, you wanna talk that kinda stuff? Dam!"

You had some integrity, LJ, maintained a rude cadre of cynics criticizing everything and everyone there. Despite the party, and the endless ritual of salaam to captivity. The endless acquiescence in the latest mode, uh! to whatever had captured us for this next few hundred years.

You build, brother, and then your own game, yr own built-in stuff aids the lame freak driftin' in at yr northern border. He sellin' some alien weird upside-down sick garbage. And you, brother, yr thing, is to try to dig it. Hey, what is this shit??

The dude tell you, give you a sample, sam. Next thing you know you trying to get in yr house, door locked, lights on, party goin' on, it's the cripple cracker boogalooin' (whatever crackers do . . . a jig is a good name) cripple crackerin' there, jiggin' and you outside reclassified as savage. Dam!

And so the party, is some essential life function, some basic worship to the lads and lassies at Colored School. And yet a few of you, some single yous (it was yo' street where you dug it) cd make it. Cd finally inch away. Always weird. Stomped by images and sounds and silences into some calculating inside singing blues singer, or maybe a reds blacks and greens singer.

You was whiter and whiter, even sidestepping like Duane Thos. Driven through the scene of the multiritual. Like a picnic ground in hell, where even the many covered-over bodies of the great minds of our fathers longing to teach us. Yet you submit to the ritual. To the stoning rite, the fraternity rite. In submission to the cracker and his moll.

You was a sphinx, right LJ? You and Shorter. God. What a combination. Shorter used to show up on the rotc field with shoes with no strings, and a war hat pulled down over his eyes. That was sweet. That shd have been recorded. There on the football field with the lightskinned niggers hooked up, jim, hooked up, prancing around that goddam field like they was the actual general double goose hisself. Yes, sweet, and Shorter. A bohemian, walking around, talking about his horn. "Mah horn, uh, man. I got to get mah, uh, horn." His eyes wd shoot up into the corner of his head. "Mah, uh, horn. Dig it?" Nobody, cd, 'cept you dug it & most of yr group. The boys. The group. That Shorter is too much, way too much. 'Cause you be so bad you be sitting on the windowledge on the inside of the room, right over the drill field, checking it out with a bottle of chianti. Hey, dig all this. Wow. These cats crazy. How do a dude get this crazy?

Wasn't goin' for it. No corny stuff. Yet whiter, bro, drawn ever toward that cold shit. A Gertrude Stein book, *A Primer for Dogs Who Are Learning to Read*. Christopher Fry. Some other dead shit. Imitating the poetry of the 17th century Englishmens. Poems to Lucasta, who I really did not know, except the movies inside me. Them Italian broads was not named no Lucasta. The encrazed Parker dying on the baronness' couch. The flyin' Bird on a garbage hamper with Lorraine whathername, the white saxophonist's wife. Snortin' dope together in Newark. You watched that on Clinton Ave.

And bohemian Shorter, he turn up at the Afrikan Liberation Day march in the park (Weequhaic) with a white woman, a pregnant white woman. Talking incoherently. A far out line he had, but it didn't work. Because objectively it was up to the international avant garde. Another white outfit. Simple stuff. Integration. Yet Bird snorted dugee with this bitch on Clinton Avenue.

You had a healthy black furnace running through you. It was and is real. It is a furnace. A fire. It scalds you. It scalds, inspires, lights up where it will. Yet all had domesticated it. Had made it fit a thousand weird designs it thought it created, and only inherited from the dead seeds of racism. How cd you come off the streets quiet and dignified? Cool. In the deepest of American Afrikas, yet have a white streak growing out of hand? Even in the midst of the coolest of understandings? What you thought was profound turned out to be dirty white people stuffen'. You was a gofer, LJ, maybe worse than a lotta' people you put down, a corny gofer, it turned out. Reality remains to be dealt with.

Yet the Colored School had go-fers everywhere. That was what it was for, to pretend you were hipped, by virtue of yr presence, to all forms of go-ferism, corniness, bullshit, undignified slavery, yet by the very fact being set up for the worst of all go-fer shit, the subjugation to white life totally, because you are in love with it.

Yas. Yas. Yas.

Cooler and Cooler.

Whiter and Whiter.

Gerry Mulligan played around the corner in our local dive, right alongside "Work with Me Annie." Side by side. And crooked niggers so corny colonialism alone could form them, talked all kind of stuff, brother, all kinds of stuff. And you grew, LJ, whiter, but somehow aloof from the death it proposed. I don't know why. The casual look from huge eyes. As if to say, "What is this shit?" And the ritual goes on. Your roommate turn up with a suitcase full of wi-kee. Right after philosophy class you rush home to check him. Whiskey in the bag in the refrigerator, in the closets, wine on ice, two boxes of waffles, and two boxes of franks to eat. Wow. A ladder in the living room, where we trying to paint. Me, Teddy—school-teacher antipoverty man; Phil—Agnew's bodyguard, Agnew about to get busted (will he guard his body in slam?); Lil Charley. Lil Charley, from sidewalk, survived, partially, me from ½ sidewalk, survive, others, scratch.

You was a sphinx and these dudes wd beat you, try to knock you out, 'cause, number one, they cdn't play the dozens and hated to lose, so they had to get mad. There was a dude who was a psychopath, name a' Larry Jackson, lightskin dude with a tuft of white hair out his face like Albert Ayler. Used to beat and beat, with a rolled up *Esquire*, baked on a radiator, after bein' soaked in water. Beat and beat.

He knew we was always laughing about this lovely sister he went with, because, geronimo, we cdn't dig why she was doing that. She was a beauty queen, Joan Collier from Jersey, and she went with this psychopath. The only thing he had going for him was that he was lightskinned. He cdn't play no ball. Personality was roach-disease ("flait"). "Say Larry, yr personality is flait." It's me saying your personality is a bit too much. Just a bit. So we laughed, tho we was just lowly pledgees to the frat. We laughed in our hands, and this cripple-brained sucker must've dug it. So he run a little light totalitarian stuff on us, on Shorter an me, especially.

"Hey man, I ain't going for that."

"What do you mean, you ain't going for that?"

"I ain't going for that."

Shorter, he just nutted out. The dude came in and tryed to make Shorter give up his lamb chop, which he cooked on a hot plate. Shorter nutted out. "Hey naw, naw babeee, you ain't getting none a' this chop, dig it." The dude didn't even really want the chop, just the power of commanding the chop. "Naw babee, you ain't."

And then, Shorter shows up in the park with the devil. A thousand bloods standing there trying to dig him. And him stumbling something to me. To you. Some ½ realized apology. Some admission of deathwish. Some gargled retreat, and did he see, brother, you think? Did he see? Do you, my man?

You can always find a "you" to point at, to talk to even. The crazy ones, the ones like bro Shorter, talking out loud to a you that day in the park. Not talking to the white woman, pregnant and ignorant beside him. "Naw, babee, no haunted house, and shit." Jagged gestures, beyond the knowledge of himself. To fend off all the shadows that could not be brushed away, all the deathwish built up in us by this 3 centuries of slavery. Cd not be brushed away like the white-looking Larry Jackson, with the tuft of dead hair. "You ain't getting none a' this chop, mannnnnn. None, digitt." Shorter pirouetted then, pirouetted our courage against all corniness. Yet brother you show up short, shorter, than reality, and you

LJ, you not even whispering the truth. You did, maybe, a snide comparison, some hope. Take care of yr self, brother, take care of yr self. Eyes not
even meeting.

The boys club cd be analyzed. All the brothers hung out together as
commentators on the Colored School, and whatnot. All the sitters on the
steps as the phat ones passed by. "Babee you are p-h-a-t," which meant
fine, Colored School talk. Because in Colored School we could talk a talk.
We cd beat a fine track down, a lingo we had, man, that was us. Sweet.
And we raged with it. You, LJ, raged with it. Is it you saying that this dude
is jiving and whatnot. It's me saying that, and saying he is jiving and is a
jive dude. Yeh. And it's me saying that you are the jiviest of the jive. And
jivier than any living cat. Your mama is jive. She is a jive mama. Everybody
know that. Don't everybody know that? *Votre mere. Votre mere noir.* Cats in
French one think they hip. An' on. An' on.

"Aw, later for you jive cats, I'm goin' to my room and hit them books
before Barnes wash me away & whatnot."

"You already washed away, you so light. You jist don't know it. You light
as air my man. You gonna float outta the valley like a blimp."

Hey, here come this dude. "Hey, LJ, you been with that bat you be with?
This cat always sneaking up Georgia Avenue to see this bat. Young Bruce
Wayne. Hey Bruce . . . what's happening Bruce? Hey Bru-uce. Way-ayene.
What's to it, cat? You still batman of the second floor?"

"I ain't starving, jive lames of the second floor. I ain't here whackin' my
doodle neither. Dig that!"

You cd streak from the streets, toodlelooin' hip on a mouthpiece
between grocery carries, transformed by a basketball game and a trip in
off Court Street to take a test for Lincoln U. Colored School upstream,
transformed to the campus of Colored School, the capstone of Negro ed.
And there to be miseducated by the capstones. There to be drawn warmly
into the middle class. And yet the petty bourgeois nigger in you, LJ, clung
to the edge and cried and stormed and fabricated another life outside
the ritual of worship for master.

Even the trips to the library, formulated a track around the sad corniness of dr. and attorney Negro, not even stated. You sd you wanted to be
a doctor. Why? It was convenient, but chemistry just kicked your ass, LJ,
farmed you out. Or else nothing at all was real or necessary but feeling.
You dove through the mists of yr self, drinking wine, falling in "love." Not
really. Not ever really going with anyone. Just thoughts ramming through

the brain like blood. All the faces of the nobodies inside you, all the voices and lifes they pursued. You & you & you & you & you. And yet, there across the green strolls someone you wanted to look at. To find out something about. A girl who was really really beautiful. A dude with nice shoes. All of them. Them other yous there, LJ, beside you, brother.

Here come AB with his stuff. "What's wit' it cat?" AB in the choir now. Later you got thrown out of Colored School for not internalizing the ritual of the master. Even you sat kinda quiet at parties, rubbed a little ever now and then, LJ, but mostly, you dug, and rapped with the other renegades and drank. I remember you all had that party tho, in the frat man's house with the Deltas. You were outside on the balcony with this Delta pledgee, an art student, with short wavy dirty blond hair, and lightskinned bumpy complexion. She was weird tho. And then, you kept drinking, LJ, and you cdn't drink then, going back, into the kitchen for more. And you and this babe were mated off by the others, and you were getting dizzy, LJ, and it seemed to you you were really getting over, and you had on a brand new Brooks Brothers grey flannel vine, rich white boy style, and suddenly LJ, the pretty babe was drifting, drifting, away, and, LJ, you thought you had a lot goin' for you. You seemed to open up and talk and talk, and get over, and then, my man, hey cat, you were drunk and on the floor and vomiting all over everything.

Ugg.

Vomit even in the pockets of your new suit. It smelled like vomit. You had to get rid of it. You had to carry the bromo in your pocket and take it for a whole week you were so hung over. Yeh.

You remember that, LJ?

And the chick, the babe, the woman, she was never that close enough to you to even speak to you any more.

Here come AB, limpin' like that. "Hey, AB, why you limp man? One leg shorter than the other?"

"Why you cats always talkin' about me? Do I bother you?"

"Naw, you too ugly to bother anybody, Bee. Much too ugly."

It was a love you had from us, to you to you from us, and the us vibrated against most of the corn. In the ivory, yellow, brown, dark and "black" world of Colored School you struggled for some kind of consciousness.

The school bourgeois dictatorship made Sterling Brown teach us jazz in the school dormitory. It was not really music after all, and a nigger would conduct the little niggers in the Ninth Symphony of mulatto

Beethoven. And so impressed with their whiteness, Mordecai Johnson, addressing the congress, wd say, "And look, yes, and look, how white, how white, how extremely white, how astonishingly white, we got 'em. Can you see it, white folks? Can you dig it?" (or however lightskin aristocratic bourgeois, to coin eff's term, say "dig"), Mordecai wd run on them. And we, all the yous, were all run into the chapel and told the holy light wd beat us into men and women, in Kansas City, or St. Louis, in San Francisco, D.C. or New York. We wd be in our clean clothes performing dignified service for the master, in an arc of unconscious ardor at the completeness of our slavery. And brownskinned girls were named homecoming queen, and Negroes said how progressive. They said, this is the first time that a brown-skinned girl was named homecoming queen, yeh. "And isn't she pretty?" Tap Stratums, ironically, was her name. They said, "Tap is lovely."

"Isn't she beautiful? Yeh, Tap is gorgeous, ain't she? Isn't she? She is." Even white people (I never heard 'um) prbly sd that. "Yeh, Tap is where it's at" (or whatever white people say in those situations, ummmmm-mmm).

So Tap married Mordecai's wild oldest son, who drank, and that was integration. A major barrier. A breakthrough. A social revolution. Yeh, boo. On the hill, overlooking the chapel and the women's dormitory (from whence I guess old Morty's son cd keep an eye on both currents of events). And yeh. She was homecoming queen, and you could see 'em on the hill making revolution on the hill, overlooking the women's dorm and the chapel, the chapel where ol' Mordecai blessed us and raised us into the image of the holy slave in love with the holy slave master, amen. They got divorced, I heard, Tap and Morty's son, I mean.

And they kept Frazier under wraps. You heard of him in wraps. And Locke in wraps, tho he rapped a sweeter line for yella niggers. Chancellor Wms, they kept him under wraps. And absolute insanity wd strut across the landscape with a Harvard bookbag, teaching classics, and being cultural attache to the Vatican. We said he's a heavy dude, meaning this Snowden, but that name should have been a giveaway, snowed-in, froze to death by whiteness.

So this is the life they give to you, LJ. You duckin' and dodging. The street pressin' in on you sometimes like beautiful blues to keep you straight, brother. You lost sometimes wondering up the avenue. Who are you? Now the Jesus image dulled. Still who are you, you asked, thinking perhaps you were the only repository for so much sadness, so much alienation.

What was it you wanted, LJ? What was it? Myself maybe. Who knows? To understand the world better? To get some direction? Some meaning to things? Why are events forcing you in this direction? Why am I being this me? Why are you being this you? You's. To choose. And you are standing now, lookin'. You ran around the track and caught the sujee boy at the last 20 and burnt him. A fan club in the windows. You fought with the mon boys one night down on Second Avenue. Some marines followed a white woman into the house, and the mon boys got down. We whupped them marines' ass, we. We. You. You.

You walked with Doll down the street to the yella boys' jeers, or let out of her car wd blow at the dorm on Saturdays. Hey is LJ the one? In her sweet sly southern darkness. Amidst the superficial garbage of bourgeois hookups, a sweet one got away to come again another day. And then, that day it was revealed that even she had been touched by the master worship madness, and was a dark social worker, working in the community, a little batty. A little turned off and on by the flash of madness. Was she still in awe of the Colored School mens?

And summers you wd go home, remember, and not really be able to touch anyone. The ritual, the master ritual, was taking up as the true faith. And we roamed all over, stretching into the darkness, imitating Symphone Sid, and *Esquire*, and Colored School, and White School, being the actual Quixote of college evenings, looking for the rituals. We looked bro. Yeh, we looked and looked, and found, did find, was finding, throughout our ritual time.

Sometimes we wd sit outside and rap about Colored School, even up north in summer. Sometimes we wd be big time Colored School students, and hope to be recognized as such. Sometimes we'd sit in the car and listen to Symphony Sid play the sounds. The sounds. Our true religion. The true mask of hipness. The sounds. Sometimes we'd go to dig the sounds. Fri nights, we'd be off, roaming.

What was all this feeling coming from? What was it for? All this silence and turning inside, or away? Or voices inside the head to compete with those inside? What was it all for? Cd you sell it? Why didn't it help anything? Except to wish. To wish. To fantasize. To be some other thing than what obviously suffered for not being understood or liked or celebrated? Or why cd it be calm or comfortable or what was it? What was it scratching for?

Sometimes wrestling with Waverly, sometimes strolling down the street to deal with lightskinned folks. Sometimes standing alone on the street, watching signs and colored folks. Sometimes going to New York with a newspaper and book, looking in windows, being what?

But reality always forced you into some direction. You got thrown out of the frat, thrown out of school, thrown out of intended wedlock. Well anyway, this old lightskinned, bigeyed girl named Shirley, you remember her? "This is my girl." This dude, a doctor now, said, "What yr girl?" All the cats was digging, and laughing. Why? And then you were supposed to go somewhere. You wanted to do some dumb shit, like the ballet or something just as white, but arty. And she had dropped you, LJ, for this doctor dude. And he was considered corny by most of yr renegade friends. Tho he was one's roommate, which made it tougher, kid. And they sat around and laughed when the night she was supposed to go to this ballet, she showed up with this dude at a Kappa set. That was some funny stuff, LJ, very funny.

Yet can you go under that event to internalize the final mortality of what it means? ("Aw, what that mean??") Mean: it was better that happened, brother man, kept you away from East St. Louis lawns and the salute to evil that you wd support it even with your life. There's something in you makes you fail at doing stupid things. Makes you unable to succeed at Americanism. You standing in the setting sun eating a peanut butter Nab. You sitting on the bench on campus watching a watermelon on the slats. You watching the reservoir, ripple. Failing. In such another way. You bet.

This period of your life was tragi-comic? You characterizing now for "This Is Your Life?" Or "This Was Yr Life?" All the way till now. But Colored School taught me about ourselves stretched out in the blue echoes of the flag. Laughing loud, being cool, dressing up, playing games, fucking each other, in the name of the cause which we kept just under our mind's tongue. It was a juicy, just like a juicy image. You understood you were moving into it, but not that it was something with a name. Something someone could say, and even finally totally negative. Really. That's why in reality dudes got into fights southwest with brothers 'cause they knew the niggers had bought a whoopie hat from whitie and wore that mammyjammer like it was pretty. It'd make a brother mad, he there trying to groove some Fri-Saturday night, in comes some dudes in some freakin' whoopie hats a cracker give 'em. But the cracker didn't give 'em it direct, which is the cool part. Was give to them by saintly Negroes. Negroes with grey sideburns. Negroes with bald heads. Lightskinned Negroes. Darkskinned Negroes, with lisps and gaps in their teeth. Negroes named Mahoney. ("What're you looking at, Mr. J?") On graduation day, they take the whoopie hat and roll it up and tie it with some ribbon and say some words. Bro look up these dudes got these whoopee hats and tryn' to squeeze they main squeeze, using the whoopee hat (NO!) yeh, the whoopee hat as the come on!

Some bad stuff (taste) you dig? Some bad (yeh) stuffuh. BLAM! "JIVE Mammy Jammy, I'll bust yo' strangle on de spangle, &c." "Hey man, why'nt yall lighten up?" (Naw, what??) Irony drifts, drips in too. "Whyn't yall lighten up?" They about to swing, bro's back up imaginary-real, dude's nose be busted. They got this to tell, and this a word from the wise . . . "Say, whyn't yall lighten up?" It's what you white guys tell us, you Americans, you racists and imperialists sailing around John Hawkins style, givin' the world a blow job. Ol' time pirates in bizness suits, be biznessin' it, & stuff rip off yo bizness, give you bad end of the bizness. Blam! They say: and this is what Colored School is for. Can you dig it, little ones ready to blow it over? To blow through and around over, this old timey madness (tho it goes on right today . . . rat naw, in our world . . . the struggle continues).

COLORED SCHOOL TEACHES: "HEY, WHYN'T YALL LIGHTEN UP?????????" Except the question marks are really lynchin' stalls, hangman's posts, where most of us gets hung up. A set of hangups to each Negrew to pass thu heah.

Readied for whiteness, black nigger, have you got on the right suit? You had a *New Yorker* magazine by then, and thot to rise, by next to last summer, slowly above all dem. Eye noticed you silent in East Orange nights at the ritual. There with big hook-nosed Sid, a white Joe White. Or a whiter Joe White. "Workin' with my boy, Sid, in the city, president of the d.j. committee . . . ," that wd roll through our nights of lookin' at the pretty ladies we held inside we haids. What is it you wanted so quiet? A special case? A special time in the evening to be looked at, or remarked on? You were being packaged, dude, that's all, bein' painted grey for use at the front, for that chair near the door of America's front on the world. And you, in perfect phrase-in with the stunt, thought you were getting sensitive. When in truth, brother, you were having your head whittled away and pointed like a shell. So that stuffin' you in the canon, as one of the makers of the canon, of all of us together, amen, loving the novel experiment. That we have sacrificed so much, and so totally, that the loudest catastrophes and obstructions on our way to the morgue are quiet shadows hovering like blue mirrors where we look. Yeh. And quiet quiet beats the night, of secrets closing in on us. Yeh. We understand. This roar, this sealed-in, cottoned roar, sensuous in its closeness to our essential natures. Yeh. (No. No. You see they have made it seem to be this way, that their imposture, their imposition, is actually your personality, but that is not so, LJ, not so. You were not just quiet and internal, not so clearly. There was always a great weight of abstraction pushing yr feelings back under waves under a wharf. It is the bloody struggle will raise our touch to feeling, our eyes to see, our lips to meaning, where we can see a tree and understand it as real people, where our total functioning lives will stretch out and open up big black flowers feeding on harmony with everything.)

You cannot say what you wd be without slavery. Readied for the white-out age 18, sitting by the curb listening to Symphony Sid. And dudes getting ready to get killed in Korea. Going over there to be killed by some reservoir by our allies the Chinese, by our brothers in the struggle, by Chairman Mao's righteous bearers of the word. "Hey, man . . . what's happening brother, what you doin' in that soldier suit?"

"Oh, wow. When they get you man?" This is Eddie. He's in that soldier shit. "Aww, man, I thought you was at Penn. They copped you. Wow. They copping everybody."

Ready for frozeland. My brother across from me is strong. He is short, about my height, but weighs a solid 147. Big across the shoulders, big legs and thighs. Fast and fearless. Half the crowd in the room comes to dig him and get ready to go down to eat at the team table and talk about the plays, about whose chest got walked up. And all of us adopted the team slang. You were having a good time . . . you wasn't outrageous with yr shit. But you stayed up rappin', rappin', watchin', checkin', rappin', walkin', broke down sometime, mad and cryin', confused, didn't know they were readyin' you to take the muthafuggin' fall. (Yeh.) We adopted a combination team slang, and just nachral blood talk. "It's me over yr chest for 50 yards and a teedee." "It's me knocking yr dick loose at the 4 yard line and sending you out for 3 months, with a fractured prick." (roarrrrrr.)

All time readying you, bro, you could never tell that this dude then wd end up guarding Agnew. You cdn't predict that. He was a good dude. You was a good dude, but the ritual is deeper, brother, the fog of Colored

School, like Brigadoon, is hidden by its very unreality, so, too, the meaning of Colored School, and the lives of Colored School men. (That now
messe Jesse can say save the children, save the black colleges and neither
will be, by that saved, nor by General Foods, nor by stacks of rice crispies
that sit rotting instead of going to Afrika to feed the victims of the drought,
who hate rice krispies and wdn't on no kind of bet eat them mammies.
That we were all being drug slowly and fastly toward the white-out.)

Kanasta: (lightskinned, straight hair, corny muff) Social secretary and
    special mantan for hiz hardware the Ag . . .

Brothers: (lightskinned, regular hair, good dude) Body guard for his dude-
    ness, the Ag . . .

Ruf Ruf Ruf Ruf Ruf Ruf Ruf Ruf Ruf Ruf/the sound of troops, gung
ho nigger troops, gung ho everywhere, fightin', fightin', for everybodies,
ruf ruf. We being drug, man, drug, straight toward the whiteout.
    Is you a dinosaur, we shd ax, is you a muffin extinct beasse?

Lowerkey: (Tall, straight, fatlipped googleface, bi-ness suits at Colored
    School, everybody clean at Colored School. Make no mistake, you
    don't be clean at Colored School. Don't dig you like they cd. . . .
    Lowerkey was big time frater-greek, *Alpha Sigma Sigma* (ASS)).

Lowerkey, he the haid of all niggers in the west, by the sea. He is the
wack by-the-sea nigger in charge of all publicans and re-publicans. All the
niggers yr eye can rest on we gives to thee to run is what his lease say. A
Colored School get you in the tune to deal with it, Sammy, it do.

Elebutt—high in his *hiney*, is a computer tuned to gibberish. It gibbers
    rhythmically it's sd, and white folks snicker and pt at him, leading
    him to rule the groups.

Babblebootie
Cardwallder Murphy
Pinky Butt
Recitin' Rodgers
Tex

Goodsuit
Dr Fang Gool
Mr White Man
Nigger Missing Tooth (an Indian)

Lined up to jedge. I ain't jedgin' 'em. You know 'em, you jedge 'em. Reality jedge 'em. 1973 jedging machine wukin' new ways. All them gone. In place on the treadmill crazy. Talking' crazy. Lookin' crazy, actin' crazy, crazy. Quiet, normal, insane, which is the worst kind, the scariest kind. That look, there they sit, faces light up by the store window, by the television, by the podium, and they are criminally insane. Look at Nixon talk now. Watch the tiny quiver of *dementia praecox* shake his upper lip, the eyes sink back behind a quiet blitz of horror meant for others. The senators sit. The agents. The jailers. The board. The little Anglo-Saxon gestures toward his creation: the world, and smiles saying that your projects are not the kind they fund, no not that one, come up with something else. . . . . . . quiver, quiver, and what you're witness to is absolute perversion, so ugly and total . . . it almost results in reevaluation of the world through the eyes of madmen and criminals. What is the world seen through the eyes of madmen and criminals? Listen to Nixon's speech through Henry's fat mouth: woe be unto you Ay-Rabs.

It is the invisibility of the process that is fascinating. That's what makes it so successful, that it looks like something else, like Toure sd of Imperialism, but it is what it is. The whiteout. The brain burn. The veil of colorless fog descends, envelopes us in it, laughing. (Slap my hand!) Laughing. Like Jews into furnaces we are led into the whiteout, with the same effect. They can do it physically, or culturally-mentally. The dead process, blind down the long tube to blankness. Unfeelingness, even among the overturned chairs and blaring record players.

You went to many rituals. You played many scenes of quiet terror, so quiet it is obnoxious to remember how easy it all was. How easy it was for them to make you take off them bell bottoms, and burn the midnight oil to learn the qualifications for blankdom. And among the herd of fellas, desert dudes all swept in upon the crown, you thought you was into sumpin', huh?? It was that, huh? And that? Oh that's the way you say this. This is the way you dress. Oh this is what you read, and this is s'posed to make you feel what kind of way, not feel, but think a' what, for what, just think thank thunk. You turn up crazy. You turn up behind red glasses, wife dying of mind cancer, a polite addict, chipying yr way across the Styx. You show up in the pages of *Ebony*, saluting what needs to be killed. You emerge more ammunition for the white boy's gun. Can explain it. Even to the lower regions. Like the lady with the elephantboombies sd, "Nah Ahma do something for *me*!" Of which there is no doubt, except it is not for you, can't you understand? Not for you, this criminal rite, this invisible savagery.

But you cd come to the edge of it in style, having passed through Colored School and gotten kicked out, because, after all, Colored School cd only be interesting enough to walk around in. Certainly you didn't think you was gonna believe all that. And it make no difference the others did, and do. Even tho they see you vaguely on tv gesturing, tho some savor the inch of life you had. They shout and wave, from down cross near the chapel, or coming out the valley with some bigeyed girl. "Hey me-an, what's to it, and whatnot? You got it, sporty, it's yo' world. I'm merely participatin' in the extracurricular activities," and on . . . . . until the curtain closes.

Walking drunk up Georgia Avenue like a movie star (1 demerit)

Falling out in yr room under the closet, with a telegram clutched in yr mitt (1 demerit)

Getting kicked out of a fraternity you never got in (1 demerit)

Staying all wk in a hotel, drunk and spending all the dough (1 demerit)

Being' brownskin and cursin' all the time (1 demerit)

Reading (1 demerit)

Bloo-doo-llya-cool dee boo . . . dababa daba daba-deeeee. (That's cool, and we dig it now. You see, Donald Byrd has become head of the music dept, but in dem days, befo' de middleclass got hip bein' at least blk enuf to be seen, therefore eminently mo' successful, in the modern worl', we had a ol' pinchbrain negra like Beethoven's 5th, Ol' Grand dad's 5th—in smallish dignified quantities—too.)

You were a demerit, in your quietness. It was Hollywood growin' in the swamps. Hollywood, which now you see has sprouted full, with niggers kneeling pumpin' bullets at a script, Jews on the half shell, coppin' dust like they was sellin' ruined port. It goes on, in another guise. In other guys. Are you a stone, to stand in the shadows wishing for something not yet revealed? Are these trips in and out of your head necessary? Did you go with Doll because you loved that black sweet chocolate flesh? The eyes. The smile. The southern music out her mouth. Or because yr life took you there, and once there the good feeling was enough to keep you, despite the yellow Agnew fronters' taunts??

What is demanded is that you reveal yourself, 1st to yrself, and then to all the other yous. Reveal yrself plain and simple, clean and usefully. That you step out of the shadows, and come clean. All the feeling you have grown is real enough. Build a world of reality out of it. The whiteout worked when it did. It crippled you brother. It drove you down crazy paths before you got back home. But the world is there to be used, to be created in, to love and live in, to triumph in. If you wd but collect yrself, yr memory and will. It is all real, and everything is really here with you. You are not like crazy Descartes in a world he created totally unrealized except for him (for "I"). . . . (we went thru that, that baby stage, it keep droppin' back, the babyhood of the world, the babyhood of humanity, which is the simple i. So Descartes there on his back, chortling like a babe, "i i i i i i i think i i i i i i i think i i i i i i i think, therefo i is. . . .")

You got to change that diaper man—mens and womens. You got to move along to discover the world. Everything is really here, as you will see (have seen if you were conscious, blood, anywhere you was). Pick it up, touch it. Speak. Say it. Understand, know it. Then move, move on it. Fight, struggle for it. You peaceful Bird. You yng big eyed Charlie Parker. You Lester Nkrumah. You Patrice Coltrane. You Miles Garvey. You Gabriel Tiedye. You all you. It come to that soon enough, with all the yous together, it come to that, very soon. This is to say that all that in you, looking. Your sunrise been in serious trouble. Let it rise, and be seen among the pain, all the possibilities of victory. Thass yr name. Dig it. You moons go in luxury dropped, drug away from yo' land, cross the sea, to kneel befo' the enemies of peace, and struggle in yr self to understand the worl's like that sometime, and still in that pit to look up and demand from yrself 1st, from yr real self, the strength to get up and raise up and stand up and build a new life. Thass yo' name, Oh Coleman Dubois. Oh Sekou Ra. O Stokely Ellington the 15th, thass yr interior self speakin' to you and all the yous.

6666

And so, at Colored School you learned how far you cd be took along the road to whiteout, how far along within the colored world the Sickness cd descend, and that here among the dancing singing ladies and gents a sinister plan was being spun, and dug! From I to you, the paths direct. You born into yr self. I you, you I. Eye see you grown now. With this terrible weight grown on yr neck. Yes. It's coming. The whole set revealed how, after 3 years of fumblin', you trudged off, drug off, kicked off, showin' absolutely no Colored School promise. And by that time some little ol' filth hair had crept out, on yo' chin. Some little ol' filth hair had crept up in you brain. And how you walked around looking at Colored School different, tho you missed it and cried for it, and wanted to be back, but by that time, bro', another heavier duty had settled on yr face. Yes. And so you split. Were split from that, by reality, the world, all the flurry of things and distance. Yes, Colored School, goodbye, we'll see you again—some way. Gone and maybe forgotten, for then, you trudge off, you drag off, you split. Yeh, there you go bro, there you go. . . .

He

The dude talking wasn't the dude I'm talking about, but then who'm I?
Who he, wd be more like it. The dude telling the story, he crossed his
legs, long limber, unfolded out the chair, and stood. He raised his hand,
and spun slowly around . . . and the room, though dark and empty,
seemed to light up at least there at the center where he was. He was in
profile, and began to speak and hum and roll words off his lips in hip
rhythms. It was the brother, the brother, the dude in green glove leather,
and high brown suede boots. He had on one big ring, and a big bush. He
spun and weaved on his heels, beatin' the sounds out bam booma bam,
reachin' into himself to raise up the image of a life bein' lived in high
emotion. Bam boom bam booma, beatin' it out with his heel. The slender strain of light beat upon the ring, and he whirled in and out of the
beam, until his terrible voice seemed to scream. It was a bad song, in a
bad motion, whirling in the dark, talking to the whole thing that listens
. . . to all who dug or gazed or cd see, or hear, to all the sensitive . . . the
sufferers . . . the lovers . . . all "the hip men" and their women . . . it was a
tale . . . a longish poem, about a dude.

He sd: If that's what you can call the world, a dude! If that's what you
can call *a* world. Worlds is size-place in the cosmos, seeds, atoms grains of
sand. Utter foolishness to mention number. Number stars suns all that
cannot be counted, come up with one, come up with one, ain't but one,
yr sun, a whole number with all the I's, all the you's, all the he's, there in
line . . . they life a song.

He and Me, me and L, first came in touch with each other in New York
state just before winter. Hawk was in the wings, and this dude get off the
bus lookin' like Joe College or Sam College anyway. A gym bag carrying
some stuff. And sad, Jim, eyes baggin', popped and dull and baggin', like
he had already dug he made a mistake. (Laugh if you want to, look up
and check you ain't makin' one, right now. You got the time??) L stood
there after gettin' off the bus, a line a' dudes there movin' to where this
sergeant wanted them to stand. L, he cdn't dig what the sergeant sd
because he was checkin' out his mistake. He probably thought that if he

corrected the shit in his head, all this wd change. He probably thot he'd
thought that shit up and it wasn't real. He standing there battin' his eyes
slowly like he'd wake up on campus at Colored School. And thas another
song, highway sadness, like he lost somethin' good, and that place just a
big plank for depositin' bloods in the sea of ugly—don't be so hard bro
. . . , but be real real.

Somebody walk up and say, "Hey blood, what's happenin'? You losing
something?" He probably wdn't dig. Just starin', and blinkin', gripping
the bag tighter and tighter. Just before dusk upstate, and cold starting to
roll up in one place. Some other dudes look over quick, or slow, checkin'
why the dude don't move and the sergeant, white boy style, go into his
number. "Hey you, over here. Over here. Hey."

L, he look up, slowly, past the dude. Yeh, past him, up toward the red
sky. It was slick and ugly. Bloody in the cold and sad too. It was happening, I guess, more than the white dude. And L looks at the sky, and invisible tears flow down his face. He standing now, staring at his life he
thought had finished. And "hey you" is what greeted him.

He went through all that from sad yng dude to silent yng dude. He
used to talk to us sometime. We'd ask the dude questions. "Hey, man,
what's this mean? What's this about? ('Dam it's like having a dictionary
around.') Hey L, where you goin' man?" We'd be out there on the field
playin' ball, L'd run through and around like a player. He cd play some,
to be so light in the ass.

In that place we was, it was funny about L, because he didn't never
seem really to want to be there. After a fast minute, Jim, nobody did. And
L, he caught all the bad duty. All the kp and double kp. Painted barracks
and washed dishes. Silent all the time. Had a hat broke down on his face
and shapeless coveralls. Maybe a book in his pocket. All the stuff we went
through, physicals, supply for clothes, assigned to barracks. Look up you
standing by some dude you don't even know. A bunch of us from
Camden got together, we find out this little big eye dude, he from Jersey,
North Jersey, one of those nastyass towns.

He came in silent, and blew up inside. It was like that. I knew him,
talked to him. We used to stand in line and jive about this bullshit we had
got in. How the hell we ever get in this jive? God, gauh dam. Pointing out
funnylookin' dudes. Tryin' to be close in a way, without knowin' each
other. Him and a few other dudes we ran with. Go to the movies together.
We be on kp together. L always be on kp too, always. 0330 in the mewnin',

L be risin', stumblin' out to the messhall. Some cracker done jacked him up. Why, it's hard to say. He didn't never say too much, 'cept he dug them. Looked at 'em. They cd dig that L thought *he* was better than them. Dig that. Yeh. He thought, you know, like wow, a nigger, hey man, that's something else, but L he walk around nixin' most of them warcats, bein' cool on them. Shakin his head sometimes was the strongest put-down. He'd say some things to us, but shake his head, maybe roll his eyes.

One time this big squarehead dude opened his footlocker and threw the books on the bed. Said, "J (his last name), why don't you be a man? Why you readin' this bullshit?" L don't say nothin'. He look at the book, a page is fell open and he tryin' to read it. A smilin' look raise just to the top of his skin and hold there like light, then the other dude, he change his number. He say, "You really read this stuff, J?" You can understand, this was some off the wall poetry L was into, hey man some ol' shit . . . L say, yeh, nodded, really. Dude throw the books back, slam the footlocker. L don't move, wait for the dude to move to the next bed. It was an inspection, and the dude didn't dig the way L had his clothes hung. He had a suit stashed somewhere and recruits wasn't s'posed to have no civvies. L don't look up or no way. He just check the open page on the bed, hung, you know. The squarehead dude wheeled around to see what L was doin' when he was inspectin' someone else, and L he still hangin'.

Hangin' there, was actually all he did that whole time I knew him then. Hang, and be hung. Be staring and lookin' all the time. Mopin'. I guess he just didn't want to be there. Nobody did, man. That war shit is pure ripoff. It's ugly. You in there, for what? Wanted to go somewhere other than where you was, or see somethin' other than what you been seein'. But there you don't be and see nothin'. You just in some dumb shit. And thass all you be talkin' about the whole time, bein' in some dumb shit. And what you used to do before.

L mention he was in HoleCard University, studying, and graduated there. Was in here to keep from goin' in the Army. But what difference do it make? Here we both is. Camden line just as straight, and I come in just to get off the f—in streets fore I get locked the f up, but L and me and Rogie the conk and Sam the doctor get on pretty tight.

To show you what kinda thing all of us was into, one time L goes off the base to Rochester. He been on the base the whole time in basic. But then he gets these clothes sent up, which you wasn't supposed to do, and he gets a pass and goes off by hisself, to Rochester. Walked around, or was it

Syracuse (he told me about this stuff later), just walked around. Put on civvies, a grey flannel suit, with a red flannel belt, and blue shirt and tie, and just walked around. Ain't nothing to see in either Rochester or Syracuse. At night some dreary buildings backed off in the shadows. Diamond ring people laughing, in and out they cars. And he didn't go down to the soul folks' turf, dig. He just walked around downtown staring at bldgs, in a grey suit. Then he started to itchin', and pulling at his clothes. Think he bought one of them pints of brandy, that cheapass brandy and the itchin' really got off. He went back to the hotel he got to stay in and found out he had crabs. The first night he went off the base, took that bus and all that, and rode those 90 miles to "the city," crabs started eatin' him up. He spent the night watchin' the neon sign blink on and off outside the hotel window, finished off most of the little pint, and picked crabs from around his balls.

It was a zero angle, like bein' enclosed in a geometrical abstraction, but it's not an abstraction. But you feel the two wings of the angle, the distance from any one, including hisself, to understand, to speak to, the absence of any real direction or goal. He was driven by nothing but situations and their remedies.

And that's what's happening with most of the slaves. The slavemaster too. All the greys, except the ones I guess who own and sell and direct world traffic. You know it's like I know what L felt, what I felt, trapped in some unmoving shit. But what is moving, and to where, for what? Even these little ol' crackers servin' you orange juice across the counter of Orange Julius, what do he know? Here I am in my shit, just come out from the midnight show, wowed 'em, bro', standin' and screamin'. Yeh, yeh, jimbo you cool. You what's happen, Hollywoooooood! And this cracker, he look at me funny, like he got something to say about what I'm doing.

L kept sayin', why this dude wanna mess with me? But then why'd you come in this, dude? But the white boys ain't hip either, except the directors. Them stupid, poorass crackers, they goin' for the ghost just as well, stumblin' round dumb and ugly as anybody. Some unclean mother-jumpers, tho' Jim. Nasty. Ain't never dug no dudes nasty as them dudes.

L tol' me about his cracker sgt, old as dirt, dead blank white over his whole body except the arms and face exposed to the sun. He got up one night, whipped his bottle out from under the bed and drank it all, drained it. Then he stood straddling the sink (in a 3-man room) and peed in the sink. Also these dudes come in from the flight line, maybe run they hands full of grease on a napkin to clean 'em. Then they get in the chow line, and scoop up that bullshit they be servin', and you see them dudes whaling, and them black fingerprints on the bread, when they was eatin', truly sickenin', bro . . . truly sickenin'. Now them dudes don't know what's happenin'. They agenda is written by somebody else. Sergeants, cops, taxi drivers. Appalachia hillbillies, lot of these dudes with these funny names, they don't know what's goin' down. They just programmed in size-places, my man, goin' for the ghost. Somebody tol' 'em they was white, and it blew they mind. So they walk around lookin' at me funny. I let them motherjumpers know they been had. They gophers, need to show 'em a copy of *Wall Street Journal*, or some shit, and say see that, simple motherjumper, you ain't in that shit. Them's the only real white folks. Dig?? And they gon' die, soon as my man get his shit together!

Another time, L sittin' at the desk, pullin' cq, some of us left. It must a' been like 2 in the mornin' we split, went to sack out. He say this cracker from New York named Martin comes in and wants to know why he playin' that music. L had this record player, and he playin MJQ, Messengers, and some way out white shit by some Russians . . . some coldass shit he dug . . . and the white boy say, hey, that shit need to be put off. L tell him naturally to go fuck hisself or his mama, in whatever order. Cracker withdraw, but later, when L go to bed, cracker sneak in with another cracker and catch L in the bed and sock it to him. Next time you see L, he walkin' around with heat under his shirt, lookin' for the white boy. We got to cool him out, and try to set up a one-on-one fight with the white boy. This a pretty big dude. The white boy copped, didn't want no fair one. So one night, L sneaked the dude outside the airman's club with the slat from under the bunk. White boys lookin' for L. Man, that shit went on for a while.

"Say, hey man, why you get so warm?" "The dude's a punk. He sneaked in my bedroom, man. Dude's a punk."

Otherwise, L never say too much.

In Nuevo Rico, he goes thru the same kinda thing. Outside everybody. Yet close to a bunch. That kind of away from everybody attitude's weird. Not like he was tryin to "ig" nobody, but like he was somewhere else, unaware that anybody else was diggin' him. They hung this dude down there. Busted him. Threw him off flyin' status tho he tried not to get it

from the jump. Locked him up. Some dudes said he had turned
Commie. Some hillbillie mfs was runnin' that. Some motorcycle billy
named Schmuck (really, man, for real), Kenneth Schmuck, sat out front
revvin' up his cycle, and L pulled a 45 on him when he tried to come up
in the room. Dude wrote a letter to the c.o., sayin' L was in the
Communist Party. They took him off fly status and put him in a flower
garden, growin' beauty for the base. Little nigger flower garden detail.
Some old sergeants in there was sneakin' greens in the plants. When it
grew, they just ripped it, and boiled it on a hotplate with some pickles and
hotsauce and got nice.

When L left New York boot camp, basic training, he went out to
Illinois, and they put him in weather school. And then they made him
some kind of gunner in a plane. Be sitting up in planes readin' and eatin'
canned spaghetti, cold and snot congealed inside these oxygen masks.
Cracker major wd call up over the intercom and tell white jokes. Didn't
dig L cause L had been to college. Dude, this major, had been to the 10th
grade, in Mississippi. He had a lot of nigger jokes he'd tell on the intercom, then crack up. Ask L how to spell certain words.

One day this dude shows up, this ol' major, dressed up in a Hawaiian
shirt and pegpants, goin' in the laundry. L nutted out on the dude, like
he didn't salute or even acknowledge the turkey was there. Then the dude
wanna know how come L don't salute officers. L told the dude he didn't
know he was no officer. He didn't look like no officer, with no pistol pocket
light blue and dark blue pants on. Dude usta dig *The New Yorker*, always
lookin' in there, and tryin' to dress outta that. Cdn't dig the flash vines,
my man, the actual hip, where the fire and rhythm is. But he my man.

The officer, Major Wisdom, nuts out, starts jumping up and down saying that L don't show no respect for officers, and whatnot. Shabby
cracker look like zoodirt. But then he started to ride L, all the time. And
passed the word up and down the ranks. These ol' nigger officers. One a'
these dudes s'posed to been in school with L, but was a officer now, nutted out. Mfers was corny, white boys didn't respect them. Talk any way to
these dudes. Some of them old fat ofay sgts talked bad to them, like they
was dogshit. Then, they gonna come up in somebody face tryin' to run
that officer shit on somebody.

He wrote me some down letters, like down on the floor, low, grumblin'
and sorry, drinkin' 151 proof rum, readin' all the time. Dude read 11 and
12 hours a day. Sitting on guard duty, out front of some chumpish planes.

Cracker general walked in on L laid up in the sack at inspection time. Had him in front of a plane till planes was goin' outta style. But then, at the same time, L got to be the asst. librarian, as an offduty job. And got in the library at night, and got some a' his boys in there, and they sit up and played jams on a brand new stereo they got the chief librarian to buy, and read books, and drank vodka and orange juice and brew.

He went through a strange linkout. (Sing it, twirl and whirl, long time, head down, light in the eye, on the ring, sing sing, blood!) Lengthened out I guess from when I first dug him traveled in from New Jersey cold-eyed and scared. When I check him in Chicago, riding up from Southern Illinois in tech school he had got quieter, sunk deeper. Deep in all those white books too. He had begun to retreat from reality, like it was too painful. Picked up from Colored School, which set some social tone, which he hated at the surface, yet it proposed a world for him to be in. And he cdn't qualify to be in that world. He didn't really get out of Colored School the way everybody else did. They threw him out, a few times on the for real side.

But like he sd, or did he? At least I think I heard something in him tell me. He'd come out of Colored School half ready to be a slick nigger cardboard man in the white boys' world and didn't qualify. He got thrown out of school, joined the service, and wasn't no officer. I think he tried out for the officer school and flubbed that. (But then I dug the white boy checkin' L and checkin' that he don't need him in that shit. Let this goggleeyed nigger stay in the back of the plane since he flubbed Colored School.) Wasn't ready psychologically. And then all that communist shit the white boy hung on him, but none of that was true. He wrote me once that "communism was stupid because it denied the existence of God." But then a few weeks before that he wrote and told me he was a communist. Then he said he was a Buddhist. One time he sd he was a patrician. I guess it depended on what one of them goofy books he was readin' at the time, but all the time his life is goin' in some direction, without a name, without a flag, just moving in that direction which he is . . . spreading the night to walk through, watchin' for the sun to rise.

Colored School with its ritual was a springboard to shadowland. Reality beat him, beat him, threw him in a corner, and he bobbed and weaved and tried to deal with trying to learn. He wanted to learn. It was in Chicago one night walking around, he said, suddenly it dawned on him that everyday he shd try to learn something else. It was clear and like a revelation that his life was changed. Looking in a book store window, he suddenly cd understand what learning was, now away from Colored School, which was a security blanket and funny farm (but all the life there too shd be saved, bro, you dig that . . . and there's them that's tryin' to save it as even today these tips and taps say that to you . . .). But it was on a cold Chicago street (hooked up to the service, having to go back the next morning to Chanute Air Base and march around in a jive uniform with some crackers and spaced-out bloods) that he dug clearly what learning cd be, the powerful opening into the world. He sd he stood there and said out loud, "Every day, I'm going to learn something." Finally, when he got down to the island he began to keep a diary of everything.

Yet bro, that move, to learn, to see. I wonder if that was the frantic move to truth, swirled around on the streets reality, unreality. Ol' fags clicking their lips and battin' their eyes under the el, and the Crown Propeller up the street with Little Richard shoutin' "yeh yeh yeh yeh yeh yeh." He sd he wanted to learn. But what, and from who. From those books behin' the orange plastic in the window of the Red Door Book Shop near University of Chicago, or the streets in which he passed with a book under his arm, those streets where the big titties swayed and sharp dudes limped in key?

For yet to keep one off the streets to seep up the knowledge of the ancients is one proposition, but whose ancients? While the streets breed religion politics history economics sociology creativity and a million ethoses. Twanged beat sucked stuck fucked killed run drank stank cool drooled dueled in a billion funky languages crazier than anything anybody ever dug to put in a book. 'Cause the dudes that dealt dealt where they was. And when they got home, they was fuckin' or smokin'. They dam sure wasn't writin'. (But who write yo' shit man? You whirlin' in the spot, hands held so hip, hat bent back like a heartless cutlass. Yeh, who writes yo' material?)

> Deal on, deal on world
> deal me in, in mister and missus
> everybody. I'm into what you into
> harmonize in and about nature as natural
> singers and swingers, peaceful natives
> of the universe.

A dude do write it. Naw I make it up. Somebody copy it. I copy it in the car, my ol' lady drivin'. I copy it in the back. Hey man don't make up no myth. Sit in yo' read chair like Isaac Hayes. Go in yo' studio, blood. Make up some pretty shit for everybody. You know everybody dig you, and waitin' for your latest side.

L mumblin' drunk sometimes . . . the first whiteout he don't remember. There's a photo of it, sittin' there under the rule of the pb's . . . on piano stools with short haircuts and quizzical grins. Later in tails with a moonfaced smile, hands behind the back, heavier, lopsided the smile had grown by then. You can actually hear corny white music in the background if you hold the picture up to your ear. Not so pb bro', they straight up into claimin', and claimin'. It all musta spelled progress, you know. Right on!

Other photos sittin' with the weird halfface smile. Frozen a little further away from reality. On the double conscious path, toward and away from hisself at the same time. (Does yus all has dis problemmmmmm-mmm? Hmmmm.) On piano stools, on stages graduatin' from yng Colored and White School, semi-mix. And then Colored School itself. For a minute it wasn't even possible to get no flicks. Thas when he changed his name that first year in Colored School, from English to French. Why? It seemed cooler. You cain't take no vampires' pictures neither. Dracula hated mirrors, he changing from a man to a beast. (Ahhh. Wait bro', you awful hard, you don't know that. Who told you that? You don't know all that yrself . . . L tol me man, he tol me hisself, these are his words, verbatim, you dig??? Ahhhh.)

Then a flick from the island, kneeling next to a buncha crackers, 1 nigger officer and a Mexican sergeant (Sahiento). They kneelin' in front of a plane. Gettin' ready to kill some other people for the Americans. Yet he made this oath on this street, windy whore-fag street, to learn. No, the vow had come earlier, and then reflected somehow as he walked, hands jammed deep in his pockets under the lights, checkin' out the sights and sounds of the real world.

Ya see, there gotta be a balance, yeh, but first there gotta be a stash of yo' own you comin' out of. You can crawl back in the backback room under the doorway of love (that's the title of my next album) and get in deep in them books. But L always jam up into the cracker books, but he read *Native Son* and *Black Boy* before he left high school. He thought Richard Wright was still wanted by crackers, that they were lookin' for him to kill him. He wondered why he put all that stuff in the book, 'cause surely crackers, the kkk, was lookin' for him, all them crazy suckers who, like, burned people, and lynched them, all them weird pictures in his grandfather's books, in those drawers, the mason books, the J.A. Rogers books, the bible with the family tree, a whole nest of lynch books, and flicks. L wd look at that stuff and figure them people who did that was fuckin' crazy, period. Smoke and Blood and weird hoods on their faces. Them Italians was just *tryin'* to be bad over by Mussolini Tech, but they wasn't that tuff out there in the street. L was over there with them and got twisted by the weight of them over there, relatin' to 'em, and bein' threatened all day, every day by some ginnie. But these other suckers were maniacs.

But people step through and around those obvious realities. And all that was in L. He had it packed in. His grandfather passed that baton very squarely, but coolly on to him. His grandfather tried to give him a dollar if he wd learn "The Creation," by James Weldon Johnson, to recite in church before his Men's 400 Club. His mother had him learn Lincoln's "Gettysburgh Address," which he did. Shows you. How right on got already ripped. The next generation, they had made so much progress they looked up they was in foolstown with the fools. The way the whiteout comes. And there on the street asking for knowledge, without your own stash and direction, you merely climbin' all the way in the nigger goon-faggot breadline, which is Mantan Moreland's code name in the pentagon.

> (Yet dig, Mantan was cool beyond even that when this sister told him when he got scared about bein' near the tombstones that the dead can't hurt you. Mantan said, "But they can make you hurt yrself") Can we dig that about crackers??

The way the whiteout comes, you askin' for knowledge. He, L, beggin' on the sidewalk to penetrate the cover of a book, was asking sincere, to find out all about the world. Ask that drunken nigger there about the world, and listen. He will tell if you can understand. So Mantan talked to us in code, as wayout as that might sound. "But they can make you hurt yrself" is absolutely correct, no matter, the context, &c. and so the art, in that what he said is real. It wails, wails. Blow, Trane, high above the deathly faggots clutching our lives in their claws.

L danced and leaped square into the unreal world of white super reality. The intellectual gag was shoved into his throat (an ol' song, but don't sing it, nobody wanna hear that shit).

In other words, having gone away from one low motive, he was given another. If this was a song, it'd rime. It'd sound like, so my man L, with so much to tell, was gonna spit it all out, for someone else's story from someone else's mouth. He was gonna shrink in growin' and grow in shrinkin'. He was gonna get high on the white folks, and lie on his own folks. He was gonna spin and try to get in. He didn't know it. He was trying to grow it, a mind, but he didn't know, so he had to blow, that he needed his own kinda mind. His own kinda mind. He wasn't blind. What kinda blood was he?

All this stated too badly. Like it happened then and there. But it was two things, a double contradiction grown up. L was trying to get away from Colored School, blindly, instinctively. There was too much glistening noisy riming love, simply by bein' able to see, to feel. And walk there, like a dancer on his way to get down. The tired formality of Colored School slavery, even hid by the slippery ritual, was just too slow, too uncool, finally, killers of the dream, for my man to go for. So he shot out into the open field. Where the street blood show, tryin' to have a go at the world. Join the error farce to dig a lemon rotting on the ground. Niggers all around, singing, "Hey hey hey, I'm tryin' to get over, will you help me? Hey, hey, hey, I'm tryin to make it. Will you cool out, etcetera." And getting sent over to Korea to die, to Vietnam to die, to anywhere they need a negrotude to get blowed away . . . and he be thererrr! But a black man, where does he go? How does he come to consciousness in this bloodstained nightmare? Mostly his blood . . . corpses strewn around he can't even identify as various hims. He's standing there, blankeyed, stunned by what he begins to understand of all the world he doesn't understand. That there is a whole world there, understood by him, unknown. That there is a passage, however, of symbols of this further, deeper world have washed across him with no consciousness all his life. Its mocking silent symbols. Like to dig, that there is a whole value system, hovering "above" him, making decisions. Calling this beautiful and that ugly. Calling this profound and that savage. Not yet to see the total, but now to sense and see some of the live structure of that thing. Having been programmed by it all his life, yet not to dig that, but now to look at its dim form, itself, not yet as itself, but as another thing than the silent flowing nigger world in which he had his birth. Silent in that he'd taken all he was given for granted. Looking at stuff, he'd half seen it. Half understood it, or missed completely essentials in the world. (It's how colonialism is, yall. It builds a construct around the colonized in which he grows head heart hands meshed smoothly into the surface of the structure so that there seems to be no separation or contrast.) Everything is as it is, and supposedly as it "ought" to be. There are no specific whys or wherefores, and when they seem to exist, they are corruptions of reality given to the colonized by the structure he has had imposed on him. Why? becomes an exotic question, tho it must not be allowed to remain so. It must be a real question from which real answers will be got.

He was like a tire rolled in some direction by mom and dad and uncle. Except they ain't but had been the rolled rolling the new rolled. Motion onto motion, each generation sprouts more of the damned and crazy. He wd look up out of the lip of the round black world trying to just know something clear. What is all this? Except it was in that shiny noisy hip swinging love set where the answers was (check it later) where they was. Trailed around the place, at all sides. In each place, an answer lay or stood or could be heard, through the broken jagged windows of eyes and memories and old men, history prepares itself constantly to be understood. A process—a dynamic process, in which we are involved. He wanted to be nothing he understood. A feeling pressing up through him whispered in Indian Summer. Vibrated meaning . . . it was flight in one sense . . . flight to get up, maybe, sometimes, sail through the twilight on the way to somewhere hip. Visions pressed him, daydreams.

He was presented with a fit of world . . . to put on, smoothly, all the images in life like it was just growin' up that was possible, and into something he wd choose, and fixed and static as an occupation. That was the only variable. Be a postman, doctor, boxer (not really), teacher, cowboy, somethin', the only variable, but all the rest was answered by what you saw . . . but did not understand.

Sayin' that, L then went into the book world. The world of make believe. The world of s'pose to be, or theory, saw himself in there with all that, hooked up in it, breathin' and shit. Yah. And walked in there, hooked up, strung out gradually on in with it. Down with it. He was, like, cool in it, cd speak the language of it. All the places flowed into one mad historic whole. He look up and 1-2-3-4-5-6-7-8-9-0 all seen and divined therefore therefrom. That interior world, seeped from books into him, a

cotton batting inside full of serious chemicals. All the stuff on the outside
which went on, from birth. (Check it out, the dude once thought he was
Jesus!!! Can you dig it?) From early on, they packed in 'round him man,
and some of that had to get inside, deep inside, and root in heavy, down,
heavy and deep. So then all this learning bullshit, sd on the ugliest street
in the ugliest city in the world, was just the significant change drop which
make the brew go into somethin' else. Like them ol' grey bells which
changed to khakis and blue buttondowns. Some mathematical abstractions L was on the pavement studying through the window, and James
Joyce, *The Portrait of the Artist* (harked back from somewhere earlier someone had mentioned this, where??) and *Ulysses*, absolute Charlie Parker
dazzle, What?? But into what land, bro, carried by its multiformed construct into the land of its source. (Trying to explain how all this goes
down, how the whiteout is made, how it seems like something else how its
form is functional to freak us. Freakin' madness, anger-now-won't-help.
See. Just see, bro, sister. See. Dig it. See!)

And understand.

Know, understand, and be

wise.

To do, what is necessary.

What is correct.

Yonder dude cd think (was that you?) that he was leaving some dead
shit, and be goin' into some deader shit. Ow. That contradiction burn
you up bro, but check it. Think he was gettin' out of nowheresville, but
he was really *goin'* there, had been *sent* there, to say it like it was! Naw, like
the dude cd end up greybearded, walkin' up some obscure street in New
Jersey with a prostitute hollerin' at him, and a horn slung over one
shoulder. And if he was stopped on the street, he wd render the world
with a description of it that blazed sadly drearily wearily with strange
machinery and taunts of great powers that cd be used to blow up the
world but for his benevolence. Drunk, or high, eyes rolled back in the top
of his head. Bein', still, hip, strung out on that vector, that mad line from
where the fake learnin' had took him. But a bus stop brother on a winding line to tiredness and extinction. He'd be babblin' and think it was
cool. He'd be talking in dumb riddles, wagging his head, rollin' his eyes,
like Mantan Moreland, only it'd be sad. He'd be high. A Jew and Italian
wd be rich from it, and give money to Israel to kill the Arabs and drive
them off their land. Which *The New York Times* wd say if peace wd only

come and the sides wd go back to the original spots, which wd be Europe for the Israelis, but the *Times* (code name "the *Jew Yoke Zions*") wd say what it wanted, and this dude wd be with one of their daughters, a diseased bitch they had picked in infancy to perform this bizarre but strategic part of the ritual.

Yeh, end there. Blank. Aw, no . . . Like them brothers that was so hip he told us about, both blow tough on they axes. But the real world wiped them clean. (It's a strain to try to say it all and complete, but you need to understand, the vines and patterns of death that grow up around us.)

So L, then, already abstract and bitter by his fall from grace—from Colored School—and its hip rituals and camaraderie of the select, soon-to-be-slaughtered. He see dudes in drawers and boots and fog cold and sharp going thru absolutely meaningless bullshit, and cd barely find somebody who dug Dave Brubeck. (Tell it!) 'cause L by then thot Dave Brubeck was pretty heavy. (Tell it!)

He left for the islands soon after his pledge of intellectual allegiance to Europe.

But it was that by default, you see. No man wants to kill himself, even those that do it are doin' somethin' "preferable," or "hip." The pledge, in its essence, was positive, but the negative side of it was the march into craziness. And like a nigger he used to run with in Illinois be carrying this Doestoevsky book around under his arm all the time. With a long benny. He approached L because he thought L was into that. That L was an intellectual. But L was a dude who wanted to dig stuff, heavy stuff. That was where that was . . . This other dude now, after 5 marriages, all to greys, actually heads up one of the biggest vineries on the set, so far out mostly white folks work in it, up on Madison Ave., yeh, a nigrew with a Madison Avenue hip white clothes store. Naw not no hippy-mod stuff, some Brooks/J Press ruling class shit, and a Park Ave penthouse, this dude, where that Doestoevsky took him. A branch of the dude in the park opening his eyes on cruel reality which mocks him as totally unhip. But for the dude, who is so big his sto' name LARGESSE, it's sweet, it seems, the same group, a little harder and crueler than the Colored School dudes, 'cause he had walked through them cold coal yards too with a shovel, and listened to them ignorant crackers play "I'm in the Jail House Now," and suffered to be intelligent in an unintelligent world. And so sought refuge with a book under his arm which now leads him into JPClarkes on weekends, and $700 leather trench coats. Yas.

But L cd appreciate all that except he knew that was (later, and any-time, really, except the superficial young time part, like a *New Yorker* mag-azine walking up the east side looking in windows or trying to find out what was playing at the different theaters, &c.), he knew it was hell and death. He thought it was nothing, he cdn't think totally in that vein. A fire raged in him from and for something, heated up his head, sometime, so he had to dance. Yeh, he'd be in the middle of some somber speech or moment and suddenly dance, or cry out, ok, all right, deal with it Jimmy. So inner wrought with love and life in spite the whiteout, worked and working. It was a glad spell, bro, like the ol' lady say, his mama. Yeh he always have these "glad spells." And that is what save us, bro, our glad spells stretched out to make a world, a life.

In the islands, L stayed in most of the time, when he wasn't playin' war, readin' incredible garbage of all kinds. He got so arty and self-conscious he started keepin this "journal," a diary he calls it, and most of it read like a grim autobiography of some sick existential cracker. "Oh, ah, this pains, this pleasures, this is profound, this is tragic, how sad, how lonely ow, aw," and more such like bullshit. Reading it today, bro, is a real trip. It read like many heavy white novels they advertise in the *jyz* (dig the code??), by they sons they tryin' to help get over, by saying they can write. "Oh, aw, tragic, pleasure, etcetera."

(Quote diary. . . .

But mostly it was books, book titles, that went into the diary, with a mere scattering of distracted reality. You cd barely tell where or when or who from the diary, except if you were some superslick psychologist, by the literary reference, and you cd deal with that quickly changing hand-writing, the vague unsure scrawl of the early pages, to the sure incisive crypto script of the thinker looking in the mirror. From *The New York Times Book Review*, to the subjugated subtleties implied by something haughtyin' the tone of something. Seeking whatever had meant whatever to whoever. What does that mean? That word? *Kafka?* Some kind of sex-ual weirdini? Virginia Woolf . . . T.S. Eliot . . . Ezra Pound. (Earlier L had checked out a name and went to look for the book on Raymond Blvd, yeh, at home, and stood there and the white boy sd, 'cause he didn't have the book in that grim workin' class town, "You're too erudite" . . . What that mean? Be run around tryin' to check that out. E-r-u-d-i-t-e, in the dic-tionary, somewhere. And then taking that on.) So L spent time bein' erudite, bein' deep. He climbed all up in that def, and got that together. Slowly, the iceman cometh inside him, cometh up into his eyes, to see, slowly, replace the flame, the glad spell, with the ice eye check. All of it come in, all the sees the cold sees, all the definitions, there shaping . . . Thos Hardy, *The Return of the Native*, Tess Durberville . . . wanting to dig how to say that, what could be happening with *Jude the Obscure*. What did it mean, with droopy hair and pilgrim hat and staff on a book jacket?

There was a list of great books, he could look at . . . in hardcover and paperback. All them heavy lookin', deep erudite books with the intelligent arty covers. The Dovers and Beacons. All the titles of heavy stuff he didn't get to in Colored School. Now he lowered himself on a silken cord, into the depths of the beast's glowing silver stomach, to check it out, bro . . . to check it out. But dig, while checking, that that does not become a groove in and of itself. *Per se.* You dig the kind of dudes that like to say that, L? *Per se.* Go 'head, bro. *Per se.* Knock yo' mofuhgn self straight out. . . . *Per se.* Yeh.

In the new groove of the beast's stomach, which reflects in cold whites, in what the victim thinks is startling "magnificence" and "freshness." He smells coffee burning in the wind (later drawn on pavements grinning at hunger, so arty had it become—a later version of pacing on pavements at Colored School, hungry but contained by that form, which had nothing to do with starvation my man, but only the leanness of passing from one class to another. Strugglin', you dig?).

L was blinded all right. All that paper bent his mind, man. For real. All that staring at etched conceits on the naked page. The piles and piles of European lives he analyzed, had fed into him, touched. He was sitting in a room in the islands somewhere, a short fat Italian in there with him answering the phone and he crying over a copy of *Farewell to Arms*. The Italian cdn't dig that, he was that closer to real by then. L over there in nutville, cryin' over Hemingway, the white boy lookin' at him, trying to get to that. White boy in a tee shirt and baseball hat, with still an Italian accent, readin' muscle books and "pussybooks," feet kicked on the desk. J, checkin' out fantasies of Europe and weepin'. Or stretched out with Evelyn Waugh, picking up the accents of the heroes and heroines of *Brideshead Revisited*.

The cakeicing life . . . those figures on top of the birthday cakes, a jiggly sweet craziness . . . so refined . . . that wd be real as reality. The flat paper mannequins that words provide, musty lives. Flashing with artificial color, these ghosts maurauded around the room, mincing and lisping. Cracking jokes and drinking "exquisite wine," and more and more we stepped into the pace, pointed toe and whirled, whirled in the dark lit by a splinter of fantasy. To be there in that world, and yet there be another where everybody walking, there like that too. Figures and sounds, the waltzes, minuets, ballrooms, rhythmic sex stalks of that world. Banged against the dum dum shatter of "I'm in the Jail House Now," which was square bizness, dust and cold and there. Washing nasty shit off white boys' plates with a little dish mop, from 03:27 to 22:00. . . . Where was that, and wd you subscribe to it? Bloom, Joyce, Pound, wd you subscribe? L created in himself, like a dynamite focus of all perfect energy hovering just a foot or so off the ground. That's a dream world. A fantasy collection of objects and lives. L read hours and hours and hours. He read some a' everything. Whatever caught his fancy, piled up like thin booty, to be internalized, and somehow filtered down into the personality. Amidst the slaughter of people. The deaths of ideas and real worlds. Nations enslaved. Hunger slashing across humanity, and death a hip slogan weird yng crackers wear on their backs when they dress up like iodine bottles. Amidst Truman and Eisenhower and the 24th regiment sent to its death in Korea. Nigger lynchings. The stench of baked brothers and sisters, bits of wool and coon grease conked on the unraveling rope.

The destruction of all life and real meaning. L cd sit twirling slowly around a planet "coming out of obscurity." In its first life being really hostile to its later sweet maturity. It was life it seemed. Like a shrunken bonsai tree. He cd be in this cloud, the blind genii dealing with the fantasies of vanished crackers, which was a code that ruled the waking world, in reality. Some Raskolnikov shit. Talking about Raskolnikov. In that diamond mist of cloud in which illusion spins itself. You be readin' all that garbage and create a garbage world . . . thin tinsel and orange peels. Meanwhile the world is churning alligators out its throat, and we are asked to stand and deal in musical fantasy. L had to mobilize hisself to stop staring off into space and spaceships. One day the mothership whizzed by his knot while he was checkin' something else, and he cdn't even dig it.

Educating himself was the name of the game L thought he was playing. Tho that had took on other dimensions . . . deadly deadly . . . gas chamber time, gas chamber time, a sly cracker face formed of all useless objects and ideas begins to form, begins to form, there, there in the dark, it forms, hideous, gruesome, yet we wink at it, we wink, it winks, wink, and there we are grinning, grinning, skinning, together. The vomit is the food they serve the further obscured, the further ignorant, who come into Reverend Abernathy's church thinking that liberlip skunk know somethin'. Hey dude yah know anythin' . . . huh? Spill it, bubble eye. You know somethin'?

19th century, 18th century. (We loved England and the English. We loved tweed and haughty arrogance . . . silence, cocktails. The icy cynical look. Criticism. Loved it.) Sucking it in in a silent stream. Reading in the suk head, suck head, suck it in. Go see look. What the f. . . .'s with this guy?? The white boy be studyin' me, trying to understand it. He was just a good immigrant running a cold red and white, meat and potato reality, and the nigger is cryin' for Hemingway.

But that is, in capsule, a lotta folks' problem. Suck up a fake world of dead cracker images. L actually wanted to be and was the hero of *No More Parades*, the swishy genius in *Brideshead Revisted*, the upperclass blank catholic of that same novel. Evelyn Waugh, who wd spit on a nigger, a nigger sat hypnotizing himself with his magic. All our problem in this cellophane world we style by, we desire, when life itself churns, chugs, boils around us, crushes us sometimes we ain't even hip dealing with the paper and cartoon the cellophane ritual, the twirling confection of poisons. The dude made himself T.S. Eliot (a reactionary white religious faggot) Ezra Pound (a flamboyant bohemian egotistical elitist rightwinger). He, L, was the aloof cool tweed and flannel English eccentric poet, the continental quietist, sipping weird wines to violins. Weeping for Doestoevsky, even got to be a mad Russian trying to assassinate the world for no reason. An existentialist. A weirdo. Oh, oh, world, oh, oh, not even digging, the what, world, and it bit him later, bit the fool, out of him. . . . almost.

And all that time, he said that stretched out bored, turned inside trying to be intelligent. Loading lies into himself, strange tastes, bizarre scenes he wished to duplicate with his own energy, and white cunts began to open like bear traps all over the universe, and yet he didn't even know it. There was no consciousness to the changing rage of interior white supremacy. It was just that his references changed. They were being changed. The old black bogged out, split open, made irrelevant, sitting inside away from the bars and whores of reality. On that smoking sweating island, he sat like Frankenstein being hatched on the late show, and fed his little boy black health to the continental pig, apple in his mouth and everything.

The stream of poison sucked into the dude's noggin in that year or so is incredible. From the *Dead Sea Scrolls* to *Finnegans Wake*, from *Ulysses* to *Auntie Mame*, and by then scuffling out from under 16th century anthology tingaling, the first tired T.S. Eliot imitations began to heave themselfs into reality, distorted, funny time, scary. L wdn't dig them a minute later. Drive Rommel, across the desert, until you get to the 20th century. And let me know when you arrives, my man. By time L got outta there, he had moved headlong into black bohemianism. Having exchanged his black childhood for a novel, and the schizophrenia was funny to L. He dug it as a mildly amusing set, the estrangement from real real.

Parallel streams of energy—one real one un—one to be totally destroyed, the other, analyzed and transformed, made totally beautiful. (Is that you goin' for the ghos' narrator? Saying "parallel," when in fact they aren't?) But they are. They the real and the unreal sit beside each other, each completely disputing the other, each contributin' to the other's discontinuity. Except one is just cultural aggression. Yeh, sitting there like that in that room, in a institution (usairforce) made available by the whites, with no alternative to that frustration, ran him out of hisself.

What is that like, exactly, being turned inside outside, becoming the other, and letting the other replace the deep beats of the real? A flashing wind tunnel. LJ, head down, hands jammed in pockets, buffeted, pushed, thrown, face reddening. Pushing vertical to horizontal, almost, it looks like day at the end of the tunnel. Daylight pulsing like a star, light years away. And yet that tunnel began a long time before that actually. LJ used to mess with them little white girls in the cloak room, grab them, nasty like, and they'd giggle, but only polite talk to the black ones like what had been taught at home, plus them sisters cd fight. They'd slap yr face 'round, tryin' to get a cheap feel. So it begins with cheap feels in the integrationists' computer. Roosevelt's pastiche of dying capitalism and Joe Louis as the world's champeen. You see, it's a hot house here, where wild plants are hooked up to the new deal. You see, it turned out (and a voice cd be speaking this in a sequence of glowing purple lights) that we were growin' them sociologists in them weird schools, so we had to let 'em dip, dip 'um (in America—what else?), like breaded gargoyles, we gotum lined up to salute invisible stuff. It appears the world is opening. It's a pricetag put on the visible, which is the philosophy of the owners. What you see is backed up by what you don't, but that don't mean it's invisible.

It just mean you can't see it, at the time. You get the price tag and only sometime the object! When you get the object, what can you do with it? Back to the drawing board!

(Dance, dance, yeh, the bro, he spins reciting history in a burst of pinky finger sparkles. He strikes his characteristic super cool stride . . . say:)

"Where and When did the whiteout come?" It'd go on like that, based on those words or unreadable scripture.

L had come into the service because he'd reached the end of one weird vague road. Going wherever from wherever. Wherever you are, my man, I'm trying to communicate. Wherever he is, he's trying to communicate. Like if L can be seen as having marched down an absolutely obscured road. (It don't matter what the superficial ideas were, like a dude on a shark's back say. He on a wet deck. It don't matter what the obscurity teaches. The shark can bite, brother. Reach up from under the water and chomp yr mittyfreakin' laig. But the shark stopped maybe?? Came to a port, or finally dumped the dude on his head . . . on another wet deck.) L got thrown the hell out of school. If he hadn't he wd've finished and become, possibly, a chamber pot for living dinosaurs. Like my man Peewee, he went to school wit, banjo playin' muhfuh working for yr man Agnew.

SONG: My man? Yeh, yr man Agnew. A yella nigga workin' for Agnew.
         Yeh.
         Agnew, Agnew, what you gonna do? (Bomp Bomp Bompaaaa
              Bomp Bomp Bomp)
         Agnew, Agnew, what you gonna do? (Bomp Bomp Bompaaa
              Abomp Bomp Bomp)
         Agnew, baby, is it real to say you blew?

His chamberpot, like Peewee, in the shadows of reality. He can be making "a good dollar," with the Hart Schaffner & Marx suit. Shoulder holster, for the Ag. Protect the Ag! Protect the Ag! He ain't a bad guy! Protect the Ag! No contest!

He drifted into the world. The world reached out from itself and dragged him round into it. Fit him into its significant edges. Tried to stick him in it. He came up without school, busted, and tryin' to get away, splitting for the airforce. Romance. Why? To get away. To think. To be other than in the obscure shadows of the obscure road, listening to songs that were so futuristic they made no sense. And the dead sirens, the minstrel-boogie, played each second in the Colored School. By the time you got there, old dead niggers were lined up on a path from the administration building to the reservoir, chanting some obscene shit about Booker T. Washington's jones. (Does the singer know that song?)

No, not the singer, but the writer, he do. Sometime he wake up, sweatin' in his sleep that the song snorts on in its uuuugly way. Ah, so it's gone, gone, for good he whispered. Yet dive down out of the clouds one day in yr shiny jet, example of the high level of yr nation's productive forces, and you will see, if it ain't raining, an impressive display . . . the tops of heads. The heads of old dead niggers lined up from administration building to reservoir. Dive down closer, closer, look at the eyes of the chanters. And now and again some youth runs in and out of the line, swatting the chanters with reefers or a whiter rap, and now and again, a dude come with a piece of good wood and lays it to them august zombies. Whap, whap, bap, wop . . . cross they head and face, and the blood seeps down into the grass, and the lawn is fed, and the students, when it is sunny, come down grinning and doing their student thing, and the symbiotic funky goes on.

The end of the line is the end of the line. Tho the line begins at a new location. Yr new base, on this island. Sucking in the jive tribe's KULCHUR. Amidst that ramble of forest life. L came out of the groves of academe, booted, booked, bewildered. He was going away, and actually got away, bad. You listen to Beethoven's Fifth three times a week, and maybe the 7th, 9th, 3rd, and even the goddam quartets a few times, and you be a jibbering idjit. Plus Bartok, and Schoenberg, and Mozart, trios, quartets, cluttered sympathies. 1st and 2nd Sympathies. You be a stutterin' lunafreak. A mad moon goon. A nigger who lost his trigger. No shot. Just lick the first trik that don't spika de nigger.

(In the crowd certain guise and doles gets up and swashes 'round de co't. De singer sings what he hears sung in de world, what he gets mashed round in he's haid—Now questions: Now Answers: Now Statements: Fragments of things, split off from practicable function, beads of do and done, toothpicks of see and seen. Questions: What was the service lak? Lak a runnaway enema the world was havin' inside mah haid.)

See it this way. From Colored School, L got thrown off the cliff of Negro respectability, into the pit of blackness. He had to become aware

of the world, because, being sensitive, he was now to be found in it.
Standing at the back of a line, of dudes who he knew, and now began to
find out what had happened to them. All the brothers he had grown up
with in the neighborhood. Most of them. Not the weird different group
he ran into in church. Church, and that church, Bethany, must have collected, and still does, another group. The lightskinned, the almost
unpoor. (Like the movie ghouls, they call THE UNDEAD, so there is this
negro we shd call THE UNPOOR, or THE UNBLACK . . .) It soon sets up
a no-life zone, hovered between the colonizers and the colonized, lingers
upon nothing save dearly revered psychosis, that they are different . . .
and they are.

Let out of the insanity house, going to the insanity open world. He cd
feel the whole deathblow super powerful society aimed at him, you, me.
Specifically it is an isolated feeling, being let out of the padded cell, into
the open world where bodies float up to the sand, drowned in America.

So L showed up blinkin' on that scene. It's history now pardner, but I
tell you. . . . It's real, the world, and ugly. He stood outside in busride
morning. With dudes with clothes rolled up in dufflebags. Standing there
all of us facin' America cold. That was it. The world had let him down, to
its cold blizzard reality. That is always the nightmare of the petty bourgeois blood, to be just an anonymous nigger in America. Just any nigger.
"You're not like the others," is the code world of bloods being led down
the stained corridor toward the furnace of absolute assimilation. Those
that are turned into the blood of America, into America's blood, its
nourishment.

Look in the jails, when they get you, famous or unfamous revolutionary, you will, as you walk toward the iron, be able to wave at brothers you
knew. Checkin' them out, this is where them dudes be. Those you don't
see at those jive meetings tryin' to be somebody in America, struggling
against being an anonymous slave nigger. . . . Dr. Negro, Professor
Jigabooo, Attorney Coon, Mr. Woogie, acting intelligent . . . The others
they're waving as you walk toward the iron. "Hey man, what goin' on?
Hey, shit ain't nothin' to it bro, you take care a' yo'self, in this mf'n
place." And the dudes waiting out there by the bus to be shuttled off to
fight for evil.

Is middleclass niggers in a baked vase? This one cracked open. And L
rolled out into America. Rolled out into America. Can we see this as a
visual sequence, L rolling out of a baked vase, a red white and blue black

and green vase baked and shiny, inside noise and cardplaying, some deep frontin' goin' on, jim, yeh, bro, deep. It's me askin' kin this be shown on the flicks for all to dig the weird color vaz of middleclass *negers*. Rolling to a stop. In the cold, eye blinkin', tryin' to check out and not daring to check out.

And all this time it took to see actually what the feeling was that moved him. He had been caught among the lowliest of Americans, niggers and poor whites. And put in line to wait for some garbage he didn't have no use for. Betrayed is what he felt. He had been betrayed, because deep down & instinctively he'd been led to believe that there was some much brighter garbage for him. He'd been at Bethany picnics with lightskinned folks and even had wavy hair hisself. He'd checked out the vulgarity of whiteschool, so po-like, and made it clean, a getaway to Colored School, and was immersed and celebrated by the place. And now this, a clear betrayal is what it was. Left out here next to a bus, with some niggers never been to no picnics or colored schools, some niggers picked up off the street like JD and them.

But even so, L cd be among them giving out answers, eyes dazed, tryin' to figure out how he lost his way, what was he doing there. Wow, you mean, where my man? Standing behind the counter of the mess hall, wrapped in old food smells, soaked through to the skin for 14 hours, on kp, and pullin' a new record kp, 22 days in basic trainin'. It was a new record he told himself, but whether it was a new record, or even whether it was actually 22 times, we will never really know.

A cracker was singing, "You in the Jail House Now," some hill-billy, a mfin' hill-bill but true enough hill-billy. He was definitely in the jail house now. "No fears, no tears/Tomorrow will always become us/Waiting is not goodbye/We'll be together, again." That played too, but those, of course, are not the real words to the song some white women like the Andrews Sisters or somebody crooned. This and "You're in the Jail House Now," over and over, the 14 hours of kitchen patrol. On a jukebox in the middle of the mess hall while L mopped the floor, or cleaned out the garbage pit.

But who was close to him then? All the bros, the lost ones, really, the real ones. The ghost part of his brain hooked him directly to Colored School. And the real bros, he sat and talked with, ran across the athletic field with, and still the ghost part lingered, and in some ways grew. It's that way now with many people. They hooked up to death, ghosts, deadness, foolishness, ignorant ratings, and the real world steams by them, us, yall. A vanished staring space in yr face and head. Looking away from reality to mazes of shadow titillation, signifying schizophrenia. Frustration. Cultural Aggression, one of the main weapons of imperialism. To replace yr healthy frame of reference with a rigged Euro-American desire syndrome, where he and she want, even unconsciously, what that frame of reference dictates. That's why these funnytime students, with gris gris wrapped around their neck and mod-Americanism shoes, have a Baby Ruth stack in their ideology, crooning about good times in America. That's why you can't move like you shd bro, these old dudes and you. Got a space in yo' face where desperation is pumped in like crude oil.

And then after the critical winter of sorrow, reality was shadows, and shadows did the forming of messages foaming out of yr mouth. American hydrophobia, a middle class nigger child, thrown out of the incubator into American reality. And now old class friends would stand an inch behind where friends stand and talk distantly about a piece of gold they had on they shoulder. A ¼" x 1" piece of "gold" on each shoulder, which had successfully removed them, perhaps forever, from reality. And L cd look at them, frustrated, not understanding the real gap that had been moved, like a stage play, where the poorly trained stage crew uses a creaking crane to transport a gap from the wings to the middle of the stage between a protagonist and his supporting cast, who have now become realer than him (to him). That gap, that leap it takes to get from reality, with a growing marshmallow of fantasy gorillaing yr consciousness, to the other side, where fantasy is the rule, and there is perhaps only a marshmallow of reality they use to sweeten their speech or regulate their walk, colored style.

L want to know then (kid!) why he cdn't be on the other side with unreality too, shit. It look dam sure sweeter than standin' in the cold near the bus with the other Straight-Out Prisoners, or in the mess hall listening to "I'm in the Jail House Now." (How do we know we're a cultural nation? Because none of us could dig that, " . . . In the Jail House Now," whether it was niggers digging Ramsey Lewis or niggers diggin' "Work w/Me Annie," hmm hmm.) But then, don't lie, bro, ain't it true that L dug Brubeck and Chet Baker and Gerry Mulligan, at Colored School? Ain't it true, that L was diggin' Paul Desmond, after, but stronger, than Bird??? Finally he gonna deny that shit, even if it's true! But that's the values of the assimilation mode, the whiteout imperialism uses. Either eliminate or assimilate, Cabral tells us, and the Colored School dudes was assimilated, yet in them still cd ring "Wk with Me Annie," and the test, bro was here you looking across that gap, they put you down. The white boy put him down, sayin' L ain't good enough for me no mf'in how. Stay in jail w/ them niggers. Yeh, and then, later, L tried to be an officer too. He wanted that gold. He sd I'm gonna take that leap. Why in hell not? Across the gap to fantasyville where Donald Duck rapes yr old lady to help you make it in Amoralica. But he failed. L blew the test, the crackers sd. You blew it, L. Stay in the barracks with the niggers.

And all this time, L had worked at stuffin' himself full of fantasy seed. Crazy books, bestsellers, just abstract bullshit of all descriptions, the whiter the better, he stuffed it in. On and in, you name it, he check it, from *The Communist Manifesto* (what? He read tha'? Well, how the other stuff get in?) to the Buddhist Bible. It all rolled in, with fantasy photographs and yearbooks of fictitious signatures till later he even changed a work to show he really loved these enemies of the sun, which finally brother, is not even true!

Left w/ reality + not understanding that's what it was. So yng & warped, he didn't dig. Nor do you, LH, in ivy league, draining hisself of relevance. ABS, in Bushwarburg, is that you, finally, laboring on a humble, while the dread beast yet remains at large? YR you he, staggering thru the world with a "revelation," a mystery shadow, to build a mystery shadowy life upon. The snowman's still at large, he still looms large in all our consciousness. DS ran away from the struggle, a fat pottbutt turning quickly into a fullfledge fag. It was the best act in the burlesque circus, a family of West Indian faggots. And on, so why not a yng man unclear of what the world is, having been taught in cotton batting that served as his shield, that he wd be of substance, of importance? If you think about it, the incubation the hatching process for the yng bourgeois. Half street, half radiodazzle. An electric feeling of wild promise. High Noon In HollyWood, Bee-Beep. (Brought to you by Ovaltine!)

And sometime, when he ain't clear, it happens yet. But he takes a great deep breath now, shakes and clears his big ol' head . . . + laughs at fantasists, idealists, bs preachers hanging off the precipice by a ol' peg leg. (You mean he made it safe?) In life where is the saftee? You jumpin' 'head of his storee, but his storee is life and its companions humdoolilah . . . Hey he got you religious? Naw, I ain't religious, not at all. I used to be, and changed up, but maybe not so much, really.

I asked L was he religious. He say, "I'll tell you this man. I don't believe in no shit that don't exist! I believe in nature, people, society." But that wasn't then, he sd that, not down on that island, standing in the sun. Maybe he cdn't have sd what he believed in, in a criss-cross place, in a criss-cross time, hours and hours he squatted on a runway and tried to sort out the whole of Europe and some of the sleeping cultures of Asia (then). So the west's publishers wd have us believe of the various swami's chose to swarm over our consciousness carrying the practiced gleaming submission of our vanquished feudalistic, metaphysical cultures. Come to think of it, L was torn then, or maybe caught in an abstraction between one entry in the diary, which says "I Am A Buddhist," and another which says, "Today I finished reading *Das Kapital.* Communism is stupid, it denies the existence of a God." But then L hadn't really read *Das Kapital.* It was too fat. He just cdn't dig the language. The sutras were easier to read, and more like poetry. God and religion were poetry. And that's, you'd think, the way the gofer-makers make the gofers go for what they sellin', which is smoke and waverin' shadow. While the gofer-makers scoop up all the dust. They not givin' up nuthin' to the chumps, maybe a liberal here and there give away smoke and waverin' shadow, and that's worse than horse. Make nigger grow pink eyes, and babble bullshit for the rest of his life.

Them pile of books was nuthin' but expedient liberal dope to turn L pinkeyed, and away from the world. (The singer takin' a hard line, now he done his split, and whipped hard at the audience groanin', WAKE, WAKE, WAKE, THE WORLD NEEDS TO CATCH ON FIRE, bangin' electric guitar behind the big sax. A hard heavy horn like we like, like a nasty Trane lightin' up the tunnel where we are. Light up the tunnel where we are, my brother. Honk Honk. . . . bow bow bow . . . Honk Honk!)

You see all this to show the pledge allegiance path to the precipice. This is the way we are prepared for the long drop through the masses and into a closed hole, amen. Cover him over. He'll turn to dirt's life. And all of this is prepared for us, in the various think tanks and imperialist institutions. We come up out of reality with a big hat and bells (22's, draped on bad kicks) and get caught on the fly, and given the uniform of our masters, if we are truly sensitive and dutiful and have an appetite for humiliation and assimilation, amen. Goodbye? But then some distance, some gap between L and the gap, some peering stance his emotions took,

to check stuff, to be checked, to check whatever it was turned all this jive
on and off and spun it in its place. Half mystical because he thought
everything had to get a play, even what cdn't be seen, the son of generations of Baptists and Methodists, one signal that the age of integration
follows the depression, because people wanted gigs. In seven years the
world itself was lit up in struggle. "World War II?" A weird concept. A
world war? What does that mean, that the contenders were actually fighting over control of the world? Chas Lindbergh cautioned all you jive old
family crackers about goin' down for that one, that Bourgeois Europe wd
never recover. Fighting amongst ourselves, he sd, is crazy. The Germans
must not fight the English. A figment of the imagination of early capitalism, decrying the lightning change into corporate capitalism. But in the
struggle, East Europe got out the whole, and as a reward fast Franklin
awarded them to Russia as new markets eventually to be rehooked to now
very slick international monopoly which sells wheat to Russia at one
price, has a wheat shortage and buys it back at higher prices. Making
money at both ends. But this is ahead of the storee.

The artsee craftee consciousness our bro developed militated for a god
concept. The idealism shook hands with metaphysics. Both looked other
than reality. L hated reality. Most people can't deal with it, except everyday they must deal with it. But how to draw information from that process
is society's problem. L believed in God, because it sounded better than
not. Tho, finally, he was a dishonest party member in the feast of the
deities. It was the culture that raised him, but like many of us, he fled it
internally. From almost the minute the preacher raised him out the water
and no searing revelation had come. "I was supposed to be changed, I
thought. Somethin was s'posed to happen. And didn't nothin' happen."
And that is essentially our rage against this life, that the owners make
nuthin' happen with all the potential world art gives.

Why leave me here in reality? Why cast me down into reality? Why am
I so turned around I keep turnin' up in reality? Eyes stretched open like
some $1.98 buddha. Here among the mass of the obscure and the anony-
mous. Among that solid mass, the defining mean of humanity. All
wedged into grey places to suffer. And called on exclusively to suffer, &
suffer the whims of the mad. But reality floods, floods. Reality floods, and
bros slink down Springfield, high and nasty. Behind them floods, bros
and sisters locked up, killed because of that, or because they lack it, sit in
offices and smile at the enemies of the sun.

So L cried and developed a fantasy jones. E'en kicked back into reality, with all the rest of us, lulling before the dungeons. He craved the recognition of the damned. And so he studied earnestly how to be one of them, and lo and behold, despite the contradictions and bellbottoms packed in the bottom of his drawer, he became one. He became a figment of his own imagination.

Lied to the authorities, created a biography they'd think was "subversive," and literally discharged himself from the service. And after the obligatory work and humiliation planting flowers, waiting tables, makin' beds, picking up garbage, painting barracks, he was on his way to Waycross to be let out.

They (Them Theirs Theyres &c)

Nobody took him in. He went to Waycross to get discharged, and had to wait there a few days at a base. During that period of time, he went into the town to see close relatives. Somehow in some spurt of flitting fragment of word or picture, he made out like one of his aunts was close to him. That he cd go to her and explain the deep division, the longing for fantasy. At the same time he was connected, it seemed, forever, and painfully, to reality. That pain of division is the exact content of the west's art. That's why it's negative. A focus of longing for what ain't. Or a willingness to prance about what is not going to be for long. "Save the Dead" cd be the title of European libraries. Tho work goes on in the world, bro, harnessing nature to the will of perverts.

So he got into town and went out to see his aunt. Knocked on the door, and came in, hugged her, asked about his grandmother, who wasn't there. And then sat like on the edge of a couch and waited for his aunt to advise him. She cdn't advise him. They talked about old times. About him as a kid, running around the outskirts of Waycross with the rest of the cousins. He threw some stones at some white boys and ran back across a field. They were shouting there behind, near an old general store, and the little girls, and little Larry, his ynger cousin, ran fast right beside him. Big eyes flashing. Ran all the way to the road, and watched the Buick pass. Then loped across and up the hill to grandma's house and the lawn and the swings, and they all jumped in the swings and swung and laughed, and wanted something cold to drink.

They talked about the Atchinsons lived next door. Four boys all got to be doctors. And L knew big old Reggie Atchinson in Colored School. Big ol' yellow Reggie. In med school, and actually L didn't get to talk to Reggie too tough 'cause med students was too hip to talk to brown-skinned undergrads, even them they knew from Waycross. That was the first time L had checked colored rich people, I mean checked out how they were really smooth and big-time, and had big houses. He savoured that too. That was an actual head whipping in a way none of them cd dig, this warm black them behind him, out of whose substance all L's acts are

301

formed. A generation of us come to the front and be examined. Be cleaned up and readied for the next step. Like Waycross. Sitting with his aunt. Running through, sorting through all the strong influences from there. She had no advice, or did she?

"How you feel, L? OK? You on yr way home, now, huh?"

"Yeh. I'm out of the service." (How did he explain that to her? He cdn't cd he, that he'd been undesirably discharged from the airforce as some kind of subversive? But actually he was kicked out for lying. But then it cd be sd he grew up to be a subversive on the real side and the lie was but the intro to a long riff of intended overthrows. They cd take you there, the top heavy pros of oppression, who finally, are the real ones yall face.)

"What you gonna do now? When you get home? Back to school I hope?"

"Yeah. I'll go back to school in New York." He was gonna say, "I want to be a writer," except he thought it was too corny to come in somebody who knew you's house and say something like that, which is the cute sickness of the west. Why not say that? Why not communicate directly and clearly to someone? Why not communicate, and build clear love and clear strength, and agree to build the world together? Living in slavery puts so many slants and turns in clear space . . . distorts, turns everything&body upside down. So you all sit and say nuthin' real, and real goes on keepin' score on ya . . . a flock a' zeroes . . . a flock of blanknesses. But then later, L cd go away and maybe say to somebody (he never did) my aunt told me to go back home and do just what I wanted, be a writer. That never happened. The tale. Just the feeling and the acts that followed.

He came home under wraps, like, under cover. The world flowed over and around him. Some other sheezit had gone down, and was partly unrelated, maybe, but it's all connected. He walked back in. His brother was there, hooked up with petty bourgeois Negroes and po' Negroes trying to be pb Negroes, and they was talkin' about teachin' school, and goin' to see stuff. L wanted to be stuff, not just see it. He wanted to be what anybody might want to check.

He marched around Lone Ranger style, hugged up in the hall with some of his brothers' lady friends. They was just like his brother. They wanted to teach school and go to New York on weekends. That's what they talked about in them hallways, bubba, the same time you was tryin' to squeeze 'em, they was talking about wantin' to teach school and go to New York on weekends. L split, very soon. He went to New York, to learn life.

He had an argument one evening at the dinner table. "Ain't nobody never got kicked out the army in this family before." Crackers in white hoods had burned down two a' his grandfather's funeral parlors, cut off brothers' johnsons and stuffed 'em into the dying dude's mouth right in front of his grandmama's eyes. She told that to L when he was 12, so he wd know it always and think about it odd times. "But hadn't nobody never been kicked out of the army, I mean, airforce, before." You know? So, like that was some deeep stuuuf. His father made laconic blood-practical comments. Like, "just so you'll be able to get a job." His mother wanted something heroic to come out of his mouth, not no vague dizzy garbage about no writin'. "Cd you write and be in the cotillion at the same time?" "Hadn't nobody in this family neeeeeeeeeeeeeeeeeeeeeeeeeeeeeeeeeeeeeeeeeever got kicked out no army before you know?" Nobody.

And then there was that time they'd found him out on the porch soggy drunk, and carried him inside and laid him on the day bed, and momma wept she had a drunk for a son. Drinking them cheap brews in a summer German course with them dopeyass white boys. Didn't know them dudes drank in no stiff way like that, where everybody had to drink what everybody bought. That's some other stuff. Hadn't never heard of no chug-a-lug before either. But then he laid out later in Colored School and got vomit stuffed even in his watch pockets. But that was everybody for hisself. Hell he had a bottle in his back pocket, trying to hit on an art student, and fell out. Not no stiff formal garbage dude be tootin' and toastin' whatnot in school.

He was drunk. They cried. But hadn't nobody NEVER been kicked outta no service before. "What kinda work you going to do?"

"You want me to be around here and get some kinda factory job. But I ain't gonna do it. I'm gonna move to New York. Me and Little Wilson."

"Little ain't goin' nowhere." L's brother had to say somethin', eatin' them p's and getting ready to teach. And after all that, this dude didn't teach but a few years, then wanted to be a dancer or something stranger. Little didn't go nowhere either. Him and Donnie Kirk, the vibes player, were L's s'posed-to-be-roommates in "The Apple." But they didn't make it. L went over one afternoon, saw an ad in the newspaper, and ran into the apartment. This foreign-talking dude was showing it to some people standing in the middle of the room, looking at the joint like they was trying to figure out what they was going to do with it, a cold water flat on the east side, truly run down, gipsies and shit running around with the door open in the middle of the winter.

Hadn't nobody in that family *never* been kicked out of the army before. Who cd visualize that? Not them. Not him. Not you, jim, if you'd been in Colored School, planning for success—vaguely but definitely. Niggers been slung around, drug around, tricked, sold into slavery, killed and cursed. But hadn't NEVER nobody we know been kicked outta no service before. And to top it off what if they knew that he had did it (L had) to hisself, cause, like, he just wanted to split? Ump!

So you talking now about this dude got busted out Colored School for refusing to take it seriously, actually refusin' to take it any way at all. Now that it comes up, he went w/ Doll, remember, that black sister at the top of the hill. Had her own apt and car. What is it in him that demands reality despite the abstraction of the white plastic melted-down and sugar on it pasted in his mental-digestive track, the wind-up toy training program complete with cotillions and reciting the Gettysburg Address in George Washington's church in a Boy Scout suit?

Then he goes off to the army, dropped down into the nigger pit of reality. To be in the anonymous crowd, the mass, as the object of some neckless white boys' scorn and then cdn't even run with that. What ain't he gonna get kicked out of cd've been the rim of question circling his parents' minds. What ain't gonna eject you, man? What ain't gonna spit you out as alien? Blind and crazy as you is.

And suddenly L was in The Big Apple, an anonymous exotic wanderin' in and out of purposively strange places. A huge I again, like a rolling me, set loose to tell the story of the world any kind of way. Later for reality, just to tell it, tell the story. Get some wood to beat together, then sit down, cross your legs. We gotta git ready to sit for a spell.

Leaving implies arriving somewhere else. L crossed the water into the east side, of stinking hallways, and, unlike any place he'd been, whites. And people who looked like they was deep into stuff, like they thought and what not. They had books and turtleneck sweaters. Cut loose, cast adrift, let out the slam to grow again. The air swept him up. The air. Coffeeful air. The air smelled like the hundreds of coffee shops. And they prepared all this for him? No, he was anonymous, again, but this time he liked it more. Gunfighter style, he roamed in another place, a weird place, a different place. Yeh, it was fantasy, now that sat around him on all sides. Fantasyland and fantasy folks. He'd reached Oz. Wizards everywhere. A much greater, much deeper, much hipper fantasy than the gold bars or the straight-out Colored School fantasy. But keep this in mind. You can reach all of them from the same road. They told him that this fantasy was heavier than the middle class Negro fantasy. That's what they told him when he started be'n w/ them.

When he first got there, they flashed around on all sides. And then bloods he met when coming through in Colored Schools, reproduced the successful travelogue of captivity. Some niggers sat in coffeeshops, frontin'. They'd go in there and sit and try to see what was going on. But look like, you know, try to look like you ain't weak and crazy. And he went from the fantasy ring who sat and manufactured a life of art and "creativity" merely to talk about it, who did nothing but sit, who got up mornings to go somewhere and sit. Or those who, even lower, used that just to get a meal, a woman (or man), who said that they were artists, writers. L found himself in that weird company momentarily, but he got them, even in that 1st crowd, to begin to produce. He put out a pamphlet and made them write for it.

But earlier, scraping around trying to wake up, trying to learn something. And the first story was on yellow paper . . . very long. "The Diary of Peter Black." Gordon Pilgrim and Francine Pilgrim sd, "Well this is better than Johnny Miller's story." Johnny, he was just somebody who wrote a story and turned it over to the Pilgrims for review or perusal.

Almost w/o question youths were absorbed in their ankles and thru their shoelaces. All the years of practice they required to become these others, were suddenly all together like a granite plaque with name and dates on it. They is blown into town. They is youths lately of the federal metropole. Wards of the state, warriors of the state. Broke except they cd see their spirit blown full of false understandin', "bloated with ignorance" (Y.R. sd), but also by the great promise of youth, its glistening perfumed romance for the world. Give or take—less or more. Whatever it was them explained, they let them loose like kites to gather in all sense and circumstance.

They hadn't told them specifically what to *be* except a general category ART! That message had come through in the airforce where they lounged, sipping 1 dolla' vodka in foreign lands, as "trained killers" & that was before they took the vow and never masturbated again.

The specific saying is not necessary, tho it happens. The walls wink at the victim, e'en the walls of the womb wanked, transmitting rays from the Beulah show that was playing over the radio while the victim's mother sat & watched. (She didn't e'en have to sit and watch, did she? Did they?) Show it all, the whole unlaughable process, as sponsored by the king of kong.

The streets wink, and project ultraviolet rays. The schools don't wink. They cry and wheeze and waddle, balled up, melted down suffering in a wet ball, a transparent pill for the victim to swaller. And they swaller what they are given by them to swaller. Hear them holler. It hollers them out, replaces brains w/magnetic tape, in which are fixed the commercial codes of the place. The police will tell you. Anonymous cute niggers. (Neegrews will tell you . . . what the game is. It's called Transform All Niggers Into Chewing Gum For The Boss! That's boss! Assimilate all jigs into the calm static of the place.) Electronic music of America, played in a bluesy drone. Strum some bux outta these coonshines. Alcohol them! Scag them! Game them! Shoot them! Assimilate them! Eliminate them!

Chewing gum for the boss cause employees helps. In the grim corridors of integrated urban America. They educated them in toilets. And all there are grouped together into a fine ignorant hatred. It turns them mad or turns them madder. If they hate the enemy they are mad. If they hate themselves they are madder.

> Some niggers hated the enemy, and they reveal that it is us.
> 1st militant, then anti-semitic, then cia!
> Now it is they that are the oppressed
> We who are the enemies.

Rayed in, sprayed on, told to them, coaxed in soft sounds, tap on the knuckles by the old witch. . . . "6+6 is 100," Hop Armstrong all-European homunculus. They taught them to love hate. And they learned to love it . . . one day woke up to hate it. Hate Hate.

But now they sat in the apartment trying to decide to be painters or writers. They had 3 typed poems and built a fold-in desk, hanging off a strap from the wall, and sat on a pile of books. This sat next to the bed and directly across from a chest of drawers in dutch oak style, corny, since the '30s, in every good boy's double decker rooom. Wooden flowers and a wooden road embossed upon the wood. They thot that signified warmth—it didn't. It was easier to mfr.

How do they be an artist? (painter or writer?) Just shadup and be it.

They quickly ghosted painting—wrote weird stories like "Peter Black." It was like an experiment, tho they'd written before, e'en stories, scaree fiction in EYE-TIE HIGH, other stuff, fairy foot Elizabethan poetry, thin bangles of English Renaissance (and that's how long they've been tied up here since somebody's renaissance—how wd a tuff talkin' cop handle that questioning? Ya mean Ya been here all this time?). Now gave way to other tides, still wrought w/Europa the bull. The white bull, the father of racism & capitalism, Amen.

They began to write because it cost too much to paint. & painting's stupid to do, it's good to look at, but what cd painting do? Hang it up somewhere, out the way . . . write them a theme of revolution, of love. Write them a constitution. Write them a pledge of black allegiance.

They didn't have to hear of them. They created them in their image. Hellow! Hiwere you, Mr. Highbrow—'n you got that out of *Harper's* magazine . . .

They that was close probably laughed at these dudes innumerable times. They hunched over, walking, carrying some idiotic book. There was a new edition of T.S. Eliot they got from Readers' Subscription. They sent them Readers' Subscription, a "highbrow" book club . . . Ulysses instead of Heathcliff. They had learned to look in glass windows at books and then tread the weird gossamer of their way. An electric scatter of circus lights, each one a message from them to the victim. On and off, live and dead, pass on.

They had them stylin', they-style, but They's-style they-style. What did they think when they saw them? Early 20's, thin, large eyes, army pants, duffle coat. A cap. Lookin' like they had somewhere to go. (They had . . . still gettin' up!) But in reality, they was answerin' a summons set up by death, rolled in on the installment plan. A tap tap tap effect, evil presence knocking inside they head.

But see this is misleading. T(He)y is they. The Them. And the other them pursue, as they have always pursued, in this society, rayin' and sprayin' minds into coiled springs of finishing clockwork. They is them, and the other they pursue.

All he's change, cross the ancient river, and become they, a warm abstract, all creation dumps its garbage on. Two theys conflict, this time in the streets of NYC, The Big Apple.

They bopped when they walked because good vibes still remained. This was the simple legacy of Dizzy Gillespie, in black Hare Krishna days. They had a legacy the others always sought to destroy. An identity, a "uniqueness," it was necessary to destroy so as better to control.

They cd be sitting at restaurants w/ their coffee, discussing their need to produce, and some wd produce only words. Remember, these dudes who sd to my man they didn't really have any compositions. Asked these dudes to write music for some jive plays. But they didn't have it. They didn't really compose, dig? Just walked around, stood at bars, went w/ women. . . . They were lightskinned and went w/ only white women. Slept with them probably . . . who knows (you got time for the story about the dude who took this broad home and later after they'd drunk they drink and went thru they lewd number, he felt something and opened his eyes, and started to raise up, and this weird bitch was sittin' up right in the bed, with a pair of scissors in her hands!)? That's why they were there. Cd it so simply be sd? They were named Frank. Composers who never composed.

They were named Fat Boy. Writers who never wrote. Oh they wrote when them folks put out that weird magazine. It means "nothing at all," was the signature. Zen Koans they used to memorize, or make up to drop on people. Veddy hip. Norman Sholom wd, always, sleepyeyed, explain nothingness. Sloped mustache, droopyeyed, Jew boy, L's 1st deep Jew (not the 1st, but the other 1st were at other levels, *e.g.* high school, service . . . but this was now at art level, most significant). And their existence in these other peoples' cribs who these dudes dug from home even . . . they been in school. These other folks, with these dudes . . . so that cd've been the strange exotic quality of the 1st encounters w/them . . . that they never expected to see nobody like that, nowhere. They walk in a house, and a bearded or weird mustache Jew boy w/ long hair talking riddles. That *had* to be hip! That was ZEN.

But how'd these other folks get to where they were foci for the mad rays of white-out? How did white folks get in there? Was that progressive? (Well that's the way it looked, and they followed them there to the bitter in. And the dude wd say they hated white folks, but nobody in their right mind believed it was even possible, much less internationally ubiquitous!) It was forward? An integrated high school did it. Or was it really progressive? There was an advance in it, but they lost themselves in it, raised above the streets' deadly box.

If they cd trace the way the other folks got to where zen white boys cd wash their sox in they crib! So the yng ones walkin' just behind them get caught in the same mix cross. (Dudes right now in Denmark march in ritual line, free free they mumble over and over in their drinks, free free the wind twists between their eyes, free free at home among the caves, &c.)

They'd set up a scene wherein the sickness the whole society had baked them in was shown as full of life and smiles. Was, in fact, deep. Heavy. Everything. They didn't know how they looked. But it was in tune with the greater them. The them which runs the place. And they'd come in, on buses, mostly, in small dribbles (now its crows & a different level twist out goin' down?). "Message from the Lower East Side, ca 1974," David Shakes living w/ an old stone lady casting spells on reality . . . reality castin' em back . . . reality always win! Next!

The Village was a liberal settlement created to let poor ideas stew, all stew eaters form mostly to the left! It is a status of confinement characterized by excessive "freedom." Mostly, it turns out, freedom from responsibility. They gave these dudes a job working for a jazz magazine (how're yer spellin that, Emory??). A rt wing white "jazz" or "jass" magazine. But like, they only dug the "real" jazz. Told them (the prospective employer) they didn't know anything about the music before Louie Armstrong! They chuckled and chuckled until finally it wasn't funny, some years later, but frankly scary. They gave them jobs packing boxes of old jazz and novelty records for cracker "collectors" who bid by mail.

Some collected Louis, some Bing Crosby. Some, that stuff—really weird . . . people w/ Spike Jones Joneses, Guy Lombardo Joneses, Paul White Man Joneses (all under the title jazz). White Man was the King of Jazz, ya know? Good Man was the King of Swing, Brubeck the Head of Cool. . . . Trane broke thru and revolution shook itself once again into view. (But Dolphy dies, Albert drowned, Ornette hooked up almost completely to the IF spirit of America as a pontificating exotic 'murican artiste, Omar still supports the juice, Archie still wid the w.w., Sun Ra using his power to mystify rather than grow the food we need, Pharaoh as yet unfulfilled, and, yeh, The Stones Roll back in place, the Beatles come out from under, and this time the greys actual put on dresses, bro, and rouge and shit, and flounce around before the howling pinkish mob, and commerce rolls and reaction sets in . . . Even Kenyatta died his hair blonde. . . . And who is the Quing of Rack? White Man Good Man &c.) As always in the sunset of America, each night the sunset of flag state people idea America can be seen as blood in sheets stretched across reality. By Blood and Slavery was it born . . . and so forth, as the moon rises, the face of the dead.

One time they had him in this basement sorting records, all the greys, & novelties, and obscure jams, plus Cab Calloway, Louie Jordan, Erskine Hawkins, Jelly Roll, Billy, Pres, Bird, Higginbotham, Bean, Count, Duke, Earl, Sweetpea, Little Jazz, Bad Ben Webster, all, like a stereo history of the race, glowed out the darkness and shimmered a panorama of meaning.

Working in that packing house–storefront for liberal conservative whites, Harvard Yale old money. They owned ol' Rolls Royces and one time took them to Pittsburgh in a snow storm w/ no heat in the car. They got there, to look at the record collection of some recently dead collector. Went down in the basement w/ his wife (she was still crying) and, poking around in the records, discovered a huge collection of pornography. NAKED dudes included, presenting the sexual expressions of capitalism, *i.e.*, perverted self-gratification. The woman's tears fell out of her like the way the parking meter snaps it to you yr time is up. She gulped. They blinked and kept checkin' records. Bein' w/them is like that sometime!

Meeting up w/ rich white boys who loved (?) liked (?) jazz (?). Weird. They cdn't let him know finally what it was involved them w/ the music, except, finally, you know, they weren't involved w/ it at all, but only them again. An old saw. A kind of unpopular non-song, *Only Them Again.* Sing It!

But it was a lesson anyway. They were watched and responded to, even, sadly for these others, imitated. The niggers were actually prepared by *New Yorker* magazines, and *The Male Animal* by James Thurber at the Music Box Theater, for this sad imitation. They rode around (this one, that one, the other one) in the old Rolls w/ Ludlow, the good guy, glasses, lock a' hair over one eye, brown tweed coat, gray flannel pants . . . , aw yeh, Rolls, old records, puppy he carried around named Xmas used to pee on the sides.

Remember the night Ludlow and them was drivin' over by the old Bohemian, Yards Johnson and his big mouth out there putting down the drummer? & dig, the drummer, whatshisname, was famous then, maybe 'cause a' Yards. Yards still famous ya know . . . yeh they still dig Yards . . . playin' way in, way out, 6 white boys dronin' & him pockin' sense thru. And them pocks is pocked . . . minute bits of reality except it's all real, Yards + them, reflections of slave world relations.

Yet them niggers sat in the back a' this white boy's antique Rolls—oh it's hip, hip, hip, cute &c, & even Yards looked up from behind his lids a moment—funny niggers—& went on putting this drummer down. Hey this dude, the drummer, was never heard from again.

See, the funny thing too was like the white boys was like the chauffeurs, the niggers laid up back sly + excited. Ya know the niggers was excited sittin' in the back a' Rolls Royce, even a 1922 one! & gettin' out like that in a crowd—Yards cussin' Eddie Yng out—Ya no-good jive nigger. Ya can't even carry a g.d. beat—then everybody look at these niggers slidin' out the Rolls.

> In the basement w/ the records
> Studying the history of niggers + niggers + white folks +
> America
> Imitating rich conservative liberal white boys
> Writing a short story on yellow legal pad
> A "critic" becoming

A few years ago these niggers wrote to Leonard Feather (they might still have the letter) & threatened him. "Dear Feather" (this was written from the island, when they was in the error farce!), "You JIVE PUNK! Why do you think you can patronize Charlie Parker? You + that faggot Mitch Miller. Those liner notes for *Bird & Strings* gonna get you killed mf!"

Later, see, bein' w/ these dudes what dealt w/ these collectors, they met all the whities that controlled critical thought about black music. David Mogen, fr'instance, who thought everything after Roy Eldridge was fake, but thought Chu Berry had the final word, tho Eddie Miller (cauc) ultimately was where it was. Eddie Miller, ya see, was him-them-they was up there playin' to they selves. E.G. "5 Stars for Them/Me! 1 Star for Them/You." That's rough. Ya gotta be lucky. You'll getta break, don't worry. Keep pluggin'. Cecil T is that for real (OK later it'll get in for sho, & then CT's our man, but he digs Bartok + them!).

There is a line of measure changes the entity's identity. What is they ID like, they real self? And how it sound? What thing are they, these coloureds who is closest, what entity for this ID? The final description of who is here under the hammer of the slave world?

David Mogen let a couple those niggers write some stuff . . . do a story or two, criticisms of records (if it was too way out, he'd get a rebuttal). David Mogen was a they too. Is a they, and theyin' on back. Let them do a criticism of these records, send them the records, the records come in the mail from David Mogen's. They boy, Sam Carstairs, the old Anglo-southern critic, a renovated closet queen in clean tweeds, fights w/ Mogen (who wdn't?) and married a dried-up snow queen, white voodoo mama made of *NY Post* editorials sewn w/ tweed yarn.

The niggers' criticism & essays caught on absently, in a way. They think so. Whites and their retainers dug these attempts at touching reality. Saying that there was breath beneath the tomb. (Was that what they was sayin'? And did them knew it?) This is the secret learnt in the basements, armed with facts and feelings kept below the surface. They emerge hugged up with Jewish mice, thinking they're leaving their shadow behind when what is left is growing every day (gradual) to be pee-you shadder. They shudder at they udder life, which passes like a train beyond their hearing, now. They'll both return, hearing and train, and the motion, like nature, is constant and everywhere.

This is the kind of movement that goes on, that go on, in 'merica. Yng dudes with a head fulla bees. Thot flick splinters stinging countless tweaks of fragments, splinters, pocks. They crawled out from under a head full of removal. Full of placed away from them. Like their heads are not on they neck in circuitry, no matter how it look. Ya see, murder is they legacy. Murder. Slavery, rape, crude yells in death. Cruelty is they family tune, and they blow all night some time to fix that image as a dancing piece. And peaceful go to sleep. Sit up smokin' boxes a' dope. They never did smoke no weed, for instance, till the Apple. That little bitta grass in the island wasn't nuthin'. Sho didn't get nobody high. But ya know, one day they was smokin' heavy, draggin', pinchin' wit' they fingers, gettin' freaked out high and gigglin' with some greys—lost time. And all that helps the murders rest away, and easy, half in shadow, draggin' when the tide go out.

From undercover, fulla startling color, thots, images, passages of music. And when they see them, they don't know how to act. Let the music play, the color mount, and lay over everthing. Comin' up from out that cellar with the rodent as a pet, people look up say oh that stuff they did's pretty good. It's got some life. But America demands all its letters to spell it. It ain't gon' be sell for short change. They is the unknown species for a minute, awright. Symphonies and stuff outta gas. Don't nobody wanna hear no music lessons too tough. And all these bitch ballet teachers needa be shot down and mashed in the shredder. So some dudes crawlin' outta cella' w/ tha feelin', gotta feelin' . . . and starts to spout

All life,
is created out of love
its raging
consciousness
or
un

People look around, some knew what was happenin', like was 'splained befo'. Jesus! Knew they was Jesus come here talking about get up, lissen to this, start ta play a low growlin' solo wit' they horn. Ya see they carried some life w/ them. From a place nobody been but them too tough. So whether it this quick hop stride or peekin' out the back of the Rolls Royce, somethin' else was happenin'. They was carrying some Jew landlords w/ them, some storefronts, red-grey windows sunset, some fabulous vines and the image and projection of fabulous vines. Preachers and murderers, new style, all with them. But the time they was working w/ the white boys, swappin' the easiest code of mutual coexistence, they was pickin' up stuff rich tweedy Yalie white boys was doin'. They scene and path is news, in a way. Death traps set up everywhich side, s'usual. It was like a career was being created. A Career! They all desert folks, and these crackers had a career as official desert folk line up.

The first career was in the basement w/ them records, but that was a career as simple buggy loader. The next was once they saw they cd speak and wasn't like the tree itself which only has a light croon, they come up with mo' careers. This theme as officially they self. What this order has to do is catch new energy and harness it up to feed itself. It must. It's the reason David Mogen, bless his passing needs (tho he will show up clear as THUG) hooked a hook in them niggers, 'cause they was tootlin' some other sheed. The job is to harness the nigger energy. From slave trade to multinational corp, the job's intent is similar. So David Mogen, the mogul of monk's dream, confines and defines that dream, and harnesses these yng wildies from the north to run it down for new time address, meanwhile constructing the exact situation to extend their own lives.

They was rollin' up a notched exact terraced hill. Apple. West. Consciousness. Ploddin' through the street at the pt of west thoughts fevered raise to its last breath. They thought they job, these really hip nigras, was to walk it right on through until the last ghastly breath, when the winged snarling griffin stops to find out what happened to Our Gal Sunday, or (in the cellar Petey Wheatstraw) the whole game is ripped off.

Capitalism falls, the racists are laid to rest, and a new epic rises. At least that's one story. At the present time, they had begun by telling them they cd use they talent to write record reviews, and they wd be known, no dough but known, and cd get laid off it anyways if they bothered. They was learning the jargon of the place. Jew Yoke. Learnin' how to deal and then, further, in case they cdn't dig, some a' these niggers had by that time actually "married" white folks.

2 *They Remember*

MICE: in sleek black leotards, they come out of Minnie Mouse Refinery where joosh chix are tampered with unsuccessfully attempting to turn them into 'Melican slinks w/ B Crocker looks. They, instead, become dreary little mice scampering under the lights of the world, constructed by history to serve as indifferent (eager) bait for the dullards in their enemies' ranks, who demand permanent moral impairment for a dying.

(Ya see they cd sit there, these niggers, and not feel nuthin' nuthin' and go on with it. It seemed to be the aroma, weather, or something of the place. They just went on. Fount they self in a Buddhist temple w/ they freakin' middleclass parents, sittin' there bewildered. What the hell's, well white folks here, go on with it, you inside, dig??? Went on with it. Pain and terror, to the consciousness as it raised to pt at they sterility in the face of lie.)

ESCARGOT: foreign other type menaces who form a line of call girls (and all the rushing phantoms with the spread open mouths, swivel hips, broken backs, halving thighs, sticky hands, hooked fang-noses, intellectual artitties whistlin' karma thru they fanger—it's way out—further further—it's way out . . . but that's where these niggers rushed headlong from soft nightmare to under the cover nightmare to a wrapped package baby. When it open they head gon' get lit! from one end of the world to the other. Cling vines of madness laid open by the death rays. Which of these dudes was it came in the restaurant w/ a gun in his belt to let some new militants know that they wasn't goin' nowhere they wasn't leaving no downy tentacles for no nigger enterprises—be they called anywhatsomeever DONT THEM TRY TO TAKE THESE WAY FROM WHITE LADIES (Wave Rod) DONT THEM TRY!

   Mice—"Whoseewhatsis"

   Escargot—Don't bother Amos, he's stayin' w/ me

The boys—No!

Yeh! (Wins)

They wd rather kill than go away. And then they just got here, just 7 years ago. Just 7 years of madness is enough. But now, year 1 is still bein' described!

They made them stars, you see? They got them to do it. They thang. But it go, it turned in to Moog over my amis. They got them domesticated like vines on bricks at old cracker colleges. They got them doin' they thing, but it was these other folks' thing. Not a thang, at all—but a Thing—The Thing. A Monster. A Monster. A monster vegetable.

Monster vegetable w/claws + subterranean eyes. An exotic tinsel self in the garden of neutral meaning. There is no such place. It's simply subterranean to those who cannot see below the evanescent surfaces to the snarling essences. Beneath appearances is the meaning of the appearances, and the appearances are meaning itself, period.

During these years these dudes rose up on the ladder of time-out-of-reality-tune into soft rancid flaccid madness. If they cd see themselves as they are seen here. (Then!) If they cd see themselves snorting scag to be crazy. To feel untied, unbricked, coming out from under the skin, so left back that splinters were all they thot they needed, splinters of the world fragments, distorted torn tips of reality. Those pocks—were all to leap from one to the other, babbling eyes, spinning dopily around, hung. They hung and were hung. Right on through the civil rights movement. When MLK was doin' his thing, they was integrating too. (Except see that the masses of peepas wasn't interested in no integration but accessibility to the huge stash of 'merica which they themselves helped up. And even the leaders which talked integration talked a gloss of pathological opportunity for they split-up sefs. See that? See? But. . . .) They, these other dudes, was such integrating militants, they didn't even see it was that. It's the world, they'd say, if anybody ask. Many body did ask, and they themselves were always comin' out with some stuff s'pose to, like, say somethin', sd a lotta stuff they now don't wanna hear. They still alive?? Yeh. Very much. But It'll come out . . . .

They was just comin' and bein' + doin'. Like everybody else, they looked up, ca early '60s, & they were covered from head to toe w/ white folks. Of all shapes descriptions & uses.

Are we to assume that MLK carried that spirit, too, that Jesus Christ & Jehovah & Angels & Halos & praying & Sin & divinity & all that are merely symptoms of the same malaise?? (Watch yo' mouf!) That niggers sitting in Andy Warhol premieres when they first premiered on 3rd Avenue on the top floor of the Green Hornet Bldg., *i.e.*, slum on the outside—grand piano + gardens on the inside. That such niggers were actually SNCCers. That the same madness which had these other dudes laid out in a loft watching 2hrs of an 8-hr film called SLEEP by a caucasian homosexual with dyed silver hair (in which a dude sleeps, & that's all) is the same madness that turned yng SNCC, address 100 5th Avenue, downtown, around. That these Martin Bubers and Martin Heideggers that them + Dr. King were reading were in fact the *same dudes* & the same process was taking place. (Is that what's being sd?)

Everybody in the world.

Are they tryin' to equate snortin' some "girl" w/ courtin' the virgin? Are they sayin' that them was the self-same faggots all them was dealin' w/? The same criss-cross, spooky smokey? That the Nobel prize and OBIE are even vaguely related? Wow! Some thot! Yeh, it is, ain't it?

They had inside jobs to do, in America. There among the many wonders. They had an exterior interior vision of sunlight and rising in style to meet it. All golden lads and girls, hooked up magnetically by they haid, rising like yallah biscuits to be recognizable 'mullicans.

They wd be working in the record stores, & walkin' the streeks to cold water flats, pinned & sliding up and down a vision like a loose moth, singing. And yes, the sun, was actually only a candle, into which, blinded by joyhighs spelled I*G*N*O*R*A*N*C*E, the wispy creatures perished.

They was sittin' in (remember the Danish Negro Tchikai who, like a knitting needle of toot, splayed a cool sophistication of the place? He recited Hamlet on his ax, *con* ribms, who later denounced the bk powr phase as many must have—shocked at Stokely, shivered at Rap), wadin' in, actually, it can be proved, gettin' in. So some are fat today & thoroughly useless. They was peaceful & removed. Ya see, music is what's happenin'. Paintin' is where it is. Ah'm sensitive—slurpin' in the buzzard cup—heap hip, high and far away, deeper than, heavier than, more powerful than, and much more profound than, reality. (A creep in a shiny suit?)

Yeh, they was peaceful and removed. (Except drunken fights in bars, these dudes e'en thot they was bad tokin' white boys at the seedy tavern— one night these dudes and Moriarti, the sympathetic Italian fascist poet, were leant against the seedy and a group of grey flannel suiters come in tryin' to rub up against the bizarre to stir up something in they putrid life. Whew. The stink from there like dead roaches, decaying frenchies patent and squeeze for outta work billionaire. Natcherally, it gets a name and is sold thru *The New Yorker*. Finally, dyed-head negresses livin' in the white house can give parties and serve these dead roaches now name *billionaire booty*. The gfsuiters make some remark abt the world, which natcherally is an insult to anybody. These other dudes, they protectin' truth, is the way they'd have everybody believe. Finally it gets tense and nasty, and the niggers spit in the gfsuit dudes' face. Actual spit, a glob of it, sticky with green in it, and it hit, and roll, some fast, some real slow down the dude's cheek. Moriarity check and start gigglin', agitating, dig? The niggers squint they eye, say punk, spit rollin' down a mf'in face, guess who? Gf suit dude say, no, ain't no spit. No, sd, There is no spit. There is no spit on a face. No one has spit on any faces. There is no spit rolling down sticky and green off a face around here. No spit has changed places, in fact.

Of course the spit was pointed at, laughed about. Moriarity went and got the rest of 'em, a grey they, and chortled in unison. Gf suits shrank and loped away, tails between they lips.)

Peaceful + removed. Either way. They was for bangin' everybody smilin'. And they was applauded for it, or sometimes just got clap. Poets. Painters. Highgetters in America. Super Hip. Cool, down, heavy, clean, intelligent motor scooters, dig? Tryin' to have *a good time*! Tryin' to blow themselves up in a million sunbaked fingers of crazy ecstasy. Anything + everything what is it? They got it! Smoke it, shoot it, screw it, lie to it, wear it, snort it, talk to it.

How did they get to that? The world had made them cool, had cooled them out. And this was the place of the cools. The many, many silent unresponses to reality. Tho they had a size and a place, and what they actually did *cd* be measured. But the celebration of the unreal. The measurement of the immeasurable. Heroic, dramatic, sole concern of the mighty world brain. Yet stack it all together, and pick up the phone to Barnabas Gotchadoe, & them, and they will not not tell you, all that stuff's good. All them screwy picha's, all them soupcans, and 8-hour movies, all that nonstop buffalo jammin' on the couch, the cellar floor, all that shootin' up or down, long talks about nonsense, dawn walks with sick white women or men, death pacts with queers, meaningless poetry, fake commitments to poverty, words on the brain, arguments with romantic conservatives, time spent unraveling literary code, imitations of nightmares, nonstop adultery, immersion in the rites of the powerful, lists of movie stars, all this is veddy good, mine boy. Shake it and bake it, and get ready to eat it, it's the s.o.s. Feces on a Shingle. Lined up for yet another strata of gofer-ho.

They were instant (a little while later) successes! They were underground but underground rose entirely up, to high sight. Like all these ladies in drag w/ boy names singin' schizm jolt rock are commercial undergrounds, tinsel dudes like what knew Allen Ginsberg, white thieves of one ilk or tuther straight from prison, catatonic transvestites, Joey Gallo, cowboys, dope addict writers from Red Hook. & Niggers like them, a very few, at first, in them circles. Circling. It's how they fount out about 'morica really. In that cellar, they aren't history. And come up to applause when they spoke and first words were of course, "cellar." They thot it was a pun you see, *seller* and *cellar*, and so the world (crowded into that halloween party at which all the niggers wore dark glasses, English caps, and jammed they short haircut haids through window shades, so the shade hung down they back like a cape. Asked what they had come as, they'd say, "Shades") applauded. And then this crowd in the underground, as it now was quickly rising to the surface like a mafia victim, were hunkies pretendin' to be bailin' out of America. This dude came around to the niggers who were pretendin' to be writers, like they wasn't in America either, except they wasn't tho they strained, by trying to be out, at actually gettin' in, and the further they strained to get out the more they cd get in, since gettin' out made you American property and no facilities were ever provided for gettin' in. (Are they sayin' Take It All. Take All of America. Rip It All Off. Fight to Overthrow Racism and Capitalism, Struggle to Take State Power. Anti-Imperialism. Anti-White Supremacy. Kill All Those Who Oppose This. Take It All. All. In the Name of All In the Universe Deserving Life!)

No.

Before that? Peaceful and Supporting Truth, as they snorted cocaine and thot profound thots. Listened to Miles' *Kinda Blue*. Trane's "Blackbird." Early hip. Slower, and cooler. Pock pin deep thrust below the Eisenhower years. Into the Kennedy Years. They come up out the cellar with opinions. Yeh. Dig Jackie Kennedy. JFK wears figured ties. Check his 3-button suit. Princeton cut. It's allright. Criticize them jokingly. After Eisenhower, Mort Sahl went into semi-retirement because he cdnt criticize JFK. That was his boy.

But this dude came 'round givin' out dope to the niggers then. Dudes from Harvard. Drs. They talkin' about let them know how it feels to get high. This ain't domestic. These mushrooms. All that scag they shootin' and snortin'. Fake cocaine cloggin' up they nostrils. Plenty bush. A chick a week and 3 steady mistresses & grey lay the queen chain strangled them. They cdnt dig they dug it. From the shriveled up ladies garment worker they first walked down 7th avenue with to a party. Lula Dutchman, with strange fingers and rings and stories of garment worker Jews fighting to create unions. These niggers didn't even understand at all that Bitches like this abounded in stories like this, were the history they were told and the history of the world. Below the surface, steady risin'. Takin' it in, they took it in, the panorama. The midnight, all-night parties. Used to pop open yellow ampules full of amyl nitrite, walk from room to room with a pocket full of amyl nitrite from any dstore. Pop 'em. Jam 'em in they nose, wheeze and scream. Goodhumor guys, room to room givin' it out, wheeze and scream. 12 in a box, 3 boxes, plus the bourbon and wine and bush and Ray Chas. They had a terrible set.

'Cause they cd get the white underground, the black no ground, updown painters, Spanish boxers all in the same jnt to scream and holler and get high. Scream and holler and get high. The cool ones get over later, some creeps tried to swoop up wit' the drawers right on the set, n.g. *86* next time.

They was mashin' w/ these greys who sd they had bailed out of America, mostly immigrants who never were in it anyway, all the way, tho they people believe they in & 'll kill anybody sayin' different. But niggers too fit that mold, now a hundred a day slide thru salutin'. But a thousan' more roll out the womb smokin'!

But see, them too, the immigrants, get ripped off, get mashed slyly sellin' out, and that was the first mention of pullback that sat in the niggers' knot. They was in this tough, was they life, how they rose out the cellar to be sold as hot commodity, opinionated sensitive everydude. They was so sensitive they skin itched and the moonlight sat on it, tinkling the soft silence of night to dawn as they retraced they steps from the umpteenth set of spread open legs, to they loft cave (loft=luft=german for *air*, *Luftknaben*, *AirBoys*, the niggers who float). They was thinkin' and writin' stuff down, impenetrable poems about the dizziness and confusedness of bein' black subjects readied for the defense of the subject matter. A shit-tawkin', high-gettin', bitch-rippin' elite. They'd carve it up, write it down, paint it cross, dance it over, all spellin' out the immersion in the blankout, and loyalty to it.

They disguised themselves more and more from the early awkward first years when they cd be seen momentarily as dark hued. The first pomes and paintings, the dance abt an angel looking to wipe out the klan, those were giveaways. But they cleant them up. They ran into some straightout aesthetes from BlkMountain College, who said, shave all that extraneous sensuality outta the shit and get down to the flat bizness of creating a new academia. (But it's all flat an' academic, even Kerouac jabbin' himself full of American highs and end up a high American "right" and white and finally outta sight!)

Stop talkin' about the nigress in the Jaguar, teachin' at 18th Avenue School. Stop romancin' abt a world of people who cain't speak ancient English, Anglo Saxon, Provençal, Latin, Greek. Stop waxin' red rushin' rhythm about a world w/o Ezra Pound or WCWms. Stop pretending the niggers can talk about the winos of Nwk or the divinities of Baptist lunatics w/o DHLawrence, and Stevens, and Merce Cunningham and John Cage and Franz Kline and deKooning and Chas Olson and the Bauhaus, cause they cain't. Get it?

It was the rules of the place. And several agents slank in the cave and laid across the couch to keep score and check the products were straight-lined, short unrhymed except the quips of Creeley, like 17th century, when pirates weighed niggers by the ton, threw 'em in the Jesus and headed for here.

They waged they war, the "romantic" underground and the "classic" underground. Immigrants led the 1st, under Allen Gberg, the joosh prophet. The last of the prophets. The head of the yowling them. The niggers read *Howl* and sd wow, how in the hell they do this? Talkin' this stuff. Niggers wrote them on toilet tissue saying are you serious? Note returned on more expensive toilet tissue sd bein Allen G is a tiresome thing, to which the assembled sd amen.

But it was the hookup of nigger rithms ragin' in America, spit out to that. Like they have stumbled here from the orange house in Joisey, through Colored School, and whiteout island, and all they had really dug was Homer to Eliz poets, and a Jew, using they own schnit, blow it back & surprise 'em all! Ghost nightmare funky ritm con matzoorinis. Stared down by reality, white boys wailin' they best to reflect the sense of come here on the afterbirth thot the streets was gold, fought to get in it, they tell such tales. "America Go Fuck Yrself w/ Yr Atom Bomb." Man that was profound! For these niggers never heard nuthin' but misunderstood they own funky soul, blowin' hot hot, but cooled out, it was in fact cool v. cool. As they were then bein' leaped on by they own soul watered down. But that's the fate of the bunch of them Afrikans caught in U.S. They only dig they soul watered down. From hippies to Jesus and the bulldaggers. Flash. HOWL! was what the niggers shda always did, and fact of it, always do, except the reportin' on these nigger graduates say they is Jesus now, they's Averill Harriman now, they's who?? Allen Ginsberg or Baudelaire? Or John Lennon? Or Karl Marx? Who? Wish the f these mfs was Karl Marx, 'fore they was any a' the rest a' them krackers tho, tell you that

> Louie—Marx was white.
> Shad—So what?
> Louie—John Hawkins, Guy Lombardo, Hitler, the
>   Devil, . . .
> Shad—aint no devil, no mf'n god neither . . .
> Louie—JFKennedy, Stalin, Bilbo, Leopold, heads of
>   IBM, Genl Motors, Heinz ketchup, Exxon, Gulf,
>   South Afrika, Portuguese, Mafia, pope, . . . every
>   lousy murderin' swine in creation is white
> Shad—Yeh, that's true. Raff Abernathy white too.
> Louie—No he ain't.
> Shad—Roy Wilkins white.
> Louie—no he ain't.
> Shad—so what're you sayin'
> Louie—fuck you

So see they hear theyself played back in decoration and hyped up with it. And fall in line behin' they self thru the white boy lips. Tarbaby jokers. Chocklate cream. Whites inside. Colored whites. No, man, Mailer the trick shot specialist, ambassador from fat soft + obvious, sd "the white negro" and that was cool both ways. The hipster was what they worshipped. Them same niggers came from where they was, to get worshipped but gypped. They cd be told what was hip about them, and the hippest part of them, was what trick shot cd steal. The rest was better kept inside or not spake about. It was frankly death, destruction, killing, torture, yelling in brutality. Guerrilla iceberg rising later smells anyway, a music they wd hum, together, or at the same time, anyway, "Amazing Grace." They stood and listened to AG be them in a yarmulca, and put on the mammyjammin' yarmulca and imitated him being them. Funny.

Anglo-Germanic rebellion was called Blk Mountain. Also crammed in its juicier times with Monk and Sonny Rollins. Pound vs Whitman was what it came down to. The same king of jazz, this time with a beard and boy-jones. For the immigrants to rally behind. Pound right back to Germanic Anglo correct vision and version. The fact that Pound was a fascist made him the true object of niggers' worship. The fact that he sd outright he hated them made him the object of fond regard. Damn, how pure can they get?? These particular niggers here whose story this is. Anything totally esoteric they dug. And even the fact that Pound was s'posed to have thot niggers simple barbarians. There was even dudes like light-skinned Steve J in Bostown who was absolutely Poundian and wrote exactly, even letters, like him, and echoed the same exact anti-nigra tone. It was weird to see and hear that, listen to them run it. Thot wow, but like they're who they're puttin' down.

But Jews was in the BM push as well. Tho the Olsons, Klines, Dawsons, Cages, DeKoonings ran with the heavy on that. That them, was the cold right wing, a'course. They had they Jews like everybody else. Oppenheimer, Finstein, &c. And they had they 'Talians . . . Sorrentino, Early, &c. And e'en they nigras . . . Jones, Spellman, &c. But these other niggers was not totally there. They was, like in all things, split. They had lines run out 'em, off 'em, like rays. Each pt touch a registry of reaction-life-meaning-movement. So the nigger-them had workings and dealings with both "sides." They crib was a cathouse for litraychure. All formed left right center, to howl and get high. Walk down the hall naked. Go out in the street. Remember Irving Phatz, serious wild academic dude revolutionary? Talked for hours, remember? Hooked up mostly w/ AG, half-married a Chicano babe, posin' as a Jew. She got 'em all into Cuba. She was half-hooked to Ronnie Cheatem, the nigger photog, who got paid back one night he returned from the South takin' pichas of the klan to find his negress draped under Scorpio Rotgut, his fella' photog. She was a dancer, the negress, and today she lives in the same loft wherein Cheatem fount her humpn' the fag. Ronnie turned away, dig it, turned away, and banged his hand thru a window. So turned away, and around, from pulsing life. Beat beat blood blood beat beat turned away to photographs, negatives, travel, mumbling under liquor. But they was they men.

And these dudes we met on side streets of our youth, hustling they way into intellectual nee bohemian America.

Cheatem was running a coffeeshop jazz club, "mugasoul," and these ol' poet niggers came in and started to read AG browner. They walked around, staring at people bigeyed. Lookin' in 'cause they wanted to find out. They wanted to feel. They wanted to know. What it is? What it is? Who are they in them cryin', inside outside? Read this pome. Gone!

The old heads who shda been in Europe w/ Jimmy Baldwin these yng niggers met and talked to. Laughed with. Followed. Were directed. Wilcox and his wife were they early influences + guides, but what was missing, ultimately, was the work. The work. The production. Not just the manque they cd dig that early. In the army they came to see Wilcox and dug the books, the white walls, the omelets and black bread, the ale, the reefers, the slim beautiful sister Lady Wilcox was (and e'en she danced till Wilcox sd no more be w/ me they want to tear us apart with dancing be w/ me, all up in here—she stopped—till years later she went off to Paris and became a novelist), but no work. And these yng niggers walked back and forth, lookin' for something to turn them on. HOWL. Jewish mice counting the steps from cellarhood. The knowledge of motion. Some motion. Action. Some action. And so they drifted away from Wilcox, because it wasn't about bohemianism, except very briefly. They were too embarrassed to show up light. They had too much to say. They had been bit and kicked. They had stood outside a mammyjammin' bus in the cold north and watched the way the world looks at its slaves. They had been locked up in Colored School and jeered at for goin' wit a brown woman. They had been trapped on blankout island and read half the motoreekin' faggits in the inglitch langwitch. They had been led off from the safe part of they tribe and separated from the heroic ones. So freak it, get it up and at 'em. Somethin' got to go, give, move. Action. Action. Move it.

They saw each other then less frequently till one night in the 5 Spot Wilcox took a copy of a new magazine the niggers were publishing called NOTHING, and turned a page to a poem them white boys had in there. Oppenheimer had a blues in there. A blues. They had writ out a white sentiment sounding half like a blues and in formal poetese had it down. They dug it, the niggers who half published the mag (with some Jewbabe's money), cause it made reference to them (the niggers) as blue, but still was Anglo-Germanic (albeit the Jew knew too . . . he was cool) BMountain

style. There was drawings, the mag had gone from sideways hard-to-see
flicks, and German expressionism, of the niggers' early influence, a weird
conglomerate of what it is they met when they was abroad in the streeks
. . . to now straightup abstraction was pawing in. The first cover like that
was black. With white contrast. Abstract Expressionism. (But what they
need is Realistic Expressionism! Yeh, but . . . take it on advisement for now
. . .) And it was a move from the naive, they thot, to the sophisticated. The
philosophical game. The pros had moved in, the litrary pros and they
litrary ideologies. They had plenty niggers in those first issues, but e'en
the niggers themselves thinned with the move to the right. Tho at the same
time AG, Joosh left, was there, wheezin' and in that axis all of it spun, then
beginning to spin. Wilcox looked at the mag, and sd to the white boy,
Oppenheimer, the right wing Jew the niggers had as one a' their closest
runnin' buddies later. . . . "What you mean, blues?" Wilcox knew what was
happenin'. He didn't make it clear to them tho, the yng niggers. He never
made it clear to them, and finally, did he make it clear to hisself, cause he
went off the fuck to Denmark to open an art gallery. He never . . . produced only a few poems that was slippery good. And soft and musical. And
at the time, the best work of any niggers the niggers had seen. Wilcox and
a dude name Postell, a surrealist, who these niggers used to run with to
keep in the snarlin' wine-drinkin' world. Both Postell and Wilcox put the
niggers down when they took up with white people, but all them ran w/
white people, but see they never let the white people hook up with them
or hook them to they flesh. Tho they slept with them, ran with them, ate
with them, even ate them, they never married none. They never sd they
loved none. (Well, none a' these niggers sd that, did they?? Well some, but
none they knew real good!) And finally the whole thing was jive.

Postell, they tried to drive crazy, and he ran down the street, sayin'
white folks was talking through his mouth. He sd, "The Jews are talkin'
through my mouth." He clasped his hands to his mouth. The other niggers didn't understand. They thot Postell was simply nuts or something.
"They talking through my mouth. The Jews are tawkin' through my
mouth." He left soon after these other niggers married white women,
and went to Cincinnati. They say he never wrote again.

Cruse was one a' that crowd of coffeesippin' bloods that shda been in
Europe with the rest a' that generation. Cruse was tawkin' about tryin' to
get a musical comedy on the boards on Broadway. Or a radio show. But
then he went to Cuba with some other a' these same niggers and came

back tryin' to produce, in fact produced, *The Negro Intellectual: Rebellion or Revolution*. He produced, and still tryin' to produce, out of that same madness, some real stability and contribution. Cruse, perhaps, was the real genius of that group, tho not its field leader. The yng niggers thot Cruse was an ol' sage and used to tawk to him and laugh at everybody. Cruse always looked like a well-to-do bum, in them days, clothes and shoes like hand-me-downs. These other niggers, like mixtures of college students and war veterans, yng and quiet. But thinkin', imagining, confusing themselves.

The pt they came to out the cellar, posin' as writers, &c., put out magazines with these Jewesses, and so were foci of impinging crossbreeds. Hooked up the Anglo-Germanic hard edge, and the Romantic effusive early Jewish hipsters. They all rushed back in front of the niggers' eyes, and through they consciousness. They were the workmen, the clerks, these niggers, for both sides, they got it all straight, a white united front, unwilling, but still the niggers strutting on a pinpoint cd see all ways because, you see, none of it and all of it was them. Bang.

A castle on the Hudson was opened with the help of a dude now heading up the comp lit dept at Columbine Univ. He cdn't move in 'cause his mother sd the niggers wd hump his wife, Dolly. So the niggers and they mice moved in. The onrush of immigrant and laidout Anglo-Germanic 'Medica sat in, laid in, drank in, screamed and howled in. Instead of marching on Selma, these niggers dragged, magnetized the whole of they brain to roll up in they crib and be picked (while they picked they own). A castle on the Hudson wherein all the roll rolled in to be counted. To be mounted. All the immigrants led (co-fratinated) by the niggers. In constant argument, lie, struggle, sloppy stuff. But the niggers actually coordinated that movement of abstract intellectual lits and awts. The nail in the heart was the niggers had become in many ways them dudes and dudettes. They did all the same stuff, 'cept they was colored and colored memories racked them, colored they style. Made them maybe cooler when cool was called for, hotter when that was needed. Like they was always running around punchin' dudes out. Bang. Niggers just punched somebody out. Tho that was death fiddle in the way that the niggers were isolated from most niggers, e'en most niggers who was sayin' they was into awt, &c. (many meant scag and white women). The niggers hung wit' these whites exclusively. In they house. They in theys. With they wimmens. They wit' they wimmens. E'en what was happening, the rise out the cellar carryin' opinon, the orange house, Colored School, the whiteout island, straight to collect $200, buy a Hotel on Baltic Avenue.

It was a big crib and they had to go out to work. Worked in a technical editing joint, copyediting technical manuals for murderers. U.S. Infantry, Error Farce &c. Came back Friday nights, to the lineup of all the immigrants and Anglo-Germans. Ampules, weed, bourbon, wine, screamin' and hollerin', Ray Chas till early Sat. mewnin'. Maybe do it again Sat. night, the same place or some other joint. Maybe go out huntin' sets, or the flicks or have more people over and scream and holler and laugh and get high and be profound. Talk about lit and awt and poets and music and wink at each other's wimmen through the fog of supposed loyalties. Get drunk, fall out, throw up, shoot up, o.d. One time they o.d.'s from procaine-imitation girl—mixed as solution with real girl. They fell straight back on the hardwood floor, in the study. Straight back. Lights out. A blue hammer poised above they head. It struck, they managed to turn just barely to one side. It struck, they wobbled just again by minute length they head out the hammeric path. Again. They twisted. Again. They moved. Again. Struggled, tried to double up, heard voices, straining, beating through the fog. They had hands which reached them, pulled them up, and wobbling in the chair, they fell back out, on the floor, and the hammer reeled again. They turned and turned and twisted, now in tune with dodging the thing which was just death.

A Good Time. All of it. Was about. A Good Time. A deep thing. Something Groovy. Simple hedonism called a million different things. But all of it together, simply that. And that was not either the final push away, tho maybe it was. Check it. It was that day after day, in some part of this world, somebody gave up. Somebody sold out. Somebody they knew sold they ass in front of the entire world, and this was difficult to understand, the selling out. Why do it? And why these niggers? Aw, some did it, but these things dealin' with, they didn't understand that. All this stuff they tawked about. What did it mean? And finally, when the biggies showed, they took the niggers easy. They had some shit they got together, some formal scholarship about the cellar (and the orange house, and ritms in the streeks, and the endless deaths in Colored School, the revelations of the island), and they bought it just as they told it. That was an intro to the final chapter of death trick, fo' sho', but not as a goofball for Rockefeller's elephant. It was what they wanted to say, what they wanted to present. It wasn't no cowboy picha' with a toupee, or drunk right wing

French Canadian kitchen for a drunk right wing French Canadian mother to say some dumb shit in.

The final word reality kept sayin', do this, go here. React to this. Look at this and make a judgment, fools. And these niggers did that. They howled and screamed, and read poetry to music. Ran w/ size-place white dudes & pulled they bitches. Even played house with some. But all the time reality pushed piles of garbage in front of them. Piles and piles of sellouts, deaths, compromises, mistakes, tragedies, mathematics. They had prepared a table before them and they were their enemies. But the table had a newspaper on it, and a tv. They sat up in rms full of whites and watched Malcolm X. They saw MLK get his butt reamed daily, and tawked bad about him. They understood it was the state. It wasn't no mere backwardass raidnake. It was the state. It was the state. The govt. And the whites chimed in.

But this is racin' faster than life to say all this now. But that ball of evolving life. Amidst and because of the fragments, the half sentences of reality, that can all be put together as a story. Trying to get all of it in, 'cause if all of it was in, every fragment, inch and minute of they lives was in, it'd be a longer rap than this, and maybe somebody'd know exactly what was happenin' everywhere or maybe not.

10 Events To Bring It Back To Death!

1. Early) They got hooked up w/ these mousie Jewish babes & then one day all they knew was lil' Jewish babes, or Italian babes—very few Americans. All them wd tell this tale. Nigresses flapped through, brown molls of isolation like they brothers, carved a lonely tale of they own. All apart and not making nothing, speeches, silences, smiles, waves, periods.

2. They started sneakin' over there to they houses in the afternoons, drinking the beer out the refrigerator, then retreatin' to the roof. But be nuthin' but yogurt or some shit in there, and white shag carpet, little wooden puppy dog with glass eyes.

Dead school books from the refinery, really odd stuff. The niggers wd be simply let in on other stuff they didn't know went on, other lives they knew nuthin' of. Black life left a different set of static artifacts to reflect the sun in empty houses. Real old blues, and deadbutt Beethoven &c. was new to them.

They got keys made and came and went. Those they was s'posed to be "seein'," these babes, yet they wd ease in and out of they house in the afternoons when they was working and simply sit around for a while, checkin' out how them folks lived. (This was when they had first entered the cellar, and it was rumored that they might be risin' up.)

They discovered then that, goin' back & forth to the cwater flat, people in bohemia was not equal either. (They didn't discover that. That's what they shd have discovered. They saw it, but it did not register as negative, only different.) Why was they so laid out in cwflat with strapped up table, open the oven for heat and these babes from the refinery in they one rm white painted joints had at least, it seemed, enough to eat? It slid off they greasy nose and rolled under the bed. Class structure in bohemia? A *Bohemian* at the time meant a lot to these niggers. It meant deep and away from the dead grey factory hell of their youth. Away from the quiet agony, the wine bandit screaming, the motionless consciousness from the street that is now named after some bad nigger, hopefully.

3. The move to cover over the past w/ mice and snails was accompanied by a trek out the cellar. They married white women. Old niggers left they company.

4. The joint concubinage, return to the blind crazy sinners of ideals, and other fantasy. Boys meets Girls. Boys w/ Garment Worker in day time, (off) w/ collitch types in evening. Garment workers say them bastids is playin' us cheap. They can be exposed, for playin' this game. Rosa Luxemburg, Trotsky, the Scottsboro boys, none of them approve of this. They was standin' sideways, talkin this trash through they fingers like a lisp. Refinery babes was "hurt." Them garment workers are weird, they're crazy.

5. Raphael Borksteen had a motorscooter and went to the Randall's Island Jazz Festival. Whereupon he spotted some mice and swept them in his pocket. The niggers teamed and went to they cold water flat, never to be heard from again. Till later that evening.

6. These niggers grew to be the stallions of requited screw. Everything and everyone. If it cdn't run, it was in danger. Bro, they'd screw it, or pinch it

to make sure it cdn't be ripped. There was dudes with eyes like chicken-eaters' eyes be when they eatin' chickens. Rimmed with teethy lust.

In taverns, nightclubs, living rms, stores, sidewalks, churches, any-where, galleries, book joints, anywhere, these dudes roamed, and they had reps.

Big Browns was one such dude. He came in they's as the circuit rose and the word got out. They tried to ridicule Big Browns and Bronx Sally. They was the new tight crew that came down on the weak end. From the train tracks, poured out the subways. Hugged up in the street. The proper bohemians, some smelled of old leather, cdn't see it. And then "legitimate" mixed couples sd they cdn't dig it. They didn't say it. They thot it. It delegitimized them, since they was "serious." Did they think Browns wasn't serious as he "stalled above them like wounded bulls"?

Browns wd walk in the seedy taverns in short shorts and a turban. Browns was not mere rhetoric, tho he excelled in it. Street slick, they ran the signifying monkey through 100 verses (count 'em). They strutted across WSPk reciting TSM at the top of their voice like Shakespeare. Yeh! It was gorgeous. Later they mighta got into Shakey Peter.

They main assault not liked by no crackers and very few of the atten-dant coons, was Browns' "crotch show." They wd stalk a certain tavern where the ultra hip was sd to lay, and lo and behold at the peak of abstract expressionist jargon, beer burps, mannered drunks (yeh, there is a mannered intellectual drunk that the white painters used to run. Where they cdn't make sense easy, but what they was runnin' was so deep you'd have to stay and try to take it in. Kline, deKooning, King, Dan Rice were the famousest ones at that, and a' course Oppenheimer, Dawson and Finstein tried 'a copy it). So here comes Browns, big like they say, abt 6'3", maybe 200 even, very hard and lean. Takin' long strides like he think he somebody badder than anybody anybody ever peeped, comes very very very slowly in. These are long long, extravagant, exaggerated strides. And all the time they walks right down the aisle, in short shorts hugging they butt and groin. They begin to slow slow run they both hands back and forth between they legs, right on the bulging organ. They got so tough they'd come right up to a table where maybe the most famous arty white folks of Euro-America be sittin' and Browns wd rub they "nuts" right in front them + they lady's face . . . oh maybe 8 inches tops.

There were flareups and such. And noise interiorly mostly, cussin' them out at other scenes, but mostly injured looks and a raised voice, &c. The niggers, tho with these crackers, were they chief defense from Browns, &c.

The myth of some of these niggers, though, was made one night in The White Whale. Browns playin' chess with some white folks. The niggers comments, they wit' AB, who soundin' like Creeley and hooked up with snailmomma. . . . Some other dudes, Marion B, the tweedley do-wee altoist, arch opportunist, gaunt muff diver, philanderer, 1st sensualist of the NYNiggs blk bohemian team.

Niggers sd somethin' 'bout the Browns' play, how they cdnt &c., nasty icy comment like they do . . . a non-momma dozen, dig? Browns raised, didn't dig it, nor the nigger particularly, but they recognized something, what? Authority? License? The names? They roared all right, but it was whipped.

Browns: Suck my dick.

Niggers: Does you have one?

Browns: Man, who you think you tawkin' to?

Niggers: S'pose to be Big Browns, The Afrikan Queen!

Bs raised completely out the chair, backs up. All the niggers' heads now in they flappy lips, hoping these niggers shuts the fuck up, or sits the fuck down, but definitely that they don't end up having to wrestle w/ no mad B Browns. These other niggers a' course still runnin' it.

N—Was a matter Browns, yall scared? Why you backin' up? (These shrimp niggers weighing less than 135, runnin' this madness. Why? Just an absolute feelin' of grim mastery. That it was nothing. That it cd be done. That it cd be run. That if it came down to blood, that it was all right. Whatever went down, let it go. Let it move. Let something move. Get off!)

B—Ahma' bus' yo' little nasty face open . . . (Then Browns made they mistake. They picks up a chain, a huge chain off the wall. The jts named "The White Whale" and has such bs artifacts laid around to lighten up the junkies' stare—Brown grabs the chain . . . the little niggers then starts to laugh and ridicule Browns.)

N—Punk gotta pick up a chain, a 1100 lb nitwit. Cain't whip a 100 lb bad nigger. They pick up a mf'in chain. You a real baddy awright, Browney, You got yr Kotex on?? And laughing they turned they back and sat down, waitin' for the music to start. The proprietors and the assorted niggers got the necessary more space between.

7. Returning at nights from Italian poet's clutches, till mulattoes arrive nonsecretly.

8. The other mulattoes who'd begun to arrive. All pts mulattoes. All pks, parties, playgrounds, schools, stores, sets, mulattoes.

One a' these niggers, a little older, almost curse age, was w/ a sister, and that happened cause the gray rodent he was with and produced three mulattoes with raised up one night and stole down the stairs with the lightestskinned one, and went to Chicago to live w/ an anarchist. These niggers used to tawk about this all the time, but later the crowd didn't even know it, but saw simply bro Bee had his number together. . . . He had a sister who claims now in her/they memoirs to have been fought with constantly, tho nobody remembers that too tough. They ran with another sister, the wife of one of the black lights. The flames that the klan which manages the art galleries killed, murdered w/ scag . . . scag and methadone maintenance.

But nobody remember no fight w/ nobody. They was pt of the big gang forming later at the castle by the sea.

9. As the gang formed, lodged in the castle, railing in all directions in pure kind of American strength, the fact of its American strength shd have loomed over it. But the splinters (they saw) shot into the gang was facts and ice cubes of American life. Old Irish folk were the janitors of the castle, and indeed the castle sat in an Irish threatening to become Puerto Rican setting, near a monastery for the oldest gay liberation army on record, and the Black Hudson.

The gang formed of the two mod-lit/awt groups, quasi popjewish romance, & Anglo-Germanic hard edge, centered on the lush life sweep of Afrika's confused youth struggling to consciousness in North America!

10. The tone of morality that lit up the interior was American modern. Speed fall to death. Stripped of reality, what is actually happening is a tiresome day-to-day reference to how hooked up to the dying specimen they are. But who knows that? The episodes and incidents, at first merely

tales, walk through their midst. Max does begin to see J's wife two days a week. All of them know this, and J shortly after. Max and J are the closest of friends. They drink together almost to extinction. They hug each other. They cry together. And apart they speak about each other lovingly. Yet two days a week, Max meets Cindy and they sneak off to fuck.

AB does begin to see G's wife. And they are respected peers, cultural workers of the land. G wrote a poem about it later, like they do. Lee left G and not for AB. AB was wit' the snail, ya see. Brook Farm, baybee. Later Max and Cindy go to the far west on a horse ranch to live. Then they find out they can't stand each other. Cindy, an American misplaced poison, Max the Jewish medicinedrinking patriarch, redhaired crazy fascist tryin'a play a nigga sax. Toot Toot. Happy as a most ta dig MB come out with toot toot as some kinda nigga' hip. It wasn't, dig, was whitey inside MB. Dig. So whitey like Max cd toot and be half toot hip. Dude drank carcinol all a time. AB tried it, and fell on the rug scratching. Scratched his balls raw the medicine so lit him up.

Industrial morality, full of new energies, but absolutely without a lasting humanity. They all were singular mad folks thrown together by lust. Capitalist morality. The rip off originals, in the name of the sainted AYE, profits from they privates. And just to keep them billions squarely in the white, they cry occasional, PROPHET, to confuse the issue. (King James or later versions.) In fact, these hungry mixmatch Americans to keep they own issue hooked w/ Uncle Samuel had deep deep covers theyself. Be poet—"Sling slong song sing bing bang bung ding dang dung kling kling kling kling klung klung . . . klang," and such, or Painter: Dance up to the empty sheet and like run into it with a wet paint brush and flail they frustration—mostly at bein' broke. They get some dust for this activity, it cool out a bit, but then all them other 'moricans hooked up likewise, so, they sympathize and trip that same path, confusin' that with emotion. But were they tryin' to show matter in motion, Kline, DeKooning, Guston, Pollock, Rice, King, and others, flailin' America. Flail, at the middle of the century, black and yellow horse stood on one leg with luminous eye at the huge figure of the Imperial Millennium, dashing in, and dashing out, amidst, yes (the dark scope revealed!) the murders yet to come!

But the matter in motion that most confronts all together is the great fleshy being of the human mass. All those faces together, all those cries, all that struggle and love or sacrifice or hatred or accomplishment.

Some of these bloods, tho, they wdn't go for the flailout, and then, since that was definitely the heavy word from groups as to what was ultimate, baby, ultimate and profound (as it all is under the cultural aggression of imperialism), they wd come out w/ nigger type stuff, like unfashionable. That's why they cd, like, stand in between the Anglo-Germans and the Jews like a plastic nut which do not rust (might split, but wdn't rust). Cause the Jews still, except the ultra hip, ya know, the makers of the new order, hear . . . they wanted some kind of recognizable somethin'. The mash of human against social emotion and new industrial agony shoot out at'cha, you check out the expressionists! Eyes. Hands. Grim faces ('specially in Germany, just before James Bond's father Adolph came to pow'). And some a' these nigs, they went for that. Them heavy lines around the faces. That jagged motion. Agony, chaos, and what have you, like it related to nig life mo', dig? Or somethin'. So then Bob and a few dudes hooked up some stuff that was like copied in form from Renaissance Italians, like layin' around with cups or in they swirls of Giotto-maniacal recall, even the dude with his pinky enlivened by de lawd from out the cloud, amen . . . Bro Bob had it, like an outline of ! "The Classic," 'cept when dudes like Bob wd fill it in, nigger stuff wd light it up, tho they wd still think they was influenced by Mueller or Beckman or Schmit-Rotluff or some dude. But they was too for sure, being there in the iron vise of the castle motion. Yet what they made, with its green men and blue and yellow ladies, was the lollypop dream of crazy niggers jugged insane by an ununderstood reality!

*   *   *   *   *

[Bob, he was goin' with A, B, C, C and E's wifes. Three of these niggers, includin' Melvin Jones, went up in one of them Klaus Bros cribs between sets (Melvin beatin' hell and heaven out the skins) to shoot up some scag, of which, only Melvin had sufficient to shoot, and Bob wanted Klaus to unbag his stash which they knew Klaus had, and Whitey Kind, the nigger poet with the tophat inside his head, was trailin' around gettin' sneaky Chippy Lightwt twisted 'cause he was drugged at being him. Right then they arguin'. Klaus's wife wanders in the room in see-through negligee, and Melvin starts to play his solo behind "Chasin' the Train," with bulgin' lumpy fly hackin' against the lamps and furniture. Melvin snatches her after early futile attempts at making small talk. The object had got out of hand, and rose above the room like a huge tyrannosaurus rex, looking to devour the world. They fitfully clung together under the shadow of it and rubbed under some jive music tootling the drama cross to all them standing there. Them other two dudes, and Klaus, drylipped, twisted. The question how the nigger cd raise such a prehistoric monster, while having just shot a nickel bag (and them bags was bigger in them days, McGhee), battered all of us, yet they swayed, and ground ground, knitty deep gritty, and when the music came to halt, a huge wet spot was on this southern lady's gown, and the gunner's animal friend lay loose and dangling on his leg! Arrgh Arrgh Arrgh (laughter, or what?) Arrgh, they fell, the other two, rapidly down the stairs, the cracker lady smiled and then cried and fled into the bathroom, Melvin and Klaus, well, they was never seen again.] LUSTED!

Human progress wd not cease! Tho the judges in that tight knot cd put the Bobs down for paintin' people, or even the big-nose Jews, wild-witted phenomenologists who trailed the nigs around because they cdn't believe the strange gargels come out they lips was actual strung together propositions to describe the world. Yet when the niggers went to the right and opted for the German Anglos, and the hard edge, the phenomenologists, the latent humanists, the portrayers of man-in-agony were hurt and slunk away, but they cd be seen carrying Husserl in their arms, head down mumbling to themselves about eidetic imagery and "the other" which haunted their steps. The double of themselves who constantly dogged their footsteps, mumblin' back, in a slightly higher key, the mad thoughts which came back from out their lips perfectly sane, yet seemingly scrambled and mad, the words of a nonexistent shadow.

They all thought that all the persons in the world were shadows or characters in books and images on celluloid. They wd go to see people dance, who wd not move, or who wd run across the stage, back and forth, run across the stage, and then plop down in the middle of the stage, head on knees, and thunderous applause wd sink the place in mischief. The niggers and the Jews, meanwhile, wanted to get out in the middle of the floor and twist they butt to Ray Chas. Or see god in the middle of the air and chant some dumb shit. And they wd.

They wd sit in halls and listen to plin plink plinky plinkyioo, and knowingly congregate on the sidewalk to bear witness to the newer technology, and the kind of Hiterlerian mind that cd call it forth, because they were of the same class!

And each step was tread, each brick placed in the road, was not that precisely seen. They was a young herd of the newly cutloose, to put together a generation's tale. To show the way from out the wilderness, to the urban center into the new society. They were multinational consciousness reflectors, circling around and around, licking and tricking each other in absolute madness. Like ants perhaps from the correct vantage. M went with h, j, m, and y, plus j's squeeze, and the newly fallen wd come to town. He had an office for checking orifices.

Criss cross, in and out, circling and recircling. Building the motif of that moment's swirl into the next. Private greedy mentalities locked in semi-public to actual public displays. Tho it wd get more and public later to many's chagrin.

From coping together, to coming together, to talking about each other, to ruining each other's lives, to going away from each other. Yet that is almost purely subjective. Some remain in partially reconstructed caverns of the castle, and speak of its mighty ruin. De Sade, Baudelaire, Frankenstein, Dracula, all, will give their lectures on their contemporaries in which they are shown as Johnny and Janie Dough. But left out, is the total life construct like any other shabby total. Of day to day, scratching out of America bowel, the inch of light and protein. The niggers became integral parts of the society. These frontiersmen build their new town. Elected new sheriffs to run it, to set the tone, white and black &c. They elected, like as not, doin' the civil rights movement some niggers to run it. New Sheriffs to run and fun, but get the work done.

The stream of petit tragedies cd mount from moment to moment, like in any life. But insanities, faggotries, humiliations in reality, cockholderie, abstract real death, jail, frustration, alienation, subjugation, all these wd pile up. Dudes wd run in in the middle of the night and find they wives sleeping with famouser dudes than them, and go beserk. That is they wd sit down and drink they self to sleep. Niggers of course didn't succumb at first like that. They'd cut the actual fool. Cut them as long as they cd see them. And this is the reason the niggers were in fact feared because they cd still feel outside the castle world to the realer world, where chumps stood in line and waited to get jobs to feed nasty children and shit like that.

The niggers wd actually comment on stupid stuff like that too. M & J sharin' the same tit, wd knock the niggers out, and they'd look out the corner of they eye at both these dudes, and then signify with each other, nigger meeting, damn these dudes is somethin' else. Until, signalling they total integration in the society of modern imperialists, it began to happen to them.

And the society of the blind, but the powerful, cd row and grow like in d.c. They march in and out of the pentagon beset by daily growing personal tragedy but continue to squeeze the poor world in iron mitts. So the society of the castle on the Hudson, shot daily communiques to the world. Art shows, poetry readings, dance concerts, new niggers in Eisenhower jackets blowin' jagged hip abstractions for their nights. Niggers name Ornette, and Albert. Provided the blood count, the pounding rithm inside they ideas, the jagged momentum of they daily stride. Dead babies piled up inside they door near the mail box, which they looked at on the way out to the bank, or the post office, or to work, when they was doin' that, or to the bar, where they held they evening office hours. Freak a baby, they might say, stumbling back, squeezing some immigrant kid's hand to show they were sensitive, or watchin' Frankie Humbauer take off his clothes and stumble down toward the convent where the rest of the fags was hid. Fuck 'em, everybody'd say fuck 'em, let him come back if he don't want to drown! Humbauer?? He started makin' movies when he got to the dock, styled himself a revolutionary, made flicks where he was the contact man in the book store for the white revolutionaries to pick up their messages. On the issue of the multinational party, he was less clear, and so he had Weathermen holding up they old-time capitalist parents explaining what is now a nigger rithm.

Has the story of Allen Ginsberg, Peter Orlovsky, Ray Bremser, Greg Corso, Philip Lamantia, and even mad ½ black Bob Kaufman been told?? Well, somebody'll tell it.

The issues of life in art, and life in life, and art in art, piled up, and they made noise in the hall too. Niggers rollin' on they bed in the afternoon with hysterical Jewesses that made noise too. Screams ran one nigger who was visitin' completely out the joint. He heard that, thot of Jack the Ripper movies. It was Jewish saxophone music actually. He split.

The talks, and lies, and artifacts they produced, that seeped into the world, and made a team of mad folks hooked on non-reality too, exact, preying, in the single shadow world of their own stink and lie. Yet in a very real way they all thought they had the key to eternal life. They were to themselves a welcome elite. They had always waited for themselves to come. They knew they were needed with a passion and put down the world because it didn't. Then, gradually some did sail down out of the clouds with the word. "Look out where yr going." Deathless stilllifes rained out of the overhanging American hell onto the imitative typewriters of pettybourgeois rebels. The urgent music this group made is that it had some workers, some black proles, some up-against-it Jews, the Italians from Mean Streets (who escaped exactly like them niggers split from Howard St., tho the ones who claimed to have stayed look like they went the same route—HollyWood! Frankie Crocker nightmare). And this quality was suspect the gradual fallout of the herd. Like they all claimed eternal life, and beatitude, but reality was more precise. And the failures cd not forever be hid by momentary invention or youth. The drunks kept on bein' drunk, and drunker, and that changed nothing. Some of the dopesters, as it stretched out over three, four, five years, actually died, or went away to cool out. Fags grew faggier, trailed off with fags, to fag it up. Dudes actually later started seriously teaching in school. Some went to Hollywood. Some actually got very nasty and denouncing all the rest. Or picked out the white ones and denounced them (which was weird??? to hear them tell it). Stalked out. There one week, hatted the next. Nobody believed that . . . at least not at first.

But the buildup, the growth, the communications of the castle and its myths, its famous persons, its fleshy projections . . . even tragedies . . . all had a historical and material nature. They met, they talked, hung out, got drunk, went to parties, screwed each other, lied, fought, adulterized, discussed &c. &c. Meanwhile the world, ever spread out past itself, poured new facts in, and common blinding change. Some did, some did not.

At first it was the art-life from its 4 poles. Aha, they recognized the possibility of commonality! Yeh, and of the utopian revolutionary forces, us so-called revolutionaries (white style) always hold out for the assimilated aggregate in groovetime. These talked poetry, music, and the life. Went to Five Spot when Trane opened with Monk, and laid there the whole 19 weeks, every night. To watch that spectrum of black philosophy, the sound of our life before us, and our minds. We cd hear our minds each night spit back at us. As we were, Miles, then Monk. Then Trane & Miles, then Rollins. Then Trane, Trane. And Ornette/Albert raggedy preacher warfare. Albert, and our own floating valley of sound. They were hooked up with the young sound men. The Ras and Cecil Taylors, Sonny Murrays, and they blew blew blew the sound of our lives. No matter we talked about Mayan letters, or Arkadian hieroglyphics . . . or stuffed Heidegger into themselves or Wittgenstein or the *Journal of the History of Ideas*. The real rush of America was the black funky beat of these yng nigger dudes in rap time.

But see it piled up is what's being sd! It piled up. One thing, one word, one motion, one copout, one death, after another, one poem, one headline, one visiting professor, after another, they piled, and piled, and suddenly it was different. It had all (the world) been shot out from under them. Or else it was simply another place they'd come to that nobody recognized!

By the time they'd got first hugged up together, as day to day contemporaries exchanging all they had to exchange, lying about their basic early existence in the U.S., to make a good story, to romanticize them, they'd actually told a broader truth, including lies, dreams, and fantasies, and the thin veneer of fact which made it like a bulging casebook of the time. They'd argue Anglo-German hard vs Jewish romantic, baseball, spade proclivities, what Jews wd and wd not do, butts or busts (leg men getting generally put down), all forms of art and what they meant by culture. After meeting each other, they met all the right people, all the rungs and ringers, the hippies and wd-be swingers, to say whatever was required to whomever to lift those individuals and by that act confer near-light on all who cavorted therewith.

From odd stuff they did to get into themselves, with themselves, to setting in motion all the likewise equally odd selves who felt magnetized by flow of late sixties material life. Robert Wagner and Dwight Eisenhower had worked their peculiar magic, of giving off the aura of total incompetence or withdrawal from relevance. They were mere shadows of antilife for the thought circus of the castle folk. They meant no harm. They were merely corny or dull. How cd anyone possibly be interested in those antics? And lightly these were some content of incipient struggle. Allen Ginsberg had sd, "America, Go Fuck Yrself w/ Yr Atom Bomb." It was profound. He sd, further, "I Saw the Best Minds of My Generation Looking for a Fix in the Negro Streets" . . . "Angel Headed Hipsters." It was profound. It was a turning onto. Look at what we all were. But first, what we all played out our lives against. Tho those specific words seemed a huge fiction life for a person who stood balding and grinning, arguing for poetry, against antique puzzles. And finally wasn't it all like the one-eyed neoElizabethan Anglo-German Creeley's "The Darkness Surrounds

Us" . . . . ? As to the exact menace of that, AG, and his sweep, were a long hungry horn.

How many days was the tone and menace of our exchange, the degree to which we cd see the one or the other vision, and promote our lives according to its preforms. Against it, Creeley sd, "What can we do, against it,/Shall we, and why not, buy a goddam big car? Look Out," he sd, "For chrissakes, Lookout where yr going." Exactly. But we did not, except we all are forced to by the fact of existence. We are where we are going, each moment we are going there. So the pileup of deaths and failures, o.d.'s and adulteries. They began to be limited by their lives, in relationship to their description of them. Some cd say "I," others "He," but it remained the same. From solitary figures trying to run they separate thang, now comes the few more (tho the Italians among them had already seen the head organized along class lines. And in velvet jackets and lace shirts), the constant interchange and cross fertilization. Of the various formations and lines reflected by the reality, our formation, they masses and feeds on the energies released by the civil rights movement . . . nonmafia Italians, nonmathematical Jews and Negroes on the half shell. A kind of class formation of the thrown together inspired. These early '60s they felt they were the vanguard of all life. But more than that, the discoverers of it. The sanctifiers. Burning their age in type and oil paint, or grease paint, wiggles, mere rhetoric, &c. All these motions first were steamed together under the great Eisenhower silence, beneath which these protests, whines, and snorts of hedonistic glee cd have sounded unnervingly honest. They lived on the last block of West 20th Street before the river, and into and out of that estate roared the forming arbiters of think, for a minute.

These particular dudes we knew, they grew as big as both sides of the world description. Shot from mistress to mistress. Collected them up like trophies, like rats run back and forth across a mind field they plucked and got plucked.

How did the ladies in waiting say they were black?? Returning from various growlingly glamourous trips, the inside folk got tricked even, and let usurpers prance through they gates as friends only to find out later, paths were beat back and again.

A. "But . . . is my friend" (falling back across the couch, arms and legs pulled akimbo).

B. "I knew you'd be like this, when they talked

about you so much. Even way off like that, I had the feeling of what you'd be like." The lights go out, grey apple shows under the bambooo.

C. "Ummmmmmm" (slanting eyes from Russia, hugged up in a loft where once Abdulah Buhaina used to hang with Bird. They talk, having had the art conversation, in seriousness the night before. Now afternoons, when M had split, these other dudes would creep and drop anchor in the Black Sea).

D. From the barstool to the back of a book store (later uptown surreal exoticism).

E. Trailing back in to take a bath, and sink back into the cardboard world.

The flow in the two directions already stated created two motions and one overmotion, of which the bloods had key and privy. Yet the motion they made themselves, as part of the history of Afrikans in America (part of the ideology) wd always find itself in conflict, in struggle, because whatever its final lurk, in that fattening society, it always sought a truer harder thrust than what hung around it describing and distorting it. Hence the constant cracking of fists into noses that helped build the niggers' myths. Like a painting in which the figures actually reach out and try to paint additions to themselves, and a bigger portion of reality. It meant, for one thing, they, the niggers, were always everywhere FIRST. And that's one simple principle of leadership.

By time the castle folk move on, a primitive formation had matured in some ways, obscure famous folk emerged, incrowd famous folk. A few folk known to them cd actually make it on they ideas, and the system hurrahed itself for sho', 'cause they biggest success symbol in that world was the dude who cd write a check at the Seedy Bar. From art loot!

It was an interracial society had formed all right. And they thot, even the niggers, that they was advanced simply because Martin Luther King was being knocked out in the streets of Selma, &c. trying to force into being what these folks took for granted. They smirked at King, not really understanding the heroic historical dynamic that King merely gave voice and leadership to. The masses of the people wanted access to the goods and services they had helped create through their slavery. Jewish hipster history, hillbilly history, blueblood rebel history and kook history didn't spell out the rising historical parameters of the black liberation movement. And besides, except for the fiction of poverty the commitment to exotic hedonism might temporarily seem to cause, they had always

assumed the goods and services. Petty bourgeois Negroes, working class
Negroes, petty bourgeois and working class whites. They watched the
stuff like weekend football or basketball, maybe a fifth of bourbon, several bottles of club soda, strong cigarettes and later plenty bush. At a distance from the turmoil of American reality, constructing instead another
reality.

But that was a society, a mode, a splinter of the urgently rotting whole.
They moved in a kind of free zone, a peculiar white (integrated if you cd
get the apt, &c.) neighborhood, out of which the same kind of thought,
but sanctified by its flashy obscurity. What is a Campbell's Soup can, after
all, but a Campbell's Soup can? And a picture of one is only valuable
through some mystification. It was that mystification that served as building block for the castle folk.

But see, Eisenhower left, and then a true mythological figure moved
onto the scene, JFK. The Eisenhower mumble had already seen a shot of
heated image impact against all consciousness. When Civil Rts marches
stumbled, one thicknecked bro rose up saying Self Defense. They used to
talk and talk about Robt. Wms down in Monroe, N.C. Standing off the
Klan! That took the civil rights movement off, especially when Unca' Roy,
the trained Jewish chimpanzee, fired Wms. from the ranks of the advanc-
ing colored people because he broke some redneck's back, who spit on
him in a sit-in.

And by that time the inner movement, and contradiction in some of
the bloods, had worked its way clearly into sight.

Arguments had gone on about the nature of reality. Whether this
included in some legitimate way politics. Elite and right, the Anglo
German/Jewish combine sd all was against any real motion. Hence the
nature of those struggles. "I hate people who want to change the world,"
was the way some of they Italian immigrant poet friends might put it, bitter at CD, a spook intellectual, for pulling his ol' lady—so she had a chit-
terling jones the rest of her life. But they was together except finally
beneath the cover of that easy collection. Hedonism Heights, given intellectual legitimacy and sufficient mystification to seem profound, still cd
not erase history and material conditions. So the bloods wd end up
arguin' with abstract painters abt whether struggle was useful, as to
whether political action, or any action was justifiable. Tho they might put
down Eisenhower in a poem, or jest, tho not too many poems! Till
AGinsberg. Inside the egg of criss cross smoky hugup & dropout, the

Friday nights and Saturday nights hooked them deeper in abstraction. (They talked about wives, gardens, cement yards where cats pee, as objects of poetry, like they were hammers of revolution.) So tired and constructed were the parameters. And the heaping of America piled on, piled on, even though these poor fools were restored to Afro-American history via Allen Ginsberg raving abt the hippy vision of the blood world. And hippy in those days was a gauche white youth trailing after sounds.

See, there was a choice they had beneath or below or outside or above and beyond the schools of the official in them parts. They also had themselves and their history, from which to draw, a world. The immigrant's path was to the paywindow, like his friend the American. The Negro's path had not been, to no damning extent, but what were King and those getting beat in the head for? In one sense it was to be Larry Rivers and paint people without no eyes for a million dollars and to walk around in a New York Rangers jersey.

The bloods, in whatever pb-wc hook up, and mass recall out of history, and the immediate slavery of their minds, wanted more. They did not merely see themselves as part of the plot thickening. They wanted more, naturally. But how much more, even they didn't know.

They had watched Dr. King get beat up or arrested everyday on the 6 o'clock news, watched, w/ white boys and girls and some cheap whiskey, the march of American society into oblivion, dragging all tails, and snags. No, but even with the creation of the Brook Farm, racial utopia, what was it that plagued them all? First, the inconsistent morals, which were the same morals as America, but given exotic rationale. Individualism, greed. Racism, even, or, at least elitism, which supports and regrows another racism. The niggers there were an elite of niggerdom. And that they had to adapt to EuroAmerican culture, tho they added spice to it, cannot be denied. They were spicier Creeleys and spicier Ginsbergs, Olsons with Negro myths to add to the pot. DeKoonings with a different cover story, Cages with a ghetto rationale. Black bohemians—yeh but Bohemia's in Europe, dudes!

All the different paths that brought the total crew together need to be studied to perhaps create a revolutionary construct out of similar materials. But maybe that's like saying create an ironclad out of tissue paper or an ocean out of a beast's perspiration. (Well how big is de beast??) The different white groups (SDS, SWP, &c.) run they chauvinistic symphony, as to why it's they, and that stuff is what the castle folk were in a sense. All run by the great Euro-style, under whose shadow the blanket of reactionary philosophy is spun and worn. By the time of the Cuban Revolution, or as it brewed up into sight, the inner contradictions in the mix-match gang took the form of arguments as to whether what Castro was doing was "romantic" or not.

They had come to consciousness, white and black alike, under the pall of dead skin called the Eisenhower years. The silent generation. So mindless in their slow bubbling weighty consumption of everything under silence. But John Foster Dulles wasn't really Dull, you dig?? They didn't. Dulles was a vicious beast, with claws for eyebrows who tried to suck up the world and destroy all that wdn't submit during Negro school, white school, collitch memories were the grim comedy of Jewish American intellectuals. McCarthy had raved (and grown both Nixon and Bobby Kennedy as the twin horns of his legacy, both hipper righties than he, like most children are hipper than they parents). Eisenhower was like a Gargoyle of Mediocrity. He said nothing. Did nothing. Meant nothing. Was nothing. A baldheaded prick with an alcoholic farmer wife. A reformed catatonic whose attempts at speech were further proof that the reform had not worked.

His (Eisenhower's) presence furthered the metaphysical thot of the group, in that he seemed unable to respond to the world, an unchanging crag of stupidity in world thot. (The defense of imperialism, that it is simply "bad taste.") But then there was a sense in them of increase, that good taste wd increase if somebody cd feel what they felt, or look at life like they looked at it. Or did they even care? Some of them wd be openly disgusted if it was suggested that a lot of people might like something they did. They wdn't have liked that, they wd have thought somebody was trying to put them down. (Gottlieb's wife told somebody once, Adolph doesn't know what he's doing either. It was defense!) And finally the election of JFK must have corresponded to this sense of increase . . . since JFK represented good taste in one sense. He was better looking. Wore better, more stylish clothes. A Princeton haircut, &c. He had, actually, the baggage(?) of Eastern education, with perhaps a strength in the face that suggested he was Irish, Catholic, and therefore (a little bit) more in tune with the needs of the immigrant, freedom, and the civil rights movement. JFK's Camelot was the camelot of those intellectuals. There were niggers who called themselves the JFK Quartet. The New Frontier. And even tho the world had changed a great deal by the time he was iced, and some minds had got opened to some other things, within the generation who shd have known more perhaps but whose history, like all blacks and Americans too, was cut off so history seemed cyclical. Brother BT wept in the streets the day Kennedy was killed. He walked down the street weeping, a big overgrown 200 lb Negro, a talented black painter. He died of a drug whip and his Jewish wife hoards today his canvases, selling them off one at a time at handsome prices.

But also even tho Camelot rose, ditto the inner contradictions, the different directions and destinations implicit in the origins of our gang at the castle. The American morality vs the need for higher morality if they were supposed to be representing something of value. The political backwardness or reactionary, even right wing, quality of thought that pervaded cd not be stomached by the shades.

A couple of them went off to Cuba (the shades) at the invitation of this dude who ran the Fair Play for Cuba Committee. Right after the Cuban Revolution. They went off to Cuba, largely reactionary, tho they had been moved by their history from time to time into some action. Whether fighting in bars, or arguing that the world really existed . . . outside somebody's head. But they were individualistic hedonist Negroes hyped by their supposed intellects. They'd fought battles for their feeling. They didn't want to be confined with white academe because they knew that wasn't them. And so they struggled against it. Ever sense the whiteout process was completed or all but formalized, down in the army base, they still recognized they cdn't eat it all. That it wasn't all them. That it was another thing being talked about that they cdn't be. And that distressed them sometimes, and other times made them fight. They sat and weeped one afternoon in San Juan reading a copy of *The New Yorker*. Some tight white verse about some dreary garden in New Canaan, Connecticut, and they cried, because they had received a reject slip from that same magazine and knew they cd never talk about no jive garden in New Canaan, in no weird elliptical language like what was shown there. They cd dress the part, wear those ties, want to go to those plays, and talk that talk to some extent, but they knew too that they cdn't write no jive poem about no jive garden in New Canaan. They don't do that. They'd dropped out of Colored School because they knew they were being readied for that. Or they dropped out because they failed the subjects, but instinctively they knew one of those main subjects was sitting still for bullshit.

The polarizing internal meanings of the Beat Mountain castle gang had sent the niggers off on other trips. They'd got in civil rights groups who were supposed to be more radical for some reason. They weren't socialists, then. Tho they knew socialists, and talked about them. But they didn't understand the reality of socialist organization. They were a liberation group. The tall yng wispy beard Lumumba blood, Challin Knox, his white wife, a musician, two poets, an essayist, a painter, were the bulwarks. Knox's wife, he claimed, was an Egyptian, tho she was just a very pale white woman. He sd that because Kwame Nkrumah was running that about his real Egyptian wife, who was nevertheless very pale and white-looking as well. Two of the poets had white wifes that they never felt the need to apologize for. They were just that removed from reality. One actually thot it aided him in his work. That Negroes wd prefer him with his white wife to Hulan Jack. And tho they got some inkling that some of the people in Harlem didn't like the fact that some of these dudes had white wimmens, it didn't faze them very much. They laughed about it, when they thought about it at all.

The group AWARE first went through some discussion as to whether its offices ought to be in Harlem. Its first offices were down on the lower east side where all the members lived. But then later they opened offices uptown, on 125th St., but much of their activities were still downtown. And most of the arty members of AWARE developed then a kind of dual consciousness that allowed them to ride the subway up to Harlem to work for civil rights and at the same time romp and stomp with the enlarging castle mob and its pincers and camp followers. They didn't know politics, they didn't know organizing. They knew vaguely they were oppressed blacks, and they wanted people to know they knew.

When Patrice Lumumba was assassinated by the nigger Tshombe and the nigger Mobutu with the support of the then Euro-imperialist United Nations, and US-Rockefeller muscle, some of the members of AWARE ran up into the United Nations and threw shoes down on Adlai Stevenson, the great liberal, and tried to hit nigger Ralph Bunche in his tomming mouth for apologizing for their "behavior." And all this went on, not really fully talked about with the greys in the castle mob. Tho they knew, and some wd discuss it. But the arc of the motion was not really internalized, 'cause there was a march of events as indices of the process. The mob was a civil rights accomplishment itself. And actually it was the interior workings of the movement, carried out to the ultimate. And instead of the open metaphysics and dreams of Martin Luther the reformer King, they had a exotic nigger band who served the same symbolic tort.

But see, the breaking off, the splinterizing of the political process away from the mix match story was a rounding of the arc of the niggers from theyselves back to theyselves. There are those that still run the same AWARE game, running back and forth, even tho the intelligence in that process was long ago exhausted and exposed as bankrupt. There are still those who labor in the mist of WHAT WE'RE DOING IS HIPPER THAN LIFE ITSELF. It's probably hedonist as well. And that framework is given constant support by the oversociety itself which is hedonistic and feeds all ideas of it. But by the time JFK was elected and hoisted on the pole of all the eastern school romanticists of ethnics making it and the society being tossed into a newer clean orbit, the tendency in some of these niggers was known and talked about but not clear and overrunning the other dominance by the castle mob Anglo-German Jewish bohemia.

They went to Cuba and got turned on by revolution, simply. By the fact that it was possible, by the force of men's motion, to turn a thing around, to throw down the negative, to blast it, to rip it off. Like they'd seen in the movies and never cd see duplicated, they thought, in America. The fact that men and women cd roar across the actual earth and drive the exploiters into the sea. Wow! To open the sixties, let that sink in! The force and beauty of that. Of Fidel Castro with a big beard, man, dig it, a big beard, barbudo! (Some of the Anglo-German-influenced Jews even went for the beard, bro!) Then Castro came up in Harlem and laid up in the Teresa Hotel, eatin' chicken, and wavin' at the niggers, and it was on. 'Cause, look, that's consciousness and the niggers there at the castle had to know it was real, that there was something that Castro was doing that was related to something that niggers shda been doing at least. And the niggers in the castle mob, amidst discussions of Ezra Pound the fascist and Eliot the fascist, and WC Wms the chauvinist, or Windham Lewis the fascist, or Hemingway the racist (who by the way had a crib in Cuba and raised a nigger from babyhood there to wait on him hand and foot. The nigger now is the host and greeter, meeting the public and telling them of Hemingway's greatness).

They went to Cuba, hung out with a blonde Mexican Marxist, but trailed around the cadre assigned to show them, the Americano artists, &c. intellectuals, what the Cuban revolution was. They looked, and found out some things. Some objective processes and facts that meant a new motion coming into being there a few miles from redneckville. But the niggers had already a few months or so before begun not only hearing about bro Rob Wms in North Carolina, but trying to raise support for him, and he was in Cuba too. So the Afro-American Self Defense movement coincided with the Cuban Revolution. The first noise of the '60s, after the civil rights movement had brought it all down forward, culminating with the Camelot-constructed March on Washington, to signal the coming together of all those forces, informal and formal, that meant an "open" America instead of a segregated one. Because segregation was dead, the industrial stature America'd attained cd not be sustained with segregated labor forces, or its power sustained with a segregated army, or the international hegemony it sought be gained with a blatant segregated domestic image. To be the governor of the world, America must put its own house in image order. Weren't the nations of Afrika, and the Asian peoples fighting for their flag's independence? Where, for too many, a flg wd be raised, and a Negro wd come into office (still hooked up to American Euroimperial capital). America had to have its own internal flag of independence for the Negroes.

But Cuba was a further tearing loose. A few months later, and handsome Kennedy threatening the Cubans for arming themselves against the insane American imperialistic fanaticism. That was not lost on the niggers either, but what we all needed to know, now, and then, was who killed Kennedy? His was a grand illusion, the great prestidigitator, for the petitbourgeoise confusees to think that somehow something in Washington represented intelligence! But that was the highlight of the mob, that what was absolutely evil could be represented for them in the boozy intercourse as JFK, and the tensions that fled up through him out of America, were all duplicated within the mob. The contradictions, lies, hypocrisies of the castle. Its own Bay of Pigs. The wives had babies, the other women had babies. Men fell in love with faggs and walked the streets with them, and made love to them in cold water flats, elegant apartments, country estates, lofts, store fronts. It foamed and built its final charge.

The marchers went to Selma, Birmingham, children were blown up learning to pray, civil rights workers were killed, and they talked about the white ones more. But fountains were opened, toilets, Woolworths, Peoples Drugstores, a few lightweight gigs, and the token business went into high gear. A token get you a ride in a subway, don't it? Below the earth. But the Cuban thing tore some a' the niggers away from their slavish imitation of the mob rule, because the niggers cd see that that was too tight. Too pointed at another softer reality than theirs. They had a thing to say, they own song, that they had riz in 'em more and more. They didn't even know what it was, but it riz. It did. It sat in their stomach and edged lightwards. They'd sit down and consciously try to say things different from the two schools that ruled the mob's thot. Scrape it, tear it out. Force it out. Force it, like sometimes it'd be only gibberish, but even so, it was free and clear most times. Outside wiggling, and so it'd pick up some of its own airs and content, some of its own history and memory. Its own life. But even so, the niggers still thought they was some kind of Euromyth figures struggling for metaphysical clarity.

Robt Wms got set up in NC, and framed for kidnapping, and split. The bloods in AWARE, tried to deal with the Trotskyites who came down trying to get in on the Robert Williams Defense Committee. The Trots had a line at the time running straight integration, and misread the rising mood inside the bloods, even the castle bloods. The Trots offered 300$ to the Monroe Defense Committee if it was integrated with a Trot on it. The AWARE niggers caucused in the bathroom of one of the leading members. Decided to keep it black (except for their wifes) and the Trots took the dough back. That was some of George Breitman's madness. The same dude who writes the distorted intros to Malcolm X books, trying to claim Malik for the Trots!

But they openly traded in self-defense ideas now, past the civil rights movement. Dudes talked about taking machine guns down South in cardboard suitcases to aid Wms in the struggle. But suddenly the fbi had coopted everything. Wms had fled into exile.

They cd use that, the majority of the folks, cd talk it. The bloods dug it and the greys cd see it. That was common. Self-Defense. Yeh, that was ok. They went to rallies, some of them, with the political types dominating. And a high shrieking tone set in to their talk, to their raps. A high shrieking settled in from somewhere. AWARE was myth, Wms & CUBA were myths, but realer.

Tim Leary came to town one night and got them all high. Psylocibin he called it. He was at Harvard at the time and wanted to get the artists high. Two niggers got high and scared and ran up the street toward Bellevue trying to get some air. When they got up there the fools in Bellevue, crazy as they are, was howling and screaming, almost scared the niggers to death. Also the table jumped around. They stayed high 8 or 9 hours and were pleading to come down by the last getdown and bust Leary in his chops if he came on with that stuff again.

They started smart little mags to talk about a wild life of open combat with the academy and corny stuff! They hooked up with afternoon women and evening women and dinner women and bar women and Five Spot women and Dancerwomen, &c. You cd see them anytime, striding with one or the other somewhere. Some were fat Jewesses with paint on they slips, nearsighted ones, Polaks with arty noses, Anglos far from home, German alcoholic heiresses, even Negroes with wigs and obscene houses or students with shiny hard hair, lightskinned madonnas practicing romance.

They sat up spinning big 45s they told frail eastern molls they'd got from a dude who took it from a klansman. And smoked bush and coughed and fumbled all night under Beethoven, til grey dawn trailed them down the street to their lofts.

They talked yoga, zen, deep image, electronic music, homosexuality, abstract art, films, poetry, and race. They smoked bush, shot scag, snorted cocaine, drank two quarts of ale a day and two packs of dynamite cigarettes.

And they did what they said they was going to do. They wrote or sung or played or painted. And some of them were for real. It wasn't just they walked around talking about the subject but not doing anything of worth in that world. After a while, they had actually some weight to throw. Some influence and opinion. And created a system of their own reference. Built with letters and published words and read words, and heard music, and seen scenes, and hugs, and handshakes and kisses and jokes, and mutually assumed cultural reference.

They saw themselves in small pamphlets, and mimeoed sheets, and even slick books paid for by arch capitalists. What they thought of as their life, was actually several lives. All jammed together, happening simultaneously, and separate. And at some pts, what was raised, by undersea contradictions, forced into the light wild contrasts, extremes. How cd they study Ezra pound the fascist at the same time they walked around Harlem and tried to play activist? Not understanding that yr ideas come from yr life, and not the other way 'round. They were themselves like black icebergs rising out the underwater American reality. Jutting up sharp and icy and dangerous. But within them were also icebergs of unrealized intensity. Unanswered questions. Unresolved predicaments. Images out of perspective. Doubts. Lies. And so when they cd feel the inner question of who were they in open "white" America? The question was being answered everyday. They saw it tossed back at them, by what they sd publicly, by what the others thought of them. And their own definitions.

The mad parties, for instance, cd still go on, but at the same time, there began to bubble forth, like glass being blown, the little luncheons with the rich patrons of the ultra-hip, the special dinners at chic night clubs they cd never go in without the tuxedoed industrialist parvenus that loved to sport them like daggers turned against the old white money. (The words were sd, the acid twist did reserve itself at the edge of their speech, to drip forward thru the tenuous "art," but the place was set. The berugged penthouse, the befagged loft, the consciousness bereft of black gold.)

They began to be actual celebrities in their circles, and the circle hefted up to be smack dab in the middle of, like, America. But then, why be a celebrity drunk, or a celebrity degenerate, or a celebrity coward? If people were going to check them, like everybody, you dig, well why. . . .

But then the other forms of sensitivity and consciousness. They ran guns to Robt Wms in the South. They knew nothing about politics as a science but talked it as a feeling and got into arguments with the others who argued against it equally as a feeling. Yet the Left was dead, was it not? The deadest thing in the world was a mammyjammin' communist. Jeez. Dig *Masses* and *Mainstream*! And that small print, criticizing some dull novels. There was no life there, no flashes of brilliant brutality! No saxophones squeezing other worlds into their skin. They walked back and forth, and never gave it a thought. It was corny. Simply.

The Cuba business tho did open it up. It threw it straight in, that he world did change, and that so rattled them, startled them, that at the same time the icy capitalist patron was steering them toward life as manque artifacts of Luscious Imperialism, they still listened to Malcolm X put down Kenneth Clark on Television. Clark sd, "I disagree, Mr. X, Negro people are not that pessimistic." Malcolm sd, the youth will not go for this, the youth will not let this go down. He meant, The Civil Rights Spectacle that we had witnessed, sipping wine. And having already overcome, being tired and looking for reality. More than cheap thrills! Watching King mashed by the state, not eccentric, unconnected crackers, but the state. The System. The Govt. They had overcome, but the world hadn't changed. When they remembered they were black, which was every third second, it forced them in touch with reality.

But they wd do something daring like rewrite Milton's memoirs in rag-time, in ghetto silken pain. They'd be tearing at the bit. Trying to extricate the calm Anglo-Germanic lyric prosody—death grip on their feeling—or trying to beat past the Jew imitation of their strung-out father/brother. Trying to get to a them which was free of all constraint, all artificial silence and stutter. It was Ornette, Trane, Ayler, Taylor, slurred around. Screaming and scribbling, interiorly raging to bust out of a value box. They fought the cultural war, in bars, on sidewalks, at the typewriter, now, screaming they were alive, they were alive, they were alive. And had come from, actual, life, not death!

The questions of the world, which the world kept raising, seemed not to be answered totally by that crowd. The mob argued. The niggers, they'd take a nigger position. That's what the dude what got his face spit in in the seedy tavern sd. "You just saying that 'cause you're colored." And that made them mad. So mad, they showed the dude was actually smooth between the laigs. But it was true.

And the questions which dragged around inside, were actions now. Meetings. Rallies. Rants in the U.N. Pickets.

It was the state. The actual govt. Corrupt. Mediocre. The enemies. At one side of the skin movie. The memory of oppression. Mostly tales, idea & images. The worst defeat had been the *idea* that white folks rejected them! Tho there were the usual declarations of utter class subjugation by poor whites in their racism, that they were supporters of the inhumanity of people to people. Rough whites killed niggers. But the real rulers killed *The* nigger. These niggers has sat up leafing through illustrated booklets they grandfathers kept in the dressers. Showing niggers being burnt, & hanged, lynched up and down.

But yeh, what'll be done? And who'll do it? What'll be done? And who'll do it? They were tiny sensitive objects created in white folks' leisure for their leisure. They were, the niggers, the enemies of the state, and they never understood that clearly. The poor immigrants, the wards of the state, daily given their share, and apparently settling for it. So to tawk to them. To say Cuba, or AG says, frantic romance, put down by Anglo-Germans because nothing was real except philosophy, leaped from Hegel, through Freud, to Pound and Joyce and the right side of the right. The only theology is excellence and surprise. NEW. The frantic romantics ended up as Jerry Rubin and Abbie Hoffman, tricktawkin' they way back to late 1950's after they got the Panthers killed believing in they bullshit, when we cd have told them then, and tried to, that that shit ain't real bros, it ain't real, it's romance, it's they trip, just like late '50s tawkin' about what to be done, and who's to do it. The niggers were left more and more to they own devices, you see? The communists were corny all agreed. They even called the niggers in they office and told them they cd run the official literary organ if they wanted to try to pump some life in the shit. "Put some yr black booty in hyar nigglow." Whose to do it? And what?

Whose to do & what = a baby gorilla writing poets insane. Dribbling
One day they held a conversation w/ T. Monk
then Iggie T
John V
Jack K
results whose to do it & what:

But late '50s all was salient bubbles. Mental Champagne & actual *career* bldg. Six Negroes & Six White Folks blend to Six Americans, period. Wkend after wkend of joyhighs, conspicuous sensuality, lies, attenuation of reality, the blacks had come from a somber reality, the poverty, oppression, mindless racism, but at the same time a culture of unrelenting *good times*. Let the Good Times Roll, bitter paradox. They were schizoid, especially (& Fanon'll tell you this—Frazier, Dubois, e'en some a' these niggers) the wdbe heavy thinkers—intellectuals—because they'd been shaped though the perversion of western thought. They traced thot only out of Europe like Europeans, except their interior reek w/ nigger history & magic.

It was an epic of growth & decay.

But at the other side of the skin movie, the values foisted on them by their training. The missionary lasso of Colored School. Bombarded by bourgeois visions of a clean cell in which to cavort & call it life. On the altar of the party. And the life they led was simply the concrete spelling out of that tearing schizophrenia. How it bubbled into objective recrudescence—like you cd see it, dig??—

To be *Aware*, yet AWOL from reality. To try to find the focus of struggle, real light, yet have their life itself bind them to sterility & insanity.

They moved from the castle to other castles. These later & bigger even, even more formal, with more of a mob, a larger group, sprayed from all nations, swirling in the confused madness magnetism of the U.S. during the early '60s. The Beats & the pauses, the black bohemians. Some now, actually, all the strands of personality hanging by the limp threads to their ego-memories, were leading 2 distinct, dialectically opposed lives.

They loved America. Really. The red, white & blue motif of 'Melican Pop had actually surfaced during the Kennedy period. Pop art freaky foolies then had "devanced" to the point that Jap Johns, a South Carolina wet cracker intellectual "painter," splashed in cold precision abstract goofons targets, yeh, for one side & abstract flags on the other. They cd only be American flags, but they were colored abstractly, hardedged flag abstractions.

It took silver hiney Warhol to actually come 'cross with the bads. The soup cans & endless reproductions of Marilyn Monroe. And after the killings, buddy boy, later on down in the team sweep gamble. America 1st! Desegregate so we can get on w/ counting the really big dough. Don't want to offend nobody, no money generations. Silver Rites is finally good for business. As such flags that do not wave such targets that have not marksmen—dudes be cleaning abstract guns—they all cd march into the outer lobby of 'Merica. (LBJ say 'Merica & that's what it ought to be. Say 'Merica! Yeh. 'Merica!)

The entire formation, generation, magnetic philosophical trance wd be bought up wholesale. & that ugly shiver run through the niggers sometimes, that they was being asked, for real, to tie up their sweet niggerhood, which, if it can be dug, is the only thing they (we, you, I, he) had. You. Turned Them!

As for "castle" & "mob" they are accurate translations of the tone, the mental image, that life there conjures up. It was a Bram Stoker castle complete w/blood suckers, zombies, mad doctors, & trapped naifs. The mob, the society-tutored bunch who fling themselves together to seek darkness, a gang of ethical criminals, a mad rush of bodies on the lam from real feeling.

There is no place in America but the whorehouse/butchershop history will show it is. Either sell ass or cut it off. Or else watch yo'own limbs fly into the fresh meat bin. Bloody & hacked up for the brief television commentary on yr "insanity."

But shadows of older history speak, memories conjugate w/ desire. They grew, some hard-faced runts, into accusers of themselves. They scared themselves w/ one-half of a sentence, because it commented bitterly on the 1st half. & all the time the hoisters did not understand what they were hoisting. Like Frankenstein for the millionth time hoisted to the top of the mad castle. On a stretcher in the midst of the storm, to let the lightning beat him in the face, & the hoisters staring up in the air at the stretcher do not really understand what they have done! Because even tho inventions take on the personalities of their inventors, these technicians had not invented Lightning, nor was their experiment finally as controlled as it shd have been—to get the desired result.

When the stretcher was lowered from the castle's vault, & the body moved. Telegram went out to the media, yng women, homosexual insiders married to wealthy painters, reviewers, all got the news & ran it big. NEW LIFE!

The rest of the tale is known—tho not totally!

* * * * *

So them razor lightning moved them, w/ its parallel flashes. And some got one face, others another. Some moved, moved, run out one joint dragging everybody 'cross town. A joint on one block, 1 liaison spot 7 blocks north, another 11 blocks south, a few blocks east. All working, sometime. Bizarre cameos in need of but a sponsor to be electronically immortal.

Maybe some others leave all known bus stops & set up new stops, using time/space hamster fashion to show up w/ a joint a minute away from another joint. They kiss & squeeze, walk a few blocks, squeeze & rub. Show up later, long flight up, giggle in the dark, be drinking in another joint later that night. Collected together, being dashing.

But also as the mob drew, & commerce doubled & got famouser, people cd pt, & run more gaw-bage. More people too cd get in on it, the rubbin' & lying & signifying.

Some a' these dudes set up in they spot & folks wd pass in & out like appointments. Sometime they'd show at the same time & rat-a-tat acid exchange criss-cross. They'd squeeze both somehow, lying to both, lying to all. A shadowed window after all had gone, & they'd long to know how to be honest.

Boomerang time, and Bam a boom in space! The criss-cross, double-cross, Brooke Farm, side saddle, jump straddle, by the numbers adultery, juvenilery, had its own vicious sum & profile. All them people sneakin' on they people got sneaked on. Not really payback, except it was, but it was goin' on at the same time from jump!

ENTER J on M&C. Two poems, a series of drinks. Fantasy contracts out. To either like them too much, or slowly undermine them. Show up G on A w/E. Moving proclamations. Remember movies of the street near the park where heroes walked alone in the rain. Wobbling a little from alcohol.

Entire sections of gangs changed they bed & board. Ending up w/ mostly entire other sections. To double up & complicate the acid commerce. Keep the score card jumpin'. Muslim Jew leaves Russian Jew for Russian Jew rolling around w/ black Benny while Muslim Jew was out interviewing some nigger bandits who had figured out a way to stomp the klan. But how did Muslim Jew get to be Muslim Jew madame heavy seat? They had a habit of watching liaisons like this in knowing silence, while RJ & BB did the nasty under the paintings. As salaam alaikum, Muslim Jew, wherever you are!

Mangy Melvin a' course picked up the phone (ya musta heard this) & caught Hirohito w/ his penis to Molly Goldberg. MM left w/ Donna Daze, but then Lana Nose showed up too to contend that Angelina Conroni showed to recomplexify plus MM w/ them others at top speed tried to be AWARE. Karl Marx's great grandson and his wife lived upstairs & they'd show w/ their daughter Molly 2 to agitate!

The rest of the niggers'd show to talk bad about things so complicated they didn't know what it was. Called theyselves The New Dudes, argued abt reality & un—its popular relative.

& they was writers liars actors musicians professors scag men cocaine con men grinning at the pile of laig they cd get easy.

They'd move again. Cast wd change. Score cards come out. Les Limp was overheard one afternoon talking to Mimi Sibelius. Whatta you talking abt? Mimi reporting she'd seen the results of 3 days a week LL had tipped on over to the Conroni spot. Angelina sat in the park after a heavily publicized pregnancy w/ the faggot of her choice, a tv actor named Reginald Mousefinger, but when the ad space popped, lo & behole, the chile was yaller. Mimi shed a few tears & said some recriminations, maybe a day's worth, & that was over.

In the real world more than that wda been shed and said. That'd drag on for years & years. Tho the heaviest irony was Angelina & Mousefinger moved right next door to Les & Mimi & they had to say hello to each other every day for the rest of them lives.

Klotzberg's coming down the stair zippin' up his whatnot. Bingo

Brown's turning the corner blasting into the same hallway. "Hey man," they say as they go by. They was that hip. And later 3 cases of clap to applaud the show. They all, at one level, cd condemn each other. Even themselves, as a form of high art. Alienation & ego. Neon solipsism. Unhappy endings—confusing abstractions to hide the essential jive quality of that society.

Yet all were pompous & intelligent, opinionated & holy. Had better worlds in they heads than cd ever exist on the real side. And the real side polarized them, drove them apart. There were the regular mixed sets & mixed conversations & slowly, on the bloods, there began to weigh a tiny separate logic, which at first only had them together at times to do something. Play ball. Hang out at the 5 Spot. Catch a set. Go to the most famous one's house to listen to sides and get high. & get high for real. 3 & four hours worth a' reefer. A bag a' scag. Some coke. And Trane Trane. Underneath over top. Describin' the motion of the time. "Bye Bye Black Bird." "Round Midnight." "You Leave Me Breathless." "Chasin' the Trane." "My Favorite Things." "Coltrane Jazz." "Harmonique." "Alabama." "Trane's Blues." "Impressions." "Expressions." A "Love Supreme." "Live at Birdland." "Live at Vanguard." Ran over & under them, pressing the time movement, the space need, the generation feeling. The logic of an era!

Be in there high w/ each other, a bunch a' dudes. They come in in twos. The whistle early w/ the smoke & maybe scag.

Famousest Friend push his chair away from the desk where he was workin' at being famous. They'd roll the smoke, & turn on the sides. In an hour, 2 more'd show. All day high, listenin', talking. Inside divided more than they cd dig. The sounds soothing, yet damaging. Talking of unrealized portents, but full of the action twist & sprint of their actual lives.

The famousest friend was always with a white woman, who'd not be there in the day. And so they gathered & got high all day & by dinner time make they move to other stops. Poppin' the white boys' wives & sisters. Or hustlin' dollars, influence, pickin' up more dope, checkin' on sets, or going to get ready for another dope-in later on.

But even randomly, what musta been sd then—the words running through the heavy Trane vibrations—what they sd had to reveal more a' themselves to themselves than they revealed to each other.

The serious ones, who pressed for notice in the outside world, wd warn they bros & be talked to by others, 'cause they'd get a rep & reference in the castle mob world, that cd set the whole group in profile as hip.

And they thot the world of each other, the niggers. Tho they ran games on the greys, lied sometimes to each other. Generally jived (& were jived by) the world. They dug each other, mainly 'cause they was there in that world together! And cd be warmer w/ each other than w/ anybody else.

It was not a known bias against the greys (except in basketball, but even there big redass Mike was respected 'cause he cd play & was rough). It was the response they got from each other that made them dig that more. (Even the whitest of them!)

No matter the winding complex jive they'd be calling they Martin Luther King era-life, still they'd ease back to each other to sit around getting super high & loaded w/ Trane. And then they'd talk about music mostly, & personalities. But other lights had come on. And Malcolm X was talked abt. Watched at night on tv. Another light came on in some heads, not blinding at first. But steady steady on & inside. The mark of time. A clincher come out and cockle doodle-doo on the roof. The camera turns. The lens smacks you. The Eyes & Ears of the World. Badada dant dan dah—dah doan—dant daaaaah.

This is all that kept them bein' merely tiny sensitive objects created in white folks' leisure. The years had glazed them w/ that, yet real commerce ran in they soul. They didn't get no better, they just kept on movin'.

So when somebody say in the big ol' world a' white professionals & class magic, these dudes is recognized as competent reflectors of the time, some a' them took it, ran w/ it. They saw themselves in others' eyes because now they were not secret niggers. People they didn't even know cd talk abt them.

They cd see now there was a society they'd help create—in the same barbarous castle. Of all nations jammed together, jivin' in rag time. But now they'd comment & someone wd comment on they comment. They'd actually be somewhere talking to groups a' people about stuff other than poppin' yellow amps in parties. They now had an objective life, you see?

Incident Two

A party in Archie's crib. Halloween maybe. Blow, blow all night. The entire mix was there, & then there was some unpleasantness. A thin nigger with piercing eyes had punched Indian Bailey in the nose (name Wall or something?). Bro ran over & checked it after & jumped in the nigger's chest. Bro was always able to turn into fire &, w/o bein' able to offer a real fist fight, burn opposition down because they sense Bro wd actually kill you—if it came to that, just so you cdn't dispute him! He stuck his finger in the nigger's face. But who was the nigger in the 1st place? How'd he get in here & who was he really? Didn't none a' them know him. But then it was revealed later that pt a' the gang did know him, as Jap Tann or simply as Wall. Simply, but not immediately dug as such, a mad man. But it let in some reality to say that if Indian cd be beat here in castle land, some other stuff was happenin'. 'Cause not only was Indian big & loud & given to fightin', but now he stood & seemed slightly scared by this mysterious Wall, who they sd had a brother who also like to fight.

It was a strange night. Later the brother showed. He showed at Bro's crib one afternoon, usually scag-up time. He was a writer he sd. He sd there were people who criticized Bro for bein' Bro.

Wall sd, "I did just what I sd I'd do—broke yr nose." And Indian hung, lookin' sheepish.

The brother, Prince or Champ, sd he was surprised to see a lot a people who criticized Bro, at the set. They were hypocrites he sd!

Incident One

At the 5 Spt one afternoon they were sippin' they early brews. Actually a ½ way station between where the greys hung & where the niggers wd get stoned. The greys had a wet culture, bourbon & soda &c. Boilermakers. The niggers, smoke & cocaine & scag. They'd slide into the bar & ease up beside they walkin' partners, sayin' "I got some dooji," & they'd split for the new hideout.

They in there one day & dude they didn't know—some a' them knew him, from further east—he slid up said, "I don't like yr poetry but yr book on music, I like that." Went into some metaphysical sidewaysism w/ another dude they hadn't seen before. Come to find out, these were the 2 prongs of another rush a' life. That Bro & Indian & Archie & A & L & M & AWARE in general had codified and calcified & rose up above the ground so far that there was actual other life come in. And it was intelligent life. It was bilateral, 2-sided, a left and a right. This was the right that talked in 5 Spot about books and spooky rhetoric.

Bro was impressed. It was a lot a' razzle dazzle. They sd they was writers. The gang thot it was the only intelligent black life in creation. But then all that talk, like that, was baroque, wasn't it? It curled around too much. The niggers got quiet & was polite & sd they talk to them 2 dudes after while, you know, another time, & they drifted into the afternoon to get high w/ some niggers & find some white boys to talk to, some white women t' screw!

Robt Wms had give way to Malcolm. They knew Rob. Billygoat went in a junk shop & bought a cardboard suitcase to carry a Belgium machine gun down to the battle zone. The junk man sd, "Why's it gotta be a special size, already? You wanta put a machine gun in it or something?"

Some a' these dudes had begun to write regular columns or have regular shows. They even taught classes in they own mixed-up minds it helped to pt them. Then a few even had some major note. And all the time, the soul sessions, scag & rap, under Trane's spell, helped put out they insides. Helped show them to themselves. But the way that life cd show itself among the mixmatch gang—at the grey side—was always either absent or controversial. Grey life & letters cd be talked of. W/ the two referenced schools as definers of the weight of the thought proposed. It became a kind of pressure on some a' these niggers that, like the pro-con Castro dialogs, they'd spin off that a comment on how they had to have "someone to talk to."

They'd been driven thru the grove of artificial trees, absorbed the common madness of the natives. And now they cd be counted as natives too. They were no posing strangers. They belonged. They were known. They cd cash checks in the Seedy Tavern. They were invited to the heaviest all-white parties. They cd talk seriously about society & give out influential opinions.

They even went to jail for publishing a newsletter, at which the post office told the FBI to pick them up, & one A.M. they spread out in the old dance hall some of 'em lived in over the gipsies, & a cop wakes them up. Insults they white wife as to whether they married or not. Famous Dudes. Beat the silly case to let in later, literally, obscene reproductions of American life.

But they stuff was forward. It cursed because 1st cursing needed to be heard. The country needed to be cursed out. The niggers' presence made the other description of curses too light.

At the same time some other ones got whipped in the head for running in the UN, throwing shoes at Adlai Stevens & Ralph Bunche when they teamed up w/ Rockefeller, Tshombe & nigger Mobutu to murder Patrice Lumumba. (Bro was working at the time for some technical editing company to pay for some babies & the vice president pulled him into the office one morning, sd, "What does Lumumba want?" This just before they killed him!)

And what they made began to show all this. The artifacts. The documents. The sounds. The cries at night in the dusk of their minds! Johnny had a play opened to standing ovation about him & some white chick. The bitch killed him. Scared a lotta these dudes. They was happy for JM but then they thot how that nigger write that stuff that's got to be him & US!

Willy was teaching art & screwin' the students. A dude lived under him sent his ol' lady to the class. Him and Willy was friends. Willy popped her the 1st day a' school. The white boy found out the next day. They was gone all day.

A wild sister in a wig pulled Richard one night out the 5 Spot, & they looked at each other cause both a' them dealt exclusively & unselfconsciously w/ white folks. But who was she? Anyway. They went home to her crib in Brooklyn under the bridge, near where the weird Jews lived. The place was like a cyclone had hit it. Stuff thrown around. Chairs overturned. Dresses on racks. Plates w/ food in 'em. Richard shuddered, popped her, drunk, & went back to his Jewess.

Bro was bein' newly famous one night in the spotlight café, at a heavy white arty set. Only one other shade. This real slim sister almost orange, hair piled up, & loose, big bright eyes, wide, when she did smile. A mocking expression always, a flash of the eyes, they locked just to the left and above the herd of important greys.

Bro moved over immediately, sd, "Yeh, hi you madame, what's yr name?" Like a lost chord reflected from always. "Yo' name?" & she lit up the room w/ this black sensuality that made him toedance around her, trying to tie her up.

What was she doin' here? This is some beautiful woman. Wow. She talked low, soft-mannered like she thot Marilyn Monroe wda sounded if Marilyn Monroe had some deep feeling.

Bro nutted. She just smiled, & knew it. & there was really nothin' that had to be said. The situation itself set it up like it was. They were there in that . . . ugly white world. But why? & touched, barely a conversation.

"I know yr name. You don't know mine tho."

"What is it?"

"It's Jan. Janet really, but Jan. I want to be an actress. I go w/ Raleigh Carstairs."

Blank. Pow. Buttery fluid smoke. Choke. Bro leaned. He thot at least he cd . . . but Bro was hooked up w/ some grey broad. For years. Not one . . . but some & he cd still be struck dumb by that. She was here, obviously needed to be together, yet she . . . & he (they) They were hooked up w/ something outside themselves.

Raleigh, the rich publisher, came over pretty soon. Did he dig that expression in Bro's face? You bet!

That stuff got bizarre. Bro went to picking her up afternoons. Jan'd stop by Raleigh's office to get money to buy new clothes. She was a model. Then they'd roar out into the afternoon. Black Confused Beauties trapped under glass.

Jan wd run w/ a white girl (she was also a little bulldaggerish some-times) & front the girl off as traveling companion & show up at Bro's spot & stand befo' his white wife and say, "Bro I need to talk to you."

And they parade off to gobble each others' face.

So too Bro wd show in front of Jan's square-topped simplex, see whirring shadows on the glass, since he was expected, push up the stairs, to thump at the door, & await both women's faces at the opening.

They cd not remember the white girl's face. Or was she, yes she was, some kind of Latin type, slender like Jan, but quieter, less explosive, but effusively implicating, ironic, "stylish."

She wd slip down the stairs into grey warm smoky fog off the sidewalks, hands jammed in her raincoat. Like a prototype wd-be woman revolu-tionary. Tho, primarily, a hedonist. And the bloods, like gifted shadows, wd flow across the room into each other, soft, ecstatic for being alive & in each other's company.

Laughing, Karenga called it. Laughing w/ each other.

Yet what cd they do finally about that world but pt out its extremes, its parametric essences. Sensuality was their philosophy, the life speed of material, in process. And sensuality cd only be raised to a point in the high arch of the dome of that world—not bust the dome. Tho, dig, it cd bring them up so close to the roof, they cd peer fast seconds at the world beyond.

And in a flash, through the grim scenes, the arch nastiness, their enemies perceived their innovative exchange. They didn't love each other—they needed each other. No love was possible within the definitions of the mob-castle society, yet need, in a scene in which all that exists is almost absolutely counter to what is needed to survive at a higher level, is the highest effective existence. And all them who cd dig it hated it w/ the precision of correct instinct.

Carstairs made faces. Bro's dumpy Jewess puffed up like a knish. They had a jewel-like appearance together. A green, exotic, 2-faceted stone. Created by years under ground. Surfaced, the clingings together in bathrooms, licking each other while they urinated, entwined on couches w/ the light coming up, in and out of places w/ the grip of their fingers commenting on the rise of new social orders, was an animal consciousness of utopia—but perfectly realized.

If they cd be seen years later, years after, the paths shot off separately, screams laughter, subjugation to the craziness of their peers, Jan cd be a muslim woman, at a bazaar, in Nwk, and Bro a dude in a dashiki suit. And their paths were separate, perhaps, described in their 1st recognition and departure. They wd pretend not to recognize each other, & each, fully understanding, the whole circle of relationships, wd merely be dazed by the meager bonds of human activity and wish each other, silently, something's speed!

* * * * *

The star's image, projected, shows how its points intersect and raise apart. They are asterisks or elections, self-conscious travelers. Crisscrossing into separate trajectories, yet part of the same elemental complex process.

Out of the mix of the times, the process made a series of opposites, contradictory correlatives. Arguments wd take on a more serious nature, proceeding from the superficial to the real concerns of humanity. The civil rts movement was breaking up.

Niggers cd be seen, quickly, for instance w/ some more. Bob was scag gatherin' & wd stop & turn on 8th Ave, crisscrossing the dope boulevard, spin on his heel, say, "Hey look at that Fox, Bro!" But the poison produced the trip. The other trip produced the poison. He wd weep when Kennedy died because it meant the storekeeper he lived w/ more & more was revealed as a storekeeper. Madame Lafarge w/ her knitting, Bob w/ miniature bullet holes all over his body, even his fingertips, which he wore wool gloves to cover. She wd knit a body glove, a shroud, when he had shot up his entire body w/ the heroin, & died in Italy, looking at Romantic paintings in a brown fedora hat & turned up shoes.

It is no accident that madame Lafarge was soulful enough to become Prime Minister of Israel.

If he had lived, they wd have had to join the NAACP in order to continue to get the gold. But Rob Wms hurt a cracker, ran the hoods out from under they hoods. Malcolm sung to them under the television commentaries of blown-up babies the productive forces of fascism. Marion sd one day, they was gettin' high, "You ever heard a' Stokely Carmichael?" A Howard student sending messages out. Bob Moses led them through the awed gasps of appreciation of the missionaries at their own creation. And having dug the contents of the Horse, which the popular liberals still tried to ride, he shuddered, changed his name to Paris, & fled to Afrika trying to escape Troy.

The contents of the Horse: Death!

But Death & Transformation.

Life holds itself over
everything—

Some a' these niggers wd be feeling on this one & squeezin' on that one, but, suddenly, out of the black, start chasing some dude across the baseball field w/ a flailing bat. At some minor slight. Or blast some white boy at a party, fu-lam, in the mouth. Or fight each other & come out unscathed having drunk a quart of vodka & took off all they clothes standing in the middle of the floor talking about Jake Lawrence & Picasso. Fuck 'em both, they decided, & stalked off looking for their drawers.

The contents of the Horse: A million Niggers on a dead man's chest!

Some watched television & wd start arguing about the results. They watched Bad Bob Johnson fight The Hollywood Sicilian & Johnson blasted THS w/ left hooks, right crosses—bloodied his nose, busted his lip, messed up his croquignole—but THS had more commercial potential for TPTB (the pow'rs that bees) so they give the decision to THS.

Now the niggers are sitting in Benny One Ball's house, ½ winkin at his wife (they probably split up now anyway—fo' they own good) not really but ½ like, & the decision comes over, after spaghetti & beer. The results of the evening, a whole buildup of sentiment and fact. The subjective & objective reality of an age changing into another age.

The niggers sd, what? What kind of BS was that? Did you see that? BOB in his shaky quavery fashion (a Jew w/ nigger hair he was), he wrinkles hissef up, pretending to be real emotional, like he tried to look like he was jumping—actually he leaned shakily in his usual tipsy dance. "What the hell you saying? That was the right decision. The black bastard lost!"

The niggers, they stunned in a weird way—"You cdn't see that, man . . . what? & why you have to call him that? Nobody was talking about that. Johnson won that!"

"Aw he didn't," BOB tiptoeing like he was bouncing up and down. "He didn't!"

Aw hell—the niggers standing in the middle of the floor saw Marva's face recede behind an embarrassed frown, turning quickly red. The niggers spun &, picking up their hat & glasses, hit the door. Later, they sd, coming down the stairs of the 2nd Ave. elevator bldg, later, & retreated toward they own spot, deciding later to get high instead.

Incidents everywhere & of all kinds. The contradiction in the American Petty Bourgeois Bohemian, that it was black & white & the streak of lightning explaining America's history had at least 2 sides.

The basketball solidarity, the jazz unity, the talking consciousness, the rhythm du dah duh dah dah dah dah—of walking Miles, clean, obnoxious, to be truly alive. Trane wake up blasting elements coming into full visibility, oracular, our-story, we tale had to be full up & opened out to be seen.

Niggers slumped across 4th St. bathed clothed soaked in rhythm. Even mad, drums bammed at them. They stopped & tried to get the right tempo—way up. Albert Ayler's anthems began—open, broad, coarse of co'se, Black flag mystical because that was the way. Blah-Blah what Trane had sd. Opened up a world so staggering. It made them disappear (to reappear as Ornette & Albert & Milford & Archie) Blast open life—& that was them too, for better or worse—& more—all.

& the public ones, took on schizophrenia that oppressed whichever audience except the mutating schizophrenic. Strange now, many times, to understand, actually who they were. They themselves, all the time, this seeming in time, to be a question mark to they self! That was life in them parts. Contemporary—profound! Yet w/ polarisms like weather thrashin' them back & forth, & from all sides!

They'd lay in white life wheezin' sweetness. & on all sides, other postures in nature formed. A conversation at the 5 Spot in aesthetics & reason wherein a scarface Negro sex fiend, petty bourgeois intellectual & plump avant right wing negret (a variant of the "gro" & the "gress" combined is the "gret," amen). They wd say nuclear criticism has arrived from EuroAfrika, hail chiefs.

All the time there'd been more bloods trickling into around castle land, Kafka hipsters, so to speak, zeroing in on where de knowledge was. And so even tho there was bloods, they'd be with whites most times. There was some'd be with whites more times, & some, like, in a group called Eclipse, who argued early to be or not to be but quietly as part of the tremor that stirred beneath the interracial bunks.

(When Kennedy was iced—the 1st one—some nigger painters stumbled thru the downtown streets weeping . . . actually for themselves, 'cause that was their signal to die. Some a' them super militant banjo thumpers yodeled a ode to jackie "who's had to eat too much shit." Ahh weak-kneed perception to those who yearn to be radical while sipping cocktails in Park Ave w/ the Jewish *nouveaus*. Woe to them who reflect suddenly, after gradually, the hacking lightning thunder of the Eagle's laugh, and are led by Malcolm into the land of Witches & Devils only to look up and be w/ them. Getting ready to haint the world!)

At Eclipse they argued whether a poem accusing Kennedy of being an Imperialist Dog shd be printed a few weeks after his ice-ing. In fact the group broke up behind that. & the mad souls who sd print the muhfuh, they drew closer together & w/ others like them. Malcolm sd, "We are not Americans. We are Victims of America." & he got busted too!

AB Spellman sd, "If all the black people separate from America what wd you do?" Talking about these same niggers, famous folk drifted thru each other's searching stares. Why did they want to be anything at all? And if they actually were found to exist—what wd they exist as?

They'd be coming out of their heads, is what it was, climbing out into the open. & so to see their names somewhere at which they were supposed to "appear." Somebody describing something about them.

That slight objectification. Verification of the existence of ——— out-side of the blankness. What was it they represented? As symbol, reality, projection of form & content in dynamic motion.

This is what the preparation was for in Colored School—to be Colored, of course & totally integrated into everything. Cool & successful. But not ravaged internally, & held up to ridicule by one's self. But that cd be sub-stantially satisfying even—you dig—western/Melican society, that even self-disgust takes on a high aesthetic, like eating rotten food (the survivors near their downed plane in the Andes sucked on rotten fingers) it had a piquance. How many prim little Kafkaesque lines celebrating mis-ery, self-hate, &c. Beautiful they cry across the lights. Terrifying!

And they'd be in lofts high away from slipping traffic, removed from all & every. They many mamas might fleetingly wonder, somebody else look-ing at a picture, but alone w/ some fag with long hair glasses among the costumes & silence. The fag's boyfriend was a "jazz enthusiast," a hippy actually. Old definition, relating strictly to music. It was a dope factory they lived in, & the fag was somebody's wife & mama, the enthusiast. He'd bring in the dope on trays, and smiling 'cause he wanted to be of service! All kinds of cocaine, procaine, scag, bush, various ups, downs, floats, flats, it was all there folks. Mexican Brown, Chicago Green, and they rolled upon the couches, minds blown scatting about nothingness. Miles' drummer, a yng whiz kid, got a set of complete works of Shakespeare (excluding this volume) to put beside his drums & signify that he went with a white woman. Harry! Pony! Names of minds in fur-nace fusion scattered among blown stars. All the time reality itself, in which their stammers formed, bit a brief silence, stretched & changed.

Was it hatred split up the castle mob? (And were they ever really split? Yes they were. But check!) They sat & smoked & snorted. Rain beat out-side, & inside intelligence & sophistication, about bullshit, about deprav-ity, pirouettes in shit ditches. Laughter in the Mad House. It was take yr pick. The world or The Shadow. The Real or Nothing at all. Tho Fantasy makes sounds like It IS Actual.—It Ain't!

They more and more sought out, even unconsciously themselves, these bloods. The white women they were with cd maybe tell a certain weird quiet developed. They never walked up & down in their barony like before or like the new breeds which embarrassed them walking in the streets like MLKing & Rabbi Prinz & co, storming Washington! This was not that evident, but it cd be felt, even if it was misinterpreted.

And all the tons of mistresses, & soft lie-raps, midnight returns, truncated weirdly too. They sought out black women unconsciously. Like Bro & Jan, accidental shots in flight gallery! Tho that was thrown apart by the same motion that brought it together. & where are they now? Struggling. In Love. Trigger fingers still burning! Separated but maybe completed, wherever they are, in the dynamic of growth.

One night Burt Corliss was supposed to go with them & his old lady was going too—down to DC to a party. Some kind a' big ol' nasty party & Corliss says his old lady Lorna can't go because she's white & they's black. What happened w/ that is Burt went with them, all the rest of the niggers, down to DC & spent all his time on the phone tryin' to call Lorna. When she got back in (she'd been over w/ the fag, she sd, but she was really w/ the Jap who banged her regular), Corliss moans over the phone about what to do. And they sort of went through some weep action. Then Corliss slides down the hall (the set was in a hotel) & spots, tho she spots heavier, Kitty Prince. He gets a drink & splits & as he's shutting the door to the hotel rm, she slides up, says, "What're you doin?" They went together for two years after that & finally separated in another town, after Burt had split from the white broad.

But people talked about that. Sisters already functioning castle time were philosophical. Lucky's wife, "Bay," sd she cdn't understand Corliss, since everybody liked Lorna. "Bay" thot Lorna gave her an education was what it was. Bay wanted to go to college, but she had to work so Lucky cd paint. So she dug to hang out w/ Lorna so she cd get a BA (Black Asst) degree. Even tho Winky left Trane's cousin for Ann Sheridan on the half shell. He got a job w/ *The Daily Fang*, writing praises of capitalism in slave gibberish.

Dudes began to form not drug groups or rap groups but conspiratorial sets to think themselves up into something. And then the summer after they made it & America sent flowers to say "All is well. You niggers are brilliant!," Gertrude Bernbaum sd she'd never speak to these niggers no more 'cause Blue wrote a song about her & her old man, how she killed him in a wheelbarrow & worked for the Slave Catchers Assn.

The castle was illuminated not as a structure but a *gens* or common consciousness. Some sisters from Eclipse middle wing slid up to Blue in front of a delicatessen & sd they wanted to speak to him. They sd don't put that garbage on. Earl Hyman stopped kissing whoever it was he was kissing & sd that can't be done while my people are fighting for their freedom (never!). The field secy of Militant Action Revolutionaries appeared on the rug to outline the path that the movement was taking. Ayler was screaming! Screaming! He sd, "It's not about you! Its not about personalities! Its not even about notes!" He carried Black Norman Jesus with him to testify with black ivory grin a silent screech of bonked teeth! The conspiracies began. They drew themselves together. The far out wing of Eclipse. New breed critics. Militant middleclass. Working class toughs.

From all the madness, a conspiracy. Against what tho? For what?

You, Yall, Ya

In 1964 Harlem went up in smoke! You might remember, some a' you.
Were teaching school off in some college, English, or at a writer's conference on the coast, down by the water at Monterey. Talking militant, sere-
nading ladies—What was yall doin' there? You remember Dunbar, was up
at Carter Tech, teaching poetry when the fires went off? He left, came
back in town. Went to some white woman's house, up the dark stairs.
Knocked.

> Linda
> Yeh
> I came for the heat
> Yeh, I figured you wd
> Thanks for holding it
> It's OK. Where you goin' now
> To Harlem

That scene was never replayed, or did it ever really happen, except if it
didn't, it still needs to. A night club session on art turns to angry shouting
thru the smoke. Lawrence Katz, the noted abstract painter, is incensed
when Daughtery told him he painted for the rich and was the same as
them. They fell out.

It was white. They heavy was put on bein' white. Suddenly white, yall
remember, can you feel that sudden absolute tension? Now it came out, it
began to come out White. It was hatred, deep, irrational, yet perfectly
logical. White. That's what it was yall came to reject. White!

It came out yr conversations w/o announcement. Yall sposed to be
friends & this! It cd be all right w/ Katz, he was corny enough, yall thot.
At least the Anglo-German aspect of fashion thot so. But weird talk got
louder & louder. What ya niggers were saying began to be heard. Not only
had Ken Clark got told off, but Harlem burned! Kennedy was already dead!
Signals. Gator came out w/ this stuff where he actually blows a white boy
away! On the stage, but even then, that shook 'em up. This Jewish Muslim
dude interviewed Rob Wms ("Negroes w/ Guns") & that was a war in real
life. Rob was the spiritual leader of forming underground armies. The

Klan cd be beat! Pay back for Dr. King's many whippings. Suspicious of bourgeois Negroes & bourgeois whites but only because of their lifestyle! Which runs to colored copouts and white murders!

When white Easley died on LeRoi's stage, it shocked you all. It shocked him. But that was emotional *fait accomplis*. Conspiratorial gatherings & loud attacks alternated. What yall sd to each other in pvt, you whitest Blacks of the time, sincerely related to what feeling existed:

Ed—You gonna get involved w/ all that?

Al—Yeh, yeh I got to, what else?

Ed—Look, you gonna stay in touch?

Al—Probably not

Ed—I dig

You had not reached past appearances to essences & reality. It came out "White"! Yet you sat there w/ whites & told them that! The mistake is you were not them, & you sd that often. But the weak link hedonism, removal from reality. And the fact that many black bourgeois ran undercover bohemian style, like the guys who's daddies pd they way through bohemia. But why white as ultimate enemy? With yall there with 'em? Aware dudes & dudettes commuting to Colorville. Earlier integration pride turned to doubt, then shame, then horror. Then guilt. White?

Except who was it asked who was killing people? They were white. Others, yeh. But what were yall there doing about it? Drinkin' carcinol, & saying politics and politicians were corny. The world was corny. You niggers cdn't sit still for that because you weren't in limbo w/ a world dying. You mighta thot that, in they company too much, laid out in "despair," staring into a cement yard under rain, or alienated from real life by the rasp of American intellectuals. Traveling between 1 "wife," 3 mistresses, & 1 anonymous pickup every 2 wks. In that madness, yall might say the world is dead, reflecting yr environment. How ya lived. Cornelius sd, "You got some a' that heavyweight champ in ya."

They were white because you cd see they ran it. The violence. The killings. The lies. The copouts. The unreality. They ran it. Were in charge of it. And these dudes & ladies yall ran w/, they only wanted to be a weird part of it. And rose immediately one or two squats they'd float up to the surface, pulled screaming into fullup America. You cd never be into fullup America. Fullup America was white. Good you sd. You remember? Good—good for them muhfuhs, let 'em be that. Cause it ain't nothin' no way neither. Look what it is? Be Andy Warhol or Lyndon Johnson—take

yr pick! & BOB or Scuchine or Bregstein &c. (not they real names!).
What the hell were they doin'? Olson died! What the hell was one-eyed
Bob Creeley doin' or 4-eyed Allen Ginsberg? 2-eyed blue nigger wasn't
dying in no hole marked "white folks" hell no!

Yall conspired & grew to harder shadows on the walls & sidewalks.
Wanderin' high thru the streets, white boys knocked yall down, yd get up
& hold them off w/ one K55 blade.

You, little nigger, went up to Columbia as "integrated thinker" of the
year, backed outta the bar after bashing two white boys across the face w/
a beer mug. Blood shot all over the pennants and pickles.

Yall talked badder & badder abt white. It was white it all focused on. Yet
all yall know yall talked day in, day out to 'em, slept w/ 'em, ran w/ them.
What yall sayin', white? White, yeh White.

& some a' these same dudes what popped Indian Bailey in the jibbs
drew close to the sound. Like the pied piper's pickups, Acid Face
appeared among the others. The hated Acid Face, the killer Negro
maniac, whose only life was to hate everything. What yall didn't understand is that Acid Face didn't just hate whites. He just seized that as perfect to run his life-paralysis. Acid Face (you mean Wall) hated everything.

It rolled up "white." Because there was no clear analysis or understanding. The principal contradiction was white. Malcolm brought it from
Elijah M. Acid face Wall wasn't w/ EM. He was later a Sunni, but his running buddy Jackie Less was the 1st Bohemian Muslim (maybe the 2nd)
yall dug. Cleanheaded, shortsuited, w/ a little hat & briefcase. He ran that
on yall because yall wasn't in the community. & all that posturing & toe
pointing was simply The Nation of Islam. & they ran it heavy. White. The
Devils.

Two sisters approached Bro one afternoon & took him aside trying to
point out how weird it was that them dudes wanted to paint pictures of
white women. That was totally strange, cause they assumed everybody was
impressed w/ the colors & shapes, but yeh it was more than "his creation"
or colors & shapes. It was white women's pictures.

Malcolm called for The Heat to Come On! & by the end of '64, Harlem
had burned & the absolute end seemed near. The society seemed to be
turning over. Around. It must be whites. White People. Malcolm sd it. It
seemed obvious they were Evil. But who were yall, there w/ them?

Pumped in with clouds & blood each day. (Conrad Cross was with his
ofay & they little children off in some cold grey community. On the radio

they described a fire in Harlem, & something Malcolm sd. Cross had talked to the leader of the Militant Action Revolutionaries. It made him feel outside reality. Like he was dwelling beneath stone under the earth or under water. There were more feelings than he had.) Ya know. You all know that twist of world's meaning? How all images fall apart, whirlwind blows them, ya hold yr breath, waiting, or jumping up & down, trying to drag them back together? The whole world, smashed, blown—no—but it had bubbled up over a period. It was his trial. It cd be traced.

White it sd. White! The laughing—behind the hand joke talk— became real. The key to health is anti-white, *Anti-white*. It was not even spoken yet. Tho it had existed openly enough. All yall had spoken of it. The struggle, openly, constantly against? What? Stupidity, you'd have termed it. Riots, certainly, now it was recognized.

But to say finally that it was Whites, All, that they were the sole source of hurt & frustration in life. The Whites! White People. Hunkies. Crackers. Etcetera. A photographer yall know *became* a junkie because of that. Took pictures, sly, perspiring flicks of jazz people. He began to take dope because he had this woman & these children. He got glazed in the eyes, the way yall wd talk. Stronger & stronger, "those whites" rang out of you. Is that what it seemed, that the enemy cd be peeled back to these white people? Is that what the civil rights movement taught? Or was it simply that after the civil rites, the jawin' & huggin' & bein', there was nothing but crazy people, egotists, new academicians? Same people explaining lines on a blk board or on a page. Same Hedonists. Same back off from the pt of contact.

It was life that was being lost. The castle, like Kafka's shadowy system, had civilian teeth for a moon, & lifeless posturers, humanoids, demanding attention by refusing to breathe!

It was life that brought some a' yall there. A sweep, like feeling of opening up into more feeling, more knowledge. A sweep of excitement, at the thought of thought. You had come from a series of streets w/ no information. Wherever yall were in America. The hallways & cotillions. Quiet schools, whiteout parties. A flash of information some way had got in. Had stood some in front of bookstores, peering in at uncomprehended book jackets. The revelation that it was all holy & deep. Seeing pursuits & concerns nowhere revealed in the idle life drift of ya family & that life. It was like the whole world had been kept secret. So yr skin wd crawl w/ expectancy! Once you'd glimpsed the heavy thing that knowledge is.

Yet the blankout in all roads exists for you. Some a' yall, thru Colored School or whiteout training on the Island! And so, screaming for life, you enter a path that is deathly. Do all yall have to be Jimi Hendrix & Ralph Bunche? For what?

You didn't understand the very construct of America. Colossus America in which you have yr life & being. The threads of yr motion are American too. From the deep slave (continuing) experience. & you ethnic greys knowing the assimilation of yr motion. In the automatic careers, there is portrayed an ultimate frustration. Be a cop or a fireman, a fat Chicago politician, or a presidential nigger-specialist.

Yall niggers didn't dig that the show itself of productive forces, & social technology were hinged on exploitation. (Ya found out!) But by rushing to it putting it on, it surrounded you like a sudden "black hole" in space. You saw thru the protective veil only the vague trailing crab being—the state. But that wasn't clear. You had all talked about the mediocrity of it— even the murderousness, but who was willing actually to struggle on? To the final bleeding & destruction. You went to the mainstream, & found it sluggish & unmoving—reflecting blackness, repetition, blind follies, mirrors.

Or maybe yall just hung out w/ the wrong crowd—but yall other ones fell away. Even on literary turf, trying to conjure & conjure with feeling, you'd come up lame. That 2-step ice finger, cameoed mumble jingles or existentialist abstraction or long tirades of nouns trying to verb them-selves into motion. You didn't want to grab holt to FIRE open. Fingers blow doors off the hinges. Always stodgy little forms, & that holy name riz to ritual control. FORM, an institution of words, &c., now falling to pieces as the thing it reflects, falling to pieces. Blowin' in the wind is a form— who's to do it was our first question. Is there a change can come? If you see the hideous world, & yrselves in it, so hideous. Blown poisons in a brief nor'easter! And then committed, at 1st, to moving to not die amongst the ruins. But all the yng white boys & girls, in varying conspic-uous ways, smashed against the construct, offering little in the way of rev-olutionary life force. That by their simple actions wd give the lie to the Yacoub myth. It seemed yall had no strength (of course this was the police, the army, the national guard, &c.) but aside from, in some cases, stimulating conversation, no strength at all. Not morally, not mentally, except cultural exercises, Smart Mo-joes! Cd correct yr grammar & stuff. But what? The criminals paraded, kept criminalin'. Some even in them

3-piece suits was thought of as hipper than thou! Even Elijah Muhammad & John Ali & them dug Kennedy—or at least they put Malcolm down. Then somebody (?) shot him down, and so forth.

But hunting & scraping, after a while, the xeroed rainbow & cigarette lighter tricks of west society gets old, very old, very quick. & yr left w/ the substance of a rotten humanity, dit dahs of communications, snide insistent sophistication blah blah, which consists of bourbon & soda in the ruins, ale, gauloises, smart talk, avant garde everything (my dear it was only a matter of time before the fags wd sally forth—they of all the you's was very liberated & deliberate about it, when I was knowin' dem!).

But for real strength & substance. On cold sidewalks of America. For anything resembling a human attack on evil, at its base, to totally, like, take it on, confront it, beat it down &c. Yeh the "new" Left came a little later, to take up the taunts. 'Cause yall taunted yall. It was heightening like lightning. From JFK's rip, it sped straight forward. All the sick killings that preceded it, mixmatched civil rights workers, Jewish martyrs, priests (& yes Black People Black People Black People), even the blown-up children in Birmingham, Emmett Till, the night faces murdered from 1441 Portuguese till Cinque 2, it multiplies the dimension of dough they get in horror, as race madness accelerates even up past its base. Po' cracker beatin' yo head to mush, not owning his own raggedy uniform, uninformed ass. But line 'em up. *Poets?* "Naw politics is stupid. It's all the same? I hate people who want to change the world." All the stripes of over and out!

Radical Pols—Dead ol' dust cake in a hall way up 15 flights, weasel in glasses, at his fingertips dead block of criticism, ole critiques of Doestoevsky, mumbled ashes of syntactical Marx. Paintings of fat people, in heroic poses. Dusty desks. Dusty glasses on desks. Quiet hallways. Not quite sunshine in sky in halls. Lips straight across. Line. Eyes. Line. Smile to greet you niggers. Barely. Spider fangs spreading. Into the throat the moving lips of Richard Wright, Aimé Cesaire, Harold Cruse, Padmore, whisper go back go back. & beyond, the heads of actual tricked niggers, zombie niggers, CP niggers, SWP niggers. Who walk like white tramps. Who never really been niggers. Unfeeling of Black to say there is nothing but class. How cd we be in the race, a race? We are workers, not black. We have no identity but workers (and we do not work)!

Or take yr pick: Painters? Are you serious? (Drinks brew—Lemme have a brew will you—I don't have any dough on me right now.) Why're you always into politics? For christsakes, You ——?

Negro wives of Colored Artist Junkies: "That's not what was meant. Not separation. Not black racism. All Together. Baby sitter & Yall!"

And all the stripes I checked on. They offered no solid foundation of struggle. Hedonism & egotism. Extended Sex & the rappin' machine! What is it. Yall provided nothing else.

Except finally, when yall got something together, Eldridge showed how carryin' that ball wd be madness w/o reculturizing. Merely to bring NY bohemian style to Calif. & spread it as the last flash before the bullet shatters the skull! And so we get a bohemian-gipsy screaming like it's the lower east side, or Haight Ashbury, when actually it's the big top, not off Broadway & for yr troubles. But Black people, real live folks, spread out waitin' for Justice in America.

It was all exhausted, after a time. Yr pretension to be alive. You niggers drove backwards by angling reality. Knife angles sharp against you, & you sharp against that little society. The big one breathed sharply too. How the civil rights movement was finally to end. The murder of Malcolm made it official. To try & close off the stream of black talk before it reached its ultimate conclusion. Before it sd *Revolution. Revolution!* (Which it sd, & had been saying, anyway.)

You niggers marched away, that's all. Talking stuff. But some of it real. & tight. & scary. Eyes popped open. In terror. Yall began to meet. To form a thing. The white thigh waved in frantic pickup. Splinter vision radar. Late Warning System. It worked once. On 17th St. an organization of young men met. Wms was struggling w/ the Klan. Blood shot through the head w/ struggle images. What to do? Little poems & paintings, teeny songs wanted to. They on a table or a bed breathing heavy.

But when you first niggers got together, one white woman sat in the bedroom & another came before the meeting was over. & then they wd have killed each other—been the only real fightin' that wd've gon on, over one of them niggers—but a' course they wdnt *fight!* And that was grits w/ milk & sugar. Strange Fruit.

And the next time yall met, the 1st defection past, the both women spangled in space. One a musical Mongolian running endless caste magic w/ the 3rd world Jew of her choice. The other married an all American model w/ child coppered by those years of complex lust.

The talk was lower, more separated, deeper fixed in a worming bitterness. The lights shown on yall, an inch at a time to reveal an epic, a pt in history, time & space.

But there was nothing at all to hold you there. Except some baffled dudes had little children that wd smile softly or rub their cheeks on their hands. No murderous confrontation.

Yall used to drift around then magnetized to black women. Remember how that grew up? With Alice & Corliss, they bit each other & laughed in the middle of the street. They knew they were hipper, for instance, than any around them. In any way. Alice was, like stunning, in that set. Slim, slender, poison tongue, hat pulled down, funny, arty, & "hung out" w/ Burt, like, hung out. Burt, quiet, serious, staring, sincere, & like a little elegant professor, when the Savoy meant England and Harlem entwined in blah blah blah! Yng Duke. Early Jelly Roll. Together they were bad bad arm-in-arm eliotic monkishness bubbling summer evenings, striding toward something new, a real Shangri-La just over the horizon—coming up fast.

The world had to blow. It had to go. We know it's got to blow & Harlem! Yeh! Blam! Malcolm! Yeh! Meanwhile silver blue scarlet streamers hoorah turning to avante, turning to, yeh, a target, a flag, a soup can—or gnarled cars smashed against reality. Blocks of unmoving colors or stagnant slashes of emotion 'n howling rhubarbs, but what of what? The ponderous Kline? The rabid DeKooning? The screaming sirenic Pollock? What were they saying? Stumbling drunk through the world in which they cd not cope except to clutch a glass & talk babble unintelligently? Why? You needed intelligence. Clear. Open. Piercing! Yall sd we ain't these peoples' sons & brothers. We must have life. Rollins, Trane, Monk, Ornette say, "life." Speak Trane! Life! Fullup.

People got smacked in the face. Cussed out. Left hanging or waiting. The tearful exchanges sped up & out. A swirling material life. Cosmic ring, a speech, to whirl out new life. New confrontation. It is nature itself that is the seed of struggle.

* * * * *

It was a gradual withdrawal from the white bohemian world. The white art. The white left & white right. Some a' yall niggers were white lefties, but some were fascists. Of one stripe or another. Yet they all, this spiraled meteoric cloud, a host of intelligences reacting to themselves. Afrikan children speeding through the desert going home!

But like all slow quantitative change. Idea, image, dropped in, dropped in—word, eyelash, concept, blue air cool—dropped in, dropped in quietly splashless tidy, filling up & then not odd ramming sounds no one understands. They begin to fight, walk out, will not be seen w/ they white wives, no understanding, no reality grasp. Yet it comes, it digs, it bangs, it begins to bulge a knot at the side of the eye, it crawls up the face to the forehead, bulges, eye-shaped. Bursts, finally.

You met Cox, Harry, CD, Roy, Walt, Jackie, Champ, Wall, Shreve, Lucky to discuss the underground movement. You had guns. (White woman down the hall washing dishes nervously, married to one in the group. Others, their white women sat at home or called Margo to see what was up, what was hey, like, happening.)

Harry laughed at the rank. Yall had nerve, Harry smiled. He laughed at that. Why? Because yall were foolish? Or what? Why? (It's explained years later! That smile, it was just separation. He never bridged from where he was, cool cool cool & clean, clean as a movie star blk ivy leaguer.)

And that was a casually observed inch of image. That smile of "benevolent" distance from the pulse. That drove us all.

Yall sd The Union of Hearts. The question, what will we call what we do? The Union of Hearts Underground in Bohemia Lower East Side. You gave out ranks to each other, Col. on down—w/ a major, captains & lieutenants. And some faded on the spot. Amongst the early mad, that went on to be in charge of nigger-stuff at YALE & other eery dumps. So they cd get a chance to wear they vines, & stretch out in all the Brooks Bros vines you dreamed abt, & finally be where you had thought the clothes called for, in the first place! Or another dude in a metaphysical sky, gibbering at yearning youth that he taught Malcolm. & next year he is going to reveal it all. What his monumental teachings were will emerge & on into the veil of peace. But don't threaten us w/ peace. We want war, till freedom comes. And then there's time enough for peace.

In all to look into the various moved minds yall was. All the ingredient persons who together were a movement, is not possible. Because besides the brothers who sat there balanced by each others' weakness, for an equation which produced, that was, groups of blackface fire egos spun together to spin an entity into being, an image into life, a time into fruition—from out the dirt, yeh, bright mad blossoms that have startling beautiful songs as they roll back & forth on tender stems in the rain.

You say there was nothing at all there to keep yall—Nothing—the ruins of Pompeii given neon signs & faggot junkies w/ pony tails. The ruins of a civilization. That Bro Malcolm pulled yr coats to. That the Cubans exposed, & niggers danced in Harlem.

You were there where they say smoky promise rises again. Perhaps a few ideas rattling near the bones might activate life, but the forms are ghosts, ghosts blown across the ice streets. To the new leftists, of which even you closest brothers, grow in that discipline. Remember the ethnocentric pale Europe has draped upon the world, how this gave birth to chauvinism & inferiority. Mad sisters tap dance up West End Ave searching for Jews to teach their children. Our people demand the right, their inalienable right, to be one of the chosen lightskinned monsters. But among the blowing ribbons & wind worked tambourines, a junior life marauds, but blue collar white boys, are with Imperiale subjectively, imperialism objectively. You was right Sam, you was right Dave, & pigeon-toed muslim w/ the propella' bow, you were right.

So trail away, stalk away, flee in buses, train subway. But get out get out—(you sitting in meeting planning, get out). Frozen trees shiver like windows, mirrors on depravity. Breakdown of hedonism. Root ends midnight bloody screams from the booby hatch. Smell yr fingers coming down the block, is not enough. Jew rolls, Italian rolls, in boxes in the store's doorway, the smell of coffee streaked like wisps of moving red clouds. It's not enough, music somewhere, it's not enough. Pause near the sleeping figure, it's not enough. The children dare not breathe— "You're one of the funny things." It's not enough, horribly. Bolt out into the day, which has no mercy at all.

* * * * *

What sealed the fate of the castle crew was Malcolm's murder. That afternoon in 1965, yall was at the 8th street Bookstore, reality complex, concrete contradiction. Persons wafted and strode. What do you want? That is a pulse that beats thru all yall. Somebody had a book party. Yall was facin' round. The little clandestine group paraded, not all, some were elsewhere, similarly parading. It, by now, had reached proportion where the crowd itself was a register of contradictions, assumed knowledge (hipness) etc. E.g., Corliss walked alongside a small Jewish woman, trailed by children. Smiling, being sophisticated, knowledgeable about the land. At one root, there spins at another tendril the mock army, hid from sight, yet instant seeable, by all but the blind. The Blind & Semi-blind, a stooped 6 footer, with wild thorny beard, Gabby Hayes hat, wobbling, correcting peoples' "English," crazy about the Mets. He wanted to say something about "what's wrong w/ the Black Movement." In that instant, separated & impotent. All of the various spectral fragments, heed up to light, an instant before the message comes. You scan the crowd, admiring court. In hunting jacket & round glasses, pulled-down felt brim, fluent in the tongue. Just before the message came. A homosexual critic, wife-husband of the player-painter Jane, thot mighty of, in the great art world. Her husband antennaes the streaks of arty lighting her way. They minces down the street w/ a ice cream soda. He climbs the stairs grimy—messages from Jock Whitney. They'd selected Corliss as the ranking intellectual of new Bohemia. Just before the message came. While Malcolm strafed & bombed the world, our island, specifically, the correspondent didn't dig the blinding flashes of actual warfare nearing. That portrait of Corliss as they wrote it & as it appeared, spoke to vanished tribes. His face a stone image of another era, smiling confidently into history & oblivion.

Just before the message came. Massed & paraded coldly, casually, calmly, antagonistically. You people float about with such detachment. With eruption masked as averted looks, the whispered conversations rise & fall. When the message came!

Malcolm is Dead!

All this time, until just 2 weeks ago. You hadn't understood how clearly Malcolm cut thru this entire society. Big Red drives across Afrika. Enters the varied phases & at each level something is turned open. Exposed. What dominoe, what relationship is further revealed? There is a message! Find out what is the message!

Malcolm opened doors & minds! He fought yr battle cry, strained, rational, hotter than Fire!

He sd, "Chickens come home to roost" to pt at the dead Kennedy. Tho Elijah sd thousands of people worship this man. They file into the barbaric sepulchre of the Romans to kneel & cry. Black avant painters walk w/ one leg firm in the gutter weeping for the blue buttondown & Princeton cut. Before the message came. The 1st pt sd Malcolm had led us *out* of America! But we cd not see it. We Blk-whited because our blood steamed & the merchants & opportunists grinned at our pain. Malcolm had let us *out* of America. Wherefore to stand take a good look & pounce Blk Pantherlike to break its back.

Malcolm had gone *outside*, to see that it all must end. Even the black prayers to black beings & little bean pie empires, all in flame away! Yeh, chickens had come home to roost! What you mean you can't say that? Why, nigger intellectual, did you write a poem in sympathy with Jackie Kennedy? You didn't want to leave America? Malcolm sent a message. That it must all end. That it was all corrupt & finally, dig it, that it wasn't even about color. Tho the raging hordes of Afrika, Asia & Latin America wd settle the score.

The Message came on a knife delivered w/o warning directly into the center of the skull. Into the bone, crushing the membrane, severing blood vessels in the brain, causing a deadly hemorrhage that poured out the ears. A sudden blow! Blinded by blood. In the mouth, nose, ears, coughing blood. A stagnant silence to hear the echo of words spoken to you people. "Chickens come home to roost."

The message came in the middle of the afternoon, mix match book party downtown. Blood on the floor, murmurs fanned around the store, welled into speech.

All jive fell back momentarily. White people spun on their heels, tried to dig up inside the silence. Eyes darted 'round to see what they main man was into. Was somebody after *them*?

The message came. Malcolm shot. He dead! Roy Lucas cried, stood in the aisle of the store & wept, dropped his head, openly wept. You others skirted to the side. Mixed couples wdn't look at each other. A jagged sigh or sob turned sharper into a high pitched radio whine. It stayed, for years.

Yall huddling crew. Exchanging tears. Whispers. Hatred. Yeh, it was I hate— kill—die—murder—rip—kill—in the tongue, rolling out, murder murder murder murder—in the tongue, rolling—

& you moved away to go yr way to pick up & split—it was all sd—too much was left to be done!

But it was only a few main ones that actually did split, & most of those were not hooked up to the white social organization, except in the casual way of easy downtown pops, flesh trades instantly evenings—all were citizens of castle land, babble over Kafka's phone, tryin' to get answers, "but none came," hence the get up.

What it did do was warn the casual mixers not to. That an era had ended. Yall w/ the sisters, in whatever circumstance, were more ready to go geographically. To leave White Folks land. But even then, failings down the line. Time that the bizarre example, CD the poet, pushing like a scared detective into the 5th Ave Hotel Restaurant, coming up behind two a' yall & showing his heat, was an exception. That was yall's answer! No one was going to force him to leave white folks—or more specifically the preying mantis who hovered over his head.

You swept out. Arrived cold late afternoon 125th street. Wind frozen. Bloods not walkin' in the center of the street (too cold!). Back & forth, carrying the crumbs of consciousness.

When the message came, you split!

Good.

What else cd you do?

In a shambles of swift motion, out, up up & away! The next few months retell lies and hard confessions. After the message came, we knew we had to leave America. Go home we felt. Uptown. Go home.

& the speed lines drawn around us give us no peace or reflection. Press forward! Raise the struggle. The speed itself you confuse w/ *form*. The rush of sharp air in our face you confused w/ program. It was a race maybe. A blk & white race. You arrived suddenly from someplace else. Arms thrown up, crossing the line. Sing dirty curses at the losers. And talk very bad about yr lost comrades. You ain't right. You can't leave. It ain't about race. I ain't black or white. Notes sent. Telephones talked on. Give ya the word! What's happening? Why're yall hunched together tight like that? Hard black fire knot. Aching to kill!

You was raising. Was you right? You was moving! Was you justified? You was motion, hot motion, fire acts—was it this you lacked to blow the world to fine ashes?

You'd arrived, bro. Streamers of lives, in yr heels. But to do what? Whatta ya mean? To do what? Askin'! To do what? To kill white people!

(& this morning you were w/ them. & some a' yall this very minute want to be in Paris w/ a red head, samplin' advanced culture.) You talkin'—talkin' why?

How did it happen? The closest became the furtherest. Think about it! Why? Yall never really left, why? Wd ya answer from dead photographs, thru pregnant widows in the interior decorating bizness? From the remaining lips themselves? Where are ya remaining lips? Now in & around where are ya remaining lips? Now in & around alluding to secret understandings. Playin' yo' horn, drinking yo' booze, doin' yo' thing, i.e., thang. Those closest to ya didn't budge. Or only a face shot through that black space, in which yall . . . what?

But what reasons now? Can you dig it thru to yrself? Does it 'splain itself fullout to ya? There was some talk, 10 years ago, a word you didn't want to hear, perhaps explained you to yrselves? Wanna listen now, but it's too late—aint it?

When yall made the move, the entire crew was only lately come together. Some staggering, flying to get there. Throw off the deadworld. Throw it at you? Playback of yrself in the dead world go by. All time playbacks, flashbacks of yrself in & as the dead world.

Cd you tell strengths from weakness? Cd you tell in that twisted state what really was good for ya & what was more of terror in the soul? Maggot baby in you got to grow.

Arrive & then thrive! Then . . . was dots that's all. You sd kill whitey. Why? He hurt us—lynched us. (Remember the yng boy whose testicles the crackers removed & shoved into his mouth? Yr grandmother watched that & reported it.) Kill 'em for that!

Name some stuff Malcolm's dead. Crying and shd a' cried more at what information was lost, what direction wasted.

W/o friends then, except, as factions, some w/ friends, some without. Who are yr friends? Who loves you? Those closest did not leave the white lands with you. You left a mad snarling herd alienated from itself. Unknown to itself—till later—or only now you begin to see—some small thing!

You arrived, in a brownstone in Harlem. All the Misfits. Wdbe whats? Killers? Agents? Revolutionaries. Black Black Black to the fore.

Black Black Black at the top
Black Black Black

You set up housekeeping. Yall sprinkled the few where you cd. More came. More noiseful shapes told the story. But they came up. Even the ones w/ the colored wives & no guilt to "cleanse." Except it was, just being in the white land, a guilt. Malcolm was dead. The message had come. (But had we understood?)

What you cdn't understand was what you knew from another way of looking, what was fact, was so distorted by cultural aggression (wherein our oppressors assimilate us, convince us that we want the same things). That all yall wasn't correct. For some the smell of blood was real. The departure into the new land, real. The clamor inside yr heads clang of violent images, to see America roast in fire. Real too.

But you hadn't studied. Not politics or economics, & not really history. Some a' you came from under white fascist wings, not leftists even. Some opportunists. Potential rulers of everybody. Johnny Coe used to talk about white slaves. Asked Corliss how many he wanted & Corliss cdn't understand.

Mad folks, plain mad folks pied pipered by movement. Mongeese for yo' cobras, man. (Who is laid dead, man, years later, after Eldridge revived Mixism or Tom Mixism as the dripping fang of SWP. Years later, yall, they dead in a shootout wit' ya symbols boss. As if Walker Vessels had never left Barrel Makers circle to find a black army.)

Sick people, acid-faced killers, trails of vacillating smoke. But still for all the staggering & indecision, lack of clarity, wd sum it all up in a phrase, there was some real movement. Some new life. Some advanced motion set up.

Union of Hearts felt the thunder & lighting of the people's movement. Shivered against it. Danced the blind rage boogie. 'Cause they hadda move.

Yall left the ruins, when the message came, climbed out from under the white stones. To breathe the air of a freer place. But some a' yall were mortally injured (siren squalls), permanently damaged like war objects, twisted survivors of the struggle to control thought.

And linked together now, stranger groups uptown full of rage. The group had *never* been together downtown. Not this group. Some a' these dudes were 'cross way 'cross town. But now yall had to put something together. All the energy & radiance jerked together suddenly—sparks & hammers—there confronting each other, yet the world obscured this & you didn't understand.

You got to 130th St. talking the same garbage you was running downtown. But downtown answers nothing! In uptown reality. Put together some forums, some new style (yeh!) confrontation. Which was real, you think, & yeh (again) positive. You remember sitting together in the newly cleared hall. Wall torn down and a new group—strands of unconnected life & energy, a productive force, the major & decisive one (of the stratum) to push the consciousness further. The questions, now, opening out. Yet who knew really what to ask? Clearing 'way the rubble of other lives. Yr questions lingered there? Reflections of the dead, the dying, the need to be or soon to be killed. It was like a heavy dream in one sense. You thought about leaving & now having arrived, real life was going on, & at a higher level. You cd see yrself. See you, faintly now, coming 'round. That indeed the pulsing rhythms, life, language in yr skulls was the world—not self-generated inside the bone, but reflection of an actual world!

But also now, it grew clear, immediate ugliness, weirdness, even danger cd be seen. Some of these niggers were crazy—crazy as America, man.

In one set a discussion of what, Music? Revolution? The Black Family? Rolled together. & a well known brother, ancient musical sage, like, spoke & what he sd. (You see, you just barely see the outline of the content, missing this street, not really, if the sound cd be heard it wd make you scatter.) But he spoke, and he too was to grow immense in that context of intense search, only to have a mad killer leap up & walk through the crowd denouncing & threatening the brother. "Tutankamen is an old woman," he threw his fingers in the older man's face. "An old woman. He doesn't speak for the rage in me." Startled, what is that? Reared up & out? Why? (This dude, tho, remember the Indian Bailey punchout, broken nose, & assault of castle Negroes domesticating on the vine? This was the same dude now stalking the crowd.) Like an agent's pitch pipe, the fear tone spread. But for some a' yall, openmouthed, what was that? No answer? Except a bitter strut, what was that? A tarboosh on a bald head. He pts to that. That's me. Where I'm comin' from. Tho a few weeks before, he strode like the rest in the foggy shadow of color obscured by grey.

But that was what the productive force produced, opening new visibility motion. Beauty & Terror. New freedom, new repression. At once at one. Those stalkers, you madmen now settled in crazy squiggles of imagination. This one madman turned completely bats & walks Harlem streets thinking he is Prince of the two lands. Murmuring curses in the rain. Ragged spectre of American insanity given to the Black Man.

Openers, sensate flesh vibrates. Colors, sounds, smells, sensate vibrations. Blood impacted behind yr mask rushing! Scalding ideas, rush of new life itself.

What developed was instant agony between the various lines. Not knowing (politically) what even a line was. Tho the Anglo-German/Jewish poetry war shd have trained you for it. Blown! You that wanted a new world! You that wanted escape from the dying colonial world. Those in search of new lust. Secret opportunists to establish nigger fascism over bloods themselves—yeh! It may come yet, bros & sisters. The cunning interlocking madness reflected of the iron beast, the imperialist eagle striking brute passes on humanity's throat. Breathing hard, crosseyed!

Consider, for instance:

Wall Peterson—Thin, iron eyed, in strangely fitting sweaters, suit jackets. Fire out the nose. Arrogant. Anti-woman. Slapped them in public places—the 1st forum, he slapped one. More followed.

Champ Peterson—His ynger brother—Half Wall, half second generation hidden bohemian. Wall, intensely jealous of Champ's attachment to white literary fantasy. Wall himself, literary Victorian, in line with the red hat. A sign in his office, "No Smoking."

Jimmy Coe—Elijah Muhammad satellite, subterranean division. Cd stand slew foot with broke brim pork pie in his hands. Mythologist. Potential white slave holder. (Later grinned that he, after torturing ½ the world to show pure hard Blackness, actually preferred "blonde women with long hair." He sd it, As salaam Alaikum, & grinning disappeared into our past.)

The 1st two hated each other. The 3rd was the go between, comrade to Champ, stooge for Wall. You others, *Corliss*, the white memoried artist, confused by the world. *Shreve* Collier, yellow boy, red head Shreve, everybody's ynger brother. The worker, the serious academic youth. Hooked up to everybody's image. He cd help no one & cried to see the Hearts cave in.

Grass Root—corny, hard, street nigger, workin' class nigger, SWP shill when Corliss pulled him by talking bad to the Jews. His two boys, Sam & Dave, drunk partisans of motion. They came too. All yall did. *Nafsi*, the Yoruba outside the temple. Wanted to be a poet, settled instead for kicking Champ's behind as Little Rock, the future junkie, kicked Wall's in the upper reaches of Central Pk, jab jab jab, cross, to end that myth.

Walter Coate—the Columbia intellectual. Frecklefaced intellectual. Really a kind of unsung hero to Corliss. Except later Coate left his wife & child to show up w/ a leather cowboy hat & a crosseyed 19-year-old, slobbering after his youth.

Bingo—shrimp, colored school accountant, BA, white woman in midleclass Bx. Saw BC on 7th Ave, split that scene & never returned again.

Alice—Corliss' playmate, lion lady, idealist, black existential beauty child. Raged like all, searched, like all, died, like most abandoned by all, except her lust for life which left in the Pacific Ocean.

The 3 or 4 or 5 or 6 bears who in these late days cd express the Hearts' life best, never having been inside, but only fellow travelers pimping yr air.

(One night Ali Muhammad scrambled up the stone steps, banging on the door. Shreve came down, from the 3rd floor, you turned on the various chairs, to hear, the night of the Harlem Blackout! Yeh. It was the revolution come down!)

All down into the streets to walk & let the people know, revolution. Corliss & Lucas hooked up a loud speaker on a panel truck & went up and down 7th Ave urging bloods to make off with the window goods! Go in the stores, & whatnot. "Get it! Get it!" Police cars quickly surrounded them, pulled them out w/guns drawn. Corliss started non-stop cursing "Mother-flugin' jelly-robbin' billy-matchin' shiney sins!!" Gun up the nose—inside the ear / call you nigger bastid! Old sister start dancin' in front the police car. "Get it on mfs. Get it on. Ain't no 'nother life no way, just this, get it on. Send you way. Send you on yr way."

People come out the shadows in the street start sayin', "Yeh—Go head," & Corliss screamin' & cops pointing they guns & talkin' fast & bad. People build up quick combination party time. Blue light. Lights out all over up town. On 125th & Lenox, the crackers crowded against a drug store window surrounded by cops. Niggers wanted to get them—Blood Brotherhood tales in the air, 5 %ers, merchants w/ cut throats, dollars dangling off the thumby scale. Couple dudes backed a cracker up in a doorway, deck him, woman screams, stumbles out. She gets slapped, thrown up against a parking meter, kick the fag in the lip, tear his suspenders & his wallet out, keep gettin' up & sirens.

So where Corliss & them spin, dancin' turned to tight hissed curses, cans looped high, hit the sidewalk near the cop, he, spinnin', dragged them out they car & flung them into the back seat a' his, weaving now from under the barrage, screamin' at these niggers how he wd kill them, cut their balls off, turning corner on 2 wheels head for 135th St. precinct.

A colored inspector released them an hour later & they walked the streets till daybreak waiting for the revolution. & that's the only time Ali ever was "inside" the Hearts! Mad bastids as you were!

* * * * *

There were w/ ya ins & outs a' plenty. Comin', goin', steamin', suckin', lickin', partin' company, drinkin'. Ya used to stand out on the steps, twilight comin', summer rappin', puttin' offensives together. Spun together so fast—nothing really planned, just fallin' in place in quick time. How all yall who dared not enter, was there, simply! And ya was, for cryin' out loud, why in hell not?

It was emotion, after all, put together. Ya was not clear. A changing motion, that severed old square connections w/ reality. Destroyed our integrated eye, & re-integrated you with ya selves. Began it!

And the essence of that time, a high political cycle, looped around for many, even further away than New Jersey to share. To Afrika & past that & back!

A generation had instinctively (?) perceived its role, to lead on out! & away! To get away from the spectres of haunted burning buildings! To run till the sky turned to blood, & the blood to children!

Arrogance too often passes for information! Tho stumbling like drunken infants, you wandered into vehicles, you made them, you turned ignitions, the streets began to churn beneath you. A buncha black intellectuals. No! You didn't hear that! You were whitey haters! Basically that. Whitey haters, spreading that. Hard-lipped line. You cd push it from yr shoe bottoms, up thru the center of the skull. Hate Whitey! (Like Hail Mary! A million times over. Over. Over.) Against the tide of sick Europe gave to ya to swaller, ya swallered!

Change the image! Inside change. Hate bring love! Can you? Fear bring strength! Will you? Madness bring direction! How?

Grey hat, brown raincoat, East German jackets. Yellow sunglasses! Hate Whitey! On the streets, 3 shows a night, all over black town—hate whitey—he hate you. Do it to him—need to kill him—wipe him out—he tried to ice you!

Hate Whitey! Street corners, playgrounds, alleyways, in front of Hotel Teresa. Stand out there w/ the old time Garveyites. Hate Whitey!

Scoop yng girls inside the joint, just above Har You. (A good question!) Upstairs above the anti-poverty machines, niggers made love frantically. If someone had stopped the g.d. noise for a minute. The people screaming for back or front or side pay—people trying to get programs started (operation boot strap). If they had quieted down baybee, all you'd heard was bedsprings bam-a-lamming & sweet moans up & down!

But what was fine was the return of the ice squad. The sickest most violent of yall—those who usually gets out the ghetto for downtown outside yr own soul. Yall had come to Harlem "to raise hell." To Kill White

People! To Build a Nation! (What about the castle crew, the friends ya left behind?

What about 'um?)

Machine gun words, hate whitey (when you recently had deeper connections—not wholesome, but deeply connected, like any installment plan Jew-nigger relationships. Buy now, Pay later!).

And part of that was the heat in the denunciations. The brutal fire fire fire to purge yr insides hooked barely but directly to the fact of world oppression. Yall was oppressed! It did affect yr very lives!

The realizations, of that, battered you down. It took you foreign to yrself, but made a new self. A stronger self (if you survive), but then the hate whitey move let in actual insane beings, from out the pit a' ya psyche. Insane red black beings that hated. They didn't produce. They cdn't. They just hated. All the white & w/ that all the black or other that didn't hate, ya hated. But they hadn't all been tricked into marrying white women—Hating that & yrself for it. For being exposed an asshole to the world. The hating let in hatings, red-black beasts seeking power to hate to destroy & never create. (They cdn't create. They weren't *creative!*)

The skull crazies—old skulkies—demons—redeyed jaw wagglers—screechers—howlers—black devils—spook worshippers—"voodoo" priests—strange islamic sects—back thru—whoosh—spaceless history—red diarrhetic images of bloody haints—baldhead zombies.

It all jingled & all yall together was the new nation, plus the reality of the politics & economics, which you never even guessed! (Tho it spelled itself out—the history of us, so we cd read later.) Every which way there was jangled together, clashed, & beneath this you sent out nightly trucks all over Black Town—of art, music, dance, drama (the revolution?) to get the Hearts back, to rebecome Black Hearted!

Democrat bureaucrats wd ease being yall, peeping. You remember Sargent Shriver's expression, getting thrown outta the joint?

Middleclass niggers peeped out they cars ya marchin' all the workers to the Teresa to scream at middleclass niggers. The ANTIPOVERTY program, in full blast.

Yet yall blew thru w/ fullout charge against yr own delusions mounted in a short space, an activist program based on federal tax dollars (as the saying goes) designed to arouse the people! And stuff you cd talk about cd be deep & way far out, long as you was in the right place. Nutty Jergen had the nerve to write a play downtown for which they gave him a Galahad

Award. Doing the same work uptown, made them (the powers that beat) spin around on their heels, chimed in w/ the certainly chorus (*i.e.,* certainly, certainly, certainly, Lord).

"Hate whitey is what they sayin'! Ya know?" In a frenzy, a veritable foam at the mouth happenin'. Seein' what was sd outside the genteel frame of they own view. City world society construct, wherein all cd be couched & cradled. Jergen sd something basic like, "This society is shaped by madness & most of the people are mad They want to kill every thing" and so forth. Which is ok in a context of the killers themselves checkin' it, being saddened briefly, philosophically, tellin' certain friends how "moving" it is—shufflin' off to a martini or even a bourbon & soda. But what's the reaction to screamin' niggers jumpin' up & down on the sidewalk, Nutty fannin' the flame (flame of "Why me-an? Aint nuttin' wrong wit' nobody is it?"). Beatin' 'em up out of the dark streets, spotlights showin' 'em to 'umselves. "It ain't the same stuff, Irv. I'm tellin' ya—It's hate whitey."

A crowd rolls down 8th Ave., chasin' a white-faced actor, led by Champ & his prop gun. "Bang," says the prop & instead of a bullet, a bottle sails up & over, smashing all over the street. Bang—twister bottle this time. Bang, orange pluck—Bang, Thunderbird, Manishevitz, Mogen David, Chateau Martin, Petri, Bang Bang Bang Bang Old Judge, Mission Belle, Italian Swiss Colony even Harvey's Bristol Creame. Colliding in mid-air & 1.00$ Brandy bottles, Reingold Beer cans. Leonard Johnson in white face gets pretty scared hisself. & he hates whitey too, for now. (Befo' the Knee Glue Simpleton, the filthiest of filthy-anthropies, opened its doors—Hail Rocky!)

In a park, the trucks stop, Joey, Billy, Tommy, Betty, jump out, put up some paintings. One of 'um got "ain't it ya' mama" with a machine gun, poppin' out of the pancake box. "Sprayin' us, Irv us! It's hate whitey!"

Tutankamen draws his court together. With strange ovular axes, they shot shattering waves of sound, fixed to blinking twirling lights. They march around the set, hypnotized by halfhidden harmonies. "What does it mean, Irv? Those lights? What's that, a code? & what's it say? Those weird gongs they strike. Like somebody's head. How they beat & beat. Hell, Irv, its frightening. Those murderers' suits & frantic turbans. It's hate whitey, is what it is, Hate Whitey! & we can't let that happen, Irv. Ya know?"

(For now Irv smiles a little painted & quizzical tone, an idea's foetus forming behind his squeezed up englassed eyes. He says, "Hate Whitey, is it? Ok, Whitey, I'll work on that!")

What you all did was keep opening up the sweep of formed motion—
the message had come. Malcolm gave the message—w/ his life, dialecti-
cally & materially—his life his murder, was the message. Capitalism, Slavery,
New World, "trianglar trade," Revolutionary War, Civil War, Mode of
Production—slavery or capitalism, North Industrial, Monopolies forming,
Reconstruction, Populism, Betrayals, Imperialism, Berlin Conference,
Spanish American War, Niggers North, WWI, Soviet Explosion, Harlem
Renaissance, Roaring '20s, Garvey's Plumes, Depression Madness, Betrayal,
Capitalism, Trade Union copout, No revolution, Eagle struts, U.S. to roll,
WW2, Niggers is needed, Factories roar, Eagle flies, U.S. uber alles, Afrika
wants out, Chinese split, Nkrumah makes the grade, Civil Rts mass,
Imperialism Clear, Self-Defense Bro!, Venceremos, Black Power, a motion
not a notion, a burning reality ya life, all ya life, you all.

To put all that in the street! Walk w/ it, Walk w/ it! Ride w/ it too. Put
it in the streets, the playgrounds, alleyways, on stoops, platform, in project lots, parks, say it all ways, the culture of the people—that's what it was—
the mythology (religion), history, social organization, economics, politics,
creativity & ethics of the people. Yall ya ya you was doin' it then. A lightning streak. A bitter nigger Yankee. A black blue tale teller, Dynamite Dan
the dark yng man, woman, youth, elder, carrying props in setting up ratings, preachin' in the street, history w/ a beat. Tell it. Tell it, JD Camel sd,
like it is. All yall together, that crimson, verdant, ebony summer, mashed
together, hugged together, straining to be born. You was then, in hot fantastic flashes. In reality & the commitment forever to be warriors.

Tho that stretches the pt. Yet it is all true & real. But not all were forever warriors. Yall know that! You, Wall, mad staggering imitating
Pharoah—drove the lightwts, ½ committed, scared dabblers out—& too
many more. Yr voice, arrogant, scraping meat off faces, a need-to-be King,
wd-be emperor, coup d'etating in each place you strolled.

& Champ, w/ ya white woman now in NYC, how ya get there, who was
the pug for black the challenger & threatener fighting main events every
other day w/ yr sick brother?

& you Shreve, lost between them, Coe, regent of race, Grass Root stabbed
to death in a cocaine bar, Yoruba Sam in a zoo in New Orleans, dancing
for nickels, Harry, Larry, Barry, Cary, & Mary in Hollywood, Shafting,
Blaculaing, Super Flying, Troublemanning, taking the Hearts to the Hoop.
Ya 12 or 15 Musketeers who revolved around words & sit in colleges

pontificating about the rest of ya faked membries. What about you? Poets, Know its, Slow its, in residence, where you at now?

Ali M., orthodox, metaphysical, hanging on the crescent, waitin' for the star. You cool? Mustapha, & Melvin who tried to hold up a bank (under Wall's later extreme sickness), yall straight? BWI sunning & funning got you now, why? Sistine, Alice (dead), Lizzie, Umafemi, Doris, Bdway, Harlem dreams, Ice-escapes, retreats to overurbs, herbs, dumb jobs, weak men, still looking, why? Except America, the ugly, until you destroy it!

But them days, as the real accomplishment, physical, mental, spiritual, roared, the doings, the boring into the brains & marrow of yo' people, singeing yr generation w/ color. W/ color! Color! The internal workings was murder, Sam. A house on a road uptown full of wd-be killers, sworn haters, spontaniacs, maniacs, real workers, opportunists, liberals, petty bourgeois adventurers, open assimilators, hidden assimilators, civil righters, actual revolutionaries, inert black meat, all together. Corliss was supposedly the leadership (no matter what anybody might put out afta' while) but you wasn't was ya? It was the times, the message, the needs of the people. You articulated it, Burt, & some a' you others did. Wall. Grass Root. Champ. Shreve. But all did not even know each other. Had no comradeship. No understanding of life or politics. Just the message, fire between the ears. Sworn hatred!

Corliss, you was guilty because ya had just left white people. Had their ways. And at the same time their arrogance, which permitted you to think you cd lead anyway.

Wall was not wrapped tight, hated Corliss cause Corliss was too white to lead yet was indisputably the leader.

Champ styled like Corliss, & Wall hated him for it, pointed out Corliss' weakness, which Champ used against Corliss to mke him Corliss's "equal."

Shreve worked for all, influenced by all, cd serve none.

Beyond this, camps, factions, go-betweens, double agents, &c. Grass Root & The Streeters, whiskey drinkers, loud talkers, working arms was w/ Corliss. But Corliss wd not tell them to stop the internal criss-cross by simply strangling everybody who made trouble. That cd have been done in a weekend.

Metaphysicians—Wd-be Elijahs, still exoticer Islams, Holy men, mystical killers, with Wall. W/ a tarboosh—no smoking—wifes in middle class apartments, out of sight. Punched out sisters who sd anything! Put Ronnie's sister (an intellectual) out her office because she was in charge of something.

Most hated Champ.

Intellectuals, whitified, went for Corliss but only sd so behind closed doors, or to Corliss, but cd take no stands. Like Shreve, who apologized years later for being so weak. Arty types went to Corliss when Wall or Champ or Coe had walked on them, then left it to Corliss to win.

What made the roar so terrifying is that Corliss was actually too weak to be where he was & Wall was an insane adult & Champ an insane adolescent. The rest took their cue, & were one of these models. The aimless intellectuals stalling in the wings.

Hamlet Corliss, ya punk, ya cd've pulled it off. Too much guilt. Why? In the face of Rockefeller, & Billy Graham. Faced w/ Chas Rangel & Mobutu, how is it possible, old friend, for you to have so much guilt?

"Whatt'a they got on you?" was the question Grass Root used to ask. "Whatta they got on ya maaaaaaaaan? Them niggers are wrong, Burt, you know it! (Or crying to them) Yall know it. Yall wanna fuck up this program? Yall ain't shit!"

But penny arcade–Coney Island explosions winding in and out. What Wall wants/wanted—Champ wants/wanted—Coe wants/wanted—Grass Roots (dead) wanted, Corliss wants/wanted, Alice (dead) wanted, Mustapha, Ali M. The Spearmint excellence group, now at Yale, Wms, Harvard, &c. wants/wanted. Away in a manger, the star stops at 130th & Lenox. Therein a babe surrounded by the mob except the reverse is true, a mob surrounded by a babe, or they keep changing places. In fact you there are the same, in it, a turning one into the other contradicting each other, yet being each other, one necessary for the other to exist.

What everybody wants/wanted cd not be put in a package—Black. You tried. You learned, all yall, that once Malcolm became the message, & Stokely picked it up, it battered & battered, raised itself, screamed till they had to do something - Whitey & Irvy ("Call Melvin," Irv sd, after thinking awhile, "Call Melvin, lets talk to him about Hate Whitey").

But it cd only be packaged Burt, yall, if it, the package, was—staring off now. Time to get into the streets, Wall & Corliss face-to-face, screaming, or Wall screaming that it was wrong to have a rally at 125th & Lenox, that the people might get hurt (Why? Why? Corliss stared). But ya don't budge in these situations, Burt, "tuff guy." Wall thought Burt cd be pushed around, but that was a mistake. That just hurt his feelings & made him mad enough to wake up for a moment in the world. If blood stung him, his eyes flew open & his jaws wd grind, & he'd die right there—simply on arrogance.

Ya know, Wall, that Pharonic madness that got you right this minute begging pennies on 7th Ave, claiming to be Amenhotep. Cd it be simply that you wanted people to do right? But that was serving yr grandiosity. Opulent mad baldhead ego. The tarboosh was a crown. & how'd that sit w/ English caps pulled sideways or broke down English private eye skimmers jammed down on sunglasses? French cigarettes dangled out the corner of the mouth? Where's the crossroads? Ya know, don'tcha, all these ancient Kingdoms gone—Even the Mad Hearts of the '60s—Time of civil war. But in each place of life or idea, the same relationship. Civil war, rebellion inside, self the enemy from a different pt, the opposite pt. Destroy it, get the music. Another scale, box yrself. Unclear pilgrim at home on the range. What you struggle for—are volunteers? See the heads & the houses, the cut of the clothes. Some a' ya wanted to be petty B in a colored way. Then some others who had forgot or didn't understand. What you want/need to be (is to be) answered! Way out civil rites is what most so-called nigger artists wanted—a little way outer than MLK, at 1st view, but looked at long enough (hip lunches in exclusive taverns) it is the same interests, not even as profound as Doc King, who was a mass man, no matter his class conspiracy to funnel goodness through Gee-Sus X (the 1st muslim). A Mass Man, reflecting a nation's need (or so it seemed). You artises representin' less—as arrogant & nasty moufed as you wanna be. Mass man, not masked man. He clearer, bro! See them abstract expressionist paintings in the bank window? You know, they pushing the same game. Obscure the process. You'll never understand. What's bein' run. Yet run it is, on you & over you. Except mass man, mass woman, break it down, break it down, break it down, power to the people all right, to interact w/ themselves, almighty nature!

You hearts was feelin' a mass line. Feed off Independence, civil rts, self-defence, Black Nationalism proclaim Black Heart, Union of Hearts, to change all entities!

You cd not analyze class forces, value-stratum differences, because you didn't know that. Except ya dug that folks committed to white folks were of less value in the struggle. Tho you didn't see it as a struggle, but an event! At which all yall or yall all wd be perhaps present (the blackest wd). You had so little real understanding, a lot of pressure in the blood, corpuscles &c. on fire &c. Smoke &c. coming out the ears, nose, mouth. Instant Killers.

But no clarity. Neither for what you struggled for or what struggled against you. Except you thot, personalities & their diversities & diversions. You thot that some were evil. Reasonless emotions, except there was some reality. There is some reality to everything real. You yous. Yall ya yall. Speakin' in a whisper, screamin' in a roar. Ya yall. Fingers pointing at the other one's chest. Girl to Girl. Cat to Cat.

Alice, the lyrical lass from colored wonderland. A lioness of art motion, which cd've been love. Except the nigger who was s'posed to raise it, too luke warm, too hooked w/ white. Lost her gentle fire in the void of America.

Maria, who was a poetesa allright, a real processional. The white man who owned her was losing fast in them days. And that was wondrous. (Alice knew white folks but treated them like they was anybody else, like most a' yall except a behooked tentacle went up even to the skull—& hooks cd be seen dancing behind the eyes.)

Alice wd laugh—these crazy crackers—& sit w/ jive Corliss in one of 'em's house smokin' weed or listenin' to Trane.

Maria was a middle class face in the crowd. In a westside coop, the dude peered down, & saw her skim across the pavement w/ Blacky Nuff. A one-night affair, but enough to send Maria screamin' into the night, her Cuban heels clicking. She wrote a little poem about Blacky in some jive anthology, cubist style, somebody knew what it was. Maria didn't you join the Father Divine Branch of the faith? Drinkin' ginger beer & flyin' round worshippin' & whatnot.

Shirley & Burlo had a set, you remember, tryin' to characterize what's goin' on. Met in west America, down by the seashore, fast car north, visited Berkeley. Burlo was "dippin'" but straight enough to pull himself out of the red mg looking ferociously intellectual. Shirley, Betty James, Bobby Seale, a stand-up comedian in them days, drifted thru, to check Burlo out. You writ a book, Burlo, about the history of niggers in love. Grey chix callin' cross country, Burlo & Shirley hand in hand casin' Berkeley. Checkin' the various good grey bards, on Telegraph Hill, lookin' down to the sea. Fantasizin' abt everything & shootin' good smack.

Eshun. Round face round behind Bembe every night. Visions of the new world coming in as she bounces up and down the fortress stairs.

Hearts was a fortress (a black castle?) of mad lovers. Passing in and thru each other. Becoming, coming, existing momentarily on fire giving light. Eshun was loved by Terry Cross, who saw her dance one night in the Century Bar. A fund raiser. You know, Terry, now think you read a poem, "Dark Hearts," in which a war was fought for America. Yr side won easy (on paper), crackers dyin' & whatnot. Look up, ya see Eshun spinnin', bumpin', "uh," a magic booty, & beautiful tits. The heat of stare goin' on in there amidst Hotness. Blast Black HEAT. HOT. SPEARS DASH OUT. BURN. BURN. Eshun pierced then by Terry & that whole world whirled & then fainted dead away.

The next day they went downtown & talked to Sammy Davis about bux for the revolution. She died in childbirth in another town. Terry off w/ another sister.

Vega—Champ's woman, yeh? Vega right? Arrived w/ long speech from Champ (in his eyes). Her name alone was love. & revolutionary? Left Champ! He fought too much. Made love to Corliss over the antipoverty program offices & gave him the claps.

In flight for what now? So swift. Years you mask you years you talk you years you mask you image—heights & sounds. The lie of yr world was hedonism, again. Yeh, it climbed up, or never left, yeh?

You.

Yall.

Boiling raptures—nightmares, complete a task of partial movement— in the speed the rush of life from light to dark (nature) White to Black (philosophy) you cd not settle on a step, even, to collect up thoughts. & plan. You yall ya cdn't put even a few words down.

Ya did

Yeh

A plot of events. Reactions

Manifestoes of Heat

Poetry

Demands

But not a carefully plotted list of life's needs for the masses of people. The being in whom yall have yr body. It was necessary. Yng hot eyes, what white boys call intellectuals, artists, triple tonguin' dozen players lookin' for light. Ya rapped, tapped (on a lotta luscious gents & ladies), grew even, argued to kill, meant to destroy the world, even some nights spat out texts that blew the faithful's minds. Kept up a spark of attack, at

Malcolm's killers. Malcolm's message that the death of America was in the bottom of them mf'n boats (Hawkins stares through night using the moon as a crystal outlined against the sea. He barely sees these words scrawled in a ledger crossing the ocean the other way. The Jesus bulks its prow toward America—Afrikans turning to niggers just below the water line. He will not warm them. Cool it!).

You cd name the criss-cross lovers and touchings

You cd picture the words bitter & sweet that ran w/ it

Cary Clark's recently divorced lady once was Jethroe's flame. Ya remember Jet—in the flaming, explaining why ya can't take her home. Why? DeeDee was there—well there & not there—She'd blew up again & fled for home. (She sd—She cd've been w/Manny Jarvis the base bass player, she "used to" love—but she claimed, mad, to have fled to daddy's house.)

Jet was at that time a moment away from proposing marriage. Another mix-match brain tryin' to straighten itself. Instead she split. Him & Clark's woman (but that was before she knew or he knew Clark of the latter-day behop horn) sat in Flamingo sippin' bourbon & listening to Mongo congolize the junkies. & he took her home anyway. Because it was too much. The yellow face. The short natural. The thick glasses. Except she was ½ lesbian, ½ because she'd roll around wit' ya all right, but when she went back to "her" spot, a burly queen slim brown sexy foxy mama who thought she was a man(?) licked on the lass. Some wasted ass, Grass Roots thought. Watching Jet dribble her up & down 7th Ave.

So Jet had one there & the other returned. A camel hair wraparound coat w/ fur collar. Pull down hat. Cigarette between 2 fingers & little bag. Jet, who is this woman?

Both yall sit down. The future Mrs. Clark made no move. She stared at Dee Dee & slowly around the house casing it. Dee Dee had both legs apart leaning forward, hat on her head, cigarette mashed out. Who're you, woman? What you want here?

No answer from th FMC. She ducks her head a little, turning slowly to Jet.

Sit down, sez Jet.

(Ya remember yall—but Dee Dee's gone)

Another time he tried to run it on Eshun & TFMC again. Eshun didn't dig it. TFMC wanted a sewing machine. Eshun dug TF was a lesbian dipper & cn't dig having 1st to share Jet & then to get squoozed by this yaller chick too. Mad-ass bitch! Another tableaux—voices—bloods floors down moving up & down 7th Ave—garbage careening into the ctyard. WHAM! Tinkle! Smash in the middle of the night.

Meanwhile you fightin' a war, right?

Crackers dyin' by the billions, right (in word, paint, sound, the projection of the bottom lip)?

But in actual street life baby, bottles gettin' turned over, legs gettin' spread open, niggers insultin' each other, facin' around Harlem, mucho lies getting told—

Yeh, you had a vision of movement, a rush of changed perceptions. Yall split a volcanic disaster. Bones buried white, ol' cow heads, dusty for years left in the desert. Ya come to the fertile crescent, the hill of high life. "Vicious Modernism." But like creatures in an egg, you grew into what thot on the drawin' bd? Eyes closed—responding to sensation. You formulated nothing. Tho by what yall did say & the turning that went on of what ya did do, formulations *cd* be made. Then & later for sure.

It was a journey to a far shore. From another country. You traveled nights & days but always the look of dawn & long summer marked the places you came to. Like the disciples travelin' roads askin' alms & receiving them. Like Paul at Damascus. Like Johnny Mack Brown in his sneakers caught in a still leaping through the window. It is a journey from life to life, which never rested except as fragments of memory confuse the issue.

The "Year of the Push," you wrote. Harlem burned. Malcolm next. The Castle next. Arrive now at the scene of the next life. (Is there a next life? No. Only life—from beginning to beginning. Life passes into itself as its own definition.)

Was there a crowd of sensitive youth responding to themselves as the world & themselves in the world. You left the village & went to Harlem. You thought less about Ezra Pound & more about black people. That's interesting! Like a sock in the jaw. A curse out. A shout. Yall cd not get it finally to live, to stand up & walk off in a winning way.

Yall was the silent power yall thot. Yall was the prophets, you 'splained. Yall was yng petit bourgeois individualists fired by ya hero's life & death. Yall wanted to be heroes too. But had only studied athletics & hedonism.

What cd it mean? Some left to die, some to disappear. Some monks still toll the bell & muddle on. (But Albert Ayler dead, William White, dead, Bob Thompson, dead, John Coltrane, dead, Vashti dead, Bumi dead, Cornelius dead—in reality.)

The rush of those years swept you out of a cold bourgeois life, "frozen roses" Lisa sd. It swept you toward yrselves. Black is—a definition you'd get to—but there were crazy people loose who wanted merely to climb up a flag pole & maybe dangle off the knob to be saluted.

Rulers, Holymen, Kings & Queens, Bs! Why is it you'd take us there & yrself? At the time you'd check the Yorubas in they clothes & know that was them—but that was that. (S put yall down for being in Negro clothes, remember? Speakin' at Harlem Circle. Yeh, but . . .)

The essential thing, S was leaving & arriving. New Beginnings. And all the stuff that went down. But why wasn't it finally right? (Why isn't you ever to now been right?) How can you say, yall, anything from where you been to where you are? How'd you know what to say? It changes so fast. Can you beep or blip blip a blur? To be in truth a blur, seed to life to death to left a blur. You need to be precise, yet can you, except to say, it's all a blur. The dialectic, that only change is constant. The material & the flappin' dominoes are reality. Real human sensuous activity. Objects in real motion, even without yr contemplation. You do, are. You are, do. Not merely to record & be in it, yeh, anyway, but to change it change it change it consciously, to do.

You didn't *know* revolution. Except yall did do somethin'. It was revolution to be in a change & say that "Us inna change, yall." But what to do? How to be correct, i.e., fully mounted to create—& create on.

By the end of the middle of the sixties. Ya'd been depression egg, child of the war (ya mama got a job, ya peepahs leaving South continuous). Where once it was steel & autos & army, now it was steel & autos & army but also Douglas, Lockheed, Boeing, IT&T, federal govt, all to make the big move, America, ya, yall gone, up on all & every, whoever, America Rule, Dig it! Rusty bloods, spookwaffe over Italy, rat a tat, 'merica rule, man, *mein paisan*—Burma, black face crawl up the hump, Germany, France, Anzio, D-Day, N Afrika, Benning, Ga, America Rule, chum get in ya skull! Knock 'em up, shake 'em up, here they come, America rule.

Yea!! (They rollin' up the street, Central Avenue, comin' back! America rule—rule America. The world's in ruins, grown up in it! Ya mean there was a time America didn't rule? Impossible! Rule America!)

Civil Rights when ya got back. People marchin'. Ghana, Nkrumah, peeped in what? College days, Korea, America Rule. McCarthy. Even Langston, the revolutionary voice of our depression years. Chanted for China. Cheerlead Lenin. Put down US mad racism, by McCarthy time had a copout—that America (Langston was the scion of petty b., like you, chum) that America was B.utiful & cd make it big. He even repudiated his uncollected self. Roar China. Lenin Is Walkin' the Earth. Die Whitey, yr name is Capitalist, ain't it?

Rush Rush, by the end of the middle sixties—Selma, March on Washington, Rob W. Monroe Self-Defense, Boogaloos, Black Nationalism Black Nationalism, Black, Black, Kennedy & Malcolm dead, a new gruesome world ya in & where ya at? Left out, gone. A note in a public place. To build a nation. Right here. Look at the streets—claim them, claim it, set up, set up roadblocks on W. Side highway—collect tolls. That easy. You *actually* thought that. Take it, take it, pick it up, Blk Nationalism, Land, implied the cracker must die, but first the cracker in you, & it struggled, the cracker, & was that spin in new black space, for all that heated mono + dialogue, finally any more than a campaign to kill off the cracker in us—& did you succeed?

One morning Corliss, after a series of hassles, the mad Wall pushing harder & harder, heavy polarism, the street program over, no dough, & none a' them'd work, they had a theater which cd make money, a schemer to scheme 'em up on some, but all maniac pressures & angles were on weak Corliss, who didn't understand what to do, or more so who to be (Himself, he reasoned, was too weak, merely to be that—as subject—as object, look he smoked black tobacco cigarettes by the carton, ale & cheap wine. He ran after women ferociously. Having just very recently sworn off the grey ones, he now was turned on by all the black ones & tried to make up for all the lost time, & purely secular, full of white reason—he'd known nothing else, except the buzz of feeling, childlike, that sustained him, which was rooted in some real black strength), yet ya you Corliss, facing the red hat hammer, which was that, a mean hammer. Purity, Body & Favor! 3 rings. It turned out both Wall & Champ thought that Corliss cd raise enough dough to support them too. & Shreve & who & whatever, which was finally true. But As Salaam Alaikum on a throne of abused sisters (brothers too) offended Corliss's humanism.

Vectors of heat & need arrows shot into each other. Ya wanted, ya say, to build a nation (Sometimes it was clear—not clearly then, tho). "I have called for a nation" in Harlem? What cd it mean—naïve children in serious play? W/ every shotgun in the world trained on them.

What was it yall had put together? A gang a' yng people—black dudes mostly & their women & that composition is precise. Betty, Sandy, the sisters who tried to function. If they cdn't be broke down like an umbrella, they was whipped, literally. For the 1st time ya saw this, clear, well the 1st Blk-run stuff since childhood, except raps & steps was always w/ dudes unquestioned. If ya was wit' a woman, ya was makin' it—but so what, in the white world the women were workin' out in public anyhow—but in a closed space, full a' frustration & incorrect ideas. Goin' to the source ya thought, equating Black w/ feudalism, mysticism. Wall wd pontificate on what Black People wanted—Black People this, Blk people do that. (How'd he know, he'd been in white town, yeh—but so'd *you* man, even w/ ya secret sister ya married (a yellow middle-class lady from Philly), tho ya chased w/ the rest, the true iconoclast—"Bobbi's pussy ain't all *that* good I don't know why yall say . . .") equating all kinds tired (new to us!!!) b.s. w/ Black. The Rule of Black Men! *Rule Rule* (In an American way!) Naw—Naw, not that—its old & Black, it's *Aristocratic*, yeh Ethiopian Egyptian Afrikan? (Wasn't ready to go there but they swirled around / was that real?) Ya knew it wasn't then, but a few years later, wow, ya went for even that! Why? To be—*black*—lost scent, trail of meees yuu-uuuus—Goldfinger music playing @ a Paris airport—

It was only logical that some joker'd take all that disorder, & order it, make it a code, a formal cult. Art, culture, Afrika, revolution. Complete w/ feudalism & subjected sisters—But that came after this particular tale—

Ya didn't know that life inside is itself contradiction. & tho yall made to fight against mighty whitey, yall was mighty white too. At least part ways, & that was a contradiction—yeh—even yall knew about. But that was cause for struggle in yall & between yall. And what was that, finally, the maddest mf'in "black united front" you ever seen & none a' us have ever e'en heard the word now!

It was a formal challenge to America tho, it was. (Don't make me cry!) It was a hurled Black Challenge. Full of invective & life & fire & even love. But ya motto cd've been "All Hate & No Planning."

The simple logistics, Buster . . . Corliss one day got up & went to see Alice, who was fighting him again. "Ya know, Alice, why're you always running away from home?"

"Cause ya crazy Corliss. Ya be w/ wimmen, run around, then curse me & beat me, & I can't stand them other crazy punks ya with is why, neither."

Alice, skinny lady, - & they went thru that. She was stayin' at Rae Lewis house. Why, who know? Alice & Rae had to go thru it cause Burt had once been w/ Rae on a Mexican trip & promised to marry her & she came East only to find Burt & Alice a going concern. Sparks give off & all, but she lay back on Rae's studio couch & spread her legs & wrapped the mad Burt in.

It was getting late, 10am now, then 11, 12. They looked up & decided to go to the movies. Evelyn Waugh was (yeh!) playin', *The Loved One.* They sat thru that & never called Shreve, to let him know & by the next day they both (Botha ya) decided to call it quits, to split.

Frantic calls, Wall, Champ, Shreve, Ali, Abdul, Grass Roots & them came less now, the money give out, they had to get jobs, they hung around some nights & most wkends. Where's Corliss, the reference—now it was clear—no matter what, was what Corliss was, *the norm*, the indicator of what & why, whether ya liked it or not. In that knot rested the balance of that mad segment of the race—when it occurred to all them—yall, Corliss, Alice, those inside the fortress & out on the street that that triangular flint upon which the whole was built was split, aye, gone (they sat there & it dawned on them they cd leave. He sat there & it came to him. You you what you what you . . . empty sentences). Alice, Corliss in Rae Lewis' house, in the E. 90s.

The next day, a soft insinuating roar edged up nr 130, & Burt & Alice, where'd yall go? It was asked like a goofy grim song, "where'd ya go?"

Nelson Lowery, the hip poet, got shot by Champ 'cause the little intellectuals had no Hamlet Corliss to reason w/ unreason, to throw cold blue on hot red. He stumbled & fell down the subway stairs. Got a job immediately at Dole U., teaching his experiences.

Where'd Burt Go (Hey Burt?
             Hey Alice?)

In somebody car they were speeding to a small industrial town upstate where Burt knew the Bloods. Bent off, broke off, no word, they'd simply fled. Bye. No, no bye, rush off, speed lines behind them, arm & arm—not a word even to them, just go, the wood's on fire, the people are crazy, suddenly w/ no prior thought—none! Just that one day, away from it, it all came down, total lockout alienation—it was all harrassment in some way. Them red-hatted kings, the brotherhood of black bullies, in the name of who knew—no smoking—a little room from which to judge the world, but what to create, to have, was testimony to yall's doing, or, as a matter of fact, what are ya doing? (Wall had sd he wanted to direct Lady Soul

Nation in one a' Corliss's things—like to let Champ know where it really was—like he, ya dig, Wall, was a director. Except ya cdn't direct Wall, never had that ready to come outta you. Ended up w/ one wk to go, slappin' Lady Soul Nation in the puss, not gettin' no puss, & then Burt had to take over last week—it cd've been simply sabotage—put it together quick like, & it worked. Leon, the boy non-wonder, sd ya can direct, Burt, ya a hell of a director.)

& Wall, probably you stared at the whirling nuts put on & hated us, them, ya self, yall. Put on a red hat & stop smoking. That'll turn 'em around. Lead 'em to what? A Wall. A blank nigger frustration wall w/ no shrubbery even, just hard & acid cold. Very conservative/corny in a snap brim (new) hat & blue rain coat, hung up.

Was what you were saying permanently corny? Or only reflective of the whole time? Petty Bourgeois individualist Corliss, years after the Mexican sister sd it, you remain so—till this day!

Driving off, looking over their shoulder, some lightweight middle class arty niggers w/ them, helping so they'd always have that as an excuse never to do anything again. "We were there," they'd say, having arrived a couple weeks before, on motorcycles, for crying out loud, you ever see a middle class nigger on a motorcycle??

Shortly after, all sides leaked out. Some downtown to retake up their old pursuits. Some to continue these same pursuits, they'd never left. Some to prison. Some to madness. Some to save themselves, somehow. Where are yall all rat now?

We

In the middle of the night we show up. Babe & we. And say hello to all around. Hello Hello. No one can answer. Thought you was somewheres else. A big ol' boy like you (we) back here. For what?

We grandmother dead, whom loves we. We grandfather daid, who we is. Wheeeee! (A leaf breaks, twirls, rain beat—water pebbles bump the glass) the lady & the gent, 2 sets peruse each the other 2. Hello. This is Babe!

We together. Our love binds us. We hot lovers, arrow hooked in laugh-venom. We cd laugh even at death. We was that hip. That really arrogant at everything! How cd anything tell us anything? Wasn't we, 1ST, BLACK, & also, dig it, hadn't we come to a place where we, indeed, did know that was *DAZZLING*, YEH alive and angry at Evil!? My friend, that is not only comforting, it's inspiring.

But see we had come from the snarling Apple. Beat by sour sectarianism we decided, like so many others, simply to walk away from fools + madmen, rather than backing them down everyday with reality!

Had we changed? A little, perhaps, humbler. Humbler than now, no. We so broken, now, we silent + scared sometimes. We not that weak really, but indulge ourselves in weakness, because we know what it is + use it to excuse our mistakes. Mistakes now are not weakness, except failure to follow thru w/ the stated objectives of the revolution. Failure to be always *conscious*. We are the subjective element of the revolution. The Human will. & we need training, more practice coming out of new revolutionary theory. (Waves of light settle on our collective hands. We *are* the revolutionaries.)

See the creation of all yall, us, is only possible to do something! We know what it is. These years we've not simply sat + waited. Not simply walked through NYC in hip raincoats.

We came away from John LeCarré revolution rebellious stance, finally all to be put in paperback, for easy delectation—but all the time we had a flower, a garden, a forest of directives—from old niggers and yng ones— from dried up white people—+ girls w/ big tits—we took direction from slanting lights, dust flown on roads, sound of railway trains. & we had just failed, our lives were damaged by failure. The 1st democratic(?) revolution, a buncha petty bourgeois arty individuals—stunned by their own ignorance. We weren't even knowledgeable that we wasn't knowledgeable.

We in our youth wanted to be moved by ourselves' accomplishment. We cd do anything. What you need? A Revolution? Wait a mf'n minute. We be right Black!

But ourselves revealed too quick + not enough. We fought each other, yet we loved each other! Like Alice + Corliss used to battle. Take 5 in the bathroom for them to box + Alice to hit him + cry + say she was going away. What we know of them + they of us, or themselves.

All of us who survived the periods of struggle to become ourselves. It began by us trying to step out of the cardboard showcase of America, where we were stuffed dummies on mock parade. From spanked children, openeyed, openmouthed, frightened of Sammy Aldrich + the Ku Klux Klan. Set upon by our parents who wanted the best for us & thus had us join the Boyscouts + sing "Ave Marie" in the midst of a raging slum. How we beat that? Just bein' bad, we guessed. & that's why we always sd we was—bad.

Sissyhood, Colored School, Whiteout Island, Bohemian antics—beneath it all readied for Hedonistic America as intellectual nigger hedonist individuals. Fight against racism, mad whitey nightly. Think about something heavy w/ one of 'em suckin' you off or rubbin' yr tits. Fillin' you full a' dope. (Archie! Hey! What's w/ it my man—is you still cool?)

The getaway was necessary + real. Among the new world ruins of humanity. You think the Becketts, Burroughs, Ginsbergs, Albees talk of anybody else but them, they, all who is w/ 'em—you—niggers, whities in this magnitudinous madness? John Coltrane can be John Coltrane. He can blow the world apart! The rest of us, tho, beat distorted hurt by America. By our attempted assassination each day + night. (*Good Times*! Geraldine!) They hung we from the 'lectric chair, our feets scraped. The cp hang, go out collectin' gol' to save the world. We is no postcard victims. We is no Scottsboro boys. We is dumb victims—yeh—true enough. But we is alive. We cannot be herded to salvation by our killers gone philosophical. We will resist. We will fight the necessary war—yeh.

The deaths in America is America itself. Fat imperialist. We, when we arrived, heads bent. People talked to us about our past. They cdn't see our present clear + dreaded, like all grasshoppers, the future. Fiddle bump—uh all night long.

But we, no matter, the death list on us, no matter our real inferiority (yes, we think it & acted it & so, was it!). Youse think, per chance, them buncha tanks is not for real—yo' fis'es won't bus' 'em—yeh but we mind will—

No matter or yes matter, we grew under it, faces full of scars. Eyes burned w/ our own shortcomings—abstract, skinny-armed, staring in space. But we love our people for real. We see them sometimes riding bicycles or walkin' w/ cigarettes or jivin' on the streets & heat up to actual animation. We say to ourselves, we gon' win, ya dig, we gon' win.

The getaway was for good cause. Who cd live in a morgue rappin' w/ corpses even if they got mean portraits of the molding rappers + pieces of chocolate wrapped in gold? Vultures half live in corners, bits of flesh between their beak, drum sticks made of maggots opening + closing rhythmically, forcing a drone circean, tho cool & imitative.

When we arrived, we'd got away from all. Even responsibility. The shot intellectual sent a message. These madmen were we's responsibleness, we's (yall him us) brung 'em to Harlem. Harm 'em it was called by niggers in they sleep.

We had a bolo knife inside our jacket. Used to carry a sawed-off shot gun inside the jacket. To stalk the vicious modern streets. & now we, us few, who made a total get-out. From Bohemia, from the never-never kingdom of frustrated wolves in red hats, from the dude what slapped women for Black Rule, what cd not create cause there was none in 'em (tho we had magnetized a host of doers), had we but found a way to understand the deed that needed to be done! WHAT IS TO BE DONE, sd Lenin. It is still the central question.

Babe split, cause the dude started seeing Eshun, again. Eshun died, then Babe died. Eshun in childbirth, poisoned by reality + this dude's seed. Babe went away in an argument, slapped each others' faces in a bar—went away + drowned in Mexico w/ a tv dude. A letter was circulated saying Corliss murdered them both because he (it implied) hated Black women + this was his revenge.

We watched + was all this, & became wholer & lesser perhaps. We'd come to a small town, a factory berg of heapin' deeps of wild south talkin' woogies. For some reason, the steel air, empty streets (nights the muggers loose), rat face po' poverty blow whistles in us. It heated us. It brought us love image somehow.

WHAT IS TO BE DONE, Lenin asked + we (you sd you hated whitey, ain't Lenin whitey?). WHAT IS TO BE DONE?

Beginning in the end—another beginning—we walked nights thru the streets, glass in hand, sat at the foot of Lincoln's stature + drove the white women out of our mind. Bats flapped between our ears, weird music, horrible organs belched dead aristocrat bop-be.

We wandered in and out of bars, smoked black cigarettes & sopped brews by the dozen. We used to go to a bar on Boatman Street + sit w/ the furniture movers, drinking boiler makers + listening to our life on the juke box. Made notes on the world around us, snips of tunes—WHAT IS TO BE DONE?

Hated, Hated, still, these crackers, yet there weren't many here. Kicked some dude in the stomach down at this ol' hotel we stayed in, Eshun, Barney, Corliss. Barney slept w/ Eshun + Corliss walked the streets. Supremes sang "Where Did Our Love Go?"— looking for lost Alice. Miracles sang "Tracks of My Tears."

WHAT IS TO BE DONE?

Slowly we saw + understood some things. We comin' from Syracuse, Brooklyn, the Village, Way into Ohio, Newark, N.J., Down Home, N. Jippolapi, Missobama.

Swiftly we saw and understood some things. We wondered if the getaway was complete? To where? We saw many things we'd done as *evil*. (Which was finally a mistake—that guilt shit is only to be exploited by some cunning intelligence or another—people want to sell you something—usually some noise—off which they made a pretty penny.) We ain't need to be in no church. But the guilt forced us to want to be *good*! Which had a positive & a negative. For pos, it meant we cd stop acting like Wm Powell or early Herbert Marshall or a Noel Coward creation. We cd put down the drink, drop the cigarette—get off the blvds + find some real work. We cd stop boozin'. We cd even stop chasin' sisters so intense we act like we had no sense. But the neg on that was we thought this was hooked to spookism. The legacy of wolf-town Yorubas w/ hot drums— Bembe brought the rhythm up—red hats mumbled, "I likem salami— hatem baloney." We wandered into our real past trying to catch up with ourselves. Slavery stopped us cold, almost drowned our heartbeat. All life froze or grew in imitation of the ice folks. & to set it all in motion again—

what? Say it! It's back! It's back! We Black!—Say it! Artificial respiration—pump + pump + pump—but will the patient (ourselves) stand up please? Black Black Black Black beating against the collapsed lungs. Will the patient (we self) stand up, please?

Lost now, in the getaway, a road led to ancient times. At the scene of the crime we want to put on robes. We was wearin' robes when we was busted—remember? Yeh? We had a buncha wives when we got busted—remember (we had a hat w/ gol' on it—cracker give me this crushed fedora he got to sell—sold a couple million to us)? But see it was just another market, witch doctor in a "stingy," mchawi w/ a monocle + tails. Like white monkey (instead of an olive in that whatname put a drumbeat!).

We argued one night, we woman + us, that polygamy meant we cd get outta slidin' around the street midnight. Have 'em all together. We woman went for it briefly and then it fell apart exposed to poison reality. The tester. Reality. *Dig The Real.* (Send a note to Nationalists!) And dudes showed from the West w/ that tale rummaging back in the centuries we thought or reconstruction except return to the source, not just the lost twains of the frozen warrior king, but dig reality. The structures we in & are. The source wd be the bros Touré, Nyerere, Cabral. The frozen warrior King is just that, a beautiful (except check the agony of stopped motion) image of *temps perdu.* (We will not bandage ourself like the mummy.) A slave can save no face except by takin' heads. Unfreeze the image. It rots like dead dinosaurs in a dance called underdevelopment.

We wanted reality. We still want it. We wanted to attack our enemies. We still want it. We were there in reality, frozen roses on ice. Readied for years for another death. Articulate stooges of the rulers. We wanted another reality. Not to suffer the fate of all philosophy, even materialism, even Feuerbach. We wanted not just to check it out, but change it. And even going back to ground zero, dressed up momentarily, shook us loose from one setup, except after a while, Yorubas dance for pennies in backwoods nigger Disneyland, Mother Ship hovers in Buck Rogers' dimension & the calls to worship anything but reality + common sense grow strikingly backward! But we knew that + it was white, that obvious truth that there was no God, no Allah, no Damballah, only the commonest truth. Maddening truth—reality—that everything, indeed, was everything—but "smilin' + grinnin'" wdn't get it, except celebrations of killed enemies. That winkin' + blinkin' won't get it—or eye closin'—or silence (except to stalk a bugger & bust 'em)—that the only thing that wd get it—is getting it, *i.e.*, getting down in reality, the concrete actual.

You see we'd fled the whiteout & went for the blackout. We don't want to be out but in—directly *in*—touchable, knowable, understandable, plain, concrete, real as trees.

We knew this once, that these dressed-up folks were just tryin' to get away from the street agony of being powerless niggers, in America. But the metaphysical element—from God humanism (Spirit Monger) to Allah + Damballah. Black Gods. But, yeh, it is misunderstanding, it is not the color of the Gods, but that there are *no* Gods. No Gods. No Gods. Reality is more beautiful than fantasy. Priestcraft killed coloreds once, is still killing us. Rev. Ike. Rev. Skinner. Rev. Sharper. Rev. Bullwinkle Simoleoncopper. Rev. Grey Ham.

Black vs. White. We saw it. Hate whitey. Put together structures to destroy him (& her). Hate whitey. The whole philosophy & by that all the same stuff whitey run cd get back, painted black. And many of the leading Blackies—well they was whitey too.

We wanted what: *Destruction of Evil.* But we sd that was simply white people + America! The Union of Black Hearts taught us the sickness of the righteous warriors. Childhood we saw the sickness of being Jesus invisible—Colored School, the sickness of the ritual & the reality of the place in America created for the lightskinned + cooled out Brownies (of whom there's more). The colored schoolers want a place in it—just a place—don't mention race—or now it's cool—Black is in—a natural too—but give us a place SAM—UNCLE SAM—you our uncle too. The isle of the zombiezation program. Enroll the whole of niggerdom in the scolding corps to scold the world in humiliation, WINGS OVER THE WORLD, H.G. Wells sd. He didn't dig Curtis Lemay wd be in there, ripped off Raymond Massey + flyin' the squad to squash the people's rights. Alliance of Warlords in the craft. (Military-Industrial complex.)

At that time of study + rationalism what turned us out was hedonism. Assimilation rather than principled relationships to build a world of reality. Layin' around thinkin'—can finally not be all rational either. The culture is distorted—racist, chauvinistic capitalist, exploitative, individualistic. No matter what, we sd we had to be all that to be there w/ 'em.

So the ashes of Babylon, & the fragments of lost kingdoms. Not enough! & Guilt. No not enough. Poetry music dance swapped love anthems. Not enough.

Slowly we understood reality had to be changed by handling it, by consciously seizing it (conquering our weakness) + seizing it. We'd put on robes, talked ancient languages. Learned the vanished customs of our stopped race. Took on religions. Kneeled at night in prayer to nonexistent pimp objects. Went forward to Black but backward to metaphysics!

We had it all tho—just get it together. We need we. Collect. No sparkling warrior singer striking alone through a world of whipped donkeys in praise of Don Q (Thass Rum, my man!) & no S. Panzas either. Collect. We we is missing! Where is we we?

At first we shadowed reality in verse + tale + staged assaults. We need to grasp reality to change it. The night Mickey + Volta fought over Sivella. Volta (lower) was scattin' Bird licks of rhythm reminiscence. Hard beautiful sound. We Mickey show. We Mickey of skinny tubular self, blowin' barbwire instead of Bird, bullets + bombs + fire + HATE—some of it burnt Volta, a school teacher w/ dirty collars + complete sway in Finland Station. And peepahs ran it Mickey's Monkey (dum dee dah dee dum dah dee / dum dee dah dee dum dah dee) evil-eyed ice lover, blackism, not sweet + sinuous, swift as wind washin' sound thru the world raw bitter blackie burnt + burning now to the ground to the ground the sound riot murder maybe rape insurrection!

And then Volta (lower) had a a hip thing when he blew his skylight flashes + Sivella danced, swung her boney black sexy self under + over the warm words. Vision Fission. Mickey, instead, beat the dark path in it & outta it. He blew barbed light bombs when asked, but wasn't really a reader or singer w/o occasion. We Mickey, he was trying to explode we self. We world Mickey no dig! And Sivella, she dig what no one ask, that world *is* here, & is got to be got at. Anti, we opposite peepah say we Mickey spooky looney, HATE everything. We cdn't hate everything. Everything pay dust love tv time, yeh?

We Mickey case around till one night Sivella checks we self Bang-Bangs on her tight + hot as volcanoe crazy. Them EYES! OW! Turn 'em off, on, anyway you gon'. We Mickey, silent lookin', somebody playin' jaggy blues. Them two we innocents (of future harder stuff to deal w/ in motion sailing toward the hoop) trail out under spell of night's hip cover.

& so to put a stop to dat Volta (lower) calls one night, & says (Sivella had canceled a duo sing dance) he's coming over to see we Mickey. He's scatting a lil hate too now ya dig. Finally bangs we Mickey in the eye & Mickey he don't even fight.

How can we be revolutionary + don't fight? Don't get mad in reality? A knife a spear a gun, but don't fight. Wrestled w/ white boys in the street + drunken fat nigger bass players. But how we gonna make a change don't seize life itself + rassle?

* * * * *

We Mickey like a rest a' us, still alienated from hard stuff. Rather think, say murder but don't be no murder. Got to cut that out—say murder got to be murder.

Volta (lower) meantime go all the way out. A priest of uncorrected sentences. Wandering between Cleveland + the motherland. Won't seize reality.

Peepahs came. Sat in ties + talk about how to swap dust for dust; tho we wasn't total hip we was tryin' to be in + seize on reality. Began to dress up, met some brothers hooked Walls' stuff up + some a' Corliss' alienated humanism, warmed it, fired it up—we went for it & was troops of the laird. Became that (tho Muslimized), a trifle put off by the purely sensuous display of bein' MEN, WOMEN, BLACK, that is.

Picture the ragtime we dudes 'n dudettes came from, put out, put on bldg & now fronts as leaders tryin' a' do, what we larned ya. We studies, goes to school, except clipped vision—yeh, a school a' worldly matters, a school of shapings, turnings, be doings—

We got a group together of dogooders now. Was artists in one group. Regular dudes that wanted "change." Then lo + behold, the redhats (older tireder version) to guard us all & we even got back in that, why, after mad Wall + the misrule of the unjust, these dudes explained what it was was a buncha mirrors. Dudes smoked & sd a prayer, cooled it out. Magic, we was into that. Called ourselves Magicians. Priests. Why to go off into that? ART of Darkness. Black Art. Black modes. But why was art about, what was there to talk about + Black art went south w/ all that came up talking magic. Why? When white boys ran the I Ching we figured they was just into they deep thang—like something to pass time. We always wanted what it was. Exactly that. But then (it was all that God talk) we was goin' for the ghos'. The world preys on the unaware.

Magic ghos' + strange lightin' for us.

Tho the whites play w/ that lightweight spookism. Peasant dresses, sneakers, long stringy hair, thick glasses, imitation cocaine. The Drones, for instance, play days at a time, slow circus stunts. Hindu hillbilly preacher. In tune w/ ease + lots of dubbling in space-time, no need to tackle the rulers of the world (they are the rulers of the world)—yes—but e'en they cd ask for a juster order—even they cd work!

We kneeled nights, made salats for victory. Acted cleansed + talked abt the need to clean up. Cleaned up even. (It's the only utility, but e'en so, we need a discipline in life that leads to life's revolution. It's this, we want this to be paradise, dig, now, here, right away. Otherwise why in Fuck be here? Except you are here, philosopher, FIGHT!)

Kneel at the moon (planes take off). Say there is no God but Allah—or there is no God, not even Allah. Kneel + say "Give me strength o mass that has no fear." Humble before people, vicious before the enemy.

And for a hot minute, man, we was there on our knees, except, listen, the sounds of the earth, we Mickey he went for it. Only seen 'em w/ a red hat once tho. Sivella never did—or maybe but she wdn't kneel & pray—listen to the carriers of the word whatta they do—well smoke? + lie + play magic + take up time + hate niggers—niggers how they get in this? "Ubangi's" they called 'em. Them whiteys knew we wasn't no regular niggers (it's about that), seen our red skies, cd mumbo a whole lotta jumbo, need you to keep the other niggers down, you can deal w/ them.

El Dahran from Alabama Sudan, spoke perfect Arab (who knew?). A tie salesman by calling, he was touched by someone pulled his coat to how he cd get more outta life—Be in this. Get a red hat. Set up a going career. Dudes + dudettes fall in, yeh, on they knees, say there is no other God, 'cept yall!

Was exposed by a class brother as petty thief (class b wanted to set up + had hooked up w/ the sheriff + gave phoney info out on black bomb throwers in exchange for a fleet of used police cars).

Corliss was in it w/ us + he was studying + came up w/ some dry intellectual refutation of Arab as the 1st human speech &c. Stuff like that move we Corliss + he drifted. The rest of us, some, still hung there, various Brotherhoods, using up energy to celebrate stopped motion. Religion is exploitation, we came to. Don't say that!

We Mickey wd say it. We thot it. Talkin' to the fat blue dude in the back a' the room. (They broke into the "Jamart" + talked bad about niggers, set up a spy system, a secret tap on us at our spiritual watering hole.) It was a GHOST SHACK, dead women sailin' up the stairways—Sivella used to talk to Muhammad Ali when we Mickey wanted to act crazy—Hi

Muhammad—White peepahs code life flitted thru. A wall a' books in the blackest hole of Finland Station, w/ Pound, Eliot, Olson, Lawrence, ya see the continued reference? In the room's center, turn facing the window (East) at which you pray, then half turn like a dancer & look at the stolid volumes.

It's the world needs changing whatever we say—we do is real. Change we do we say change too. Change we do.

Stokeley came, spoke in the park, sd "Black Power!" Was the spinning of god's business that business. Simply to tell us get up, stand up, clean up, back away, we walk away from American values which include nigger wipeout. A way of life? A cleaner, stronger way of life. We had to go to unreality for that, why?? Because the world—reality you call it—is so fucked up. & so, you reason, to be at a higher pitch, a cleaner direction, you had to point at pure speech—vision—tales—Be in the real world man, sister, + get a cleaner version. That's what revolution wants. A cleaner version. A better, stronger way of life. Not UTOPIA—a fantasy. Not paradise—another fantasy. Not Heaven or the land of the Deads. But life itself can be raised, we thinkin'. King Faisal got slaves. As Salaam Alaikum. Pope Pius killed the Jews. Hail Mary. Rabbi Pincus curses the Arabs, + gladly helps the Palestinians die. But wait:

A street in future reality.

You wait there for a light

A car pulls up, w/ 4 round hats

The vegetables have come to check us

Veg = Sandwich!

Us = Sandwich!

Veg: May the urine of the ruler cleanse yo' habit

Us: Yebo

Veg: What group you bros w/

Us: Primitive Nationalists Chauvinist Atavists

Veg: Ok, pass

Us: Is all well

Veg: Except some negroes w/o smack, slidin' around tryin' to subvert our just role. Brothers yall our allies & you must preach the partition is just. The Devil (PBUH) has relented & we are victorious. The Black Man has come into his own right.

Us: Sandwich!

Veg: Where are yall bound?

Us: To the Pathmark & then to the Exxon Station to fill up
Veg: Teach!
Us: Sandwich!
Veg: Sandwich, good bros
                    All leave—

Convert to reality, to change it (if we is real). If we is real, matter in motion. What is the matter. We need to get we mind straight. Need to get straight. Be in reality—even if it means using yr writin' table as a barricade to fire on scum. We must convert to reality. Try study. Investigation—of we world. So we dig who's in it, us in it, as a seriousness in motion.

Corliss, Mickey, Sivella + them split from red hatism, other obvious metaphysic. We rest, cut eventually too. Dudes for change. We was runnin' w/ now. Actin', rappin', walkin' around to meetin's. A local warlord (white) dispatched he 3rd rate thugs to get cursed out regular. We began to use that gift for callin' people out they names. "Green mammy lumper—creature wit'out no pappy—you best to hang out w/ diarrhea rather than frig with us who is actual haid mashers!" Was a wearying wop warlord we faced in them halcyon days. Halcyon now it seems because the conflicts was so cut + dried. They still supported Hate Whitey! Knot 'um up—if you cd, bro! We wasn't seeing how the shelf of self-projection we was born to (we & it a solidarity of notions in motion—to form our inch of nascent singularity) was the same bizness, Kar-Mike-Key-El (French pronounciation at Conakry Airport which made it impossible for us to, like, get in Guinea later). But these other ginnies (named cause they was dark enough to be lightweight mulattoes) was colonial warlords in FS. But we had approached, yes, another ledge of the same shelf as the Union of Hearts. Simply another wing. Both wings enable the beast to fly!

The Screaming Wall, Sullen Champ, Stallin' Shreve, & the intellectual-arty dominoes (yeh square—black w/white spots!) was all an aspirant PB formation. Either from there or going there—dig it? (Ya can't? Dig yaself then who we is a-talkin' to? Who we—you is and so forth . . . ?)

The arty-nut wing, union of arts—w/ every petty bourgeois tendency known in the world. Liberalism, individualism, ultra-leftism, ultra-rightism, putschism, mountain stronghold mentality, roving guerilla band-ism—all collected together in g flat, sound like Hate Whitey in mo' time. All that flailin' & boxin' & shadow worship. Confuse craziness w/ revolution if we wants to, but it ain't. We ain't say nuthin' of a revolutionary nature.

Cdn't go on, but it's a general tone most likely, compared to plain-out lie tellin' for the Bush-War-See. The straightout made mad by bourgeois cultural imperialism. Yankee nitwits—traitor groups! Apologists like then + now, the group increases. Whoever recent got a few pennies, a gig &c. Yeh, we left some apologists for international boushies. Now later some a' black runners turn out to be, now in change time, merely apologists for the native boushies.

But it was a same group lads and lassies. Arty wing + civic affairs wing. They bees together. Fat Tootsie, who is alligator Lesbian's hookup, cd be in Irving's Coalition (Irving to cool out flaming nigs) + scribble sloppy fat prose poems w/ Alli lesbian, Italian spookette celebrity, C.I.A. strophes in Africa, yea, clearly emerged as poetess lariat of congressional black caucus + bureaucratic capitalism.

And all, check it, the unconnectors with the workers + peasants is become now apologists, cool-out artists, for the native agent niggers.

Dudes United for Change turns out to be—well, consider this—to say we for change—is veddy coolt. It cd mean but a change of hue. Consider the group, any Sunday, we consists of.

Old politicoes, snarling now. Tried to get it maybe—& didn't. However, pavement caught 'em & there they be. Grey slightly at temples, pre-Nixon Republicans. It never really mattered, like whose pocket we got we pennies from, dig? But to get 'em was we question. So Republican, Democrat, in a strict sense, so what?

Civil servants, serving the city, at whatever low capacity—wanted mo' howsomever—But the black power mode cd, at one pt, get 'em all.

E.g., Oily Hairs, the above mentioned politicoe. In the middle of the floors, arms akimbo. No Bux—I'd run bro—smiling—had just opened Pork Works—ribs for ya jibs—smokey bones to make youse groan. Long history of deals + whatsomever cd be got into. Yet Hate Whitey was the militant edge + behind that all manners of particular benefits.

Bro Carmichael sd "Black Power." Wasn't it? Didn't It? Yet it needa be! Still needa be. Ain't yet, but check it. At a lower level just only + Gip Fatson, sat, Sweety Wade from way back when, on a leash for years by FS colonialists, be he wit' we snarlin' team. Turned out to be the other wing (left or right—maybe right so cd be left of same petty bourgeois—was yr doctors, lawyers, accountants, school teachers), met to say, in they way, Hate Whitey—getum outta there.

On second floor, a window brought in some light. Sundays holy streakers to churches let out a light low, low nonroar—churches don't be that filled no more. Like these, we s'posed to be Godfearin' folks—yet they we don't be wit' the hymn hummers, yeh? Watch 'em from the windows, clean, & when we need ta go get 'um we know where they is, dig? 11am go get 'um in there. Them ol' dungeons—kinda hip tho—one dude in a Afro wig, white knit vine (got indicted later for bribing a public official) preachin' in a contemporary mode. Came in, he rarin' back, a finger in the air, he jiggles + crosses his legs to turn to stare at Jesus—Jesus hip enough not to be alive in all that—bad boy swings back. "YEH," we let out, the move was so hip. Like JB, w/ holy ghos' in it. Preacher call the real showstopper. Huge "'fro," a real one, w/ strands mashed down on his forehead Charley Diggs style. He raise the ladies + gents, hummin' + bendin' they knees in time—talking 'bout Jee-suz &c Jee-suz Jee-suz, hands in double fists, stretched full up—place be rockin', be rockin', & look—

There's Perry from "The Toilet," a deacon now, his sisters, both the married + the unmarried ones in the cool chair chortling colored chants. Years have rocked, slanted, wooden angles, they behind us—yall—what we lose by not bein' here wit' 'em moving w/ the gospel. Workers. Black People. Yet God does *not* exist. And in the sullen ritual—tho it is a high hysteria make you leave the ground baby, make you dance on float space. We "happy," we "moved," we "touched by the Holy ghost."

Goddamn bro—just like you shrink back away from struggle. We donno, a worker in the energy corp, yeh but what can be seen Sundays from the pulpit lookin' at the new suits, the pink hats, the shiny shoes—wherefore prancin' preacher holds forth—what is seen, what shown, but unworldliness, gullibility?

"Hey bro"

"Hey, man"

"What's happenin'"

"Hey, nuthin', man, work, you know"

Is this the same (a question hang inside we drippin' lip)? Is this life like we knew it? Why you traitor to feelin' we had, man? We remember somethin' else, don't we? 'Member me bringing the ball down, faking to the right the left, movin' sideways, letting the pill sail over the front man's fingers where you elbowed into the key took the pass wheeled + either gave it to Billy Peace or went in yaself—when "dunks" 1st came out. All that real excitement in life. Life lived full up + open. "Mickey! Hey!" & we Mickey leaped + threw it to you fast, for you to wheel + *deal*! Two. Big man!

"What's happenin', Bro?" The talk is space consumer + little else. What can you say in a church while dudes sit on a second floor talking 'bout Black Power? Huh, Stokely?

"We gotta run somebody for city mgr. + councilman. Who's it gonna be?"

These are the people, it seem—all walks of life. Black United Front. Blue blazers grey pants. Blue shirts open at collar, sneakers. Sunday AM. There's Neddy Pinkett, from where? Colored School. Yeh we went to school together.

Big ol' Ronald Pucker, he's bigger now, my man. Jes' got in last wk. Made it finally. Gip's main man. Like Maulana sd, "my body nigger." When what was really sd was Mbadiliko, he comes to change. Cd be either one, hung at the mistake. The internal dichotomy, take you either way. Ronnie's an expert on drugs. Smoked some bush once. Expert mean cd get up to 20 big ones, talking abt it. Like a couple yellow dudes we know got rich off Black + meant it. Like we just got here + it was, frankly, work! Now you gonna tell us something else! The system?? What? Don't hand us that!

But den, Black, was the cutting edge. Black against white. Principal contradiction. Against which our united front.

We stand on the porch some evenings + people came over. Little dudes crowd around the steps. They parents come over. "How ya? Hey Miss J. how you feel?"

"You seen Harry? Where's he now?"

"He inside running off a flyer for the show on the weekend. You comin'?"

"You know I'm gonna be there. Wdn't miss it for nuthin. I'ma find out just what yall doin'."

A basketball game gets off at dusk. Hoopin' up + down the streets. A gang a' folks suddenly in the game + watchin', the street. Street light summer nights.

We, you + I, all us, had been burned + turned to see what was really real. What it is. Arc of the ball descending. Street folks howls. We walk back late night, hands dirty, a couple a' dudes trailing, see sisters on the stoop. Get a lemonade + talk to people go in. Police car occasionally drifts slowly up the street. A little quiet settles, except the kids, who call 'em what they is.

We thot it was the correct line. And Corliss, we seen him more than once on the stoop watchin' the street. He was teachin' little kids to run a

mimeograph machine. One night checked him in an anti-poverty meeting. Wondered was he still paintin' them big head people w/ the guns
shootin' fire into abstract space—America it looked like. Blood + purple
skies. We seen him argue w/ a dude abt who the program was for. Corliss
sd You ain't representing the people, man. You represent the wop warlord. He'd changed a little. Talked louder, pressed issue like he meant it.
Wondered why, how he got to there. But we backed him up. Sd yeh, ya
dirty whatnames, you in Bernardinelli's pocket, thass all.

Hall fulla bloods. But who? Some people who followed that? Bloods
lookin' for some kinda lift outta dirt. Some hustlers. A few workin' people. Hands go up to vote. Numbers + nonsense. We cdda' known, we
didn't. Like comets sailed into the sidewalk. Smoke + fire. Black power
pushers. Hate Whitey, the cutting edge.

The folks hunch forward. A fat nigger stooge is talked bad to. He slinks
out + look at the faces, some you'll see again, now broad smiles, the
hands held up. Yeh, Yeh, we win.

We draw some yng folks w/ us. Meetin' as the months moved. Events
stacked up. A time of particular ideas. Currents of thought, at the tips of
all imaginations.

"We gotta go down city council + talk against this dog-bill.
Bernardenelli wanna bring in dogs, ride around w/ the pigs."

Go down there, a crowd of blue collar whites, loud women, dema-
gogues stuck in for good measure, to keep the laird's word. Hail
Prudential, Holy Father. Yr monopoly is so cool. We salute you w/ our
lifes. They frightened whites led by a heavyweight w/ a 2-ton tummich
who, it turned out (of course), got to be a state sinner. In both crowds,
mercury headed rise above us all. 4 years from now at the level of the
blue collars, + the black muscle in the crowd, some change. Some talk. A
few got gigs. But for most, for the whole world, dumb, static nothingness.
Why are we in here for this? To go for what? Is your life ever pleasant,
whoever you are? What have we created?

But what we is lookin' for? From all we travels, to be there on a city
council floor. The lips beat fictions across. Dot. Dash. Sun. Sky. Water.
Corliss tit tats. Mickey close his eye for word to come. Do you work? Who
is making the world go? What they want?

Smoothies come + climbed on we back. Rt wing of art pb's ran w/ it.
Used us. Put on new suits (Ivory).

We need to see this. All our lives (yall) we been used. Ok go to the back a' the bus. Befo' the bus. Back in time space, to where the black giants walked. Drums bang smoke rings. We ain't there, is we? (Dude's wife home, never seen her, we need 50 women, this ol' fantasist sd, she need ta be put as number 50, somewhere deep in Malawi forests, w/ Ubangwe & feudalism.)

All our lives, blood, we been used, + used by everything, except we self. So darkness flee to top of wall. Sun slant crying thru window, old dogs half step up a street. It's good ta be home, home. We feel we won that much. That we knew a place, even, we wanted to be. So it wasn't all flying shit, & contradiction. There was a solid branch of life we cd pt to & say, yeh, thass my mf'n home!

But metaphysical nigger—from Holy Ghos' to the Allah peepahs. Idealistic nigger—drawin' forts for president Roosevelt, to stick in the radio. Its green light stream on the rug. To thinking that 'cross that river lurked, in the small glistening greyness of yo' home, a thing apart from the world.

& so the contradiction, is life, is always, in Finland Station too. We home up country. Cross de water, where what?

Take we Mickey f'instance: he came back to F.S. loaded w/ idealistic crisscross. Didn't know from nuthin' 'cept he was gone + now come back. Whited out by 'Merican life. A black man grow up, tried to kill 'em, bleed him. With us in the Union of Hearts. Wanted to be a racing car driver, but never thought about it enough. A magician, he cd throw cards in the air + they fall all over the table. Thought he was a singer, but never did that. Mostly we Mickey checked stuff. Played a trumpet. W/ Carl Stiles group. & they were bad bad, not just one time, but bad bad. Low & slow cool & blue. And sometimes they'd get high up in it. Twow! Beat a wall a' glass splashes. Chromatic wiggling knives. Talk about yo' mama + her mama + all a' mamas a be. + they set it up so when we Mickey blow, he blow stuff don't nobody be thinking about, except the shape a' our world is made a' these notes, baby—turned on these sharped + flatted breaths.

But Mickey was w/ a white woman in the Apple. Split when Malcolm died. Wdn't talk to no whites + sd he was gonna kill 'em all. Hung out w/ us in the Hearts. When he checked Burt + Alice hating, he got his sky too. To the same jeezoint, Finland Station. Funny name for a town fulla bloods.

Mickey still check music. Know about it. Play occasionally when we ask, or somebody say, for real, "Hey Mickey, play somethin'." & he blow something about the destruction of America. Cause that's all Mickey inarested in.

One time all we Mickey play is burn 'em up, burn 'em down, Hate Whitey. Now it's America got to go. Tear it up, rip it down, America. But how in a note of abstract sound can that be there? It's there—fool. Words are not all life, friend. Are there scary sounds, sounds of warmth. Night sounds, daylight, streaming into a room. Youth, old folks—the woods—the city. All can be told. So the story of Die America was also blown.

But wait that wasn't Mickey. That was Barney. No, but Mickey married Sivella finally, right? Or was it Barney? Who? The two of 'em mash together in we head.

Barney was w/ us blowin' his hot horn. Scared folks. It was a musical w/o words, only gestures, mime about how man emerged, the creation of the earth, the 1st civilizations, & the destruction of Black social order by the Barbarians. That subjugation, humiliation. And finally, the restoration + reconstruction. In that time, what was told was the subsequent subjugation of white. Racism had drove not only themselves crazy, but those who they humiliated these centuries now rose + humiliated them. At sword's pt, the European was made to kneel to metaphysical power. We made him do salats & that's how the story ended. No new life, but a salat, from the old oppressive metaphysical shuck. To continue the same death march in life of societies. Put to the sword for the mullahs, khalifs, priests, & bd members + their families.

But Barney anyway wd chill ya up. Hair stand up on yr neck. Watchin' the life begin. & the imprisonment + release of Black life—That night there was an incident. White girl come w/ a dude sd she was a Russian Indian. Sister Reza talked bad to the woman + the dude too. "A Russian Indian. Well, the Indian can stay, but the Russian pt gotta split."

Went on, that stuff did, all over. & wasn't it what, felt good. Needles + pins. Black + Hard. To say, Naw ya cain't come in. Was fightin' hard. We even had a set doctrine, notes 'splained why ya cdn't let 'em in, but it was simply payback. Like we 'splained ya—payback is hard.

At another level, Gip was the one we sd was gonna run for city mgr. Sittin' in that Sunday circle. Same time, from city to city, white folks cdn't get in the sets. We cd tell who was for real or not by how they ranked crackers.

At Hearts, tho we ain't never had that problem, 'cept for Sargeant Shriver. Rep went out everywhich way.

Barney hooked up w/ Mae, changed his name to Malik—Mae to Lateefa. Raised 5 children in Finland Station. Taught them to Hate Whitey, & they'd stop 'em in the street & run 'em down till they later dug somethin' else. & what's that? Mad Wall what it was. Hassan, white woman, slew foot, bowtied. All of 'em. Motacycle twins. They w/ Oily Hairs + Otto Ice + Gip Fatson. (You think it's just that white boy w/ the leather bag tied to his dungarees, balding already, in blue jeans an' a 1000 dollar cross-Atlantic flight? That bignosed blonde stewardess, w/ haughty chauvinistic stare? Think they the enemy only? Not lookin'. Deeper look. You can't see 'em. Sits above us. At they long wood tables. Countin' dough they stole. Ya see a line, a shelf a' bloods, hooked ass to nose around a chain. We see a buncha puppets—but check it out—)

The whiteout all our lives took us to a brick + we left, split. We was there inside where all of it pointed. From day one. For what we mama grunted for. Success in America! Dig?

We fled a whiteout. Blackout fulla knives + deaths + madness. A rat-faced madman cd tell ya all life + understanding flowed from him. We seen him later in front of Count Basie's, bleak + washed out. These words a' Volta (lower), Wall's, certain white boys we toured the northern note with. All these tales wd light a match to the present. What they say about cowardice, stupidity. Heartless last.

Like the night we was w/ these dudes in New England at a harbor town. Midnight, we sit drunk in an ancient mansion (How many a' these in the world?). A hidden castle, furnished complete inside w/ scrolls, rugs, vines, balconies, trays of peanuts + nothing but fags enter same. We the aesthete, let in to turn us out, but what happened in the midnight, a naked dude above our heads went to the balcony's edge + dove shining into the vine-covered pool. An organ began to play distorted Bach, twisted notes, + drunken fags quoted 16th century verse + fell out on the floor. Boushie Cultural Imperialism.

But then, to escape that, breathless all night we turned, nose runnin', all night, dawn found us home.

Not home, but in a Afrique town, Harm'em. We talked of that. & the corrupt circus whirl. & Home. To get to reality. Barney thought.

Barney loved Mae. Malik loved Lateefa more. Lateefa from Finland Station, had never left. Went w/ musicians & heard a' Barney. Now Malik. She asked him to play sometime. Why he didn't is what she asked.

From day one she show w/ this other dude. A half baldhead genius of the joint (they says). 'Cept M, he don't like nobody, and love everybody, which is hard to deal w/ being around them the same. Dig it. She is long and skinny, boney even. The dude he talkin' but you listenin' to that? She dark-lookin', smooth-skinned, walks like she practiced and even big head O, the Marketable Moss-lim sd at the Stokely set, she belong to you? & M blushes—"belong." A weird concept. Does this sexy lady . . . &c. Ya ever hear a baldhead ('nother) hustler talk? Tryin' a say if you don't deal with it mah man, ah mus . . . at first sex and circumstance . . . sly nights they hugged in the dark like others do. The smoothness, incredible sensuousness, pulled him. Yet the world, in its hookups, had other plans . . . almost. Except in the tide of their feeling they rolled over them, smashed the barriers, in FS it meant what people "thought." And love boiled in them. From feeling, to admiration, to need. And they, between the icepick words they cd hurl at each other, forced a relationship so broad, a world, an epic, depended upon it to survive. And they did.

Define that, then. Like pins and needles in a novel. Dreadful reality, it builds itself and demands itself for precision. The fierceness of love. The hot oil thrown upwards out the eyes nose mouth ears, interweaved, grown inside, corresponded into. They wd hate each other inside love, burn each other's playhouse down to build a fortress wherefrom to kill the dead. She picked pimples off his face to try to make him better and he was so shy she felt sometime he didn't even love her. Which was just the space they come to each other across—from way 'cross town, and then some. But then read a history yall, of we together raised ourselves to free. Our love was an explosion slowmotion double time played back in the eyes of the anonymous freedom fighters slow poets in doorways celebrate, high note, hold it, crooning. Soft night, we hear ourselves. Amidst the hard days to struggle just to be close. Can you feel we in this? Our growth. Our desert time. Our coming inside each other's heart. Our births. Our tragedies and deaths. Our dogged, stay on it, pump waves of life and mysterious force explain themselves in our arms, in our hot hard tones. Can you understand how finally they were not in love but were love, sharing themselves with anybody. And finally they shared themselves w/ themselves. And had a buncha children who cd quote Lenin at 6.

Malik now more & more went to meetings, demonstrated for peoples' rights & against the Italian colonialists.

Barney knew he cd make a statement w/ the axe, but other work

seemed clearer, more direct. He got w/ Corliss + Mickey + we rest a' niggas to do. What Is To Be Done, Lenin asked.

We worked hard ya know. Posters, flyers. Believed in Black Power.
Mickey got married that same day he went down the street to make a
speech. In Finland Station, America came to rest. Its various angers colliding + heating each other. Harlems, Watts. Went off befo'.

We had come back + sat on a step to get up + work for Black Power. We
sat w/ some dudes we thot now didn't understand everything in the
world. Nobody did. Experience became superfluous. It was hard to talk
about deep feeling. And the Hearts. Bohemians. Both irrelevant like. But
life need a be analyzed, not turned off. Not fled from.

What was it in all being sd? What steel rods bound us? What pyramid
life was combed together? In the coming together, being together, departure of things. Look at it. Tell us what it is.

Barney sat in a meeting talking about meetings. About some evil folks.
About what need ta be did. Not black music, poetry, drama, or strange
lights off water. But a meeting, + then light stuff. Superficial jive. Pleasant
insults. Jockeyin'. Not really what you were reading, what you felt, who
you were. How we spent our inside life. What we finally wanted the world
to be & if you don't hold no conversation like that w/ folks, why're you
'round 'em? Like they was little children in the world. All unformed,
uncool, save what we flashed inside we noggin. Patronizing the world.
The pb intellectual sickness. Stand there, let it go down, is it real? The
idealist phenomenologist claims it all is real—what goes on in his head—
but past that he don't vouch for nuthin'!

If you not talkin' to 'em, why you there? We cdda sat + sd what is it we
want. & heard the contradiction. But who knew really, 'cept superficial
one-sided abstraction? As forces build, our movement seems to grow. All
forces collect (again) to attack the white man - & the woman! A higher
level tho, we all come. The other wing, my friend, is all, the other wing.
Are we learning the whole? Except we had some analysis cd save us.

Jack Roach is a good example, brats and sassies. Check it. Roach came
w/ wife (again had left a white woman (French lady)) & he not arty sec-
tor. He sold suits door to door, pots + pans. Wore them now, when we met,
shiney mohair vines of different fluorescences. A stiff turkey, always.
Laughed like a grimace. Wife a slender giggling yellow noddle who we felt
cd never be about what? Seriousness. Well, what was it we were asking?

Revolution? Ya see. Is that was it still what we're asking? From Hate Whitey. Flames sear the universe. But now we felt this is practical work. We working in the community. Ya see the fact of this work "in the community," from our twisted pb reference, let us think that that work cd be less "revolutionary" because 1) we didn't know what revolutionary was except rhetoric. And that had rose to the top of the ladder—fire & smoke. And when the busts came in the rebellion of '67, we tailed off maybe—not backing away—but unclear now, since America had been assaulted, but had not fallen, as what to do. So now look at Jeanie Roach, 2-lb wife of Jack Roach, who inna shiny suit, comes to talk of Dudes United. Smoke clearing.

They lived in Flithaven, a suburb of Finland Station. & so the fires of '67 never touched directly. But what cd be talked to w/ them? We had a theory now from the advanced west coast. From the land of Watts, where fires licked the sky. So weird a land, a movie star stepped off the screen to run the joint—or was it that the whole set was a film? (Work 10 hrs a day at some humbling gig & tell me, bro. Turn a lathe, punch a press. Stay on the line 10 hrs, twisting screws + getting a screw twisted in you—tell me as the flecks of steel curl around yr heels, red odor in yr nose, yr fingers harden, hands turn to rock, tell me bro, when you come home & sink into yr chair, is it real, or is it a flick?) But ya see the petty bourgeois arrogant abstraction. Like Corliss, Mickey, Barney from site to site screamin' full up. "Burn it, burn it, tear it up, rip it down! America must die. & all you niggers which dig it must burn up too."

W/ what reference? We mental workers, aware of the evil of white America. The "whiteness" of niggers. (That shd be analyzed, what that means, not run w /in abstraction—but go on mid-'60s roar.) What reality? Intellectual? Student? Artist? Saying yo' time has come, America. Malcolm was working class, degenerated to Lumpen, restored by faith. Ya see the connection? So the Panthers worshipped the Lumpen—sd everything is coming from them. We had a school afterwards for the corner Lumpen. A couple flashy ones'd throw number gold into the pot. They flew up the street. Shorty Moon, outta jail, come over talkin' Afrikan or Arabic, wherever we was. Had a name, Muhammad Jamal or somethin'. Until scag rise up, his eyes begin to close. What's happenin', Mo? He's gone again, dope bust, 6 mos.

The people, we were saying. Drunks. Bums. A couple of junkies. The people. (Tho we did reach yng people who were the actual. But them others—all lumpen, those society has ground to the ground.) The people? They at work!

Dig it, Dig it, Dig it. But we didn't. A bro showed talking Swahili, Dan Mwananchi. Ran it down. Systematized our collective ravings. Student reality.

PB reality. Deep + profound, organized all the free factors that wd. Arty section hung till fire ruled.

But look at it. Malcolm, our cross & message. As Salaam Alaikum, one form it took. His biography too. When Harlem & Watts took off. A lumpen expression. Bust out windows, run in the street. Hemmed up the crackers in Yoruba Land. We thot the people were "in the street" but that was just one class of them.

PB wuz in w/ lumpen. Match came, check it. Romance. Bros + sisters on the corner. Patronizing distortin'. Our people at work bro. Not composing music or poetry or hanging on corner. Those are 2 classes. But Allah connects us. Cain't deal w/ Allah. Even w/ Malcolm. Got to go on. Really. What it is? Who knows? Talk to each other about it. Dan Mwananchi came + ran it down. The enemy + how to do it to him. Watts rights. Mad infernoes in the night.

The lumpen + Islam. Run by the pb. Metaphysics + idealism. Patronizing abstraction. The people on the corner. As Salaam or what have you. By the time Mickey was in California, the armies of the lumpen had formed. Led by the PB. In black uniforms like the people in the street. (Whites, of course, ran w/ it, gave it a formal non-meaning, like rock group fantasy—The Street People—a white youth lumpen—really! Too much! Mickey Mouse gone mad. Donald Duck the governor! & we Mickey + Sivella fist fightin' 'cause he draggin' her around callin' her his wife + hadnt married her—true bohemian style.) Volta (lower) sd, "That shit Mickey + Sivella doin'," to say what?

All this walked in the nigger house. The west coast Union of Hearts. Spook shack other places. Woogie Manor. The Jig Bldg. Coon House. And then Huey Newton innovated w/ the actual heat (after Rob Wms + Deacons did a real Boogaloo for JB to cop). They stood w/ rifles at a poetry reading. PB + lumpen—some working class youth—arty wing impressed & so set it to music. But the same contradiction in the nigger house. The gun carrying wing & the arty wing. Tho that wasn't exactly it before. We cdn't get a double line. It never was that clear. A buncha elites, in big red hats. Sd you cdn't smoke and some a' us smokin' two

packs a' gauloise a day—arts group—but that aspect created nuthin' &
demanded authority but had no skill or talent except for disruption. All
they cd do was block stuff & march around. Drivin' folks away. They was
so great.

On west coast, it at least had come to arty vs gun but the artys didn't
even dig it except Everett Hatchet, newly released from the slam, where
he had rejected the blatantly metaphysical idealist wing of Black über Alles.
When Malcolm was killed, Hatchet sd openly it was Elijah Muhammad
killed him and became openly anti-Muslim.

But the ripoff was the Trots got to him then. Like we ran into the Trots
1st, dealin' w/ Rob Wms. They offered 5 bills to get on a committee and
make it interracial. Heroically, we refused after caucusing in the john.
Ironic + halfway Looney Tunes, 'cause the chief spokesmen for our group
were married to white women! (Tho Carl Lloyd sd his wife, like Kwame
Nkrumah's, was *Egyptian*. We blinked. Why was that?)

And thru the women they'd struck again. Sicked a female lawyer—who
eventually "freed" him. Went to see him all the time. Wrote him. & that
formative stage of the mind opening to its liberation—cd be connected
to the white lady. Paragon of the left. So weird tho that Hatchet's woman
later, a lightskinned pb student world killer, sd Everett was gotten out of
prison by a white woman. We cdn't do that. Yeh but he was put in there by
one too. By a ruling class of 'em.

Ya see, Trotsky ain't had no home. If he went for that, he'd been a
Zionist. Its opposite was to go straight out the other way—wasn't no
home. Ain't nobody got nairn. It's the world or nuthin' + ain't nuthin'
revolutionary except it says we stealin' a world. Except that turn into its
opposite, 'cause if don't nobody never be revolutionary, then a world full
a' counterrevolutionaries 'cept yr style group. & finally all you talkin'
about is elections, not even that, but a flat rate gadfly style. & its actual
form is Jewish culture. In fact the whole left sometimes, white version, is
just one form of Jewish culture or another. From pop to op to cop.

Everett was copped by the Trots or Poptrots as it turned out. Poptrots
called themselves the new left. (Now, from side to side, all agrees we need
a new Communist Party. We needed one for a while ago. But most a' them
sayin' it is the reason it's needed + they need not be in it—ya askin' us!)

The Blackies—were arty, metaphysical (Islam or Cosmic) pb mostly.
And Everett cdn't cry Black Black Black &c. (He meanwhile easin'
around corners—some nights the whole house knew he was yodelin' in

the canyon w/ the Jewish Trot. A pregnant colored lady polarized w/ the artsy black metaphysicals. But this ain't the one we quoted. (What happened to the child?))

The level the confusion occurred was likewise like it was. A gun to the head. Advanced now. W/ lumpen + WC gunmen backing it. The lumpen transformed to PB, Trot style, took it all, for a time. Really to: Trot PB idealism. Left Bohemian. Even to protectin' white boys goin' for revolutionary. Paper came out w/ a notice sd, "Do not bother our friends." Trots all over the sky prob'ly lit up. How far that box took 'em. Some box + some books, like indians + booze. Let 'em rip off the world.

No talk at all. One wing, northern Calif. Dispatched. That shit that Leroi Jones + Ron Karenga talked. Offed. Threw some PB arty metaphysicians out on the street. & the get down got down.

But dig, Everett was balanced till PB nationalist elements romanticized, got took off. What Black there was, Black Nationalist Idealism, got took off. Roy Johnson got popped & that part of west coast Black Power was put inside and the new PB Trot ideas, White left bohemian, got to do its thang.

We all was in that. From new wing, old wing, left wing, right wing. A shelf of twisted idealism. And as an answer to screams of the whole of the PB, from "Hate Whitey" to "Whitey Is Revolutionary," the lumpen leaped & got it on. Yeh. Remember the mid-'60s, bro? Martha & the Vandellas sd "Dancin' in the Street." Was banging in our blood. We'd rule our world. Yet? Not full up like before we'd hit the actual street, but this was what set up the calm downbeat later. When we'd say we got to work w/ the community. Run from the lumpen + picked up w/ the other wing of the PB.

The reason. All the screamin' didn't go out into a void. It hit the VanAllen belt & come back. The lumpen raised, the metaphysical Blacks + Idealist Blacks screamed on of war cries. In Finland Station the ground caught fire.

Mickey Corliss Barney rode around in a car shooting at police. Shot out the windows of a shoe store. Saw two plainclothesmen at Maple + Cummings + sprayed the car they ducked behind. Glass flew out in one of 'em's face. Turned the truck + beat it up past the big fires. Saw the police in a war. W/ fire + running bloods. Store bottles + now + again shots banging at their heels. Two shots into the radiator of a prowl car. Aimed at the twirling red light, missed, tore out a supermarket window. Turned the corner, one cop cd see them as they moved, firing at him, his body was facing the store where 3 bloods hit the big glass w/ a shopping cart.

The cop turned + fired hitting one in the face. He died then. The others, with six packs piled in the wagon, split in the smoke.

The 3 PB artists parked behind a project where Corliss worked, went down the cellar, took emergency stairs to a store room. Lowered a frosted window + cd see in the closing darkness the panorama. The whirling red eye. Emptied 2 32 pistols at one police car, shattered glass, sent them sprawling to the ground. Poked a rifle to fire & the cops were answering, 3 stories higher in somebody's house. You cd hear the glass + children screaming. Mickey emptied his rifle, a 22, at the cops, up under the front wheels, blew out the tires, drove the cop under the car. Then the three of them split, ran out in the hall. By this time, families had moved in the hall to keep from getting shot. A dude was whippin' past them, goin' upstairs, w/ a 44 shotgun. A start, a wave, stiff + fluid, too fast to stop, "Hey" like a thrown greeting & called behind. They know somebody's shootin' from here. The blood on the steps goin' up sd, "I got another way out." And they kept goin' down to the car. Pulled off, goin' anywhere. Everywhere. 2 pistols, a rifle, a box of bullets + the war of the worlds was on.

Who're our allies? Whatta ya mean? The people. You see 'em! We know the enemy. Whitey, whitey, kill whitey! It never occurred to us that the people had no guns. That the people crouched in their homes. Or were coming from work, to get jammed in the streets. The lumpen roared. And a few PB adventurers popped a couple rounds. & thot that was the war. That 46 shots was a war. Against 46,000. Against whitey? But where do whitey get his stuff? Is it merely whitey? The cars, troops, rules, fire power. Is it him?

They came up a side street to get around to the other side, looking to the corner, a violent tv show passing at one end. Now, at the perimeter, they cd see police cars racing back + forth trying to stop the lumpen from ripping off. The 3 stopped at a small white mom + pop + pulled open the gate—broke the window, took petty cash out the cash register, & a couple cases a' beer. Rolling down the hill, fire stood on the roofs & made shadows on the walls + jumping in the streets. From the outskirts of the action, they circled + popped away at cars, frantic pigs, whirling them around at the sound of close-up gunfire coming at them. There was a blood wounded in the streets, legs dangled out off the curb, moaning + crying. Next to him a case of Seagrams 7. They picked him up, put him in the truck, wound through the maze of killers + victims, to the hospital, where the blood was detained, arrested immediately because of the gunshot.

In the hallway, bloods full a' blood. Bandages soggy. Stretchers carried in streams of wounded. Some of 'em dead. Frantic workers, cynical doctors, frightened cruel police, all mashed together by a dying social system. We thought it wd die that night! But it was & is today dying, carrying so many in its fall.

Adventurists really came to think about it + we did, that's what we were. In a new truck with new pistols firing into the night at fleeting hate forms. Gettin' kicks at a higher level. We didn't kill nobody (wd've been our whimperin' answer), tho Mickey tried, it shd be sd. He brought the bead directly to rest on the neck + face of a resting piggy. Blam. The shot hit a house, tore out the glass & made the face there wheel around + start to fire. We'd never even got to a point where we cd even shoot. Which is why these bloods always be losing on the streets—the cops practice shooting bullets, we practice shooting bull—

Energy wound round + round. Bullets spent in walls + poles + windows, alerting the porkers to the fact of an unseen malice. That they cd then respond to massively, like U.S. troops in VietNam, just shoot shoot shoot. The tires go down, the grass gets wounded, the ground, the stones, all shot up. Just shoot shoot shoot till all life is gone & then they felt they did sumpin'. (Like the one-eye puppy the baldhead barber had. He snap his fingers. Shorty his name was. "Do sumpin'," he sd to the dog. The dog'd sit up. "Ok, now do sumpin' else." The admirable response to the formal circumstance of training.)

Our training, individualistic petty bourgeois artists, trying to kill America because we hated it. No, hated white people! Why? Because they were evil! They killed & hurt people. & they were weak + never followed through in principled relationships. Mickey shot again & missed—bullet slammed into a fire hydrant. Bloods skipping 'cross the street w/ boxes, a dude w/ a new motorcycle blasts by, "Mother fuckaaaaaaaas," disappear into the smoke. Instead the gestapo shoot into a window where the 3 pre-Marx Bros cajoled + split, + hit a mother of 12 square in the throat, killing her instantly. Her children ran in the hall, screaming + falling down the stairs. Her oldest son, 17, gets down to the street & we see him come out the door running straight at the police cars w/ a butcher knife. Corliss cries as the crackers kill the boy. Barney vomits. Mickey shoots & hits one of the blacks fleeing in the ankle + drops him to the pavement in murderous pain. The police run up on him, shooting straight into his screaming.

A spastic slow motion, Mickey, for a moment tried to turn the gun on us. Finally, on himself. His eyes slid around, like something terrified and dead at the same time. It all came down. At that minute, moment, a life, lives, together. And the mad people we dodged all our lives got their fullest laugh. We weren't sure that what we saw had happened, but it seemed a signal, of our sterility and weakness. That what we called ourselves, doing theory on roller skates posing as action, had already turned into something else. And we. And we.

We pulled off then amidst bouncing feedbacks, tears vomit & frustration. The results of our own real training. & Corliss wheeled the truck down the street. To a door where Barney sd Ricky Carter, the tuba player, was workin'. Ricky was on the stand playing. Hell danced outside a few blocks away. Old women, yng boys butchered. & hip niggers in sharp clothes blew dead dreams to catchy accents. At the tables fairly yng + middleaged niggers snappin' their fingers to the roll of sound.

But we were there too, our training sd., & stood at the bar & ordered bourbons + beers. "What's happening my man," the bartender sd. "The motherfucker's burning," sd Mickey. "Let the motherfucker burn." The bartender looked up w/ a sly smile. "It'll be here tomorrow."

Rickey finished + a few people dug it and clapped. It was chilly in the joint, for summer. Probably the air conditioner. Rickey sd, "Hey yall what's to it? Them folks still burning up the ghetto?" A whore uncrossed her legs + tried to pick up somebody's eye.

At Rickey's house, they smoked bush + talked about the end of America, not heeding the bartender. Rickey had good smoke. The three, now blind + silly, got in the truck + crashed into a police barricade, were beat up, arrested & booked for possession of deadly weapons.

* * * * *

In city jail we cd look down at the street. By now, on the 2nd day, the yng faggots of the national guard were called in to make believe they were the army + frighten somebody. They guarded the corners, smoked, & wished they were back in college. Occasionally someone shot at them + they hit the street & then shot in that direction for the next hour, hitting nothing and wasting the taxpayers' money. Plus they were shooting at the taxpayers at the same time.

We saw them shoot one sister in the breast, then throw her against the wall, gun at her head. Dragged her dead husband or boyfriend out the car—then let the woman pick up her baby & hang on the wall till the ambulance came.

The 3rd day the police swore they were going to kill all niggers. The words seeped even into the jail. A white fire chief trying to put out a fire on a Tom McCann shoe store was shot in the back of the head + died instantly. Also a white police sgt was in critical condition w/ a bullet in the stomach. Two or three also suffered lye burns, 2nd & 3rd degree, from some sisters who dumped pots of lye on their heads from the window. One sister, alone in the house, heard someone storm up the stairs, & when the door slammed open, the lye flew, mixed w/ cocola + alaga syrup! When the cop recovered, he be a ugly mammy topper.

The 3rd night shots came into the jail downstairs where the screws hung. Lights out. Cops shot out a streetlight. Joni James sings "Love Is a Many Splendored Thing." A group a' dudes slip out they cell + down the back stairs, go out through the latrine + split. We stayed.

The 4th day Johnny Green is killed in JoRae's bar, shot 35 times.

Finally calm is restored blacks & whites. We then are freed on bail. The Black Power Conference, Karenga, Jones, Rap Brown, McKissick accuse the U.S. of Genocide, and ask for the U.N. to enter. We were there hanging on the walls. Days + nights of foolishness + terror. Rebellion, yet where is the rebellion in us? All that we did was in us to start. Idle, finally, tragic ineptness in reality.

The U.S. says the problem is Racism! And we agree. Hate whitey. Whitey in yall is what ya really hate. Whitey in us is what we really hate.— But don't hate it enough.

We are sitting now w/ a group of dudes in ties or even sport shirts deciding who will be city mgr.

After we got outta slam, we passed out leaflets, opened an office, talked millions of words about Black. About Hate Whitey. Black is Beautiful. Black Power!

In Ct. The judge was a crazy man, try to send us away. An old Jew, who thot we talked too much. Too arrogant. Barney brought a mouthpiece to court & wd play "Chasin' the Trane" sometimes. We booed when the prosecutor passed. They lined up cops + they testified to seeing the vehicle + being shot at. One cop accused us of killing officer Zizza. It was stricken from the record. One cop leaped to his feet when Barney called him a dickless faggot. Barney told him he used to screw his wife till she got the claps. First person he ever met w/ claps around the mouth. The cop reached for his piece + the lawyer called for a mistrial.

We were convicted & the judge read from a book Mickey wrote to sentence us. He read it w/ passion + meaning like he knew exactly what was being sd. Tho Mickey made fun of him & called him a senile old Jewish fool . . . whose mama went down on any Arab she cd find!

People cried + Corliss wanted to fight the cop. They put us in a speeding car w/ the siren screaming, light twisting, + zoomed 40 miles to the prison right away. 3 days later we were back on the street, agitating against white folks. Hate Whitey!

We decided today that Gip Fatson is to be the city mgr. Oily Hairs, Jim Porter, Ray West are councilmen. Good funny bros. Comical—don't hate whitey, exactly, but see the need for black power.

The next time we went on trial, we beat it. Case thrown out. In D.C., a short dude w/ a white pulldown hat + dark glasses meets w/ Jim Coates, spec. Gip Fatson's flick, Oily's, Jim's, change hands. We picture too change hands. We in dashiki now. Learning Swahili, "Habari Gani," we say we greet you. Short dude dress in "perfect taste." Noel Coward for sure. Coates comes to Finland Station to look around.

In a hallway, the sister's face lights up, we say black, a city mgr will change this. We need change. Coates looks in store windows. Sees us. The sister says yes. I know.

The children have a newsletter. It has a flick of Gip—Oily Porter + Ray. They run down the street, laughin', giving them out to all who pass. Black is Beautiful!

A truck, like Harlem sound, w/ JB "Black + I'm Proud." We strut arms around we love one, handing out leaflets. At night a crowd of yng folks, students, sons + daughters of the PB + some W. Class. Streamin' in and out of our place.

We speak. We must control our destiny. We must have Self-Respect, Self-Determination, Self-Defense. 300 years is enough. 300 years, we ain't going for no more. Forget it, Whitey, we ain't going for no more. Dig it! No more! Gip, Oily, Porter, + Ray come on next to speak. We end it Black Power (the fist). Soul session music plays Black delusion. We see the world changing before our eyes, dancing through our fingers.

An old brother, Tom Russell, meets w/ us, run down how we gotta get Gip + co to promise what they gonna do for the people. Have a convention, we figure, where we choose from all who want to run, see if the people we want really have the support of the people. Posters, signs, sound cars. Celebrities. A hip comedian comes in + tells jokes about white folks. After the session, he leaves w/ a boy + girl, both yng + white + hip to what's goin' on.

A slick jazz preacher in cowboy jacket + jeans. "Love is the Answer. Love each other + Unify. Unity Is the Answer. Love + Unity." He has a big wood cross around his neck. He checks a reefer out his breast pocket & mashes it down quick. Nobody sees it but Barney, who just gave up reefers last week, so he talks bad about the preacher.

"Everybody join hands + swear to love each other + be unified!" Everybody do. "We can beat them what nots + what have yous." He didn't wanna say white folks. A yng girl had a orgasm when preacher Cole stretched in his tight pants to say, "We're on God's side." It was real good tho, a real warm feeling settled on everybody. Cole Younger sd, "Give it up. Reach in yr pocket, give it up." Another sister got wet, a dude laughed + clapped. Everybody got a little dough up right quick. Which was good. We hadda pay the dude's carfare & what not + still a couple nickels for posters.

A black woman politician w/ hard wig under a red hard straw. A lisp + buck teeth. She says she's fighting against the inequities of society. She gets thunderous applause, slips into her chauffered Lincoln + splits amidst the cheers.

A short, bowlegged politician in blue striped suit. Weeps as he preaches about "This is the Black Man's finest hour! In Congress where I am the 1st Black man to represent my state. Didn't you black people get together to get me in? So yall here in Finland Station can get together. Unity is the answer. And in coming together like this we show we know the arithmetic of power. We're ready for presidents, not only city mgrs. But prove yrself, Finland Station. Get behind yr leaders. Support yr righteous Black Bros & sisters to lead us all to freedom." He then started singing "Somewhere Over the Rainbow" in a weird key in a weird falsetto. Old women fanned between they knees.

Corliss + Mickey met w/ Fatson + he promised a black superintendent of school + police chief. Conversation was like this:

Corliss—Ah—you know we supportin' you. W/ everything we got. We gonna really push this total commitment.

Fatson—That's good. I've got confidence.

C—And we think certain changes you see ought to be made. Like we been talking about.

Tom R—Yeh, black police chief, & black superintendent of schools.

Fatson—Yeh, of course.

Of course, it sat there, a grey flower amidst the colored ones. Was this, of course, power. Of course. Black. Of course. (Let the sun stream through the broke window of the little office. Let the faces of the candidates + then the circle of united brothers be seen + digested. The teachers, yng preachers, storekeepers, salesmen, yng doctors, students be seen smiling. & the here + there refracted stare, albeit ensmiled as well, of a few like Corliss, w/ knives in their skull forever. Hate whitey buttons replaced they hearts who hope—instead of struggle—but the only struggle is against the iceman, whom we've come together to kill!

Show old niggers, some yng, in open collaboration w/the wop warlord. Threatening people. Collecting bribes. Trying to live it up like old times, except an ICICLE we were pressing in their ear.

One Sunday the red hats, just before we broke w/ them, rounded up all of the warlord's niggers & herded them together. Actually Dahran, the leader of the red hats (still another wing of the aspiring PB) knew the chief of the stooges & he merely asked for a meeting. Corliss felt such a meeting, a unity meeting, was good to see if these bloods cd understand real Black power.

W/ red hats, w/ kaffiyahs draped around their faces, like Sheik assassins, they lay on the walls menacing the stooges. Mickey, Corliss, speak, urging unity. The stooges grin. One raises a hand, "Why?"

When they leave, the ynger ones & some of the old go to the same bars the united dudes we with be in. They sit & discuss their mutual fortunes. Mickey, Corliss, the others lecture a small group about no drinking, no smoking, no meat-eating, even. Some agree, some grin, some look at the floor & they leave. Some to the same bars to drink. Some home to drink. Some w/ chicken legs in bags they eat in the car. Hate Whitey!

The small group grows, in dashikis & sisters in bubas + lapas. Mwananchi speaks + lays the ideological support for Hate Whitey. "Buy Black, Think Black, Live Black, Sleep Black, Love Black!" & *that* crowd goes hysterical. Outside the bldgs are shot up.

We & All

Boarded up, silence hangs heavy at night. Killed place, life beats tho. Beats in us. Who are the sons + daughters of life. We sit & listen to Mwananchi tell us about our beauty, our history, our potential for new life. The Impressions sing, "We a Winner." The Dashiki wearers + the suit wearers are on the same shelf still, huh? From one end of the shelf to the other. Rhapsodized by our image, crying "Power, Power."

And the power came! Posters. Flyers. Sound Cars. Canvassers. Phone Squads. Parties. Speeches. 10 sisters sing. Now Is the Hour for Black Power! Movie Stars. Politicians. The Cream of Black + progressive White Hollywood showed.

And finally on the day of the election. We walked. Rode. Flew. & 10 hours later a buzz caught & lifted. A drunk wandered out the bar and by his self til another appeared. A sober sister, smiling, still danced with him when he sd, "We got power, Baby—Dig it. We got power."

Horns started to sound. Cars dizzy in the streets. Niggers started stumbling out. Phones. Radio. TV. Mouths. Upstairs. Downstairs. In the streets. Bars rang. Drinks turned up. On the House. Yng boys danced in the playground. Old ladies wept. We sung. Where's Gip? Front ta TV. Corliss smiled. A crowd gathered. Cole Ynger spoke to them and sd how he had planned this victory two years ago in a Holiday Inn.

We hucklebucked down Main Street. Finland Station turned big nigger funky. We, 10,000 of us or more, jammed the streets and jerked, Boston monkied, horsed, twisted & mamboed.

The man in the cool cute suit with the dark glasses smiles. He picks up the phone and calls his man. His man in a hotel room looking down at us. Phone to his ear. Not even a pistol. Still he carries some kinda heat. A grimace. A menace. A connection to the ultimate danger. Smiles, down at us. We dancing, M + the V, in the streets.

We were, he said, yeh, of course talking. And the man in cool hat called Fatson. He went of course. Tom sd, you know. Yes. That is expected. In the street. A big bus poured musicians out. They tumbled into the Hall. Cole Ynger spoke, of the Holy Ghost, & the words bounced off the wall.

435

Mitchell & Nixon & Agnew & dying J Head Giver Hoo Art in Heaven.
Heaven has to be full of FBI men, if the streets are made of gold. It must
be just like America. A capitalist state w/ a racist culture.

Dancing, dancing until tomorrow. We beginning. We be feeling good.
Real good. We be walkin' up the street, feelin' good. White folks last
night start to fighting. Some busted each other in the lip. Bopped CBS in
the face & lit up the Jews thereby. [This is not meant as an anti-semitic
remark!] They start running in the streets like niggers . . . like niggers.
"Let's go get 'em," somebody says. "Naw, call the police. Let them do it!"

In the sunshine days that follow, when dancin' turns to grins, Fatson
flies to D.C. & talks to Mitchell. When he enters the office (& this is
hearsay) we man, he sweatin' he hands. To meet a big white dude like
him. Even a ugly baldhead rascal like Mitchell [He's Powerful! Was what
they tell you.]. Crazy wife & all. She look like the kinda crackerette buy ol'
niggers' underwear to put 'em under her pillow + sniff when JM cdn't cut
the mustard, which was, ya' have to admit, frequent as a mf!

We hear they tol' Fats he was part of 'Murica ('Murica, 'Murica, God
shed his grace on thee). That he, thas what we heard, betta be cool 's the
way we heard it. Either be cool or be cold. The street talk laid this out. A
wolf ticket from the top began our brother's reign. But maybe, a dim of
red lights & dark glasses, w/ heat w/ a silencer in the desk, a file electronically selected shows Fats naked w/ the Fat yaller bitch he sleep with
(ain't his wife), 'specially the one of him pearl divin' in the vulture's cup!

A sweep of low imagination.

The truth.

We ran this to ease ourselves. "Mitchell ran a cold game on him," the
brother'd say, to make us feel better. But I thought we felt good. I thought
we was walking quick + light on the street. Ready for anything, is the phrase.

But ya see, ya' wasn't

But we see, we wasn't

Was not payin' attention.

Poppin' yr chest in Swahili, what was the turgid reality? Whatta you
mean—the laid-out rap? Amilcar Cabral sd in 1965, in Habana. We was in
1970, & cdn't hadn't didn't dig it. Nkrumah sd [wiped out in '66 because
the book in '65 was the whistle, the wakeup we didn't understand! Except
the space began to appear. The concerns remained in a way the same but
new happenings far away from the real happenings. The new concerns of
the day were the same concerns in different place]. Black power.

One morning we met w/ Fat after the inauguration. They played one a' Barney's tunes at the inauguration. The one Barney called "Progressive Perfection." Some Jew dude put words to it a little sister sang. "Gip Fatson, our rising star. Gip Fatson, our rare example. Gip Fatson, take us to yr bosom." Complete w/ high trumpet part (an octave above) just like Mickey's.

There was no room on the visitors' stand. So we took one of the empty seats. Two dudes sat in it; the other stood. The grey preacher droned on. Too stiff to summon the Lord, no doubt. Crowd surged around the stand, new life in our town, the world.

Meet w/ him in his office, the next time, later. Meeting was a thing, we didn't want to experience it. But we were coming there. Going in there. Where was here? Who were we?! There was others there. Some never left. Some wd always be there if there was, according to our man in the cute cool suit, Civilization. But others. Italian Patriots. The dross we knew. Throw 'em all out, was a good line. Throw 'em all out! Grins. Why not? Civil Service! Name some other stuff. But who was there in the shadowy fill in to. Who was not the old Italians waiting for retirement! Somebody—always—respond. A later letter. Who? We saw yng dudes—white boys suddenly—technicians & the peace corpse. Dead body Jesuslike inserted on the scene. Social Tampax. Stop the flow. Were they the CIA? Or just the Woodrow Wilson fellows? And the difference? Between straight ww fellow + CIA—Well CIA dudes carry guns. Yeh but if ww fellows carried guns, they'd be the CIA. There has to be some distinction.

"Mental aid," is what Touré called it. Sd some a' these dudes always asking mental aid from imperialism!

It was going down so cool tho. Militants, why the sudden calm? The super cool in place of—well, ah well. Just that—the confusion. Cd you see the skin scraping off + beast mouth foam? What? Naw!

Only the cool "low key" movement. What kind a' movement? Adjustments. Many cool meetings. Cool. While we put great stock in the fact that the city mgr wd come big shot here. (Yeh, but outta whose gun?)

Machines coming in. Like stuffed animals on wheels. But yng underfoot. A fog of positive feeling, like fog around our ankles (or heads, like the way Brigadoon look).

We were enjoyed. Full of it. But savored, finally, by others. Jewish opportunists. Irish opportunists. A-S opportunists, swiftly moving, in the set up.

Gip sits one day & relates a dream (traum). He is a dreamer (trauma). Less profound than, less sincere, less militant than Dr. King. But he wd quote King if he cd remember stuff.

Gip's Dream

"Suddenly I was walking in the halls of the white house. It was dark, but Nixon accompanied me. Shadowy figure, trying to push the shadows aside by smiling. He begins to explain the role of people in his kingdom, of the me's, the you's, the we's, the him's. We walk in a slow circuitous route. What we looking for? But talking abstractly about everything. Finally, at one pt, he made some pt. Reached out his hand & gave me a bill. Money. I looked at it close. The dream cleared. It was a sloppily folded five dollar bill. Well that was, like, empty—but significant. Empty, 'cause 5 dollars ain't nothin'. Significant because the president, Nixon, gave it to me. Ya understand?

"And then we went out the dark corridors & through the press room where the pressies assembled, looked up, staring, then past that, we went somewhere else. Nixon at one pt holding my hand or at least it seemed like it. I didn't understand."

"Then what happened?" we asked. Gip sd, "Then I woke up. I was back here."

Yah, those days fell in place like invisible dominoes—carrying the message. Not Malcolm but another message clear.

We wandered back & forth, talking the positive. But in the corners an unresolved question. Talk the talk I 'splained you—out + carry message. Suddenly we cd see that Gip had other folks suddenly assembled from somewhere. Not just the old hats + heads. Varicose-veined hunchback Italian women or the yng ones w/ the hard upsweeps. But a herd a' dudes from somewhere else. But we knew what Gip Fatson really knew abt the world. Ya knew. We knew. But, but—we was to be there, you know, w/ the word. Ah, ya kidding. Unprincipled hypocritical relationship.

[A dude appeared in front of city hall w/ a uniform on + a badge *GOD*. He sat & checked people out. He wasn't shy tho. You say, "Hey man, what's happening." He explain the whole thing to you. But in a military uniform, dress cap + all. We dug that.]

But a relationship based on yall's correctness is just elitist Jesus nigger stupidity. All shd be correct. We didn't know no incorrect really, tho. It was just that we knew Gip Fatson wasn't Lumumba.

But how did Kenyatta get to where he's at, the sacrilegious Baptist asks putting the roach into the end of a gauloise. It is slowly explained.

Hey—like dig, remember the culture committee. Create a Popular Culture. Transform all cultural institutions for the use of the people. At the 1st meeting—Fats actually had put Mickey on the committee. The dude from Prudential, Al DeRogatis. He says he can't be on no committee w/ Mickey. Ya know DeRogatis, he's the good guy in the NY Giant TV football games. But see how electronics transforms—like a weak guitar player they wanna say is Freddie Green behind the electricity.

But the Fats cops! Yeh, he just cops and lets the thing die.

He was goin' w/ this two-ton yaller lady at the time. A swollen ladyfinger. His secret squeeze. Hell, we seen 'em paddin' around the park trying to drive some a' the OZs away. One night his ol' lady flush mallah yallah out—outside her crib in the lowrise. Start to jawin' & cussin', sd if she *evaaaa*. But ol' plump lump move to another crib. High up this time—to search the night for her lovah.

But that's relevant. But see if you can dig this. We was used. Not just be here thinking abt somebody turned right on you or stuffed dummies did the trick. We was used very consciously—as naïve unpolitical individualist petty bourgeois punks who cd not enforce what was in our heads because that wasn't nothing but idealist nonsense. It wasn't based on material conditions. What it is? We begin now, huddled, to ask.

The meetings wkly began to falter. Some on the committee showed up w/big jobs. Nathan Wms the 3rd became Poobah Almighty of Poverty. He was a exSNCC (maybe?) nigger who, having been worked clean in Yale + Amherst was compleat w/ law degree. To show the depth or height of his collaboration. So hip was he that not only was he part of the oppressed nation (oh yeh? for how long?) but he also had a degree in understanding the oppression! (Yeh, but dass who they you we was.) We is. No, the move to kill it, kill it, smash that rubber-coated wire leading from yr heart to they designs. Class sick. Like visible dominoes they join up. Rank in the ranks of. Those wd-be enemies got gigs as soon as the clean partisans. Dirty partisans had to get secret type gigs.

Put 'em all together, they spell Sell Out!

"Why are we with these people?" later she sd. "What do we need w/ these people?" later she sd. As it rolled out. Not all at once but later. A year—the smile had closed & opened at the same time. It poked out more was what the whole face under the lip protracted. "He looks like a pig to me," later she sd this. Not the 1st days. We were happy. But even then, the night we won, she argued w/us about the celebration. Abt how Cole Ynger got there, to give orders.

Always we want it easy. We want to think up stuff + that be the answer. We thought it up, so here—live in the MF. But subjective egotism is not struggle.

It grew more + more obvious that Fats had they own agenda. & that he was putting distance. Like us in a way, he watched his words, supported us. But no not really. We *always* totally supported him then. Except ya didn't, you never really believed nothin' except ya knew him + cd talk to him. The peepah didn't (they sd they did you told 'em they did) cdn't see him (ya told 'em they cd).

You can't Hate Whitey. We isn't all black. We for white. We for all. They sd it. And finally thass logical—you can't beat it. Ya gotta be for all the people. Yeh but . . .

Yeh, but nothing, we for all the peepah! Two tons a' yella meat shiver in apostasy. A naked one-ton yella man on tiptoe in front a mirror. A loud-speaker calling out instructions, he bend before the mirror. The one-ton yalla woman has a similar set up, calesthenics + chocolates on the bed. To eat during breaks. Crawl roach. Run out. Eat sickness eat.

Meanwhile these curlecues of power. And all the assembly toss a haughty bow. All together. We can't hate whitey. And we are backwards pointing out the injustices of the whites. In a working class town like Finland Station, amidst the spiraling towers, madmen lurk at the tips inside. Trying to kill us for certain. Going over they books to scrutinize they game. We went on, even knowing that. That they up in them towers watched us die on closed circuit. That they orchestrated it. The composers, choreographers, directors. All hedged in those towers to regulate the rest. Yet we fought fat crackers in the street. Like the dude they call Captain Spaghetti. All he say was Pasta! + Boom a spaghetti lightning shoot across the sky + low + a hole, a 300 lb dummy in a red white + green jumpsuit w/ a red white & blue flag appears, eating a bowl of pasta fazool. His first intelligible words, "Martin Luther Coon!"

But the irony of that. The poor white, fighting for Marty Begnana's bit. His opening into the stock exchange. As turf.

While we wrestle on the pavement, exchange ethnic cusses. You can make it off dis, muskeeta-knee, at home on tape + on the air. Witness the crowd at which the mighty carabineri thrusts his emotive troots. It's named after the survival genius of America—who came into the world as peepahs + left as Amelicans. TOMS! Speaking to the surging crowd, "NIGGERS Ain't Shit." Or "Niggers *is* Shit." "They lie stink steal rape shuffle. They ain't like us, Yeaaaaaaaa!" Meanwhile, cross town we, righteous bloods sd, "White motherfucker need ta die outright. They lie steal hurt oppress rape enslave. They ain't like us, yeaaaaaaaaaaaaaaaaaaaa!" Albeit, my friend, the slave ship is no myth. The death by fire + hanging. The tar, the feathers. Niggers eyes rolling in the dirt. Clean-ass white-suit cracker!

But Gip rolls over singing in his sleep. His wife turns on a tape recorder hidden in the pillow trying to get the goods. Framed Z's paste themselves to the walls as flicks of he mind mood. We peepahs says what it is what is.

& look out a cloud at us, from a high, & smile or somethin'. Laugh, fall out, roll over, har har har har —

Spaghetti wrestlin'

Har har har

We wrestlin'

We even cain't talk with we wimmen. We can't even talk with we mens. We can't talk to we sometimes. Alligator lay out laughin'. Rain all down yr back.

Two sisters wrasslin' in the street w/ a pair a' scissors. One yng sister gets stuck in the neck, bleeding. Her white starch blouse turn blotchy. But then she turns the scissors round, against they huge black cow, + severs the fat woman's jugular. They both collapse. My god, my god.

We comin' up the stairs looking for junkies. The junkies + junky-pushers doin' they number. We call out, "Hey whatta ya niggers doin'?" They drop the shit + split. One trips, we kick 'em in the face. Two more, clean ones, head upstairs, & one wheels w/ a piece in his hand. Us hit the walls + hold there. The bloody one runs behind us, down the stairs, + breaks into an apartment + calls the police!

They come & bust us all. The junkies + clean pushers split.

Har Har Har Har.

Dress up get ready go. Now say all the stuff we need ya to, Har Har Har Har.

Heaven is a place where the laughers be.

Hell is a place where the laughed at can't flee.

The ones w/ the jobs were the ones to fight us streeties first. That was they gig. & some a' them, like N Wms III, had a streak of white individualism in them that wdn't even let them submit to colored no way. But see, they needed to be treated like the TH's* that showed now everywhere.

And inside the souls of the wd-be. The seriouses. Among our closest circle, which was not as close as it needed to be. There crept the contradiction, which aspect wd dominate. Because we were bourgeois, petty bourgeois, & workers. Students & intellectuals dialoguing about Hate Whitey. & now whitey was beat, at one level. But draw the curtain and reorganize so in a minute it'll be paradise!

Har Har Har Har.

Nathan Wms, ex SNCCer, he sd. Now High Poobah gen'l poverty div. Line up the troops, Nate—Hot Nate. He's a activist. He was w/ us. His main squeeze still is. But he no tie-wearin'—tie open, now be close, took tie on, tie off. Post-free. Pre-free. Was you in SNCC for real, Nate? Sure. But then that was college students.

Like the sit-in, where in the end Lloyd marries the white waitress who called the police to throw them in the street. They started chatting. She liked him. He sd he was a college student. That was bizarre enough. Freakish as she was. Her hair stood up on her neck, a cullid collitch studenk. She was from rib, georgia. & was only used to cullid like you usual see.

And Nathan was one a' dem. Trained in law. He now flowered. He cd strut + prance + think of stuff to say + do. He cd fling his sensibility open full up + *create*! Because that's what it finally all's about, Creation. Production. Linked to nature + people. Life, Creation & Production.

Nathan cd now be in charge as he was taught to be. Specially that he was in charge of all us. We . . . who were we. Bohemians, workers, petty bourgeois students like hisself, only he was dressed up, some dropouts [and the PEOPLE!].

He sat by Barney's old-lady-to-be one night. & talked his stuff. & why Barney don't like him. Mickey just thought he was corny. Corliss tried to

---

* Trojan Horse.

talk to him + Nate 3 wd say irrational kinds of egoistic things. Corliss didn't feel Nate cd *do* anything of value. Nate cd only talk to Corliss.

Mae sd one night, "Burt you don't love me, you love white women still. You put me down. You hate me. You always treat me like I'm stupid. You never talk. You never answer. You always w/ yr head in a book or newspaper."

This was like lye in the face 'cause Corliss had only one link w/ reality & that was his desperation to be correct & real in it. Tho reality escaped him because he wdn't insist upon it. That's why the confrontation w/ Fats came obliquely & through press releases, rather than face-to-face in a room, you fat traitor bastid. Mickey had to do that! You fat traitor bastid. You yellow roach-faced motherfucka. You big jelly apple lookin' muthafucka. That fat-assed bitch ya laid with, I hope Mamie stick her w/ a icepck!

Mae cdn't dig Corliss' ice-cold style. He was in headquarters, dealin' w/ the world. The world was in his head. Like he was Descartes in technicolor (as Grass Roots wd say, if he was alive).

Corliss had had the top layer of his skin seared off by tons of paper cuts. Proust, for instance, sitting there eating mountains of bullshit abt a French faggot swathed in bandages going back in time + space behind the taste of some tea, 8 volumes of that—cut away his hands, arms, legs— all outer extremities were shaved of sensitive skin—or was it the opposite, that the volumes gave off an invisible sticky liquid that covered the flesh + cut it off from feeling.

She smashed her hand through the window of a door + scarred her arm w/ criss-cross slashes. Right after they married, these eruptions— madness, crying, curses—began. "Go back to that white woman. I can't be white. I can't shrink + be no little bow-legged Jewish bitch."

But even so, Nathan's world sprouted life he also didn't understand. He also w/ us was a manipulator. Great Brown Father from Eastern School. Tho funny abt Nate, he never really got that look, you know, the *real* authentic Ivy that is the A-S badge of authority + excellence. Why? Still maintained a kind of Cecile B. DeMille–Robert Hallish style of post-anonymous ignominy. But his gig was to seal off us as anti-program. He was the right wing of us spelling out the transformation. The office was big, wide-windowed. He opened the blind more. Offered us a cigarette— we don't smoke—took some coffee. He then sd some stuff cd be done, but we can't do everything at once. Fats does some strange things—but we can get some things done (where is whitey?).

After we fight our way to the palace + mount the wall. Slay the sultan + drive out his viziers. One of our warrior-officers says, "We can get some things done."

Later he told someone them programs we had was OK, but the white man wdn't like 'em. In other words, he was the messenger—Naw, bro, he was the message.

A year later, Nathan was gone because he got too big for his britches. Thought he cd tell Fats what to do, when Fats, as Fats pointed out, was city mgr. That was Fats' final word on anything. He was city mgr.

A white light bathes you. From Jesus days. Drones silently its social magnetism. We has risen in it like Zombies & marched smiling thru the years.

We all had our chance [on this one shelf] 'round the corner—some others' shit. A bubble-eyed pimp get you pregnant. You shoot some dope in yr heart. A policeman blow yr ass loose. Thass 'round the corner, where Mae's folks live (& some of them see the light riz up nights to practice bein' Lauren Bacall models w/ Audrey Hepburn complexes). The white light say-aye, "Come on Neglews ready for the judgment. Ready for the good news. You can make it Jesus, kinfolks, just be ready to take up the cross" (a song).

So each minute it be bathing you (the white light). You feel this song imitatin' you in you, dancin'. Singin', "Come on Neglews, ready for the judgment. Ready for the good news. You can make it, Jesus, kinfolks, just be ready to take up the cross."

Like Fats had crossed us.

And each stop, there was another time to deal. To get on bd, the freedom train, where slick heads + yellow jewelry was created for the folk. Get ready, for the judgment.

The judgment, by whom? The editors of *The New Yorker*, probably, checking the labels of yr suits.

We cda been preachers, stomping around the circle of gold. We be saying singing our song "Come on Neglews." Straight out, for the folks to dig or run away from. Mad man killed Dr. King's mother had another message. Garbled. Distorted. Maybe give to him by somebody. But it was a message.

We didn't wanna be no preachers. Too tied up w/ ol' folks + face powder. Too many shiney shoes + jewelry. The shouting when they fell out was an event. Spooky. You cd check it, like was they gon' die or some shit.

Like the dead yng nigger. 30 years old + embalmed, a preacher + phd in education. Now he's qualified to go to heaven + be somebody. Take up the cross!

Cdda been in Colored School style. A doctor. Lawyer. Or Agnew's bodguard. Or head of equal opportunity program. Small Bizness Association. Head of all nigger Republicans or sumpin' sumpin'. Cda been sumbody + not no flashing image the people might some day need—Coughs blood. Wipes forehead.

What's the Image? Blank?

Naw its not Blank. Its Black. Black + in motion. Somebody. A mass. A body. Biggest body. The mass. Body of the people who are the life of the planet. "The major & decisive productive force." The People.

Or a pilot. We cdda been pilots w/ goggles on our forehead & leather jacket. But everybody have to be at the base to see us walk around hooked up so clean.

At the isle of the dead, we cdda been that. Cold away + gone. A vulture sit on our chest + sing Ohoo "Take up the Cross." We tried out to be a officer & they thought we was crazy & flunked all a' us.

Cdda been officers in his majesty's SAC. Cdda had gol' + bars + been in a little cement house on a island in the middle of the Caribbean. Or in Germany. In Arabia. Anywhere. Whattabout Japan?

"Take up the cross."

Cdda been artises. Paintin' + pantin'. Bitch pullin' in technicolor news-reels. Jet set. The Set set. Profound feces ticklin'. Isolate breath fumes. Everything abt us then is up for grabs. Cdda been immortal. Like Babe Ruth + Tex Ritter. But more serious, cdda been really important to the growth of Wesern Civilization!!

(Dig it?)

Look, there we is wit' we robe on. Wit' we square sky. We's gettin' a deep pluma, says "WATCH these motherfuckers"! No says you is who they is *Now* (Dig it?) or WELCOME, TRAVELER or Dig it! Whatever, amongst the folds of dazzling gown. We staggers toward the bathing light. The light now saying, openly, warmly, so all (amongst our tribe) cd hear, "Take up the Cross!"

No, boys, mine boys, dig it, de deep pluma says, "TAKE UP THE CROSS!"

Whatta you think about the world, Mr. We? Well we ain't in it. But we is. & so we cdn't been artises (quote this, *NYT*). We cdn't been artises cause we peters was too long.

And now the other side, the other wall, the other layer, all on the same shelf. To confront the self on the shelf in the hell of those who cannot flee.

The self on the shelf must die. Kill the self on the shelf. Yeaaaaaaaa!

Us cdda been still on there. A rheumatic cardboard Negro agent of imperialism, like we man Nat.

Mae kept saying she wanted to leave. That we ways was too cross + corny, too white + cold. We cdda been w/ Fats' inner sanctum. Party of the 1st part. The lifter for the tower sultans. A Man.

"Fats Fats Fats Fats Fats Fats Fats," cries through we brain. Fire now anew. As the minutes tick. The day, leans into we memory.

And amongst us there walk the gold watches + suits—a stream of ghoses from the stops we left. Them various margins, boy. Them joints was tomb towns. The niggers come. Line up. Hands stretched scary style. Race relations is hip now, ya dig. The Black + White Bourgeois get on fine, shit, they even fuck, so what? But let 'um find out they can't be that, they'll scream a minute. But now they cool. Sell you AfroSheen + live like anybody they want! Buy this *Ebony*, nigger! Eat this Parks pork sausages, mom. Hate whitey (yeh, Vaseline, *Time*, & Hormel!). Our father, who art in Heaven (yeh), give us our market + stay in yr own. Our Black Nat battle cry.

But the ghoses come. They drawn into place. They was always in place. They the cream of the race!

Take up the cross!

We tried to work & study. We fight nights about our lives. Were we crazy? Did we think that world cd be changed merely by our example? To withdraw from itself. To divorce itself. To leave itself. To purify itself. Educate itself. In yr head is only as much as can fit in. We in the world, only a little of it in us. We is nature too.

Mwananchi had a Swahili wedding w/ Miriam Makeba records. Southern Calif. Sunshine. We ran it straight. From one end to the other. Self Determination. Self Respect. Self Defense. While Fats drove on, to pull the left, the lost, the was, the used-to-be, the never was. To success. In slick Clyde style, or Afrikan dress, Muslims of all flavors, preach together in the light guiding all together under the showy dome. A huge party where they can bump till they bumper break off! Music was Yeh "Take up the Cross."

Har Har Har Har.

It was nuthin' against nobody (except the uncool). Just tryin' to get over. Can't do that worryin' about everybody. Dig it. If they was swift enough, they be here.

And that was one a' our inner circle talkin'. We in Afrika time. Nation time. In Afrikan clothes. Talking Swahili. Tryin' to find a way off the shelf. Joy split, man. World come back. Niggers in line, clear white light beaming.

In his office one day we went to see Gip Fatson. Calm talk exchanged. Abt the cross. The bio swift unfold. Not that he cd say Shazam & do something. Him. Like Us. Idealistic non-sense Ego voyage beyond the stars, Star!

A mass of small acts, like a nail being driven in. A piece of stone hacked away. Each sun, the pig snout grows. We cd sit at night over fish + orange juice + talk about it. Will again. Except the needles dig through the vein, a wet pop, the blood shoots into the dropper. The knife comes down into the chest. A yng dude falls staggering toward the door + flat outside on his face. Joint man attacks again—opens his raincoat to show his joint— runs the sisters off the elevator. A child floating face down in the pool. Drunk teacher curses the other children.

Every night, we study Mwananchi. As Mwananchi say, Hate Whitey &c. Take that white girl's head. (Corliss was still guilty.)

But downtown bro, you dig it.

Har Har Har.

A caravan of claim stakers. They were readied for this for long time. Just step forward. Step forward. Face up. To the light! We was 'splaining to 'em. The difference between, see, the bohemian petty bourgeois & the civic petty bourgeois. Dig, like, Jay Wilkes, the writer. Playwright. Used to walk around w/ books, went home. But see he never left. Never went + got fully burnt down. Never really committed "suicide." But that was just, say, to go to be weird. That wasn't real suicide. (Remember *20 Vol Suicide Note*? It was class suicide that was meant.)

Like, one may write a novel glorifying the cops. The other way'll be a pr man for the colored police director!

But it raises out the water like a huge sick behemoth. A bejewelled + vulgar rotting whale. Astride its pus, oozing back, Fats chortles + beckons like Ahab as the thing leaps into the air!

But, like, the garbage was piled up. The heat + flies. On the streets day thick as smoke. Everywhere the talk went on. Niggers came to testimonials. Every wk, some blood was giving a testimonial. Collec'n' the dust on a sly.

We gettin' to talk about what ain't. Hate whitey peaked, bro, cause we look and ain't no whitey right away. They off harharin'. But Fats, you look at him, a pig now. He waddles + lies like a pig. He screws around like a pig. Tryin' to make it in America like wasn't nobody here. Nobody, just him + whitey + ain't no him, ain't no whitey, just the game they both be runnin'.

Like sit + die on yr porch, 'cause ain't nuthin' happening. Nigger landlord poisoned two babies w/ his walls. Can we get him? Lock him up? Naw! Landlord was *Black*, was w/ us. One a' our boys, Gip says.

Schools dying need to be taken over. Seized! Teachers Union isolated they fascists. Hitler might still be chief organizer. The School Board one blood, a yng dude, 18, the rest the old line creeps + new wave of stuffed animals. And finally talk open + land different places! What this nigger doing? Cdn't see nuthin'. But he ain't done or is he? Where is it? Where is it? A crowd of cleanies go in cty mgr bldg. Another tesimonial. Partee. Frankie Crocker appears. Partee.

The students gotta buncha people to march on city hall w/ the garbage. Actually the stuff that piled up over the many months. Now the show was on the road. The ice cream suits + gleaming wigs. The Lincolns, the GTO's. All marshaled as a force for them. A class for themselves. Our civil rights days are over, massa. We ready to take up the cross,

And so leaflets went 'round + the peepahs came together + marched. A lotta talk before the newspapers. As to what was going down. Agitation. A confrontation. An' Fats, he take a moment beween chicken bites to say don't throw garbage on the ground! Garbage *on* the ground, nigger. We bringing it down here for you to clean up! When you gonna do somethin' for the people?

Fats is bumpin' up + down on mella yallar + hears this on the radio, on "the peepahs speaks," an his jaw tighten but he butt keep motionin'. Uhh.

That day a crowd of 1000 peepahs came down w/ old baby carriages, tires, junk, vacant lot garbage, dead cats, from the disaster area most of us live in. The police trail the crowd. Slowly down the street till city hall is close up. Laughing everybody is only ½ serious. Serious about the fact they live in dirty holes, but only ½ serious about today's danger. Because we know Gip Fatson for years. Grew up w/ him. We got to give him a chance. Shelfsitters waiting for gigs run on the peepah + they can repeat it, except the actual trampled on who know. Except Fats got warm cause he sd them dudes begin a make him look bad.

When Mae go back she lay flat + you have to pump a while. Her legs rise—a sign it's time to root down heavy & twist it home. Barney got a sign, thinkin'. Blooey, the police vamp + the baby carriage touch a step. They leap. Come down. Hard. Hard. Sticks wailing, flying fists. Yoked in the chest. Two black policeman w/ the marchers get mopped. One got his badge in his hand, tryin' to show it. They see it. Mop! Mop! He drops it + himself to his knees, covering his head. A nigger cop on a horse & two or three others whirl around on hind legs, snortin' + bitin'. Like a giant beast ballerina. Kickin' + stompin' people. A woman w/ a child in her arms kicked in the face. Split open legs. Sprawled on their backs. Like ol' time U.S., billy clubs splat open heads. Wrestlin', fallin', strugglin' against whitey. Not whitey, against these people here killin' us. Against the thing that sets them in motion. Against that inside ourselves, that thing we struggle inside of. Struggle is normal now, tho—the eagle rises. The black bird shat on us. We learn in the modern world. Heads staggered, knees crossing. Down. & jailed. Complete. Complete.

Mwananchi says—but we here in Finland Station knows the game— Black Hearts Sing. Against the game. Away w/ all pests.

The circle shrunk + wavered, and at once it was the opposite. In changing from the shelf folks. They went to Fats for gigs.

The crowd of black nationalists hating whitey cd hate em, from the inside. Walk thru the city mgr's joint. As Salaam Alaikum, Habari Gani, Right On.

The circle turned itself inside out. The traveling salesmen, poverty pimps, preachers, all hadda go. We studied yangumi, trained, ran around the lake, read revolutionaries from conference to conference. What was it we wanted? Who *were* we? (Read it again!)

Were we lost now, reeling back + forth, learning love + unlearning romance? From the left wing to the right wing of the petty b. And the advisors change in that regard, perhaps. We had at that space, that space's advisors. Speaks same language. We same-same (they say).

We had come back to Finland Station to find the revolution at its root. To run out on the diminishing return of nigger nazi fantasies. & run into another set w/same-sames. Yet the struggle inside us, but a reflection of the world's struggle. Let us locate ourselves properly in that world & fight against the enemies. & who are these?

Endless series of selves resolve, and at each pt of progress, we are whoever we must be to develop + reunderstand reality. Out of the fire identity of a decade, we understood our black life, our Afrikan life. Around the world shift blinding prints from shoulder to shoulder, to ask why we on our knees. And look into our brother's face who is in charge of it. But can you stand to know this? Can we know this?

In our circles, we had inherited the will to identify ourselves as Black. The drums + rattles, & geles and bubas. Afrikan warmth, & self-respect we reached for. Against the madness of racists who told us we were just they waste matter, against the already enghouled, our brothers, sisters, suffering bourgeois cultural imperialism, *i.e.*, had they minds blown loose & bounce when they s'posed to bump.

We sought in ourselves for Afrika. And because of this, it was idealistic. We cd not create Afrika or recreate it. We cd only comprehend what really exists + existed. We cd comprehend it.

We needed to be Black-Black maybe, why? It was a wave of Afrika, swept us up. One day we felt, looking at our sisters, this was truly beauty.

Why? Cause we cd see *them*. Because all the colors + line fell together as harmony upper level. But now some people question the relationship between culture + aesthetics.

It was a cool rage on yr eye. Nice. Umm. Yeh . . . like. But the yeh was a recognition that that cd be in today reality, cd tell us about Afrika but wd be simply as itself somethin' gorgeous. (But can we be "gorgeous" in a war? You mean we shd be frustrated even by what we know is beautiful at the time & consign ourselves to grey husks to fight? Why do you doubt it?)

Except we needed to show Black. We needed to be it in a gorgeous way! Yet you was in Harm'em during the smokin' sixties & you looked at the Yoruba as a cult, a sect, a group apart. In our pull-down grey skies + yellow shades. Urbane. Cosmopolitan. Half white (yeh, turned to that, in that world. We struggled. Linked by flesh to the Bourgeois & when they wd not fight, & Devils Devils Devils was the cry, Devils . . . we fled). Yet, given the industrial west, wherein we is, was. We tried to fight, even then, to struggle. Yet the cry of Black, of Afrika, must not be merely some self-immolation, but the call to struggle, in reality, against the Enemies. We had been so guilt-ridden, we'd gone for madness 1st + then mediocrity + then a combination of both!

Feudalistic rituals, from Afrika, to complete w/ imperialist technology? No, to turn us around from cosmopolitan existentialism. Hedonistic Bohemianism. Exotic Bourgeoisification. Pickled in heroin cocaine stoppers in our nostrilless nose. Weed incenses & Cecil Tayloresques at the funeral.

And now we clothed in the neo-cloth of our ancestors, calling for— Hate whitey? No, Fatson rolls on oink hoofs setting us up for the kill. The links we make w/ unprincipled nigger pigs is sausage links! They are exploiters too. That group of niggas posing in storebought alienation, they ain't just come 'round. They come here from way back, a tip, a tap, an inch, an inch more. A dip, a dap. Preacherhood reality made them. Chump down on the sidewalk made them. Colored School made them. The white light bathing them. Bathing them down. The officer lurch. The full embrace. W/ silver bells on yr shoulder. You know they are clean cut + think that the world can be understood in they USA suit. They think. From Colored School, ya see there's a place, a good place, to lay yr quiet head. Ya can be in that + be peepahs. No, be important. *Recognized*! The Bohemians made them. The real, the semi, the quasi, the Fake. Civil Rts made them, the conservative wing of the pb group. Doing their routine in front of the stage. Their flawed needs. They is somebody, now, sho nuff. A bourgeoisie.

The Enemy . . . who is killing the people? Who is hurting us. Who is against us! Who has locked us up? Who sits ridiculing us. Who above all others is in control of our miserable lives.

But our circle grew. One day Mickey was standing in his parents' house. Sivella came w/ another dude. A painter-poet. She was still married to a dude managed a shoe store.

Rudolph showed up in a shiny suit + wife look like Olive Oil. They left because Rudolph dug Fats' program + the pb reality. Runs the local anti-poverty program. They winnin' antipoverty fight 'cause Rudolph boss got a silver Mercedes + Carl Michaels, other local Poverty Pimp, got a green one. They winnin'—poverty being whipped in our time!

Ernie + Faith. They left. Ernie wanted to be a cop. He works in the parks, chasing birds on a motorcycle. He also studying law.

Katibu, Majadi, DuUwezo, Mfuasi, Taalamu, Teule, Tarik, we here.

Buddy + Billye left, Buddy hadda jones he hadda take care of. Billye used to fight w/ him. When he split, she split. She skinny bulgyeyed, bad tempered. He higher + higher.

Onaje, Risasi, Dhati, Angulifu, Komozi, Kalamka, Ngola, we here.

John, Willie, Leon, "Colonel," left in the middle of the night. Bags packed. Ed, who we wdn't let sleep w/ his mama, sd he wanted to take his bass to his cousin. He split.

David Wiggley, wanted to be a bohemian. He + Whiteen, left, one at a time. Whiteen makes pots on E. 3rd St. w/ a Jewish pianist + Wiggley teaches hydrocephalic caucasianism at a commune in Altamont.

Got his picture on the cover of the *Rolling Stone*! Carl Barren, the government agent, was here a minute. Made a couple of babies, named them fierce revolutionary titles, split.

Nyamavu, Sudi, Hakika, Halisi, Elimu here.

Amina, Jaribu, Furaha, Akiba, here.

Jackie victimized by polygamous returning traitors from LA. Handsome priests w/ cut foreheads where the U.S. security force had sd they were agents. We disagreed & had dope inside a wee revolutionary—almost killed before a month went by. They left trying to kick the leg jones. Thirty-year-old college students, ersatz socialists now.

Judy who hated water + had to have the bottom of her baby's ear cut off because she wdn't clean him. A welfare stiff, blowin' plenty smeezoke. Legs spread eternally for the incorrect bystander.

Remember the student w/ the low-slung revolutionary jaw? He & some looney tune woman made plans. She sd, "Wherever Irving goes, I go," to split, leaving the watoto in the cribs alone. To keep from getting kilt he called his father, who looked exactly like him. "My son gotta come home + look after his wife—mother. We ain't together, his wife—mother & me."

We sd, why aint you home? Why can't you take care of her?

"I'm a traveling man." Jr. Walker nightmares. No fathers on the block. We begin to scream at the nigger. Lord. Lord. Irving begin to cry. We spit on him + he left.

[Mwananchi, Stokely C, Malcolm, talk Nkrumah. Nkrumah. Osagefo. PanAfrikanism. Unification + Independence of Afrika under socialism.]

What about the Muslim poetess what put the pork in the ice box! She wasn't no Muslim then, blood. But now she say, "In the name of the Hon Elijah Muhammad who met Allah in the person of Fard Muhammad, *on a street corner*" (Watch out Nwk here come Steak + Take!! How are you smelling that?).

Penny, whose mother saw ghosts + was hurt that our philosophy wdn't make us serious abt them. In our own house. They wanted a rap where ghosts + spirits wd be, at least, respected.

Enemies?

Of what?

These were the shadows, dreams, shadowers, dreamers, middle class kids & working stiffs—even lumpen jivers + jivettes going thru.

Hey what about Ulozi & Fundisha, hip royalists, waving they wands at it? Is it waved at? These were 2 dudes, dashiki-ed down, one extroverted, Ulozi, hand always out. A warm dude, but completely outside reality. If they ruled the world, it'd be worse than capitalism. Fundisha, a weird silent nut. Stared at flame on candles & sd it lowered, simply by him staring at it. We never seen that. Cut carrots on yng dudes stomach w/ a huge sword. Absolutely perfect. A few unexplained weirdos. He was a karate expert. & they, we've found, are just artsy fartsy dudes, w/ no values. Like art for art's sake. Train! Train. For what? For when the shit goes down. Train. But what will you make?

Fundisha + Corliss argued abt whether bros needed political classes or was the karate enough! Fundisha was like Wall, a destroyer type w/ an ego the size of the pyramid—Also what is it abt these types that they hate women?

[Mao too we looked at. Under the barage of Panther deaths + our accusation. Mwananchi implied in it by the opportunistic paternalists arranging our intertribal death matches. One group saying we is Black 1st + against white. The other saying sometimes that but then that the enemy is capitalism! & the Racist Pigs that benefit. But they thought to know that was enough. To say it wd do it. They sd "Pick up the Gun. Pick it up." & finally all of it was right, except for petty bourgeois subjectivism. You cd not shoot capitalism w/ a rifle. It had to be millions of rifles + masses of minds moved against it by their experience of it.

And we who had so lately embraced whites cd not so soon admit of it!]

Ulozi had a lying problem as well. He always had. About any + every. Mostly how great, knew so much, what not. Fundisha just looked mean. Mean at everything. Thru stone + air, mean baby. The leak was when he tried to talk. Like what was hip to him was passed by some a' us hardheads on the way thru Alcatraz. Music for Zen meditation. Like to cut this carrot + make the flame diminish w/ his stare. One night a whole bldg full of people dug the carrot get cut. A yng brother lay on his back & slowly, tense silence, the scimitar raised, he suddenly, brought it down full force, cut through the carrot, umph! Applause.

We are we doing . . . what?

Who are the enemies?

Why are we here?

But then the flamelowering bit. Darkness. Only the flame. Breath held, but a little trickle of air made the flame waver. Begin the stare. Some of the sisters bit their lips after a while. Later he wanted to attack them for lack a' respect.

They marched people up + down. "Disciplined" them to smithereens. Black! Kill Whitey! Afrika! We cdn't see before we were just angry. But Mwananchi gave us a formal stance to take. Destroyed by racism. Culture taken away. Language destroyed. Mixed tribes. Our families destroyed. We crazy because we want to be our oppressors. (It fit our own guilt!) Create alternative institutions. Defeat racism. & we worked.

At a soul session, filled w/yng bloods, clapping to "We A Winner." Black People gonna rise we sd. We gonna break these ties. We gonna rise. Yet as our lips moved the city mgr's daughter cdn't stay when his face grew a snout. She cdn't say it was a snout. It was her father, his snout, in fact. Daughter of the Bitch in charge of special programs or son of the negress exSNCCer who w/ two children who had gone to *private* elementary + high school (exSNCCers), assumed the role as Board Chair-Neo. Soul Session. Black clap + shake, we a winner!

But all of this as it pointed at out. At pt. To be open & out. The whys. The whys + hows.

Fundisha had sent some dudes to get yng Harry Nelson one day for some fraudulent reason. Harry, a arty yng pb, nevertheless sincere, had sd something or done something. The main reason is that Harry was like Mickey, Corliss & us. Tho ynger + more life flexible, leading w/ great speed for reality. Fundisha wanted to punish Harry for being hipper than him. (It used to go down w/ Hearts Union always. Threaten the bright ones. Who will see the sham. Who will struggle eventually for what is correct, for the real reason.)

Harry wasn't there, so the dudes broke some records, tore up his room (like the Union—sick Wall + co.). Corliss + Mickey this time didn't go for it. Corliss sat thinking. Mickey started cussin' when he found out. Sivella talked bad abt it. Corliss knew it meant step up, gotta feel + move.

That night in Corliss office, Fundisha, Ulozi, Rudolph + the old man came in line to confront Corliss. [Now Fanya-Kazi.] The struggle had been abt the visit, also a wk ago, some women being screwn by Ulozi, Wiggles + co came to the circle Hq + started laughing loud, talking to the bros, didn't say nuthin' to the women.

What that mean? It means they—we wimmens—talked hot abt that & like why didn't Wiggles + Ulozi take a position to deal sideways w/ these lazarines. Why did they hate we wimmens? They wimmens? Ulozi divorced or separated. Children came over once a week. Fundisha separated, but during this period he came together w/ the sister, a mousey quite mediocre housefrau he had consciously kept that way + then consciously made a beeline away from. Picked up a sister in the group they had, but she was ignorant + smoked. Tho a big ol' fox, if we cd perform the preparation process.

They sd they was tired a' what was happening. Especially they didn't dig what Mae was doing. Or Mae, now Malkia, + Rose B, who they sd had a big mouth. Always, we have found, they attack the woman—to attack the leadership, they attack the woman.

They went on. Talking. Rudely & the old man listened. Corliss half-listened. Now whatta you gonna do? Umh, shot by. Sick Wall. Champ. And now the need to find the enemy.

Barney gave them a piece of paper. A memo. Sd. "Reduce Rank. Turn over all authority. One organization." Same struggle. One leaped to his feet & woofed orders at a subordinate, "Get yo shit, + pull security on Ulozi, if anybody does anything weird? Kill 'em."

But to say that to Corliss was saying nothin'. It just didn't excite him. It just didn't reach him that it was dangerous, &c. He sd. How long yall want to deal w/ this memo? The big 45s sat in the holsters, by midnight the Ulozi-Fundisha group, which had been called Bloods for Community Determination, was movin' out they stuff & whatever else they cd get. Bloods for Community Determination moved into a black suburb + continued they policy of physical training, lying + Bp'n (bitch pullin') all in a nationalist red black + green Swahili-greeting style. So they now bees As Salaam Alaikum (Baloney hatem) Habari Gani (Ulozi-Fundisha w/ us w/ dat) + Right on! Stream of perception. Response. To the enemy, if we still at it. We've come as far as to say there is an enemy. Will it be fought in the heavens? In hot space, amongst the clouds? Red Black + Green angels w/ switchblades + way-out beanies swoop down upon our enemies. Destroy them + create—what? Red Black + Green cathedrals of Coltranesque obscurantism? [But Trane wasn't obscure, we all grew through exposure to the Fire Prophets, Malcolm & Trane. They had the message. They *were* the message.]

But in pointing away from the degeneracy of this—look at it—we pointed into the sky, lacking a hard-nosed ideology of struggle for reality. And what was then the answer to the degeneracy was *the spiritual* & away we go—into obscurantism, absurdity + sleep! Priestcraft, nonsense, & lack of progress. "Amenotep," the great genius of sound, is trapped into non-materialism + reduced to clown shows of Egyptian metaphysics. The sound is real! Material! Turn it to reality! Be in the world! W/ us! We are all in the world! Be real!

Concrete reality must change. We came to change the world. The corrupt greedo-crats in charge must be arrested. Put under a dictatorship. A new society must be born.

Ulozi + them now training for "matches," demonstrations. Exhibitions, like all artists have since the Impressionists. Running that suburb's [West Lemon] venereal disease program. Their slogan, "Screw Safely."

We came to Blackness w/ whiteness in hot pursuit. It was just America-total & the bohemian wing of the expanding nigger middle class. When we walked in to speak at the Colored School Alumni meeting, one nigger, a black psychiatrist, pointed out Barney didn't have no tie, & when Corliss spoke a' Malcolm (dead just a few months before) the niggers booed!

We built our circles out of guilt + over-compensation. But truth rooted in. In those hours, we sat w/ 45's crossed on our knees, wondering abt the duplicity of Ulozi. A wave of regret that we were, none of us, clear. Clear enough to join, if any of us wd, in the ultimate battle against the structure + nation of this, this boundary of frustration + degeneracy. Wasted promise, lies, sell out. All the faces in a carnival stacked like milk bottles to throw at.

The circle went on. Nkrumah, Mao. The sisters studied authentic Afrikan social practice. Our AfroAmerican fantasies balanced off. And the goofs + doofs + goons of Finstat Police or *Administration: 4 Essays in Philosophy.*

Asali, Anasa, Makini, Karimu, Kimya, Utrilulin, Tabasamu, Nadra are here.

Circle to the real. Ask the questions. Read the volumes. Digest the experience. Try to get it out.

Anti-Dogma. That the real is in and is change. Including us, we real. Oppose the eternalists who running a game wherein they always come up, year after decade, on they feet awright, but they feet in yr chest. We love the world, finally, Love it. Its red dusk skies stray through blue ghost-like silence. Plane trails wavering, its sound among the motorized noises + human yells of the coming night.

We had come to Black, but finally if yr investigating, eyes open, not just getting high or low on yr own subjective, ya gotta see what goin' on. We were always ridiculed by folk on the west coast for being people influenced by the Muslims. But that was our understanding of discipline. We want the old world to go—all of it negative—We believe in a judgment day—but the judges are people, working men + women throughout the world. The oppressed of all races. The oppressed people of the world. & we came to this through struggle w/ ourselves. 'Cause trails go by the things through processes. Our trail's a process. Someone accuse us of having forgot the pressure. The whiteout terror. Only wake up sweating, ½ gone, + reversed that. The white light shining in our room onto our bed had made a person, a white woman, a hedonistic fetish, & in flight, we began the slow work of reconstruction. Trying to understand the effects of the whiteout. But its deep number is it gets you to be it as you. We ain't gon' whistle that tune, we say—vehemently—& so we start whistling a direct opposite tune, opposite for opposite. Be same tune, different octave, different key. Like we doesn't want no other God. No different Nationality savior—none at all. Not to take up the ankh instead of the cross, but to put down all invisibilities. Get a better life goin' for you + me. Remember, you wanted beauty. We still want it for real. It was always we wanted out, or away from ugliness + stupidity. But in hating the ugliness + stupidity done to us, we were almost tricked & made a part of it. It cd go either way. They got it, baby, on one side or the other, either be crazy or be crazy. Look, man, I'll get you one of these bow ties or another!

Some a' our people still crazy. Some shellshocked. Some too white, too white to make a comeback. Mwananchi even got sick on us for a spell from too much pressure from the leopard men. Began to drop pills. Talked unintelligently on the phone. Opposed our giving some conference. When we was trying to "unify all the Bloods." Even the reactionaries is Black. But 1970 was a time to see the civil rights movement go into its next phase. After the democratic revolution, *neocolonialism*. The rise of the native agent. Ya wanna know the difference between a Tom & a Coon? Tom run the town, Coon the police chief! Mammies is Title One Coordinators. & the mulattoes . . . who you think malla yalla is? Tom's main (secret) squeeze.

Mwananchi sent some dudes w/ attache cases. 6 dudes w/ identical attache cases. Before the hijack regulations everybody flew w/ heat. These dudes walked around + looked threatening. But that was all.

But that cut us on our path. We didn't not sit there at the fact of mighty Shaka, nor understand all the darkness that was left. We had to move on— restless about the stream of reality. It bends + contracts, ever signaling.

What the outside is, what we perceive of it, & are by that, we think, take that (what we have perceived) & build our theories, our lives. The world, relentless, grows—changes. All the Mwananchi nut-out did was root us on our path, paradox. A moving root. Rooted motion, talks to everything. Resembling everything, as it changes. So we had ideas by our view, our history, together, as growing elements of Black Heart, international Black mind, worldwide. Our life a root. Our seeing a root. A path, flat, is our- selves. Man is the brain of the world (says Touré), but the world is the brain of man.

We had to go on. Past all the whiteouts + our own grim history. We had to grow clearer. "Study," says Mao. "On Practice," he sez. Develop a revo- lutionary work style. Be in the world to change it, all this piled-up stuff— out of history. Establishment institutions. We were born to live + grow + blow up strong with reality. To sidestep the many planned dyings, the slaughters bossman had set up. On the streets of our time, we can say the dinosaur beast, the old dinosaur, is openly condemned. Though South Afrika, Rhodesia, Guinea-Bissau, Mozambique, Angola, Namibia are still to be gained, that work has changed our motion. And we want more than a flag + colored bureaucracy. A national anthem when all the native agents can raise their fists + swear oaths against colonialism (emotional pleas for job security!).

It all meant go ahead. Link up later, go ahead. Look steadily. We breathed heavily + quietly, poring over the texts. Our past? Exposure to bad ideas is like being vaccinated, sez the Chairman, it readies you for some really bad ones.

We studied Cabral. And took the stride, even in our dashikis & sisters doing "Salimu," hands crossed on they chests. Amidst our feudalism + male chauvinism. And our guilt + alienation. We studied Cabral. Who had been on a similar trek. "No complexes, Comrade." No complexes.

All the weakness + lies. We seen it, some of it. Been some of it. The Wabenzi (tribe of the Mercedes Benz drivers) left (most of them) the same niggers undermining in Tanzania. Rudolf the insect w/ his shiny suit fighting against poverty + winning. The petty bourgeois survivors of the beginning of the long march, blushing, they are told the truth. We try to show them it is a fabric of exploitative relations. And our arms, when we really check, huge black muscled masses beginning to mature into the advanced social force of this America. A picture w/ Leroi Jones, Ron Karenga, Rap Brown + Floyd McKissick comes to mind. The rush of the '60s another message. To go on. To keep at it. Seeking the real answers.

We cd even see then, that "Afrikan" sd only where we came from—ideology save us from the backwardness of "Afrikans." These heap dead dudes 'n dudettes keep draggin' our lack of development out like a charm. "Turn off the computers, bring back the bones," our backward giant friend from Brooklyn whined. Yeh, well get out yr car niggra, take off that mammyjammin' watch, and while you in that airplane, you must be a yur-ope-peeeen. Culture save us from the backwardness of yr rope, which has been given us despite Fanon. And which we continue to hang ourselves wit'. But all of it, the sandbag empire of lust and pinnacles, in all its toaddy reflection, is wrong. Needta be ripped down and trampled. Except do not go backward to befo'. We know forward is the direction. Take off our Ancient Robes, come out in the street w/ the people and struggle. We have helped create this very technology that dazzles us, but let us bleed a little more to control its uses.

And gradually, baby, we come out our complexes and tripouts, our excessive black and Afrikan shit, except we is blk socialists, say it, yr lips poutin' this mornin', but say it, black revolutionaries, however we look. And look at us, yall, when we comin', you might cain't tell except when the words say. No robes, No crowns, just the nobility of the mass, and the light of struggle toward truth, reality. Yeh we black w/ Afrikan names, but the words are in everybody, the life we want for everybody, all all all together . . .

We organized. And when we do not argue, struggling like blinded light addicts for illumination. The building. The school. A nursery where the children are kept to free up our sisters to be our comrades in struggle. The advocates drawn together by struggle in which our reality will emerge. Our enemies show themselves. The wheels in the sky. Crisscrossing the globe for profit & sometimes fun. We wd go up in the tower + see the ring of fat men finishing lunch. The white-haired dignified man invites us in. An Italian ex-linebacker, his aide + specialist in community relations pushes a button to let a little light on the subject. The stained glass window cruises back into its receptacle! Looking out the picture window, we can almost see these wise men's houses, high among the hills. And directly below our miserable hovels. They show up their maps (24 of them stand then sit at the 100 ft oak polished table, their pictures gold-framed in the hall). They recite their statistics. There is a whir, a screen pokes down out the ceiling. A projector emerges from the table. The stain glass closes. The film w /music, a 10-minute explanation of the divine right of the corporation. It is impressive. We look into each of the white gleaming faces. Ah. There is a yellow face too. Mr. Koyimshobashi returns the glance. But, there is a brown face too. Mr. Harris Sullivan, the noted black poet, is now poet-in-residence to this largest insurance company in the world, he explains. He rises + reads his latest epic, "Whitey Better Increase the Stock Options." The meeting comes to an end.

Down a ramp there is a reception, tonight for Baba Mkubwa Aminifu, the president of Lower Gonda. He explains how the whites who were thrown out of LG + the Asians had to be looked at as simply signs of a progressive time. Eyes darted uneasily across the claret. He went on, but Barclays is cool ain't it, White Cross + Sharing? Whichever? We must understand we have a class of quality Afrikans rising who must share in some aspect of the wealth. But (in gold leaf) you have the reports. Greed must not be tolerated at the expense of profit! We can all get over together! A positive grunt like in a Xtian Scientist prayer meeting. Look at the Books! Uneasy but positive feeling. Finelooking womens coming in now. And important other peepahs. Plus some important black peepahs. Mayors + shit. Ambassadors. Congressmen. M. Moreland from the Apple, in a sheep blue tuxedo, in fact the black caucus minus the dude from California. A group of black mayors, Teddy Kennedy's Mississippi nigger, the red nigger what endorsed Wallace, plus bad Johnny Cheviot Mayor of Monkee, Ala., all the 1sts. 1st nigger mayor w/ a white wife in Ala. + (he added) who supported Wallace. 1st nigger to do this. 1st nigger to do that. Plus Daughters of Zion. Harvard Alumni Assn. Democrats for New Populist Majority were there. Kissinger + a blonde woman are still w/ a Rockefeller button. "Yas, give up the dust, give up the dust," a couple colored businessmen sd later, after they had gotten past their limit of one scotch & milk.

They owned hair sprays (AfroRip) + a magazine empire (*Colored People*), respectively. Both had red black + green flags in front of their brand new office bldgs. Oakyard Melting, the homosexual democratic "socialist" stooge for big capitalist labor, showed w/ a naked white boy on a leash. The chant began. "Look at the Books. Look at the Books." It spread. Gip Fatson appeared w/ mallow yellow dressed in ostrich feathers, dress, glasses, shoes, cigarette holder, rings, earrings, all out of ostrich feathers. One of her boobs had a U.S. seal of approval stamped on it, but she didn't seem to try to hide it. Was weird tho.

Ya see, my friend, the two inebriated jigaboos began in unison, "Vaseline can't hog up our market too. We can keep niggers heads greasy. Know how to do that! & *Time* can't tell it like it isssss," he slurred, dropping whiskey on the rug. The owners of the NAACP appeared w/ Golda Meir. They escorted Roy Wilkins, ex-director, w/ a patch over one eye. A sister stuck her welfare check stub inna nigger's eye one evening. A swirl of new stuff. Nixon was taken to prison this evening. Agnew was living w/ Roscoe Green, Jr., the American Negro Actor. Sammy Kvetch Jr., the Sambo tap dancer who tongue-kissed Nixon last election, passes out pictures of Green + Agnew embracing nude in a fountain. The Nigrita poetess, Niggy Johnsonetta, lets forth a few notable lines—"Ah money + fame you are warm + sexy. A rolled up dollar will make me hollar. & fame is not for the lame. Nothing is good but the rich. Nothing is exciting but the powerful. Would that the new women had penises, as bananas go down too quick."

At the end the books Aminifu's intensity + sincerity were accepted, & one of the board members led the singing of "Solidarity Forever." Aminifu presented the corporation w/ *a shrunken Afrikan.* An entire person shrunken w/ a hoe on a plot of earth about 12 inches wide. The brother worked + worked w/ the hoe + his efforts brought howls of serious delight from the crowd + an awed draw of breath. Aminifu was clearly a hero. Austin Wilson, head of the board, sd they wd get a major sporting event to L.G. to signify the emergence of AMERICA. A whisper goes thru the crowd. Nixon committed suicide. It grows to a happy jovial roar. Change the Guard! Change the Guard! More discussion ensued.

And finally we came to understand this is the real world. A world of facts + processes. A world in process. We began to read Lenin. What Is Imperialism? Huge monopolies. Export Capital. Raw materials + markets. The beginning of colonialism. Bank + industrial capital become Finance Capital. We read Marx. Boggs. Stalin. Touré. We urge ourselves to be real. To come into the world + struggle before it's too late! Come + build the weapon of the masses. Organization.

And when we, in our travels, meet our raggedy-headed brothers in red black + green dashikis still raging at the devil. When the blue devil slides. "Vote for me & I'll set you free," sez the Temptations. The Blue fascists raise in funny hats w/ funny names. "Away with all pests," sez Mao. The sixties are over my brothers + sisters. Our bourgeois revolution has already been done. Consolidated. While nigger Caesars + cockteasers abound & are at large throughout the land. Black. Afrikans. Against all pests. The energies are the people's + they will eventually seize + control them. The wealth & all that's produced. The people. Our agony + alienation can be pointed at & its source destroyed. Our social lives, our day-to-day reaction to man nature + society, determine our ideas. Too many of us struggle under the weight of the fat old men in the tower. Dance to their dirty tunes. The preachers resist. The Colored School victims. Gladiators of Alcatraz + Devils Island. The Bohemians. The Civil Rights Successes. At every space we hear + see their mischief. "Mischief for profit." America turns + we turn in it. Our people classify themselves, consciously or unconsciously. Their needs make them who they are.

We were reading *Afrikan Red Family*, when the sister sat down on the bed. We were stretched out & the whole brigade came in, age 7, 5, 3, 2, 1, plus the 13 + 10 peepin' in. In our struggles, is part of all our struggle. Our roads to get to here, where we are Black + Green + Red. Where we are revolutionary nationalists, struggling to see Afrika liberated. PanAfrikanists fighting for an end to world oppression. Socialists pushing for a new beginning for all people. It is a long warm slow embrace today. Amidst the children's noise. They are looking for the ultimate weapon. Organization. The only one the people have. Victory to all peoples, we are singing to each other, just before lunch, Victory to all peoples.

1973–1974
NWK